P9-DFX-888

Starting Out in Futures Trading

Updated and Expanded

FIFTH EDITION

MARK J. POWERS

IRWIN
Professional Publishing®
Chicago • London • Singapore

©1993, Oster Communications

ALL RIGHTS RESERVED. No part of this publication may be reproduced, stored in a retrieval system, or transmitted, in any form or by any means, electronic, mechanical, photocopying, recording, or otherwise, without the prior written permission of the publisher and the copyright holder.

This publication is designed to provide accurate and authoritative information in regard to the subject matter covered. It is sold with the understanding that the author and the publisher are not engaged in rendering legal, accounting, or other professional service.

ISBN 1-55738-506-8

Printed in the United States of America

IPC

CTV/BJS

6 7 8 9 0

Dedicated to
E. B. Harris

The guiding light of the IMM and CME and under whom this author gained a "post-graduate degree" in political economics. His wit and wisdom made it all fun.

Contents

List of Figures xiii

List of Tables xvii

Foreword xix

Chapter 1 Stocks versus Commodities 1

A Word about Your Suitability for Trading 2
Trading Stocks versus Trading Commodity Futures 2
Margin and Leverage 3
Relative Size 5
The Time Factor 6
Daily Price Limits 6
Market Analysis 7
Selling Short 7
Method of Trading 8
Size of Account 8

Who Trades Commodities and Why 8
Social and Economic Benefits of Futures Trading 10
Electronic Trading—Globex 12
The Crash of '87 15
Stocks, Bonds, Currencies and Commodities—
It's All One Market Now 16

Chapter 2 Speculation Is Not a Four-Letter Word 21

Why Do Speculators Speculate? 22
Speculation or Gambling? 23
Do Most Speculators Lose? 24
No Winning Formula 25
Practice Trading 26

Chapter 3 Managed Futures—A Good Alternative 27

Growth of Managed Futures 29
Selecting a CTA to Manage your Money 34
The Value of Adding Commodity Futures to Your Investment Portfolio 40
Getting Help—Use a Trading Manager 41
A Long-Term Perspective Needed 42

Chapter 4 Commodity Index Futures—
The Basket Approach to Investing 45

The CRB Index Futures As an Investment 48
Real Time CRB Index Futures Performance 51

Chapter 5 The Trading Plan 53

Your Attitude toward Risk 54
The Plan 54
Part I—Capital 55
Part II—Initiating Positions 62
Part III—Exiting a Trade—Liquidation Strategy 66
Part IV—Review of Results 68
A Word about Diversification 68
Seasonality and Trading Plans 69
Summary 69
A Final Warning 70

Chapter 6 Choosing a Broker 77

Where to Begin 78
What to Look For 78
Consider the Firm 79

What Not to Look For 80
Problems 81
Opening the Account 82
Types of Accounts 82

Chapter 7 The Order 85

Time Element 85
Price 86
Stop Orders 87
Combination Orders 88
Placing the Order 89
Electronic Trading Orders 89

Chapter 8 Forecasting Prices—Supply and Demand 91

Fundamental Analysis 92
Consumer Is King 95
Where to Get Data 96
Government Policies 97
What to Look for and Where to Find It 97
Government Information 98

Chapter 9 Basic Price Patterns—Forecasting Tools 101

Seasonal Movements 102
Cyclical Movements 103
Trends 104
Statistical Techniques 105
Analyzing the Data 109

Chapter 10 Technical Analysis 111

The Bar Chart 112
The Point-and-Figure Chart 113
Intrepreting Bar Charts—Basic Chart Patterns 116
Defining a Trend 117
Cycles 119
Chart Formations 120
Technical Analysis, Chart Services, and Software 124

Chapter 11 Technical Analysis—The Tools and How They Work 127

More on Moving Averages 128
Moving Average Oscillators 128
A Survey of Technical Indicators 129

Warning 136
Mimicking the Mind—Neural Networks 139
Additional References 142
Futures Periodicals 143

Chapter 12 Volume and Open Interest 145
Finding the Information 147
Intrepreting Changes 147
Seasonal Patterns in Volume and Open Interest 148
Fundamentalists versus Technicians 149
Random Walks versus Trends 150

Chapter 13 Commodity Hedging—A Primer 153
Who Hedges and Why? 156
Several Benefits 157
Commodity Characteristics and Hedging 158
The CFTC and Hedging 158
Hedging Is Not an Automatic Reflex 159

Chapter 14 Hedging—The Basis 163
The Important Difference 164
Calculating the Basis 166

Chapter 15 Your Banker and Hedging 171
The Loan Package 172

Chapter 16 Commodity Hedging in Action 175
The Short Hedge—Cattle 176
Hedging Hogs 178
The Storage Hedge 181
Trying Other Examples Yourself 183
Selecting a Hedge Broker 183
What about Delivery? 184
Decision Making on Hedging 184
How Much to Hedge 184

Chapter 17 Energy Hedging—Some Examples 187
Hedge #1: Refiner—Hedging the Sale of Excess Inventory 189
Hedge #2: Forward Sale to Hedge the Purchase of Inventory Needs 190
Hedge #3: Selling Inventory in Transit 190

Chapter 18 Fact and Fiction About Spreads 193
Semantics 194

"Time" Spreads 195
How Profitable? 198
Perishable Spreads 198
Inter-Season Spreads 199
Spreading Location Basis 199
Spreading Quality Basis 200
Inter-Commodity Spreads 200
Spotting Spread Opportunities 201
Suggested Rules 201
Options Spreads and Trend Changers 202
More on Spreads 203
Spreading and Taxes 205
Carryback and Carryforward of Losses 206
Summary 206

Chapter 19 Financial Futures—An Introduction 209
Money 210
Money in the Economy 212
Money, The Machine, and The Banking System 213
Inflation 215

Chapter 20 Money—Trading the Ultimate Commodity 219
The Price of Money 220
Recent History of International Monetary System 221
The Spot Market 222
Evaluating Foreign Exchange Rates 223
Interest Rate Arbitrage 226
Capital Controls 228

Chapter 21 Understanding the "Yield Curve" 231
Why Study Yield Curves? 232
The Changing Shape of the Yield Curve 233
The Futures Yield Curve 235
The Strip Curve 236
Compounding Factor 237

Chapter 22 The Interest Rate Contracts 239
Eurodollars and T-Bills 239
The Contract Terms 240
Comparing a T-Bill Futures Quote with a Eurodollar Futures Quote 241
Spreads Between T-Bill and Eurodollar Rates—The "TED" Spread 242
Hedging with the T-Bill and Eurodollar Futures Contracts 242

Delivery 244
Treasury Bonds and Treasury Notes 244
Treasury Notes 245
Factors Affecting Rates 246

Chapter 23 Hedging Applications for Financial Futures 249

To Hedge or Not to Hedge 249
Hedged Ratios—Dollar Equivalency—And the Maturity Adjustment 252
Hedging—Currency 254
Applications of an Interest Rate Futures Market 256
Hedging Against Falling Interest Rates 257
Hedging Against Rising Interest Rates 259
Reducing Basis Risk 261
Hedging the Prime Rate 262
Hedging the Fed Funds Rate 262
Prefunding a Portfolio 263
Corporation Hedging Sinking Fund Obligations 263
Bank Issuing CDs 263

Chapter 24 Stock Index Futures and Options 265

What's Traded and When 266
Computing a Stock Index 267
Volatility in Indexes 268
Circuit Breakers and Crash Protectors 269
Trading the Stock Indexes 273
Hedging Illustrated 273
The Portfolio Manager and Hedging 274
Stock Index Options 276

Chapter 25 Commodity Options 277

The Language 278
The Greek Language and Options 280
Options versus Futures 281
Picking an Options Broker 283
What's an Option Worth? Determining the Option Premium 285
Futures versus Physicals versus Financials 290
Are Options for You? 291
Creating Synthetics 291

Chapter 26 Strategies for Trading Options 293

Using Options in Business 294

Strategies for Speculating in Options 296
Using the Futures to Convert a Call to a Put 298
Options on Financial Futures 299
Summary of Options Strategies under Various Price Scenarios 300
What Option to Trade? 303
Calculating Return on Investment 305
Summary 306

Chapter 27 Historical Development of Commodity Futures Trading 311

Characteristics of Organized Futures Trading 312
Emergence of Organized Markets 313
Early Futures Trading in Japan 314
Development of Futures Trading in the U.S. 315
Midwest Grain Market 316
Development of Chicago Commodity Markets 317
Chicago Mercantile Exchange 318
Other Exchanges 318
What's Traded and Where? 319
Commodity Futures Trading and the Law 324
The Commodity Futures Trading Commission 325
Self-Regulation and the NFA 327

Chapter 28 The Commodity Futures Exchange 331

Nature of the Organization 332
The Trading Floor 335
Execution of Trades 335
Dual Trading 336
The Clearinghouse 336
Finance 338

Appendix I Commodity Trader's Scorecard 339

Glossary of Commodity Futures Terms 343

Index 363

About the Author 381

List of Figures

1.1 Leverage Illustrated 5
1.2 Daily Average Number of Contracts Traded 14
1.3 T-Bond Futures versus CRB Index (weekly data) 17
1.4 S&P 500 versus Bond Futures (weekly data) 18
1.5 Dollar Index versus T-Bills Futures (weekly data) 19
1.6 Dollar versus Bonds (weekly data) 19
1.7 D-Mark LIBOR verses D-Mark Futures (weekly data) 20

3.1 MAR Trading and Dollar Size of "Qualified" Universe 29
3.2 MAR Fund/Pool Index Dollar Size of "Qualified" Universe 30
3.3 MAR Qualified CTA Index 34
3.4 Fund Structure: Efficient Portfolios Optimal Portfolio Size 38
3.5 Efficient Frontier with CRB 43

4.1 Average Annual Returns 51
4.2 CRB Index Performance (June 1986 = 100) 52

8.1 The Demand and Supply Structure for Pork 95

9.1 Cash Seasonal Omaha Pork Seasonals 102
9.2 Pork Belly Seasonals 103
9.3 Changes in Hog Prices and Pork Production 104
9.4 US Hog/Corn Price Ratio 106
9.5 Scatter Diagram of Correlation 110

10.1 Chicago December Wheat 113
10.2 Point and Figure Chart 114
10.3 September Eurodollars Point and Figure 10×3 116
10.4 July Cotton Point and Figure 40×2 117
10.5 September Soybean Oil 118
10.6 September Corn 119
10.7 Corn Price Cycles 120
10.8 "Head and Shoulders" Formation 121
10.9 Comex December Silver 122
10.10 October Soybean Meal 123
10.11 July Lumber 124

11.1 Elliott WAVE Count Illustrated 137
11.2 Neural Network Illustrated 140

14.1 Basis Relationship 167

16.1 Cost-of-Carry Illustrated 181

17.1 Crude, Heating Oil and Gasoline Futures Prices (weekly data) . . . 188
17.2 Heating Oil Less Gasoline (weekly data) 188

18.1 CME May–August Pork Belly Spreads 197
18.2 2:1:1 Crack and 3:2:1 Crack Spreads (weekly data) 205

21.1 Yield Curve 232
21.2 Normal Yield Curve 233
21.3 Flat Yield Curve 234
21.4 Inverted Yield Curve 234
21.5 Humped Yield Curve Shift 235
21.7 Futures Yield Curve 236

22.1 TED Spread (weekly data) 243

24.1 S&P 500 Index Spot Price History 268

25.1 Option Pricing Probability Diagram 287
25.2 Normal Distribution Curve 289

26.1 Long Futures 307
26.2 Short Futures 307
26.3 Long Call 307
26.4 Long Put 307
26.5 Short Call 307
26.6 Short Put 307
26.7 Short Call/Long Call 308
26.8 Long Put/Short Put 308
26.9 Long Call/Long Put 308
26.10 Short Call/Short Put 308
26.11 Long Call/Long Put 308
26.12 Long Put/Short Call 308

27.1 NFA Organization Chart 329

List of Tables

1.1 Globex Trading Lineup 15

2.1 Profits and Losses—Individual Speculators 24

3.1 Comparison of Annual Returns 1980–1992 35
3.2 CTA Returns 37
3.3 Multi-Advisor Correlation Coefficients 39

4.1 Average Annual Returns 49
4.2 Volatility of Annual Returns of Domestic Assets 50
4.3 CRB Index Correlation with Inflation 50

5.1 Payoff or Mathematical Expectation 57

9.1 Building a Moving Average 107

12.1 30 Futures Market Ranked by Tendency to Trend 152

14.1 Allowing for Basis 168

16.1 Summary of Short Cattle Hedge 177
16.2 Futures versus Cash Hog Prices 179
16.3 Worksheet for Live Hog Hedge 180
16.4 Hedging Corn 182

17.1 Refiner's Hedge of Fuel Oil Inventory 189

18.1 Tracking A Spread 201
18.2 Put Ratio Back Spread 203

21.1 The "Strip" 237

23.1 Hedge Decision Model 252
23.2 Swiss Franc Buy Hedge 254
23.3 Canadian Dollar Sell Hedge 255
23.4 Hedging Short Term Investment Rates 258
23.5 Hedging Commercial Paper 260
23.6 Sell Hedge Eurdollar CD's 260
23.7 Bank Hedge For CD's 264

24.1 S&P 500 Index 1986–1992 267
24.2 Coordinated Trading Halts . . . .

25.1 Options Futures versus Physicals versus Financials 290

26.1 Summary of Sell Futures—Buy Call Option 301
26.2 Summary of Option Strategies Under Various Price Scenarios 302
26.3 Scenarios Summary of Bull Spread—Call Options 304

27.1 Exchanges 319
27.2 Commodities and Instruments Traded Financials 321
27.3 Commodities 323

Foreword

When Mark Powers first wrote this book more than 20 years ago, it was literally a month-by-month, chapter-by-chapter effort. It appeared as a popular minicourse series in *Commodities* magazine during 1972 and early 1973. When the series was pulled together with the new additional chapters, it became "the first book of its kind on commodity futures trading," according to Todd Lofton, co-founder and editor of *Commodities.*

A lot has changed in the futures industry since then, including the demotion of the term "commodity" from both the original title of this book *(Getting Started in Commodity Futures Trading)* and the name of the magazine, now called *Futures*. Yet, the essential elements that the beginning trader needs to know remain much the same as they were when the first version of this book appeared in 1973.

Getting Started was easily the most popular book to come out of the magazine and was the first basic text read by many new traders in the 1970s and 1980s. Over the years, it has been reprinted at least half a dozen times and revised several times. In each case there were lots of new things to talk about—contracts and products and strategies that weren't even around when the first version was written.

Powers had already written about "Money, The Ultimate Commodity," in the first edition before most people had a clue what the new currency futures market was all about—or why it was so significant. Later editions brought new chapters on interest rate futures, options, stock index futures, managed futures and many other new developments that have marked the growth of the futures industry over the years. This completely revised—and renamed—edition retains all the basics and brings you up to date on how a new trader can approach today's marketplace.

Few people are as well qualified to write about futures and trading as Mark Powers, whose career path closely parallels the development of the futures and options industry. In getting his agricultural economics degree at the University of Wisconsin, Powers wrote his doctoral dissertation on pork bellies—at the time, the new frontier in futures trading.

Moving to the Chicago Mercantile Exchange, he wrote many of the contract details for currency and financial futures, helped to launch the International Monetary Market and became one of the "founding fathers" of financial futures. The next stop was the new Commodity Futures Trading Commission where, as the chief economist, Powers was instrumental in helping to establish the policies of this fledgling government regulatory agency.

After a stint as director of commodity trading for a major Wall Street firm during a turbulent era of new products and new players, Powers started his own firm, Powers Research Associates. It is the prototype firm of the 1990s for the futures industry and is highly regarded for its sophisticated strategies and trading approaches for banks, financial institutions, corporations, and pension plans involved in derivative markets.

Given his institutional thrust in recent years, Powers can get very complex very quickly when it comes to trading derivatives. But his style, reflecting his background in education and teaching, is to get to the heart of an issue and make clear what it's all about. Perhaps because he knows so much about so broad an area of the futures and options industry, he is able to convey to beginners the difficult concepts they need to grasp if they are to be successful traders.

Unlike the situation when the first edition of this book appeared, traders—even beginners—have a number of choices today to learn how to start trading. But it would not be surprising if this new edition, like its predecessors, again became one of the most popular volumes for the beginning trader.

Darrell R. Jobman
Executive Editor
Futures Magazine

Chapter 1

Stocks versus Commodities

The late Vince Lombardi, legendary coach of the Green Bay Packers during their glory years, once said, "Luck is what happens when preparation meets opportunity."

Lombardi was saying that, in the long run, people who are successful make their own luck by being prepared to take advantage of favorable circumstances...and those who rely on "chance luck" have very little hope of continued success.

The purpose of this book is to introduce the beginner to the world of commodity futures trading and to aid in preparing one to take advantage of favorable circumstances that arise in the trading of commodity futures. This book will offer no sure-fire methods for making money, nor will it predict the prices of any commodity. It makes no promises to turn you into a successful trader, because a successful trader needs more than knowledge about the market. It will, however, provide you with an understanding of many of the basic aspects of futures trading—knowledge without which only "chance luck" can work in your favor.

The word *commodity* is used herein for the most part interchangeably with the word *futures*. Futures contracts are now traded on many goods and services that are not strictly commodities in the traditional sense. The concepts, ideas, and descriptions in this book are applicable to futures whether the underlying "commodity" is agricultural, industrial, financial, foreign, or domestic.

A WORD ABOUT YOUR SUITABILITY FOR TRADING

Commodity futures *trading* is not for everybody. Commodity futures investments managed by others, however, have a much broader suitability to many investors.

For example, you should not trade or invest unless you have money you and your dependents can afford to lose. If you are in the proverbial "orphan or widow" class, do not trade, and select your managed futures investments carefully. Some studies have shown that the probabilities are quite high that after a customer pays his commissions and calculates the interest income lost on money deposited with his broker, he will not make money.

You should not trade unless you are psychologically suited to taking large risks. Most commodity futures transactions involve a great deal of risk. Unless you are certain that you can accept that risk and still sleep at night without worry, do not trade.

You should not trade unless you are sure you can control your ego and your greed. High risk and high profit potential go together. If you cannot discipline yourself well enough to admit a mistake on a trade and close it out at a small loss or to be satisfied with a moderate gain on a winning trade, do not trade.

If you tend to live on hopes and dreams instead of on the realities of hard facts, do not trade.

If you think you can make money trading futures without doing some hard work, do not trade. Making money consistently is not easy in any line of work. And it is especially hard in futures trading.

If after reading the above you have already concluded that *trading* is not for you, don't give up. Read on. Investing in a professionally managed futures product, in which you don't have to do the work, may suit you fine. In that case, when you have finished with this chapter, go directly to Chapter 3, "Managed Futures—A Good Alternative."

As you read the rest of this book, keep these points in mind and try to determine your suitability for trading.

TRADING STOCKS VERSUS TRADING COMMODITY FUTURES

Most of you have probably invested in stocks so you understand something about exchange markets and how exchanges operate. Stock exchanges and commodity exchanges are similar in many ways. For example, they are both membership organizations established as a means of facilitating the investment decisions of large and diverse groups of people.

The stock exchanges act to bring people with extra capital together with those who need capital to develop a business. They facilitate the transfer of ownership of corporations which are engaged in various productive activities such as steel making, auto manufacturing, banking, etc. Property rights change hands.

The commodity futures markets act to bring people together to transfer the price risk associated with the ownership of some commodity, like wheat, or a service, like an interest rate. No property rights to a physical commodity change hands at the time the futures contract is entered into. The transaction is a legally binding promise that at a later date a transaction will occur involving the property rights to the actual commodity.

One can "invest" in commodities in the same way one can in stocks: e.g., buy a share in a commodity limited partnership. In that sense, according to the dictionary, investment is the "committing of resources with the expectation of making a profit." On the basis of that definition, it seems apparent that one also "invests" in oil wells, real estate, and a whole array of other things.

It would not be accurate to leave the impression that investing in blue chip stocks and investing in commodity futures contracts are exactly the same thing. The two activities can often reside on different levels of the risk spectrum.

MARGIN AND LEVERAGE

Commodity futures contracts, when traded with high leverage, fall in the high-risk area of the spectrum near speculative stocks, rights, puts and calls, new issues, and "penny" stocks. But if you trade them using low leverage and carefully select trades that provide favorable probability payoffs, then futures trading can be at the low-risk end of the spectrum.

Just as there is a risk spectrum for all investments, one could set up the same sort of spectrum for commodity futures contracts. That is, you can select commodities for trading that have less risk associated with them because of higher margins (less leverage) or more stable prices. For example, trading futures in a commodity like pork bellies is normally more risky than an equally leveraged position in lumber. Lumber prices are usually less volatile. Equal leverage with lower volatility means lower risk.

Further, the method of trading you select can affect the risk you assume. For example, you could use a "spreading" technique, which refers to the simultaneous purchase and sale of contracts in two different markets or for two different months. This usually, though not always, has less risk associated with it than an outright long or short position. We will discuss spreads in depth in a later chapter.

Why do commodity futures end up so far out on most people's risk spectrum? Is it because the prices of beef cattle or pork bellies fluctuate so much more than the price of blue chip stocks? Not at all. In fact, the prices of many commodities fluctuate less than many stock prices. During one six-month period of 1992, IBM's stock moved down 20 percent, up 20 percent, and back down 50 percent. That's real volatility. Meanwhile, no commodity changed that much. The important difference is in the leverage of margin—the amount of money needed to control a given amount of resources.

When an investor buys a stock on margin, the margin represents an equity interest in the security and the investor owes the unpaid balance as debt. In futures contract trading, the trader is not buying or selling the commodity but only agreeing to buy or sell it at a later date. In one sense, you could look at the purchase or sale of a futures contract as the purchase or sale of the right to participate in the price change. The margin payment is considered a "sign of good faith" or earnest money such as might be used in acquiring a piece of property. In other words, the purchaser promises to fulfill his contract during the delivery month.

Use of the term "margin" to describe the security deposit posted when trading commodity contracts is somewhat unfortunate, since it suggests that "margin" in the securities market and "margin" for commodity futures contracts are identical. In fact, they are quite different in concept and in practice.

The purpose of margin in commodity trading is to act as a security deposit, thus providing the broker and the exchange clearing house with protection from default by the customer or the brokerage firm. The level of these security deposits is set by the exchange on which the commodity is traded.

Margins on securities are set by the Federal Reserve Board, and their purpose, as stated in the Securities Exchange Act, is to prevent the excessive use of credit for the purchase or carrying of securities. Recent federal legislation gives the Fed authority to review margins on certain financial futures.

New purchases of stock on margin generate credit in a way that adds to the national money supply. When stock is bought, the entire purchase price is paid to the seller a few days after the transaction. If the purchaser is buying the stock on margin, the balance of the purchase price must be borrowed in order to make his full payment. Ordinarily, this balance is borrowed from the broker or from a bank and, in either case, the effect is to expand the national total of bank credit, leading to an expansion of the national money supply by the amount borrowed. This points up a major distinction between margin in commodities and margin in the stock market. Margin in commodities does not, in and of itself, involve the borrowing of money nor does it affect the money supply.

Leverage is high in commodity futures trading because, as a percent of contract value, margins are low. In the stock market, margins are currently at 50 percent. In commodities markets, margins are usually less than 10 percent and in some instances less than 1 percent of market value. Because of the low margins in commodities, one can control large amounts of resources with small amounts of capital. Hence, a slight change in the value of the total contract results in a substantial change in the amount of money in your account. For example, a 1 percent change in $10,000 invested in the stock market via a non-margined account will equal a 1 percent change in equity or $100. A 1 percent change in a futures contract valued at $10,000 is equal to a $100 change in account equity also, but in order to control that $10,000 futures contract, you probably needed to put down $750 as your initial margin. And a $100 change in $750 is equal to a 13 percent change in your equity (see Figure 1.1).

It is this leverage factor that causes commodity futures to be considered a high-risk investment. Of course, there is nothing that says you must use all of that leverage. You could arbitrarily set your personal margin higher, say at 30 percent and trade more conservatively. In other words, the riskiness of futures trading is a self-selected risk. The institution of futures trading does not necessarily mean more risk by design.

RELATIVE SIZE

A very basic difference between the stock market and the commodity futures market, however, is the relative size of the two markets. The stock markets are overwhelmingly larger than the commodity futures markets, and the number of people who own and

Figure 1.1 Leverage Illustrated

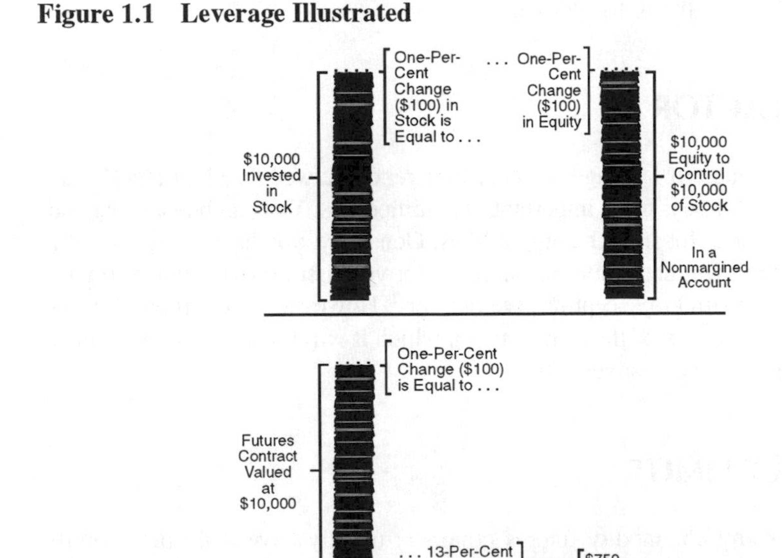

trade stocks far outnumber those who trade commodity futures contracts. Although newspaper stories frequently portray the commodity markets as being "vast" with "millions of people playing the markets" where the dollar value of trading frequently "exceeds the value of stocks traded on the New York Stock Exchange," such statements are misleading.

In the case of the value of securities traded on the New York Stock Exchange, most of those securities were paid for in full and delivered to their new owners; thus, something approaching the $500 billion in value of stock traded was actually exchanged in cash through the Exchange. On the other hand, futures contracts are traded on margin, and less than 10 percent of the value of the contract is deposited with the broker in cash. Hence, only a fraction of the trillions of dollar value of futures contracts traded annually in recent years actually changed hands.

Since the early 1970s, several market profile studies have been completed by the Commodity Futures Trading Commission in Washington, DC, by the exchanges, and by the Lind-Waldock brokerage firm. All of them have concluded that the total number of futures accounts in industry is no more than a few hundred thousand. Since many traders carry more than one account (one trader was known to have 17 different accounts), it generally has been estimated that there are at any one time about 150,000 individuals and business firms who trade commodity futures contracts. These estimates include members of exchanges and brokers. On the other hand, in mid-1990, the NYSE survey showed that about 51 million people own securities, or about 21 percent of the population and 10,000-plus U.S. institutions (banks, universities, investment companies, pensions, etc.).

THE TIME FACTOR

Besides the difference in leverage, another difference between trading stocks and commodities is that time is more important in commodities. You can buy a stock and put it away for years. Not so with commodities. Generally, you have to get out of a commodity position within a matter of months after you first make the commitment, or you are legally bound to accept or give delivery. However, at the time a futures contract is created, you know the exact date on which it will mature, so there is little excuse for being "caught" inadvertently.

DAILY PRICE LIMITS

Unlike stocks, many commodity futures contracts usually have daily price limits which prohibit prices from changing by more than a certain amount on any given day.

These daily price limits are instituted first, and most importantly, to limit the financial risk to the clearing house. Clearing house members must settle with each other each day, paying in or receiving the amount by which the value changed of each contract they owned that day. Second, limits act to constrain hysteria in the marketplace and let all parties have a breather when prices are changing by substantial amounts. Some futures have no price limits while others have formulae that dictate the imposition of price limits and the suspension of trading when markets get too volatile. Perhaps the best-known example of this is the cooperative effort of the Chicago Mercantile Exchange (CME) and the NYSE regarding price limits of the S&P Index and the trading of the underlying stocks at the NYSE. When the stock market gets volatile and the S&P futures index advances or declines by 1200 points, trading is halted for half an hour. If the Dow Jones declines by 50 points, there is a trading halt.

MARKET ANALYSIS

Market and price analysis of commodity futures is similar to and yet simpler than for stocks. For those who are chartists, the techniques of charting and chart interpretation are nearly the same for commodities as for stocks. On the other hand, fundamental analysis of many commodities is much simpler, because there are far fewer commodity contracts than there are stocks, and some of the best fundamental research organizations in the world provide free data, for example, in agricultural commodity futures the U.S. Department of Agriculture; in interest rates and currency the Federal Reserve, the U.S. Treasury, and Department of Commerce.

SELLING SHORT

You can sell short as easily in commodities as you can buy long. A short sale in commodities can be a speculation or a hedge. It is not necessary to borrow the commodity in order to go short in the futures market, since it is not a sale of the actual commodity, but only a promise to sell and deliver the commodity at some future time. If you close out your position prior to the close of trading in that contract, no delivery is required. In the case of a short sale in securities, you must borrow the securities sold. Ultimately, you would have to obtain a similar amount of securities and return them to the party from whom they were borrowed.

Another difference: Contrary to the securities market, going short in futures does not normally require an uptick before initiating the position. Nor does it involve dividend payments.

METHOD OF TRADING

The "specialist" system used to maintain markets on the floors of the New York Stock Exchange and American Stock Exchange is not used by any U.S. commodity exchange. Commodity trading is conducted as an open auction, where settlement prices are arrived at by open outcries of "bid" and "asked" prices. No single person is granted the right by the exchange to "make a market" and keep a book on all the open bids and offers. The commodity markets have a number of members, each contributing to the making of the market through open competition.

In commodity trading there is no receipt or delivery of certificates with which you have to be concerned each time you trade. That happens only if you decide to make or take delivery at the consummation of the contract, in which case you will receive the physical commodity not on your front lawn but rather in an exchange-approved warehouse or depository. Many futures contracts now have cash settlement meaning the product is never delivered. Instead, at maturity, the two parties simply settle by exchanging cash, the same way as daily mark-to-market settlements are conducted.

SIZE OF ACCOUNT

Most commodity accounts are small. From surveys conducted by the Commodity Futures Trading Commission, by the exchanges, and by brokerage houses, it is clear that a majority of all accounts contain less than $10,000 in equity.

Nearly 90 percent of them have less than $20,000 in equity, and only a few have equity in excess of $100,000. About three-quarters of all accounts are categorized as speculative.

It seems apparent that most people risk very small absolute amounts in trading commodities. Less than one in four accounts is a hedge account, and even the large accounts (those in excess of $100,000) are small compared to accounts in the securities industry where $100,000 or less is considered a small account.

WHO TRADES COMMODITIES AND WHY?

Some people trade commodity futures as a normal adjunct to their business of producing and marketing a product. For example, if a meat packer wishes to establish the prices he will pay for cattle to slaughter in his plant during the next six months, he may buy futures. Traders who fall in this category are called hedgers. They buy and sell contracts as substitutes for merchandising transactions they will make at a later time. We will deal with this topic at length in subsequent chapters.

Other people trade commodities not as a normal part of producing or marketing a product but only in the hopes of making a profit on their transactions by correctly anticipating price movements. These people are generally categorized as speculators.[1]

There are different types of speculators. Among them are the "scalpers" at the exchanges. They buy and sell contracts continuously, minute by minute, in large and small amounts, hoping to make a small amount on each transaction. They seldom carry a position for more than a few hours.

Another type of trader is the "position trader." He takes a position in the market and holds it for at least a day and frequently longer. He tries to take advantage of short- and long-term trends.

One of the questions frequently asked is, "What sort of person is this speculator?"

In a Chicago Mercantile Exchange study conducted in the 1970s (the only modern-day, full study done on this topic), some 4,000 customers were surveyed. These customers were trading in all types of commodity futures listed on any exchange in the United States. It was found that the typical trader looked something like this:

- Male.
- About 45 years old (56 percent of the sample were males between 35 and 55 years of age).
- Middle to upper-middle income class.
- Good job (54 percent were professionals such as doctors, lawyers, dentists, top management people, or white collar workers).
- Well-educated (68 percent of these 4,000 traders had gone to college; 60 percent of them had graduated with a bachelor's degree; 18 percent had graduate degrees).
- Tends to be a short-term trader (85 percent were holding their positions for less than one month and 55 percent of them for less than 10 days). This could be interpreted in any number of different ways. It might indicate that many of them are trading without a plan.

---

1. The terms "speculator" and "hedger" are unfortunate choices as they have strong emotional conntations for many people and do not always convey an accurate sense of an individual's activities in the market. A more accurate and useful classification of participants would be on the basis of "commercial" and "non-commercial" users of the market.

- ➥ Tends to be a small trader (55 percent of these 4,000 customers were trading one contract each time they traded; 75 percent were trading less than five contracts each time they traded).
- ➥ The individual trading commodities generally had a securities account also (70 percent of the 4,000 had securities accounts).

This does not mean that these characteristics are required in order to be a successful commodity trader, because it takes a special emotional and psychological makeup to trade commodities. But it does help to remove some of the mystery about the type of individual who trades commodity futures. He is probably your next-door neighbor.

SOCIAL AND ECONOMIC BENEFITS OF FUTURES TRADING

Although economists have not yet found a way to accurately quantify all the social and economic benefits that flow from futures markets, a number of them can be identified.

The basic economic functions performed by futures markets relate to competitive price discovery, hedging (offsetting) of commercial price risks, facilitating financing, and allocating resources.

Prices on an organized futures market reflect the combined views of a large number of buyers and sellers, not only of current supply and demand but also of the relationship up to 12 or 18 months in advance. This does not mean that a futures price is a prediction that will hold true. Instead, it is an expression of opinions concerning future supply and demand at a single point in time. As conditions change, opinions change—and, of course, so will prices. These changes do not make the market's pricing function less useful. On the contrary, keeping the supply/demand equation current makes the system more useful than a one-time prediction.

Information generated by futures trading through the price discovery process is invaluable for planning at every stage of commodity production, distribution, and processing. Planning is a normal part of every commercial business. It is necessary to achieve maximum efficiency and to minimize operating costs. To the extent that futures markets improve planning and efficiency and reduce operating costs, the benefits should accrue to the consumer and the economy.

The second major function of the futures exchange is risk shifting. A futures market is a market in risk. It is the risk of price change, not the physical commodity, that is being traded on futures contracts. The futures market allows risk to be "packaged" in special ways and transferred from those who have it but may not want it (commercial businesses) to those who do (speculators).

The risk of price change is ever present. This risk represents a cost that must be borne by someone. If the merchants or middlemen have to assume the risk, they will pay the producer less, charge the processor more, or a combination of the two. If the risk is assumed directly by the producer or processor, they will need to be compensated for bearing the risk, and they will pass the cost of that along. In any event, the cost of risk assumption will become a charge on the economy.

Numerous general economic benefits flow from the hedging function. These include reduced finance charges in carrying inventory. The larger banks that finance producers, distributors, and processors give their best terms for the value of the inventory that is fully protected by an adequate hedge. Most merchants, for instance, finance their operations on borrowed money. A fully hedged merchant with a good credit rating may obtain a loan of 90 percent of the market value of his inventory at an interest rate of say 10 percent. Such a merchant has a great advantage over a competitor who obtains a loan of only 75 to 80 percent on unhedged inventory at a cost of 12 percent interest. If this latter merchant is to survive in the business, this added cost has to become a charge to someone in the economy.

Market participants who do not reduce the risks through hedging are speculating. In assuming these extra risks, they may be increasing the costs to the consumer.

A futures market acts as a focal point where buyers and sellers can meet readily. This improves overall market efficiency by reducing "search" costs. Buyers automatically know where the sellers are and vice versa. They do not need to search each other out.

A futures market in a commodity should lead to less segmentation in the market or, to put it another way, it should foster competition by unifying diverse and scattered local markets. Local monopolists will have a difficult time maintaining their position when national markets easily accessible to all people offer their customers other alternatives.

Futures markets help to tie all local markets together into a national or international market. An integrated national market means that prices in all local markets will tend to move more closely in unison with the national market. Price relationships (basis patterns) for a larger number of locations and a larger number of related products will become more stable. This makes for more effective and efficient hedging of a wider number of risks. We will talk more about this in a later chapter.

How much is the service of the futures market worth to the consumer? That is hard to say precisely. Some studies of the use of futures markets have shown that those who use futures for hedging purposes over several seasons have a more stable income pattern than of those who do not. They do not get the peak prices, but they do not get the bottom ones either. The futures market provides them with the opportunity to stabilize their incomes and allows them to obtain a competitive advantage.

Of course, a futures market can't do all things. Some people have the mistaken notion that futures markets establish prices. This is incorrect. A futures market does not cause either high prices or low prices. In an open market, prices are established by supply and demand. The futures market simply reflects the supply and demand factors and their interaction.

If a consumer boycott of a product becomes operative, if a foreign nation raises its export tax, if the foreign policy of a nation is intended in some way to affect world commodity prices, the futures market should reflect those influences, if it is working right. A futures market cannot guarantee a businessman a profit. If the businessman cannot control costs or is inefficient, the futures market will not magically make his operation profitable.

In short, a properly functioning futures market should foster and improve competition throughout the marketplace, thus encouraging efficient use of all resources.

ELECTRONIC TRADING—GLOBEX[2]

The most visible and exciting part of the traditional exchange is the trading floor with its pits and hundreds of people milling around.

The electronic exchange replaces all of that physical hurly-burly with a computer screen and a keyboard.

Electronic trading is conducted by video display terminals tied to a central data processor where the bids and offers are matched. Electronic trading attempts to duplicate the process of pit trading and to provide instantaneous confirmation, clearing, and settlement of the trades.

Globex is an electronic trading system developed (it is not called an exchange in order to avoid certain regulatory complexities) jointly by Reuters News Agency and the CME. The CBOT has also recently become a part owner. Electronic trading of futures has been on the horizon for many years and emerged only recently in Europe.

Globex began operations on June 25, 1992, several years behind schedule and behind other electronic exchanges. Individual traders do not have direct access to it. Only members of exchanges can join the Globex electronic network and enter orders directly. Certain members can act as brokers for individual traders.

The advent of Globex and electronic trading was hastened by the trading scandal that erupted in the Chicago futures pits in 1989 when undercover FBI agents operated a trading sting and arrested dozens of traders for alleged violations of trading rules. It was clear to CME management that regulators and congressional critics of the futures

2. For more about the organization and operation of exchanges see Chapter 28.

industry would impose possibly burdensome regulations unless the exchanges moved quickly to provide a cleaner and clearer audit trail and an ability to prove that customers were not being unfairly disadvantaged in the trading. Hence, Globex was announced as a responsible move toward improved market surveillance and as a recognition of the inevitable move toward computerization. Increased competition from foreign countries who were creating futures exchanges linked electronically also helped hasten the move to Globex. The foreign competition threatened the continued growth and success of Chicago exchanges.

Regulators like electronic trading because it leaves a clearer audit and paper trail than any floor trading system thus making it easier to detect wrongdoing and violations of trading practices such as trading ahead of a customer, non-competitive trading, and attempted market manipulation.

Defenders of floor trading on the other hand argue that the open outcry system is superior to screen trading because it is more transparent, provides quicker response to new information, and allows more flexibility in executing complex strategies.

Screen trading of futures and other derivatives may have been late arriving in the futures industry, but it is here to stay. First of all, it has been working successfully in stock markets outside the United States for years. Second, the increase in communications technology, the emergence of a generation of computer literate people, and the sheer inefficiency associated with physically cramming more and more bodies into limited exchange floor space makes the continued move toward electronic trading inevitable. Third, the growth of competition from, and among, rivals to Chicago exchanges has made it clear that for Chicago to survive as the industry leader it needs to link foreign rivals on electronic systems owned and controlled by the Chicago exchanges.

The success of financial futures in Chicago, unstable world financial markets and the spread of capitalism spawned many new changes around the globe in recent years. LIFFE (London International Financial Futures Exchange) started in the early 1980s and has grown rapidly. On September 16, 1992, when the currency turmoil hit Europe and both sterling and lira fell out of the European exchange mechanism, the volume of trading on LIFFE exceeded the volume at the CME and the CBOT.

Marche á Terme International de France (MATIF), the French futures exchange, has also had phenomenal growth and success in developing financial futures on the continent. The Germans have recently launched DTB, an electronic exchange for trading futures on German government bonds. MATIF and DTB are forging an electronic link-up. In mid-1992, some of Europe's smaller options exchanges (Stockholm's SOM, Amsterdam's EOE, Zurich's SOFFEX, et al.) also announced an electronic link-up that eventually will enable all of their products to be traded on each other's exchanges.

The growth in futures and options business in European markets is mainly the result of increased business from European banks and institutional investors who are using futures and options, as well as other derivatives, to manage risk associated with their balance sheets and their investments. These institutions are big hedgers.

Perhaps the most important factor is that communications systems know no geographic boundaries. The attraction of electronic trading is that it should increase trading volumes and liquidity in individual contracts, and it also offers a ready-made opportunity for emerging countries, which might otherwise think of building their own futures exchanges, to immediately be linked into the world dealer network. The world dealer network in turn can better offer or customize risk management and investment products to these emerging markets.

Indeed, the growth of an electronically linked exchange and dealer market is good for the exchanges because it generates new deals, and those deals are often based on and hedged through the exchanges. Electronic trading linkages allow smaller financial institutions welcome access to the exchanges' clearinghouses, which stand between a deal's counterparties and enhance the creditworthiness of both sides. In the future, dealers who devise products with sufficiently standardized terms to attract a range of buyers might well find it most convenient to have those products listed on the electronic exchanges.

So far the trading activity has been low (see Figure1.2 and Table 1.1). It is likely to take several years before Globex's real potential can be assessed.

Figure 1.2 Daily Average Number of Contracts Traded

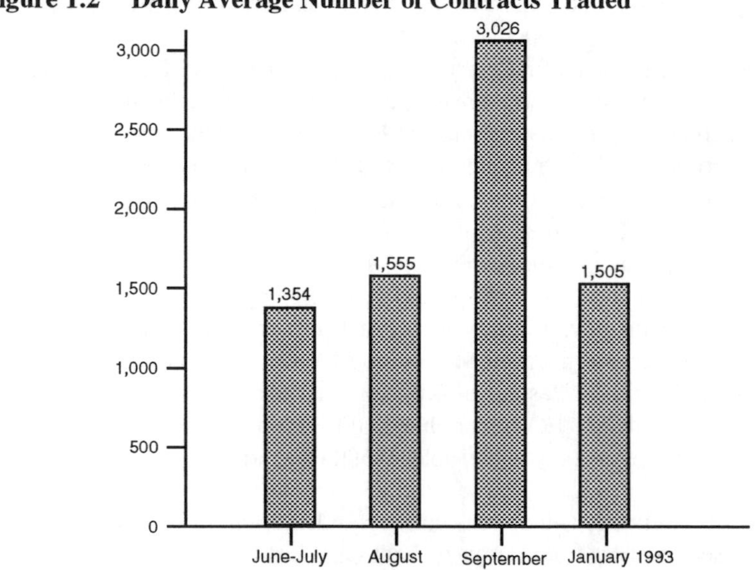

Table 1.1 Globex Trading Lineup

Chicago Time	Greenwich Mean Time	Contract (Futures & Options)
		CME Products
5:45 P.M.	2345	Eurodollar
5:49 P.M	2349	LIBOR
5:51P.M.	2351	90-day T-bill and interest rate futures spreads
6:08 P.M.	0008	Japanese yen
6:10 P.M.	0010	Deutsche mark
6:12 P.M.	0012	Swiss franc
6:14 P.M.	0014	British pound
6:16 P.M.	0016	Canadian dollar
6:18 P.M.	0018	Mark/yen cross-rate
6:20 P.M.	0020	Australian dollar
6:22 P.M.	0022	Currency futures spreads
		CBOT Products
10:30 P.M.	0430	30-year T-bond
10:34 P.M.	0434	10-year T-note
10:36 P.M.	0436	5-year T-note
10:38 P.M.	0438	2-year T-note
10:40 P.M.	0440	Interest rate futures spreads

Note: Starting in March 1993, Globex was scheduled to begin trading on an afternoon session beginning about an hour after floor trading closed.

THE CRASH OF '87

The crash of October 19, 1987, was a major public relations disaster for the Chicago futures exchanges. On that day the Dow Jones Industrial Average dropped 23 percent and the news media immediately blamed it on the trading in futures. Subsequent

Figure 1.3 T-Bond Futures versus CRB Index (weekly data)

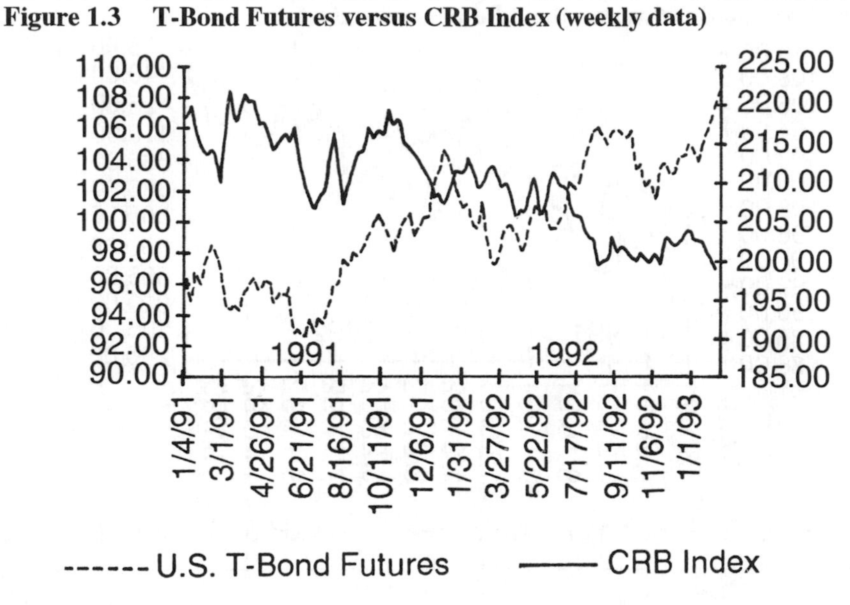

modity Research Bureau's Futures Price Index's (CRB Index) close (inverse) correlation to bond yields (prices). He demonstrates that the CRB Index is a leading indicator on changes in long-term interest rate trends. When yields fall (bond prices rise) as they did during the last half of 1992, the CRB price tends to begin rising (see Figure 1.3). As bond yields (prices) broke out to the downside (upside) without a similar break-out in the CRB Index, Murphy would argue that, given the close historic link between these two markets, such a divergence suggests that either the bond market's fears of inflation from a Clinton presidency are overstated or the commodity markets should begin to move higher.

Bonds versus Stocks

As noted above, commodities have an impact on bonds. Bonds, in turn, impact the stock market. Figure 1.4 shows how the bond futures have tracked the S&P 500 from 1990 to 1992. The bond market is often viewed as a leading indicator for stocks: i.e., a rising bond market has generally indicated a rising stock market in the coming months, and a falling bond market (rising interest rates) generally indicates that the stock market will soon follow. Due to lags in the economic system, of course, these things don't happen simultaneously. At the end of an economic expansion, bonds and high-dividend stocks usually turn down well before the broader index, and during recessions, when inflation is dropping, bonds and interest-sensitive stocks rally well before the broader stock market.

Figure 1.4 S&P 500 versus Bond Futures (weekly data)

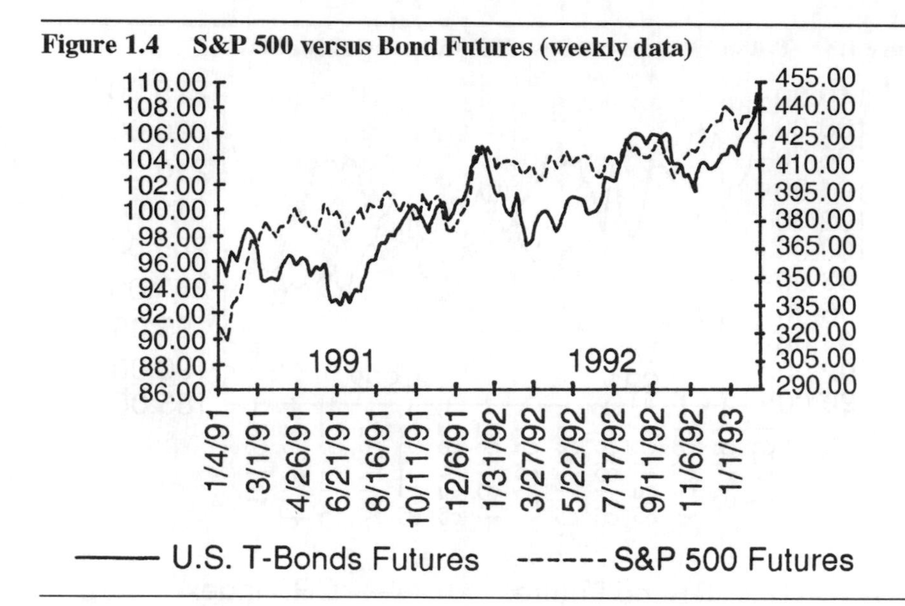

Currency

The third inter-market relationship can be seen in the comparison of currencies to interest rate futures. As noted elsewhere in this book, the value of a currency obviously is influenced by the direction of interest rates in a country. For example, falling U.S. interest rates have a negative impact on the dollar, while rising rates raise the value of the dollar. Thus an inverse relationship exists between the values of currencies and those of interest rates. Figure 1.5 shows how T-bill futures have trended in the opposite direction of the U.S. dollar. As T-bill futures prices rise, short-term U.S. interest rates drop (see also Figures 1.6 and 1.7 for relationships between bond prices and currencies and deutsche mark interest rates).

Thus when you see the dollar going up, it may be a bullish signal about the economy, but it also may be bad news about interest rates. They are probably increasing.

For those of you wanting more on this topic, I suggest reading John Murphy's book.

Figure 1.5 Dollar Index versus T-Bills Futures (weekly data)

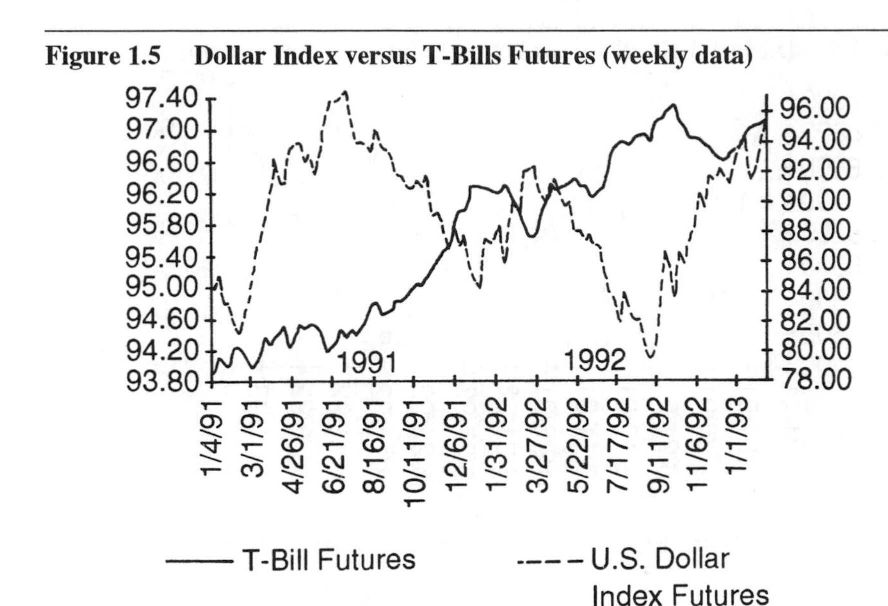

Figure 1.6 Dollar versus Bonds (weekly data)

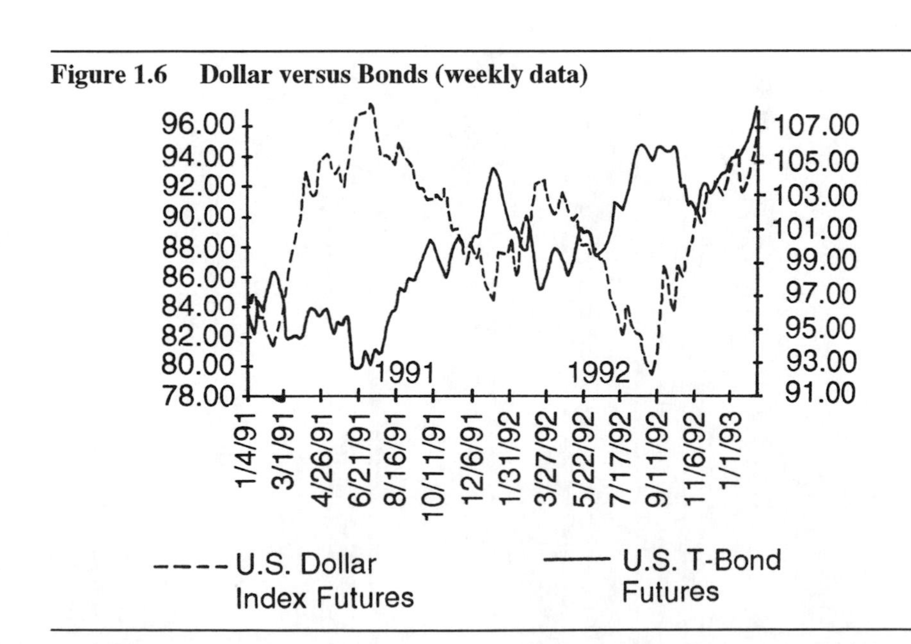

Figure 1.7 D-Mark LIBOR versus D-Mark Futures (weekly data)

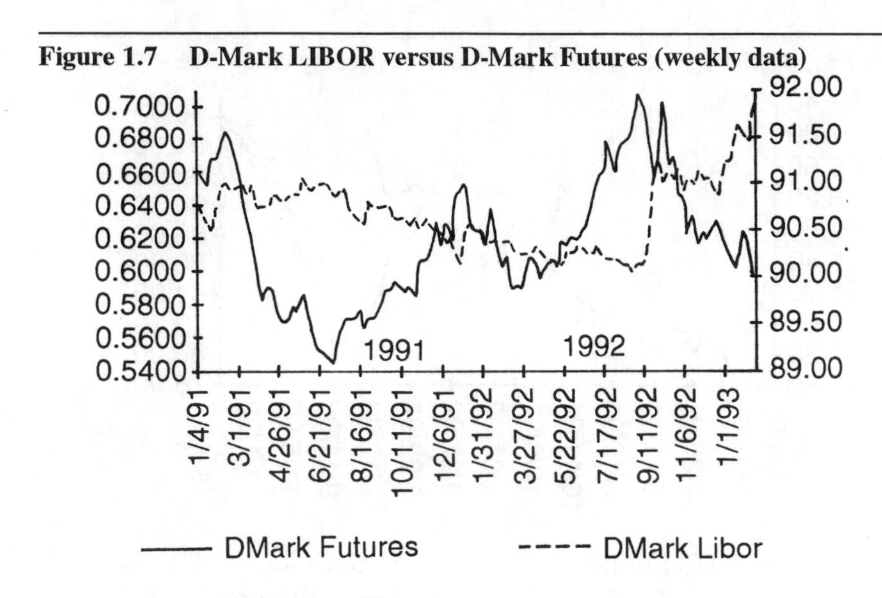

Chapter 2

Speculation Is Not a Four-Letter Word

Commodities . . . ? that's Russian Roulette!
Commodity trading is only for "high rollers."
Anybody who trades commodities loses.

Mention commodity futures trading to a group of strangers at a cocktail party, and the comments above are the most likely kinds of statements you'll hear.

So let's consider some of the reasons why people trade and the more common reasons why many, if not most, lose.

To review for a moment, in the first chapter we outlined two basic categories of people who take positions in commodity futures—hedgers and speculators. Hedgers are those who trade as a normal adjunct to their businesses of producing and marketing a product or in the case of financials buying, selling, or holding a portfolio. They buy and sell futures contracts as substitutes for merchandising transactions they will make at a later time. Speculators take positions in commodities only in the hopes of making a speculative profit by correctly anticipating price movements.

WHY DO SPECULATORS SPECULATE?

Many speculators trade simply because they want money, and the high leverage in futures trading affords the opportunity to turn small amounts of money into big amounts.

But it goes deeper than that. Some people trade because they seek a sense of excitement and risk not available to them in their daily work. The derring-do that had survival value in frontier days is still extolled in our society; yet it is often unavailable in everyday life. In an industrialized nation where most jobs are routine, a person cannot win status through on-the-job valor.

The commodity markets, though, give a person the risk, the feeling of a "man-alone-against-the-odds," that is not available in the everyday world. There is a certain mystique and romance associated with commodity trading. To be able to pick up the phone and call a broker makes a person a participant in an exciting, international game. It pits his skill and judgment against that of all others in the world of futures trading. To win is more than the making of money. It is a reaffirmation of his own ability and acumen; it is food for his ego—and therein lies the danger. When the ego takes over, rational decision making is impaired. A man whose ego won't admit a mistake tends to stick with a losing position too long. Consequently, people who fall in love with their positions become big losers.

A successful trader knows and understands the importance of his ego in trading, and he learns to control it. In fact, self-discipline is an important key to successful trading.

Some of the basic psychological motivations for trading can be explained by the greed/fear complex. People trade because they want money. Yet, by trading, they fear losing what they want the most. Sometimes the greed motivation becomes so strong that they overtrade. In other instances, fear becomes so overpowering that the ability of an individual to make rational decisions is impaired. A good trading plan will help control this greed/fear complex.

Another motivating factor is sheer gambling instinct. Some people trade commodities because the market is like a "Las Vegas" for them. They enjoy the excitement of the unknown, the taking of risks, and money doesn't mean that much to them. Usually these people are losers.

There also seems to be a basic need-to-own drive in every individual. This drive manifests itself in the decision to trade futures contracts and, undoubtedly, helps explain why the general run-of-the mill trader prefers to be "long" in the market and hesitates to go short. He would rather have no position than a short position.

Before you trade, ask yourself whether any of the reasons above describe you. If so, think carefully about your suitability for trading.

SPECULATION OR GAMBLING?

Even relatively sophisticated investors and investment counselors have been heard to refer to commodity futures trading as "a close relative of a Nevada casino." Gambling and speculation are distinctly different economic activities, however.

Gambling involves the creation of a risk for the sole purpose of its being taken. The dice game or horse race creates risks which would not otherwise be present. If the police raid the dice game or the race track burns down, the risks they offer no longer exist. Gambling involves sterile transfers of money between individuals. In the strict economic sense, it absorbs time and resources, yet creates no new value.

Speculation, however, deals in risks that are already necessarily present in the process of producing and marketing goods in a free, capitalistic system. As livestock and crops are grown and marketed, there are obviously risks of price change that must be taken by someone. It can be those who own the actual commodity—or someone else.

For example, let's suppose you own a small ranch and decide to raise beef cattle. You know how much young feeder cattle cost, and you estimate how much it will cost you to feed them up to market weight by next fall. Based on these calculations, you decide that if you can sell your cattle next fall at 60¢ per pound or more, you can make a fair profit and the enterprise will be worthwhile to you.

The day you buy your feeder cattle you are assuming the risk that by market time next fall cattle prices will be below 60¢ per pound, which could mean no profit, or worse, a loss to you.

The futures market enables you, by selling a futures contract, to shift at least part of this risk to a speculator who is willing to assume it in hopes of profiting from a change in that future price. The point is, the risk was there. It had to be borne by someone whether the futures market existed or not. The futures market served an economic function by facilitating the transfer of the risk from someone who didn't want it to someone who did. (This is, of course, a highly simplified example of a hedge. A much closer look at this operation is the subject of later chapters.)

This does not mean that no one treats commodity trading as gambling. Anyone who approaches futures trading without a knowledge and understanding of commodities and their markets is doing just that—gambling. And it shouldn't surprise you that these people tend to be losers in the long run.

DO MOST SPECULATORS LOSE?

Perceived wisdom has it that most commodity traders lose money. In this case, perceived wisdom is correct. All studies conducted over the years on this topic yield the same conclusion: most individual traders lose. Studies done by the University of Illinois and others, as well as private industry surveys, have concluded that overall about twice as many people lose money as make money. Or, to look at it another way, roughly one-third are winners and two-thirds are losers. On the average, each loser lost more than each winner made.

But such broad generalized conclusions can be misleading. Elliot Bercovitz of Lind-Waldock, the largest return discount broker in the world, surveys the firm's 16,000 customer accounts periodically and he's found some interesting results (see Table 2.1).

Table 2.1 Profits and Losses—Individual Speculators

No. of Trades	% of Traders with profits		Successful Traders's Average Profit		Unsuccessful Traders's Average Loss	
	'91	'92	'91	'92	'91	'92
1–20	22.4	29.5	2,456	2,483	2,808	2,306
21–100	26.3	32.2	8,000	7,126	8,408	7,716
101–200	33.5	36.7	15,888	18,501	16,686	21,989
200+	44.5	43.2	37,656	44,347	31,731	40,460
All Accounts	26.1	31.7	9,514	7,340	6,942	6,106

Data from Jan–July each year.

a. Overall more than two-thirds of the traders lost money.

b. Those who traded more had a higher success rate. But even in the most active category (200+ trades), the majority lost.

studies by the U.S. Treasury supported that view. But in 1988, Alan Greenspan, Chairman of the Federal Reserve, released the Fed's report, which suggested that derivatives did more good than harm on that day. Indeed, since 1987, dozens of academic studies of the crash have been completed. None of those studies supports the case against futures trading, and most of them agree with Chairman Greenspan's conclusion.

In any event, the Chicago exchanges and the stock exchanges moved quickly to put in "circuit breakers." These were intra-day price limits and trading halts that were designed to slow a fast-moving market. Between 1988, when the circuit breakers were installed, and the end of 1992, they have been triggered approximately 23 times. As of this writing, the most recent was on October 5, 1992.

In addition, the stock exchanges, commodity exchanges, Fed, Treasury, SEC, and CFTC have established better procedures for collecting and sharing information about who is trading, the size of their positions, the flow of arbitrage, and the extent of basket trading (buying futures in a stock index at a commodity exchange and simultaneously, or nearly so, selling, individually, a group of stocks on the stock exchange).

STOCKS, BONDS, CURRENCIES AND COMMODITIES—IT'S ALL ONE MARKET NOW

All markets are linked. One really cannot do a thorough job of analysis in one market without studying what is happening in related markets. Hence, if you really want to understand the bond market, you need to analyze commodity markets, stock markets, currency markets, and interest rate markets. And if you really want to understand stock markets, you have to analyze bond markets, currency markets, and commodity markets, etc. Since the futures market covers, worldwide, all four of these major groups—commodities, currencies, stocks, and interest rates —the futures are convenient laboratories for conducting robust investment analyses.

To illustrate, consider each of the four groups in turn.

Commodities versus Bonds

Basic commodity prices function as a leading inflation indicator and so do bonds. These two markets are linked and should be studied together. As you will see in Figure 1.3, bond prices and commodity prices usually trend in opposite directions. Commodity prices are reflective of low inflation and when people expect low inflation, bond prices rise (interest rates fall). John Murphy, in his excellent book entitled *Technical Analysis of the Futures Markets,* provides a very readable explanation of the Com-

Although this survey is not scientifically sound as a random sample and it suffers from "survivor bias" (i.e., the losers leave and the winners stay to trade more actively), it probably reflects reality.

Even the most experienced, most successful traders make losing trades. In fact, in my experience analyzing professional traders, many have more losing trades than winning trades but still make money because the losing trades represent small losses and winning trades represent large gains. For example, if you had 10 losing trades averaging $100 each and two winning trades averaging $600 each, you would be a net winner of $200, even though you had more losing than winning trades.

NO WINNING FORMULA

Since there is obviously no magic formula for winning, it is important that the beginning trader understand some of the more common reasons why inexperienced traders may lose money.

1. Undercapitalization Experience has proven that to begin trading with too little risk capital (and risk capital it must be; a trader should trade only with capital he can afford to lose) is almost a guarantee of failure. A position not adequately backed by trading capital may be forced into liquidation by a temporary adverse market move, which results in a call for additional margin that cannot be met. More on this in the next chapter.

2. Lack of Knowledge Some traders, of course, lose simply because of lack of know-how. It is easy for in-experienced traders to misinterpret or miss altogether important pieces of information that affect prices. The result can be frequent mistakes in market analysis and errors in trading decisions. Before getting involved in trading, one should know the methods of fundamental analysis and be able to detect errors in trading decisions. One should know the methods of fundamental and technical price analysis, learn the different types of buy and sell orders and how they can be used, and study the production and marketing system for the futures you want to trade. (Note: Yes, even financial futures like T-bonds have a production and marketing cycle!)

3. Trading Too Many Different Commodities Many new traders try to follow too many different commodities. It is difficult for even an experienced trader to keep a close watch on more than a few commodities at one time. It is good advice when starting out to stick to one or two commodities and learn them thoroughly.

4. Lack of Discipline A lack of discipline is another frequent pitfall for a new trader. As was pointed out earlier, human ego is an important part of trading. When you take a position in the markets, you become emotionally involved. You defend your decision. Unless you are exceptionally objective, you can trap yourself in an unprofitable position by refusing to admit, even to yourself, that you have made a mistake. Successful traders exit quickly when they suspect they are wrong. They do not fight the market.

5. Lack of a Trading Plan Probably the single most important mistake new traders make, however, is to embark without a trading plan. A plan is like a road map. Just as you would not set out on a cross-country drive without a map, so you should not embark on commodity futures without a clear-cut trading plan.

An adequate plan forces you to set objectives and develop discipline in meeting those objectives. An adequate plan removes speculation from the personal realm of gambling.

PRACTICE TRADING

Before you open an account and lay your money on the line, it is a good idea to test yourself and your abilities by making some hypothetical trades. Appendix I contains the "Commodity Trader's Scorecard" work sheets and a set of instructions for doing such practice trading. Results of your practice trading may help you decide whether futures trading is for you.

A word of caution is in order, however: Success in paper trading is no guarantee of success in real-life trading. If you are like most people, you will probably react quite differently when faced with a real trading decision than with a paper trade. This is a major reason why one should be wary of placing too much faith in hypothetical or simulated trading results.

Chapter 3

Managed Futures— A Good Alternative

The definition of a successful speculator is one who picks the right time to die.

Most people who trade futures and manage their own accounts lose money. This is especially true of speculators and of first-time traders. The reasons are numerous and are recounted throughout this book.

There is another alternative, and, if this book does nothing else, it may help convince you that a more sensible way for you to get started trading commodities is to do so by hiring a professional to do the trading for you. Professionals (those who make their living trading) also lose. Sometimes they lose a lot. But a larger percentage of professionals than of individual small traders make profits.

There are a variety of vehicles available for participating in futures markets. You could:

a. Open your own account and manage it yourself.

b. Open your own account and manage it yourself by relying on trading signals and guidance from a third party—usually a broker or advisor.

c. Open your own account and have it managed by a third party Commodity Trading Advisor (CTA).

d. Purchase an interest in a limited partnership or a commodity pool, which is managed by a professional CTA.

Commodity pools are groups of individual traders owning an interest in an account or group of accounts all trading identically. The organizers of such vehicles are called Commodity Pool Operators (CPOs) and must be registered with the CFTC.

CTAs in the futures world are also registered by the CFTC and act in a similar fashion to investment advisors in the world of stocks and bonds. CTAs are granted authority by the client to make transactions on the client's behalf.

Collectively, CPO and CTA activity is known as *managed futures* activity, and the limited partnership vehicles by which they collect and aggregate client funds for trading are generically referred to as *futures funds*.

Managed futures vehicles, whether individually managed accounts opened with a CTA or interests in limited partnerships, are an especially attractive means of getting involved in futures investment vehicles because:

a. Professional money managers have the expertise individuals lack.

b. Individuals often have too little capital to trade successfully.

c. Individual traders lack the time needed to do adequate research and monitor the market. They are too busy working and making a living.

d. Individual traders have little bargaining power in lowering commissions. Professional managers and CPOs with large chunks of money can get the most favorable brokerage rates.

e. Individual accounts have unlimited liability and are liable for all losses in an account even if the losses exceed the amount of money in the account. Limited partners are liable only for the amount they invest in the partnership. They have limited liability.

f. Professional managers usually have more timely access to information, research results, and the markets than do individuals.

GROWTH OF MANAGED FUTURES

During the 1980s the managed futures business grew rapidly from only a few million dollars in 1980 to in excess of $14 billion at the end of 1992. Figure 3.1 shows the growth in money managed by the CTAs included in Managed Accounts Reports (MAR) Trading Advisor Qualified Index, which represents dollars managed by CTAs who have at least 18 months experience, manage at least $250,000, or who are acting as a CTA in a public fund. These numbers do not include many private pools, offshore pools, or individually managed accounts. It is likely that such private monies bring the total to $20 billion or more (including so-called "guaranteed funds").

The number of funds has increased dramatically as well. In 1980 there were only about a dozen public funds—each only a few million dollars. Today there are hundreds—many of them with tens of millions of dollars. Nearly every major brokerage house, especially the large securities brokerage firms, have regular public offerings of such futures funds. Figure 3.2 shows the growth in monies invested in funds/pools as measured by MAR.

STRUCTURE

Generally futures funds are formed as limited partnerships. The securities laws prohibit the use of mutual fund structures in futures. The limited partnership structure has the major advantage of limiting the liability of the limited partner investors to the

Figure 3.1 MAR Trading and Dollar Size of "Qualified" Universe

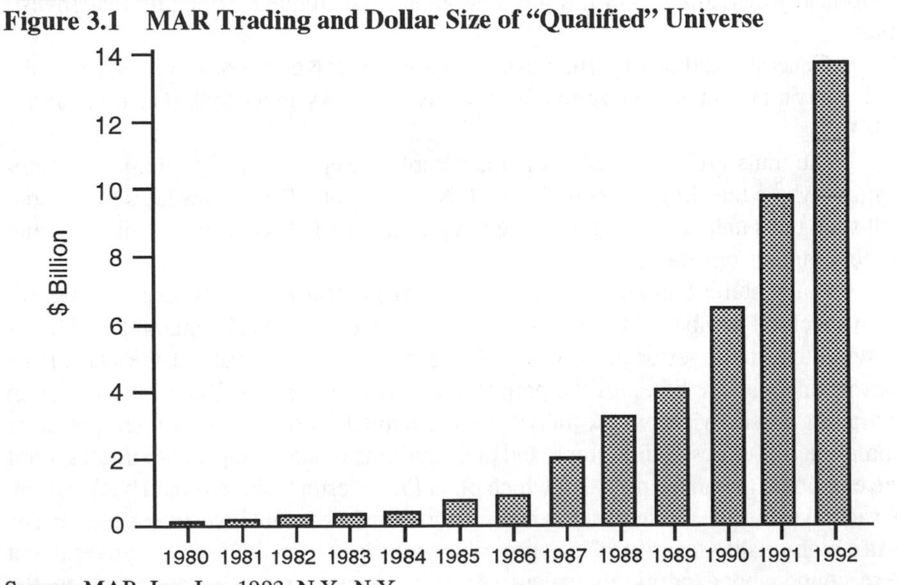

Source: MAR, Inc. Jan. 1993, N.Y., N.Y.

Figure 3.2 MAR Fund/Pool Index Dollar Size "Qualified" Universe

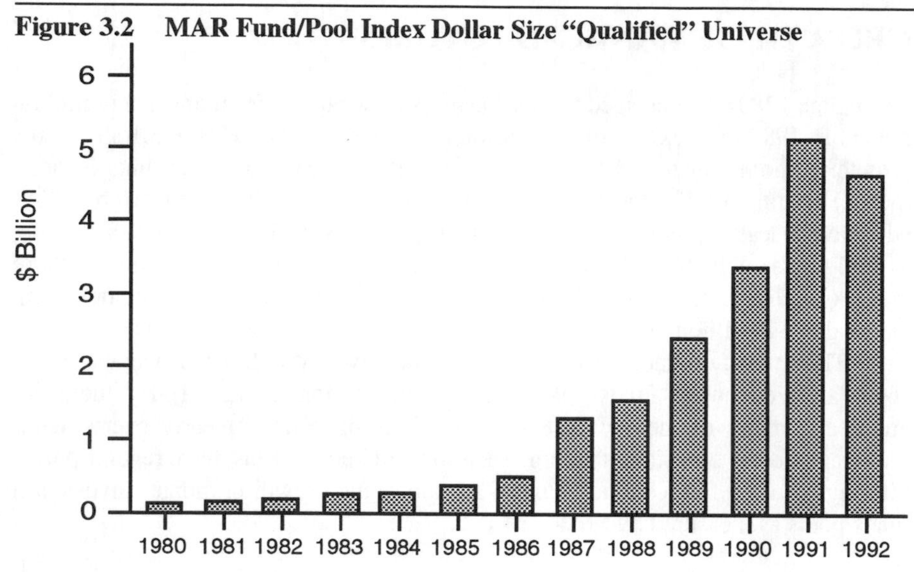

Source: MAR, Inc. Jan. 1993, N.Y., N.Y.

amount of money invested. In that sense the partnership limits the losses in a manner similar to the limited liability of a corporate shareholder. Such partnerships normally are open for investment for several months and then are closed for good or open only periodically thereafter. Very few are "evergreen," i.e., regularly open for new investment.

Generally, a limited partner can sell a unit for its Net Asset Value (NAV) at the end of any month or quarter by giving a few days or weeks notice to the General Partner (GP).

The units are not tradable or transferable except under very unique circumstances where the GP gives permission. It is a violation of securities laws to buy and sell such units unless they are registered as publicly traded securities—a difficult and unduly burdensome task.

Many futures funds provide a "money-back guarantee" if you remain an investor for a specified number of years, usually three or five years. Such "guaranteed" funds provide that the investor gets all of his original investment back at the end of the partnership's active life, plus the proportionate share of profits, if any, from trading. If trading losses wipe out the initial trading capital before the guarantee period is complete, all futures trading stops, and the remaining monies simply earn interest until the end of the guarantee period at which point the investor's share is paid back to him. To achieve this, the GP sets aside a certain portion of the initial investment and invests it in a high-quality security of an appropriate maturity. Often this is a U.S. government zero-coupon bond or its equivalent. As this amount grows in value due to the compounding of interest earnings it eventually, at maturity, reaches the value of the initial investment. The difference between the initial set aside for the security and the initial investment is the amount available for trading futures.

The "guaranteed" futures funds have one wonderful advantage. They assure you that you will get your money back at the end of X years and, therefore, the most you can lose is the interest or earnings on your money had you invested it somewhere else. The disadvantages are as follows:

a. The loss of five years of interest earnings can be substantial. For example, if a five-year Treasury bond can be purchased today to yield 5 percent, at the end of five years each $1,000 you have invested will be worth $1,276 before taxes. Your risk in the guaranteed fund then over the five years is 27.6 percent.

b. There is no liquidity in these funds. If you want to sell your unit before the guarantee period is up, you generally cannot. Not so with a share of stock or a bond. You can sell them at any time. Further, in cases that do allow liquidity, there are often penalty fees that must be paid if you liquidate early.

c. You pay a substantial fee to have the GP use most of the money to simply buy a zero-coupon bond or other security. For example, if five-year interest rates are at 5 percent, then out of every $1,000 you invest in a five-year guaranteed futures fund, about 78.4 percent will be invested in the T-bond and only about 21.6 percent will be available for futures trading. Many people do not need to pay someone else substantial fees to buy T-bonds for them.

d. The total return on guaranteed funds will be much lower than on other funds. Of course, your risk is also much lower because in non-guaranteed funds you could lose all your investment. For example, if out of $1,000 invested about 79 percent ($790) of the money earns 5 percent for five years and 21 percent ($210) of it (the futures portion) earns 20 percent *after all fees*, the net average annual total return to the investor on the original $1,000 is 8.7 percent. If you had all the money being traded by the CTAs instead of only 21 percent of it, your return would have been 20 percent.

But look further. How realistic is that 20 percent return? What are the probabilities that the CTAs selected to manage the money will indeed return 20 percent after all fees?

Suppose you think there is an 80 percent chance they will earn 20 percent and a 20 percent chance that the CTAs will lose all the trading capital and you will only get your initial investment back, thus losing the interest earnings ($276) on the original $1,000. If the $210 traded by the CTAs increases at a 20 percent compounded rate it will be worth about $522.50. The mathematical expectation on this investment is:

$$
\begin{aligned}
522.50 \times .80 &= 418.00 \\
276.00 \times .20 &= \underline{-55.20} \\
& + 362.80
\end{aligned}
$$

The mathematical expectation in the alternative investment in 5 percent T-bonds is $276.

Would it be worth it if you think there is only a 10 percent chance the CTAs will return 20 percent per year and a 60 percent chance they will return 10 percent per year? The answer in this latter case is that the mathematical expectation would be against you.

Fees

The fees associated with futures funds are often quite high, but when compared to the costs of trading a small individual account or compared with fees associated with many other Wall Street products, they may not be so unfavorable. The fees in most such products will generally include the following:

Sales fees: Equal to about 1 percent per year of initial investment. Sometimes these fees are taken out in a lump sum up front. So for a 5-year fund they could amount to a 5 percent or more front-end load.

Brokerage Fees: Usually about 5 to 8 percent annually of the futures portion.

CTA Management Fees: Usually about 2 to 3 percent annually of the futures portion plus 15 to 20 percent of profits. Sometimes profits are measured exclusive of interest earnings on the broker's margin deposits.

General Partner Fees: Usually about 1 to 2 percent annually for providing the Guarantee. Sometimes the GP will also get a percent of profits.

Administrative Fees: Usually about .5 percent annually. These fees cover audits, legal, correspondence, organizational expenses, etc. Sometimes these fees will be stated in dollar amounts rather than percentages. Thus, the larger the fund, the lower the percentage. Generally for large public funds, the organizational fees can run half a million dollars and annual administration fees half of that amount.

In total, the fees associated with public funds will generally range between 10 and 15 percent annually for the futures portion and between 7 and 8 percent annually on the net asset value (NAV) of guaranteed funds.

Clearly, therefore, in order for CTAs to return 20 percent annually after all fees, they have to perform extraordinarily well. So well, in fact, that you should not count on it.

Performance

There were about 3,000 CTAs registered with the NFA and CFTC at the end of 1992. However, there are fewer than 50 of these that have been acting as CTAs for 10 years or longer. In fact, the registration category of CTA did not appear until the late 1970s. Hence, you are dealing with a very young "industry" here and a group of people most of whom have very short track records.

Many of the 3,000 registrants are brokers who have the CTA registration as a convenience and an adjunct to their brokerage business. This, of course, raises potential conflicts of interest if the broker collects both brokerage fees and CTA fees for his work as a CTA. Only about 300 to 400 of the 3,000 registrants have published track records that reveal how well they have actually done in managing their own and other people's money. There are several organizations that collect and publish these track records and the performance records on public futures funds. These organizations include:

Managed Accounts Reports (MAR)
220 Fifth Avenue
New York, NY 10001

TASS Management Limited
40 Catherine Place
London SWIE6HL
England

Barclay Trading Group
Fairfield, Iowa

Stark Research, Inc.
Palatine, IL

If, in 1980, you had invested $1,000 in the MAR Index of Qualified Universe CTAs (which represents CTAs with at least one year experience and managing at least $500,000 or managing money as part of a public commodity fund), by the end of 1992 your $1,000 would have grown to $8,637. Clearly, the growth in the index is not representative of how you would actually have fared because you could not invest in the index. You would have to select individual CTAs. Nevertheless, it probably represents the best estimate one can obtain of general industry performance during recent years (see Figure 3.3).

The data in Table 3.1 provide a comparison between the returns achieved by the MAR Universe, of Qualified CTAs, for each year 1980 through 1992, and the returns for investing in the S&P 500 or bonds for the same years. Note that although the CTA

Figure 3.3 MAR Qualified CTA Index*

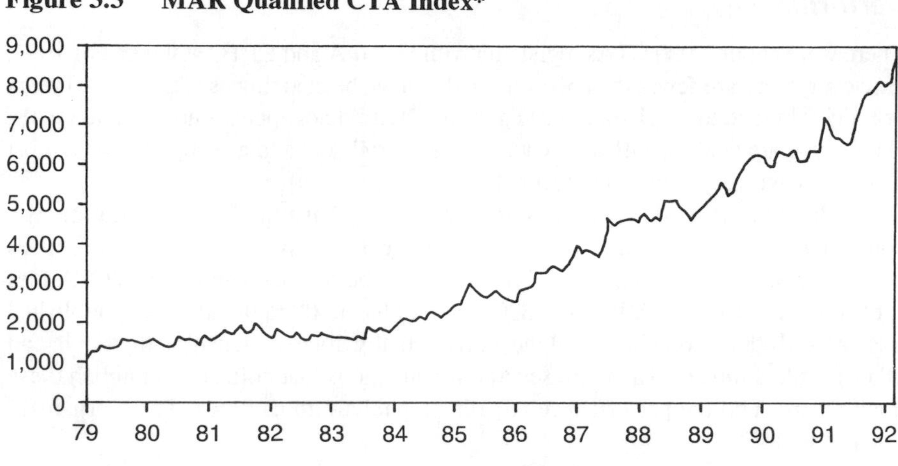

* Monthly returns compounded. Data Spirce: MAR/Laporte.

returns were higher, their volatility was also higher. Nevertheless $1,000, compounded at the average annual rate and invested with the CTA's in 1980 would have grown to $6,813, while the same $1,000 invested in the S&P 500 or in Bonds would have been $5,911 and $3,871, respectively, by the end of 1992.

SELECTING A CTA TO MANAGE YOUR MONEY

Selecting a CTA to manage your account can be a puzzling process. First, you need to know who is available as a CTA. Second, you need to get information about them, and, third, you need to negotiate with them.

Finding out who is available can be done easily through any of the services mentioned above such as MAR or TASS. Subscriptions to their monthly reports are expensive. However, a good independent broker can also help you identify possible prospects.

Once identified, contact your selected CTAs and ask them to send you their current Disclosure Document. That document, which is required by law to be presented to each investor at the time of first sales efforts, contains all the basic (generic) information about the CTA—e.g., full name, address, educational and business background; number of years registered as a CTA; the method of trading; futures contracts traded; specialties (spread trading, arbitrage, financial futures only, agricultural futures only, etc.); minimum size account; fee schedule; affiliation, if any, with a broker; statement regarding civil, regulatory, or criminal suits or actions during the

Table 3.1 Comparison of Annual Returns 1980–1992

	MAR CTA Index (Qualified Universe)	S&P 500	Bonds*
1980	52.99	32.45	5.17
1981	1.11	(4.95)	9.38
1982	5.09	21.56	27.75
1983	0.28	22.55	7.40
1984	18.05	6.27	14.48
1985	27.11	31.75	20.43
1986	3.08	18.68	15.31
1987	57.78	5.26	2.19
1988	14.63	16.61	7.03
1989	7.25	(31.68)	14.23
1990	27.29	3.12	8.72
1991	16.82	30.48	15.33
1992	9.90	7.64	7.17
Ave. Annual Rate	17.34	15.96	11.94
Volatility	20.56	16.32	6.69
$1,000**	$6,813	$5,911	$3,871

* Shearson Lehman Long Term Government Bond Index

** $1,000 compounded annually at the average annual rate

last five years; and, finally, a track record if he has actually been managing other people's money.

The track record, if one exists, must be presented in a certain way prescribed by the regulators so that potential investors can do their own analysis of the results (see Table 3.1). For example, the record must clearly show for each month how much money was actually being managed, how much of the month-to-month change resulted from trading gains or losses, and how much from additional investment or withdrawals; the brokerage fees charged; the interest earnings; the management and incentive fees paid; and the net return on investment after fees, expenses, etc., stated either in percent or as the change in the value of a unit investment.

It can be difficult to get precisely comparable analyses of all track records but the CFTC's required 13-column format for presenting track records helps. To get the most realistic picture of the CTA's performance, you should deduct from the profits all interest earned. Table 3.1 depicts a sample track record report.

After you have the numbers adjusted, do some very basic calculations of each CTA and compare them on:

a. Compound annual return.

b. Largest single losing month.

c. Largest loss from peak-to-valley.

d. How many months were involved in (c).

e. How many months it took to recover to a new high.

f. Sharpe ratios.

The Sharpe ratio, named after Nobel Prize winner Professor William Sharpe, measures relative reward and risk by subtracting the monthly average T-bill rate from the monthly average investment return and then dividing by the standard deviation of the monthly returns. The higher the Sharpe ratio the better the reward/risk ratio.

$$\frac{\text{Investment Return} - \text{T–Bill Return}}{\text{Standard Deviation of Investment Return}} = \text{Sharpe Ratio}$$

Statistical analyses and number manipulations will take you only so far. It may be misleading to use statistical analyses that are based on less than three or four years of data as reliable guides about future performance. Indeed, several studies have shown that past performance of CTAs is a very poor guide to future performance. Hence, you have to rely on other qualitative factors.

Which CTA Is the Best?

Consider the data in Table 3.2. If you were going to give your money to one of them, which would have provided you the highest average annual return over the four-year period shown?

If you are like most people, you would have answered A or C. The answer is they all provided equal average annual returns—5.5 percent. At first glance, that seems preposterous, but look closely at C. If he started with $100, at the end of year 2, he

Table 3.2 CTA Returns

Year	A	B	C
1	–6%	+7%	+20%
2	–6%	+6%	+25%
3	+20%	+5%	–30%
4	+17%	+4%	+18%

has $150. After the 30 percent loss in year 3, he's back almost to $100. The 18 percent return in year 4 brings him back only to equal the plodding, but positive, return of B.

Actually, from the data shown you cannot answer the question posed above. Statistical data, and especially returns data alone, can be very misleading. To answer the question you need to look also at the volatility of the returns, the Sharpe ratio, the trend in returns, etc. Further, you have to consider qualitative factors.

Qualitative Factors

You should meet the CTA if you are hiring him to manage your account. If you are putting your money in a futures fund, the CPO or GP will take care of this for you. Just check the fine print in the prospectus to be sure that the CPO, GP, and CTA do not have conflicts of interest that reward them in a mutually beneficial way while possibly harming you, e.g., brokerage arrangements that reward the CPO, GP, or broker for selecting a CTA that tends to trade a lot.

The best guides to selecting a CTA are:

- Number of years experience—the more the better. He's a survivor.
- A record of stability in business procedures and methodology of trading.
- A record of consistency in returns. High returns are not so important as steady positive returns.
- Attitude toward risk and discipline or attention to detail in controlling risk. This is best reflected in (a) the CTA's responses to questions dealing with how he leverages and de-leverages an account as he makes profits or suffers losses; (b) the explanations of the size of the largest loss to date—why it occurred and what safeguards are in place to see that it won't occur again; and (c) the Sharpe ratio.

Single Advisor or Multi-Advisor?

Almost all individually managed accounts are managed by a single CTA. Most commodity funds issued are private placements and most of them are single advisor funds. Almost all large public futures funds are multi-advisor funds.

Even casual perusal of the records of individual CTAs reveals the very high probability that with any single advisor there is a very high risk of having very substantial losses at any point in time. Diversification across several advisors, whose trading patterns are non-correlated, provides a substantial reduction in risk, reduces the peak-to-valley drawdown substantially, and increases significantly the probability that one will have a superior investment. Of course, such multi-advisor diversification can be accomplished only if you have enough capital to do it yourself, or if you participate only in multi-advisor funds where the CTAs are selected with diversification and risk control in mind.

Figure 3.4 illustrates the point. If you select a single advisor, you live and die with him. The Sharpe ratio (reward to risk) will usually be lower than if you select two CTAs. Similarly, three will be better than two, four will be better than three, etc., all the way up to seven or eight.

Figure 3.4 Fund Structure: Efficient Portfolios Optimal Portfolio Size

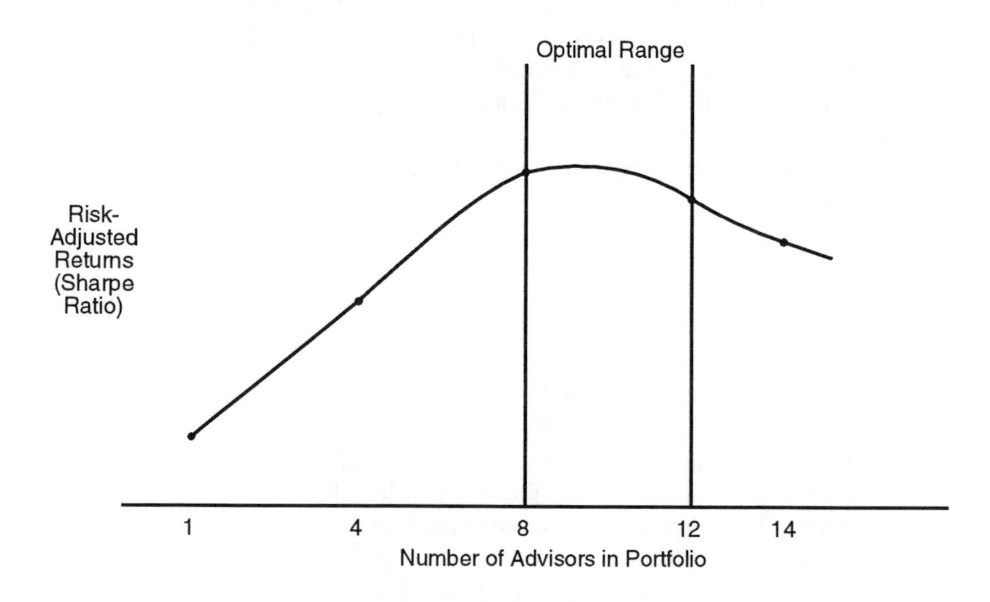

If you spend some effort in researching and selecting CTAs that are truly different, it is easy to see how you can really improve the quality of your investment.

One important measure to use in assembling a diversified group of CTAs is correlation. Conduct a correlation study of their monthly returns. Select the group that has the highest returns and the lowest correlations with each other. Generally, you would not want any two CTAs that have an inter-correlation of returns above 60 percent unless there are other offsetting factors. Select one of them, not both of them. The data in Table 3.3 illustrate the point.

CTA A and CTA D in Table 3.3 are so highly correlated that to select both of them is almost like doubling up.

Of course, you don't need to make equal allocations to each CTA. Varying the allocations among CTAs also adds to diversification.

You can also diversify within a single CTA. Many CTAs, especially the larger, more experienced CTAs, offer several different programs, thus allowing one to diversify within a single CTA by selecting several programs and allocating monies among them. Putting equal dollar amounts in each of the separate programs could provide substantial diversification and lessen risk significantly, while still providing reasonable returns.

Table 3.3 Multi-Advisor Correlation Coefficients

(Eight Trading Advisors)

	A	B	C	D	E	F	G	H
A	100	1	–1	80	33	–27	5	8
B	1	100	–39	0	4	9	–6	12
C	–1	–39	100	–30	–6	–29	17	10
D	80	0	–30	100	12	5	11	–2
E	33	4	–6	12	100	2	31	15
F	–27	9	–29	5	2	100	21	2
G	5	–6	17	11	31	21	100	13
H	8	12	10	–2	15	2	13	100
Average	14	–3	–11	–11	13	–2	13	8

THE VALUE OF ADDING COMMODITY FUTURES TO YOUR INVESTMENT PORTFOLIO

Many studies have been conducted over the last several decades to determine whether it was worthwhile for an investor to add a managed futures investment to his total investment portfolio. In other words, whether the Sharpe ratio (reward/risk) would be improved if investors diversified their investments by allocating say only 90 percent of their investments to stocks and put 10 percent in a futures fund.

The answer has been a resounding yes. Virtually all studies, academic as well as commercial, agree.

The earliest of these studies was done in the early 1980s by Professors Bodie and Rosansky of Boston University and by the late Professor John Lintner of Harvard.

They applied Modern Portfolio Theory, named after Professors Sharpe and Markowitz, who won the Nobel prize, to the question of efficient allocation of dollars among investments to get the most attractive reward/risk combination. They concluded that allocating even a small percentage of the investment dollar to futures funds improved the investor's return/risk ratio over keeping all his investment in stocks and bonds. They established the concept of an "efficient frontier" which is created by plotting on a graph the measure of risk (standard deviation of monthly returns) and the measure of reward (monthly returns) for various combinations of investments in stocks, bonds, and futures funds. The combination that lies furthest to the right is the best reward/risk combination, i.e., highest return/lowest risk. The line connecting the dots representing the different combinations is called the efficient frontier (see Figure 3.5 for an illustration).

Many other studies have concluded that one's investment quality could benefit by allotting as much as 20 percent of a portfolio to futures funds.

Recent studies by the Russell Corporation and Powers Research Associates concluded that a passive (buy and hold) strategy involving a basket of world-produced commodities would improve the reward/risk ratio of an investment portfolio, even if the basket contributed a return as low as only 1/8 to 1/4 of 1 percent per year.

All the research points in the same direction and says the same thing. Investors can improve their returns without making their risks worse if they allocate some small percent of their money to an investment in a managed futures product.

Clearly, some qualifiers have to be added to that statement. First, the results reported are based on a presumption of long-term trends where the returns from futures funds are very lowly correlated with stock returns. Second, it presumes that the CTA(s) selected or the fund selected will be at least as profitable as the funds or the average of funds the researchers selected in their research.

Figure 3.5 Efficient Frontier with CRB

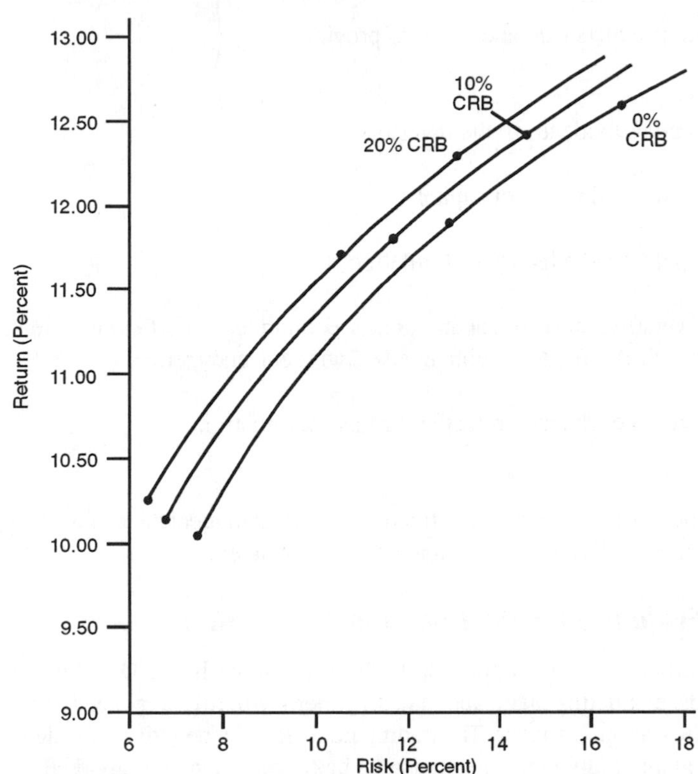

GETTING HELP—USE A TRADING MANAGER

If all of the above discussion leaves you feeling uncertain as to how to proceed and still asking, "How do I select a CTA or a fund?" or even, "How much improvement should I expect in my investment reward/risk ratio if I allocate 5 percent, 10 percent, or even 15 percent of my money to futures?" There is help the—Trading Manager.

Trading managers are like investment counselors. They are supposed to act independently in evaluating and selecting CTAs, futures funds, and brokers. They are normally paid a small fee, plus a percent of profits, so they have great incentive to hold your costs down and select CTAs who do not lose money. Normally they are most appropriate and affordable for large investments seeking to place several million dollars singly or in a fund.

The trading manager normally provides the following services:

1. Product Design

Futures fund products can be devised to provide:

- Annual dividends to the investors
- Guaranteed return of capital
- A potential hedge against inflation
- Diversified investment in foreign economies, i.e., German stock market, French Bonds, Australian bonds, Swiss currency, etc.
- Foreign exchange protection against devaluation

A good trading manager can structure a product to meet the needs of the investor whether it be an individual, a pension, a trust, or whatever.

2. CTA Evaluation, Selection, and Negotiation

As noted earlier there are about 3,000 CTAs registered in the U.S. Sorting through their records, evaluating them, and matching them with investors needs and desires is the job of the trading manager. The trading manager also negotiates the deals with the CTAs. Often the trading manager can get a better rate than an individual.

3. Allocation and Re-Allocation of Assets

Selection of the appropriate CTAs is only part of the job. Equally important is determining how much money to allocate to each CTA. It is rare that one would want to allocate equal amounts to all CTAs, and it is even rarer that one would want to keep the allocations the same after trading starts and profits or losses accumulate. Trading managers do that job of monitoring CTAs' trading activity, gains and losses, and adjusting the allocations among them.

4. Administration

Clearly, research has shown that an investor is better off with more than one CTA managing his money. Sometimes investors need a special product. Oftentimes, they want the limited liability of a limited partnership. All of this requires someone to gather the documents, see that the proper legal niceties are followed, that all signatures are in place, and provide all reports about performance, net asset value, etc., back to the investor. The trading manager does this.

In short a trading manager makes futures investing convenient, easy, and personalized for the investor.

When selecting a trading manager, ask about their independence. They should be protecting you from conflicts of interest and should not be compensated by brokers or CTAs for bringing them business.

Trading managers can be very worthwhile by reducing your costs, protecting your interests, and improving enormously the odds that you will not lose money with your first foray into managed futures.

The author's firm, Powers & Dubin Asset Allocation and Management Co., is a trading manager. Figure 3.5 represents the investor returns on multi-advisor futures funds after all management and incentive fees.

A LONG-TERM PERSPECTIVE NEEDED

Did you know that if you missed only 20 days of being invested in the stock market (S&P 500) during the entire decade of the 1980s, your average annual returns would not have been much better than if you left your money in Treasury bills during the decade?

The average annual return on stocks from January 1980 to January 1990 was 17.5 percent. The average return on U.S. T-bills during that period was 8.9 percent. If you were a market timer (i.e., buying when you thought the short- or intermediate-term trend was up and selling when you thought it was down and standing aside when you thought there was no trend), and you were standing aside when you should have been long, your return would have averaged 9.3 percent. It would have been much worse, of course, if you had been short!

Unless they are very good at market timing or very lucky, long-term investors tend to have the greatest probability of making extraordinary returns in the stock market. The same thing is true in managed futures and selecting CTAs. Get help in selecting good ones and keep a long-term perspective on their performance. That does not mean ignore them.

Chapter 4

Commodity Index Futures—The Basket Approach to Investing

One of the challenges facing all traders and especially new traders is selecting one or two commodities on which to focus attention. Most traders can't trade everything. They do not have the time, the money, the information, or the inclination. That is especially true if they are just getting started.

Enter the commodity index futures. A futures on the commodity index is exactly what the name suggests. The index represents the price movement of a basket of commodities. The commodities' prices may be weighted or unweighted in the index. The futures represents a contract on the expected value of that index at some future period.

Commodity index futures have been popular for another reason. Those investors such as institutional investors who want commodities in their portfolio perhaps as a hedge against inflation can cover a broad range of commodity prices with a single product. The commodity indexes represented on futures contracts include futures in the Commodity Research Bureau (CRB) Futures Price Index, the Goldman Sachs

Commodity Index (GSCI), and the Chicago Board of Trade (CBOT) International Commodity Index.

The CRB Futures Price Index was developed as a commodity price indicator in the middle part of this century. The index is traded at the New York Futures Exchange. Price calculations in the index are based on several futures contract months for each of 21 different commodities. The base year for the index is currently set at 1967.

The GSCI is based on a single, near-month futures traded on the major exchanges in Western countries. At present the index is composed of futures prices for 19 commodities. The weighting is based on world production. It started trading in July of 1992.

The CBOT International Commodity Index is very similar to the GSCI except that the meat components of the index are based solely on U.S. production and it uses largely U.S. government sources for production weighting. This contract has been approved by the CFTC but, as of the end of 1992, has not yet begun trading.

The oldest of these indices, the CRB, is an equally weighted index. None of its 21 commodities has any more influence over the index than any other. A 10 percent increase in the futures price of any component of the index will cause about l/2 percent increase in the index itself. So if soybean futures go from $6.00 to $6.60 a bushel, the index will go up roughly one point; similarly, if crude oil goes from $20.00 to $22.00 a barrel.

Developers of the GSCI wanted a product that was more specifically designed to reflect the impact of commodity price inflation on the cost of living. Ideally, they would have liked to base their index weights on consumption, but that is an extremely difficult thing to do, so they settled for weighting on production. They selected world production as reported by the U.N.; hence, the GSCI is heavily weighted toward energy, since crude oil is the single largest produced commodity in the world. Only five commodities compose nearly three-fourths of the index.

The GSCI also embodies one other unique and very important concept called "roll yield." Five major commodities included in the index are subject to a tendency called backwardation in the price structure. [Backwardation refers to prices in excess of futures being successively lower than the futures month preceding]. Since the GSCI is based on only the nearby futures month, when a contract expires the index automatically picks up the next futures month. In a backwardation market, one is continually buying futures months that are cheaper than the month just "rolled out of." For example, if one had kept a constant long in heating oil since January 1, 1983, and, as each successive month matured, rolled into the next month, the investor would have profited before commissions by about $6,783.00 despite a 37 percent drop in market price. These profits emanated from rolling the positions over into lower-priced futures. Since the Goldman Sachs Index is heavily weighted toward commodities whose futures prices reflect backwardation, this creates an extra "investment yield" for an investor in the index. Although this yield would technically be available in other indices, it is virtually impossible to achieve it in the CRB because the CRB reflects equal weighting among all futures, and because the CRB is based on several successive futures price months rather than a single month.

Those who like the GSCI insist that it fits nicely in an investment portfolio because it can act in a way similar to real estate—a hard asset class. The GSCI is negatively correlated with stocks and bonds. Second, it can act as a hedge against sideways whipsaw in the market. That, in fact, is the attractiveness of the roll yield feature of the index. Third, Goldman Sachs has created a class of bonds whose yields are based on changes in the GSCI. These bonds are a proxy for a hedge against a change in interest rates as a result of fears over inflation. Lastly, there seems to be a definite seasonal pattern to the GSCI Index as a result of the weightings of the individual commodities; and, lastly, the GSCI Index is designed to facilitate arbitrage between individual commodities, or baskets of commodities, and the index. This arbitrage is designed very similarly to the so-called program trading in stock indexes.

Defenders of the CRB contend it is a better balanced product and better reflects a fundamental commodity world and general commodity inflation. Its equal weighting does not make it susceptible to price controls or other external events that might more directly impact a single commodity that has an inordinate weighting within the index.

The CRB Index

The CRB Index is constructed from the prices of a series of futures contract months for 21 different commodities. The commodity contracts are themselves divided into sub-indexes. The commodities and the sub-indexes are as follows:

Grains	Metals	Meats	Industrials	Imports	Miscellanous
corn	gold	cattle	crude oil	coffee	orange juice
wheat	silver	hogs	heating oil	cocoa	
soybeans	platinum	pork bellies	unleaded	sugar	
soy meal			gasoline		
soy oil			copper		
			lumber		
			cotton		

Building the actual index price is a two-step process. First, the futures prices for selected delivery month prices for the 21 different commodities included in the CRB Index are arithmetically averaged. Second, the geometric (or harmonic) average of the 21 arithmetic averages is calculated. The result is the Index.

CRB Futures Price Index futures ("CRB Index futures") represent the futures contract that is based on the CRB Index. The contract is traded on the New York Futures Exchange from 9:45 A.M. to 2:45 P.M. New York time every business day. The contract's value is $500 times the CRB Index futures price level. The delivery month trading cycle for the contract is March, May, July, September, and December. The last trading day for the contract is the third business day of the expiration month. Since the settlement at contract maturity is by cash payment, one need not worry about getting delivery of a physical commodity.

THE CRB INDEX FUTURES AS AN INVESTMENT

A recent study of the potential role an investment in the CRB Index futures could play in an investment portfolio concluded the following for the period 1960–1992:

a. Adding the CRB Index to an efficient portfolio, representative of existing institutional portfolios, had a positive impact on the portfolio's Sharpe ratio.

b. This positive impact was most clearly evident at CRB Index allocations between 2.5 percent and 20 percent and clearly disappeared at allocations above 40 percent.

c. This positive impact was seen even if the CRB Index contribution (not including interest earned on margin deposits) was as small as 0.25 percent per year.

d. The CRB Index, as defined, was an excellent hedge against inflation over the entire period and shorter sub-periods studied, except the period 1985 to 1992.

e. A continuous, fully collateralized, buy and hold, passive investment in the CRB Index futures, since its inception in June 1986, would have reaped a total return of 33.90 percent or an annual return of 4.59 percent.

The study constructed a typical investment portfolio held by a pension fund, and then evaluated the CRB account relative to the individual assets of the portfolio, and as a part of the portfolio. The typical portfolio was assumed to be composed of stocks, long-term U.S. government bonds, U.S. corporate bonds, and Treasury bills.

The CRB investment was assumed to be a passive, buy-and-hold investment in a fully collateralized CRB Index futures account. Fully collateralized means the equity value of the account is equal to the full dollar value of the CRB Index futures ($500 multiplied by the Index). Since approximately 10 percent of the funds are assumed to be used to margin the actual open futures positions, 90 percent of the collateral is available for investment in T-bills. Thus, the return on the fully collateralized CRB

Index account is the sum of (1) the CRB Index return plus (2) 90 percent of the T-bill return.

During the period 1960 to 1992 the average annual returns for the CRB Index account were better than the returns for corporate bonds and U.S. stocks but not quite as good as the return for long-term government bonds (see Table 4.1). The arithmetic averages of annual returns for the period 1960 to 1992 were:

Table 4.1 Average Annual Returns

CRB Index	9.37%
U.S. Stocks	6.40%
Government Bonds	11.30%
Corporate Bonds	7.29%
Foreign	9.22%

In general, the CRB Index returns were more stable than the returns on stocks and were slightly negative in only eight of the 32 years. The years of peak CRB Index return performance coincided with periods of agricultural and energy price shocks. During the 1980s and 1990s, periods of falling inflation and rising stock prices, the CRB Index returns fell behind returns on other assets.

Correlation to Other Assets

The correlation among assets in a portfolio is an important measure of diversification. If two asset classes are highly correlated, they have similar price movements and, therefore, provide little diversification. Hence, the lower the correlation between asset classes in a portfolio, the better the diversification and the lower the risk associated with the portfolio.

The correlations between the CRB and all other asset classes were very low, or negative, indicating that the CRB acted as a natural hedge and diversifying element in a portfolio of these assets.

Risk Associated with Asset Classes

Risk is measured by the standard deviation of monthly returns. The data in Table 4.2 summarize the risk associated with the annual returns of the other assets.

Table 4.2 Volatility of Annual Returns of Domestic Assets

	CRB Index	Gov. Bonds	Stocks	Corp. Bonds	Foreign Stocks
1960 to 1992	14.24	10.77	15.71	9.41	
1960 to 1969	5.90	6.00	13.20	4.90	
1970 to 1979	18.10	8.70	16.90	8.70	16.70
1980 to 1992	10.90	14.40	18.80	13.00	21.20

In general, the risk associated with the CRB account was comparable to that of stocks, though it was clearly lower from 1980 onward.

Inflation Hedge

In general, the correlation between the CRB Index and other measures of inflation suggests that it is a potential hedge against inflation, because as inflation increased so did the return on the CRB Index account.

Table 4.3 CRB Index Correlation with Inflation

	1960 to 1992 CRB Index
Consumer Price Index (ALL)	0.99
Consumer Price Index (COMMOD.)	0.92
Producer Price Index (ALL)	0.99
Producer Price Index (FARM)	0.93
Gross Domestic Product (DEFLATER)	0.99

A well-known asset allocation model was used to select and allocate the portfolio assets among the model portfolio assets on an unconstrained basis. The results show that adding the CRB Index account lowered the risk and increased the return. This is shown in Figure 4.1 by the leftward shift of the curve as successively greater amounts of the portfolio's assets were allocated to the CRB investment.

At A, with 0 percent of portfolio assets allocated to the CRB investment, the risk is 10 percent and the return 11.25 percent. When the CRB investment is increased

Figure 4.1 Average Annual Returns

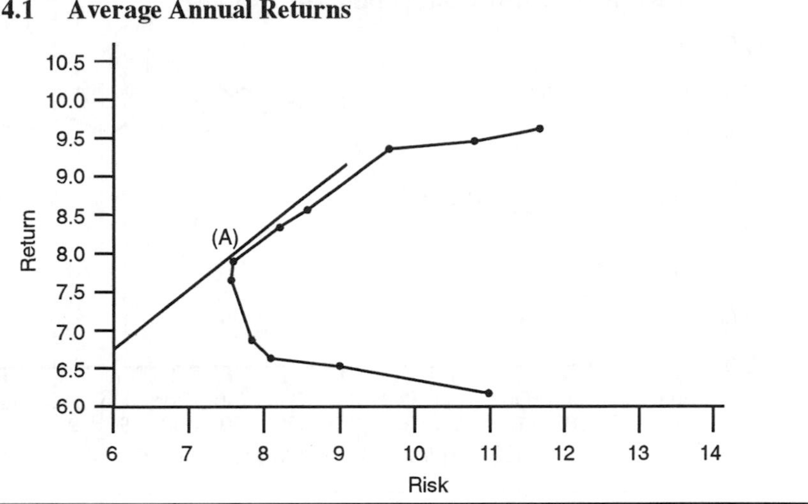

to 10 percent of the portfolio, the risk remains at 10 percent, but the return is increased to about 11.4 percent.

REAL TIME CRB INDEX FUTURES PERFORMANCE

Figure 4.2 illustrates the performance of a hypothetical passive, buy-and-hold, fully collateralized CRB Index Futures investment from the beginning of trading of the CRB Index Futures in June 1986 through 1992.

The account would have opened with the index at 204.255. Multiplying the index by $500 means the fully collateralized account would have been valued at $102,127.50. Of that amount, 90 percent ($91,914.75) would have been invested in T-bills and 10 percent ($10,212.75) used for margining the futures contract. In calculating the performance index for the CRB Index, the combined returns are compounded.

Note that the CRB Index opened at 204.255 and closed at year end 1992 at nearly the identical level of 204.00. The Index rose substantially, reaching a contract high closing average of 261.754 in July 1989, and then declined steadily thereafter. The T-bill rate was positive through the period and declined substantially the last two years. Nevertheless, the combination account would have provided a reasonable hedge against inflation. A continuous, fully collateralized, buy-and-hold passive investment in the CRB Index futures since its inception in June 1986 would have reaped a total return of 33.90 percent or an annual return of 4.59 percent. The GDP deflator, as an indication of inflation during that period, averaged 3.10 percent.

Figure 4.2 CRB Index Performance (June 1986 = 100)

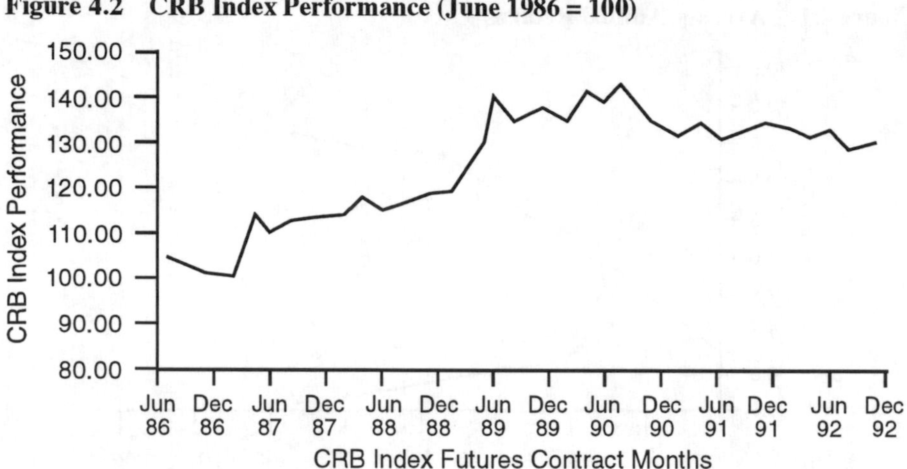

In summary, a reasonable case can be made for including commodities in an investment portfolio. Their inclusion seems to have a positive impact on portfolio reward/risk characteristics. Those who would like a full copy of the CRB study can obtain one by contacting the New York Futures Exchange. A similar study on the GSCI can be obained from Goldman Sachs.

Chapter 5

The Trading Plan

People who trade commodities without a plan are like Christopher Columbus. When they start, they don't know where they're going. When they arrive, they don't know where they've been. They differ from Columbus in one important aspect, however. They usually aren't as lucky in their discoveries.

As was pointed out in Chapter 1, many speculators lose money because they trade without a plan. All good traders build trading plans. If you are a beginning trader, put it on paper. That way you will be less likely to forget an important element and you will have something to help instill discipline. Your success as a trader will depend, to a great extent, on your ability to minimize the common mistakes made by losers. That ability grows and develops with well-made written plans and experience.

A good subtitle for this chapter might be "Money Management," because a plan forces you to think about how you will manage your money. It is also an excellent way to control the emotional involvement that clouds the judgment of so many traders. A plan should help reduce the frequency with which one takes profits too early or lets losses run too long. It should also help you determine your suitability for commodity futures trading.

A well-prepared plan considers all aspects of your participation as a commodity futures speculator, including emotional as well as financial suitability and the strategy you will follow in achieving a goal. Plans range from the simple which include only general considerations to elaborate systems with completely mechanized or computerized rules of action. Some plan is better than none at all. Even a poor plan is better than none, because no plan would provide for losing all of one's capital.

YOUR ATTITUDE TOWARD RISK

Certainly no investor or commodity trader wants to lose money but when one takes risks, one obviously has a chance to lose money. On the other hand, there are few opportunities to make money without taking some risks. Considerations of the nature and the amount of risk that one is willing to take are the real key to determining customer suitability and to designing an appropriate money management plan for a commodity trader.

Exactly how much risk should a trader take at any point in time? How does he protect himself from the risks he has taken? In answering these questions, keep in mind that *your need or desire to take risks seldom is equal to your capacity to take risks*. You need to evaluate whether you are in a position to take risks separately from whether you should take risks. One should always distinguish between potential of loss on any one transaction and the consequences of the loss to the trader. Look at a transaction always in terms of the appropriateness of the risk in view of your need and capacity to assume risk. In making that evaluation you want to take a cold and objective look at your family responsibilities, your financial circumstances, and your overall emotional suitability for trading. Weighing the consequences of gain against the consequences of loss is ultimately a subjective calculation, but it is absolutely essential in determining how much risk to take.

THE PLAN

As noted above, plans may be simple or complex, written or mental. The best are simple and written. The ideas and procedures for developing a plan, expressed in this chapter, are illustrated in a set of sample planning forms included at the end of this chapter. Use it for your own plan or as a guide to developing one of your own.

The elements of a plan can be separated into four broad categories:

1. Capital availability and needs
2. Getting into positions

3. Getting out of positions
4. Review

We'll cover each of these in turn.

PART I—CAPITAL

What Do You Have and What Do You Need?

The basic questions to ask yourself are:

- How much money do I have available for trading? Put another way—What is my financial suitability for trading?
- How much money can I afford to risk?
- How much capital do I need to trade successfully?

What Do You Have Available?

Like a building, a plan needs a good foundation. The place to begin is with a complete review of your financial suitability for trading by determining your net worth and liquid assets. Net worth provides a guide to how much you can afford to risk in trading, and liquid assets are the only ones you can use in trading. Part I of the sample forms at the end of this chapter are for determining your net worth, liquid assets, and income available for futures trading.

You should ascertain the amount of money you will need to meet your fixed living expenses—food, clothing, shelter, education, life insurance, savings, retirement account, and investment portfolio. Only the extra money left after meeting your regular needs should be considered as eligible for use in commodity trading.

To put it bluntly, prudence dictates that you segregate from everything else you own the money you deem available for use in trading in the futures market. This makes it easier to control the urge to overtrade, and helps you to manage your money intelligently.

How much of this extra money that you allocate to trading commodities depends on many considerations. Among them are your age, the size of your family, the type and security of the job you hold, the attitude of your family toward trading, your emotional suitability, and your own personal desire for risk-taking. All of these factors should also be considered in determining your own personal trading philosophy.

If you have a family and a net worth of less than $200,000, you probably should not be trading. But if you insist, a good guideline to follow is to commit no more than

10 percent of your liquid assets. If you are experienced and have large amounts of capital, you may want to go as high as 20 percent of your liquid assets. It would seldom be recommended to commit more than 25 percent of your liquid assets, no matter how great your assets are.

Once you have determined how much capital you have available to risk, you next have to decide how much capital you need to execute your plan. Scale your plan to your capital.

How Much Do You Need?

One of the most important reasons people lose money trading commodity futures is they base their trading plan on too little capital.

As a trader you want to establish favorable trading plans based on logic, probabilities, and sufficient capital. The first two will help you establish the last one.

Risk and reward should be studied only in the context of probabilities, e.g., what is the probability that I will achieve a particular profit versus the probability that I will lose a certain amount. Our purpose here is not to make you an expert in probability theory, but rather to give you an appreciation of how knowledge of probabilities will help you establish a plan that gives you a successful trading experience.

A word of caution is in order. Although the illustrations that follow use gambling examples, don't be fooled into thinking that the certainty with which probabilities can be calculated at the roulette wheel can be applied to trading in futures. They can't. And it is dangerous to think so. You will always be tempted to place too high a level of accuracy on probability numbers that are themselves loose estimates based on other loose estimates. At best, the probabilities you generate will be numbers that emanate from an ever-changing market environment and an ever-changing set of market conditions. Thus, you can get only rough estimates of probabilities. Nevertheless, the exercise of establishing a set of probabilities will make you a better trader.

Probabilities[1]

If you go to a casino and look at the roulette wheel, you will find that there are 38 squares on the wheel, eighteen red, eighteen black, one "0" square, and one "00" square. If the wheel stops on "0" or "00," the casino automatically wins the bet. If you bet red (black), then you have 18 out of 38 chances of winning, and 20 out of 38 chances of losing, i.e., 18 black (red) plus a "0" and "00." So the odds are against you on every spin of the wheel. Roulette bets are not fair bets because the odds of winning or losing are not equal. A fair bet is one where the odds are 50/50 each time. A fair

1. Some excellent references to the concepts discussed here and throughout this chapter would include Teweles & Jones, 1987. *The Futures Game*, New York: McGraw Hill. Also, any basic statistics book on probability will be helpful.

bet doesn't mean you win. It only means that you start out with an even chance of winning each time. A bad bet does not mean you always lose or that you can't win. It only means you start out with higher odds of losing than of winning, e.g., 49-51. In trading futures, successful traders figure out how to get the odds in their favor *before* they enter a position.

Knowing something about probabilities also will help you establish the appropriate level of capital you need in order to trade successfully.

A couple of things about probability numbers that you should keep in mind: First, probability calculations don't mean anything unless they are based on a very large number of repeated experiences or trials where conditions are the same. Second, in any long series of a repeated activity, there will be periods where "runs" will occur. In other words, the roulette wheel may stop on red five or six times in a row.

What's especially important to remember about runs is that with each successive trial that continues the run, the probability that the next trial will continue it decreases. Hence, if you develop a trading system based on estimated probabilities that a particular trading strategy will be successful 60 percent of the time, and you find that it has given you six or seven successive profitable trading signals, then you probably should not be leveraging your profits or increasing your position on the next trading signal. The chances are increasing, as that run continues, that the next signal in your trading system will be a loser.

Mathematical Expectation

The mathematical expectation of an event is equal to the sum of the amount of money you can win times the probability that you will win, minus the sum of the possible amounts you could lose times the probability of losing. For example, if you have a 50 percent chance of winning $500 and a 50 percent chance of losing $1,000, your mathematical expectation is a –$250. If you have an 80 percent of winning $500 and a 20 percent of losing $1,000, your mathematical expectation is a +$200 (see Table 5.1).

Table 5.1 Payoff or Mathematical Expectation

Sum of Possible Payoffs × Probabilities Of Each Payoff = Mathematical Expected Value

e.g.,

50 percent Chance of Winning 500 = +250
50 percent Chance of Losing 1,000 = –500
–250

80 percent Chance of Winning 500 = +400
20 percent Chance of Losing 1,000 = –200
+200

Often I have heard (and read) that a trader should only enter a trade when he expects to make twice as much as he expects to lose, e.g., make $200, lose $100. While setting explicit profit and loss parameters is laudable, it may not be smart because taken alone that advice is incomplete. To make it complete, the trader must assign expected probabilities that he will achieve the $200 gain and the $100 loss. If he has a 30 percent chance of making the $200 and a 70 percent chance of losing the $100, his mathematical expectation is a –$10. This is a bad trade. If the reverse is true, his mathematical expectation (.70 x $200 – .30 x $100) is a +$110, suggesting it is a better trade.

The point is that you have to consider *both* dollars and probabilities. You cannot ignore probabilities in setting your trading plan and policy, but simply knowing probabilities is not sufficient. You also need to know and apply the concept of mathematical expectation, which looks at both sides—the dollars to be gained or lost and the expected probabilities associated with each event.

Risk of Ruin

A trading plan that starts with a positive mathematical expectation but is executed with too little capital creates a high probability that overall the trader will lose all of his money. If you start too small, you will lose it all. If you over-reach (trade more aggressively than your capital and the probabilities allow) you will lose it all. If you fail to realize that eventually you will have a string of losses and trade accordingly, taking small risks, you will lose it all. The probability of runs of losses or gains increases as time passes.

The concept of risk of ruin refers to a probability calculation that a series of losses will be devastating.

Studying the risk of ruin calculation provides insights into:

- How much capital you need
- How and when to leverage or de-leverage your capital commitment
- How and when to leverage profits

The formula for calculating the probability of ruin is complex but easily understood:

$$\left(\frac{1 - \text{Trade Advantage}}{1 + \text{Trade Advantage}}\right)^{N} = \text{Probability of Ruin}$$

Where:

The trade advantage equals the difference between the probability that this trade (trading method, technique or decision rule) will be profitable in the long run and the probability it will be unprofitable. (See later section of this chapter for determining the trade advantage.) So if the probability of a profit is 60 percent, and the probability of a loss is 40 percent, the trade advantage is 20 percent. N equals the percent of your total capital you are willing to make or lose on this trade before you would exit from it; your stop-out point in dollars. Suppose you had $20,000 total capital in your account and that on any single trade you would not risk more than 10 percent, or $2,000.

Then this factor would be $\frac{\$2,000}{\$20,000} = 10\%$

To illustrate, suppose you had done a lot of research on several of the technical trading rules discussed in Chapters 9, 10, and 11, and you had discovered that over a large number of trials, whenever a rising pennant chart formation coincided with an RSI of 75 or more, a short position was profitable 60 percent of the time. Your trade advantage would be .20 (i.e., .60 – .40 = .20). And if N = 10, your risk of ruin is:

$$\left(\frac{1-.20}{1+.20}\right)^{10} = \left(\frac{.80}{1.20}\right)^{10} = .017 \text{ of Risk of Ruin}$$

In this example, there is a very low probability of losing all your capital.

Let's presume you are willing to risk $5000 per trade with the same trading system. In that case,

$$\frac{\$5,000}{\$20,000} = 4\%$$

$$\left(\frac{1-.20}{1+.20}\right)^{4} = \left(\frac{.80}{1.20}\right)^{4} = (.25)^{4} = .1975 \text{ of Risk of Ruin}$$

Essentially, this is a 20 percent chance of ruin, which is too high. Reduce your risk.

Assume your trade advantage drops to 5 percent with N = 4.

$$\left(\frac{1-.05}{1+.05}\right)^{4} = \left(\frac{.95}{1.05}\right)^{4} = (.90)^{4} = .656 \text{ of Risk of Ruin}$$

This risk is totally out of the realm of reason.

This exercise clearly demonstrates something good traders learn quickly: take small risks. Don't expose large amounts of capital to risk of loss on any single trade. Trade to survive. It is easy to make money trading commodities. It is hard to keep it.

The above examples assumed that the account was kept at $20,000. Suppose though that the account actually grows to $30,000 because 60 percent of the trades really are winners. If you keep risking only $2,000 units the probability of ruin drops. With $30,000 you can withstand a run of 15 consecutive losses —

$$\frac{\$2{,}000}{\$30{,}000} = 15.$$

The probability of ruin here drops to $\left(\frac{1-20}{1+20}\right)^{15} = .00228$. Not very high.

If you decided to leverage your profits and start risking $5,000 per trade your probability of losing all of your profits would jump to very high levels. You could withstand only two successive losing trades.

The risk of ruin increases dramatically as more available capital is exposed on each trade. Risk of ruin is highest at the start of trading. Suppose you have $20,000 and commit $4,000 to each trade. If you lose on the first two trades, you have only 60 percent of your capital left and probably need to reduce the size of your trading commitment. If you lose on four of your first five trades you are in very serious trouble, and the time it will take you to get back to even may be long. You will need a string of winners or a winner that provides an immediate and astronomical return on your money. The probabilities of either occurring can be calculated, but you will find they are very small.

Sequential losses are not the only concern. In the example above, if you have a pattern of two wins and three losses repeated four times you are broke.

Adding to Positions

If you double your position each time you double your money the risk of ruin increases. Conversely, if you trade at the same scale as your profits accumulate, the risk of ruin decreases. So to have probabilities work with you, scale up your positions but at a decreasing rate.

How Much Capital Do You Need?

There is no absolute number. Clearly you need enough to meet initial margins and margin calls up to your maximum base loss point. That question can be answered only in the context of how large a trade advantage you insist on in your plan *and* what percent of your capital you will risk on each trade. If you use common sense, do your homework to get the best estimate possible of your trade advantage, and then risk small amounts of money, you can have a profitable trading experience starting with as little as $20,000.

Once you have determined the amount of money available for trading, you should think seriously about your philosophy of trading. By the mere fact that you have decided to trade futures, you have also decided to accept relatively high-risk investments. Nevertheless, as pointed out earlier, there are varying degrees of risk in trading commodity futures. You can trade conservatively by reducing your leverage, by judicious selection of the commodities you trade, and by your method of trading. For example, trading a normally less volatile commodity like wheat, a storage commodity, may be less risky than trading a perishable commodity like pork bellies or cattle; following a "spreading" method of trading in storable commodities is normally less risky than taking a net position in a commodity. Spreading refers to the assumption of long and short positions on the same business day in the same or related commodities for the same account. See Chapter 18 for more about spreads.

In summary, before you start trading do some careful studying of your trading methods. Examine and research their effectiveness over the long run. Assign some level of expected probability to them and then calculate your risk of ruin.

Hypothetical Is Not the Same as Reality

Testing of trading methods, rules, and techniques on past data is of great value. However, hypothetical trading or simulated trading seldom turns out to be reflective of reality.

Seldom does the future course of a market exactly mirror the past. The market participants are often different in one time period than in another. Emotionally and psychologically, people act differently when faced with making decisions with real money than they did when it was hypothetical.

The lesson to be learned:

1. Don't place too high a confidence level in your probability calculations.
2. Back-testing a trading system and then testing it by paper trading on live data (or out of sample) is most important to determine your probable trade advantage. But after you start trading, keep a reality check on your system to see if it provides you the trade advantage you expected. If you expected to get 60 percent winning trades, then keep a tally to see if you do. Calculate in advance the probability that you will have X number of losses out of your first 10 trades.

PART II—INITIATING POSITIONS

The most exciting part of a trading plan is entering positions—deciding what commodities to trade, establishing the criteria for being long or short, deciding how long you should wait for your expected market move to occur, etc.

Deciding What to Trade

This choice depends very much on your interests, background, and knowledge. Pick the futures that are most familiar and the easiest for you to follow. The list from which to select is rich and varied—stock indexes (like the S&P or Major Market Index), bonds and Eurodollars, corn, wheat, hogs, cattle, gold, silver, etc., plus a lot of foreign stock indices and financial futures.

Once you have picked the commodity(ies), the real work of market analysis just begins. Before you are ready to enter a trade, you should dig deeply into the market information. Get "inside" the market. This means you must know the types and sources of information that are important in making judgments.

Some traders base their trading decisions primarily on the "fundamentals" of the market. That is, they evaluate possible future price movements on the basis of such things as a commodity's estimated production, carryover from previous years, and estimated future demand, utilizing the wealth of information and data available from government and many other sources. (See Chapter 8 on "Forecasting Prices" and "What to Look for and Where to Find It.") Fundamental traders often tend to be long-term traders. That is, they trade relatively infrequently, and they tend to hold positions, once established, for long periods of time. Such traders need larger amounts of capital to withstand margin calls. These types of traders have to be very patient and willing to wait for fundamental factors to work their way through the production/consumption cycles.

Some traders take the "technical" approach, using price charts to predict future price movements on the theory that familiar price patterns tend to repeat again and again.

Technical traders come in all stripes and colors. Some are long-term traders, some short-term, some very short-term traders, like day traders. If you are not on the floor of an exchange and don't have immediate access to quotes, don't try to be a day trader. In fact, a beginner is probably well-advised to aim at being an intermediate- to long-term trader, i.e., select commodities that trend, utilize your research tools to identify potentially emerging long-term price trends, establish a very small position using only a small proportion of your capital, and be patient, but watchful, to see if the trend emerges.

Some blend the two approaches and take a position only when their interpretation of both the fundamental and technical factors are in agreement with respect to market direction and timing.

Still others depend heavily on the advice of a broker or advisor in whom they have confidence.

Regardless of the approach taken, to make the decision-making process more objective and to add discipline to the approach, develop a checklist of key technical and fundamental factors, and evaluate each set of factors in light of their probable impact on price. For example, are the general supply/demand or economic statistics basically bullish, bearish, or neutral? What do the technical market factors indicate? How does the current price level compare with historical price levels? You can then assign weights to each assessment and ultimately end up with a basic indicator of whether your analysis supports a long position, a short position, or a neutral stand-aside position (see Part II of the trading plan).

Developing the Expected Trade Advantage

Once you have a good general understanding of the expected direction of price movement, you need to assess the extent of the price movement and the probability that it will occur. In other words, you need to establish the expected trade advantage. This is a very subjective process and has to be discerned from past price action, and the expectation that past interactions of the fundamental/technical factors affecting the market will be repeated.

Although this is a difficult step, it is a most important one. It forces the trader to think hard about how confident he is that his expectations of price movements will be met, and it provides a more definitive way of determining whether this is a worthwhile trade.

By combining all of the information about technical/fundamental factors and the expectations about price movements, you should get a clear indication of whether the weight of the analysis suggests a long, short, or neutral market position.

Calculating the Trade Advantage and Expected Value of a Trade

One of the most valuable things you can do in planning is to assign probabilities that your target prices and either gains or losses will be achieved. As noted earlier, the mere process of assigning such probabilities causes you, the decision maker, to consider the strength of your faith in prognostications. It forces you to think about whether your chances of achieving a gain or suffering a loss are 90 percent? 60 percent? 40 percent? etc.

This process of calculating probabilities has to be based on past experience (yours or someone else's) and the testing of your decision criteria on a historical data series.

This essentially means you need access to several things: a data base, a computer, software, and/or a set of price charts.

You need the data base of past prices so you can check out past price activity and patterns and so you can test your decision rules.

You need the computer and the software if you are interested in doing any substantive data analysis. The calculations of most technical indicators are so complex, time-consuming, and fraught with potential mistakes that attempting the task by hand is generally a discouraging exercise.

You need the charts, if you decide not to utilize the computer. Of course, you can use the computer to develop and build the charts and do the other calculations, too. (See Chapter 10 for more on criteria for selecting data bases and software.)

Let's suppose you get access to the computer, software, and data base. Let's assume also that you decide (a) to conduct your study based on five years of past data (a good time period to work with); and (b) to test the following moving average rule:

- Buy if the nine-day moving average crosses above the 18-day moving average
- Sell if the nine-day moving average crosses to below the 18-day moving average.

You conduct the study and find the following:

# of Trades	100
# of Profitable Trades	60
# of Losing Trades	40
Average Profit on Profitable Trades	1,000
Average Loss on Losing Trades	700

If this is a reliable sample of how you expect this trading rule to behave in the future then your trade advantage is .20 (i.e., .60 - .40).

The mathematical expectation associated with this rule is:

60 percent × $1,000 = $600
40 percent × $ 700 = –$280
+$320 Mathematical Expectation

If you expect that the future will unfold like the past and have confidence that your trade advantage is really .20, then you can calculate the risk of ruin associated with this trading rule.

Let's suppose, though, that you consider the trade advantage too low. So you decide to add another rule to your trading model.

Assume you apply the same rule as above plus the following condition:

- Execute the Sell order only if the 14 day Relative Strength Index is above .70
- Execute the Buy order only if the 14 day Relative Strength Index is below .30

Let's further suppose your results turn out as follows:

# of Trades	50
# of Profitable Trades	40
# of Losing Trades	10
Average Profit on Profitable Trades	$1,200
Average Loss on Losing Trades	$900

Again if this sample is a reliable indicator of the future performance, then you should expect (a) your trade advantage to be .80 –.20 = .60:

$$\frac{.40}{.50} = .80 \qquad \frac{.10}{.50} = .20$$

and (b) your mathematical expectation for this model to be:

$$\begin{array}{rcl} 80 \times \$1{,}200 & = & \$960 \\ 20 \times \$\ \ 900 & = & \underline{\$180} \\ & & +\$780 \text{ Mathematical Expectation} \end{array}$$

This model gives you a much improved chance of making money in the long run. Of course, if you decide that this model is so superior to the first that you can risk more money per trade on it, you may actually increase your risk of ruin! Remember, eventually you will get a string of successive losing trades and you need to husband your capital to survive those periods so you will be able to participate when the string of profitable trades appears.

It is important to consider commissions in the calculations. A $45 commission and a potential profit or loss of $100 before commissions is really a potential profit of $55 ($100 – $45 commission) and a potential loss of $145 ($100 + $45 commission).

The expected potential profit must be compared to the expected potential loss on each trade, and each trader should decide on a general rule of thumb he can use as a guideline for decision making. Some traders prefer to have a mathematical expectation of potential profit to potential loss of at least 3 to 1, after commissions, before they enter a trade. Others prefer a higher ratio. No matter what ratio you select as a guide to your decision to enter the market, you should have a profit objective and a loss limit in mind when you take a position.

Now you should be ready to implement your plan. The above procedure should have yielded sufficient information to provide a sound basis for your decision. It is important to remember that the objective of the plan is sound decision making. A good decision may indeed be a decision not to trade, to stand aside until the market trend becomes clearer or until the probabilities of a successful trade improve.

An important factor here is patience. Pick your trades carefully. Do not rush in out of fear of losing an opportunity. Another one will be along shortly. Be prepared to recognize it.

The number of different commodities to be traded, the size of the initial position and the conditions under which one should add a position are, as noted above, also important elements of any plan. For the inexperienced, it is better to trade conservatively in only one or two different commodities with an ample cushion of cash in your account and to add to positions proportionately on strength rather than weakness. A good general policy for the beginner is to add to a position only when he has a profit on the original units, and never carry more than three open units in any one commodity. The financial graveyards are full of inexperienced people who took a plunge and overtraded.

PART III—EXITING A TRADE—LIQUIDATION STRATEGY

No plan is complete unless it also considers a way out of the market or a plan for determining when and under what conditions you will liquidate the position (see Part III of the planning form).

This means you have to consider how long you intend to hold your position. Some traders feel that if they do not reach their objective within a few weeks, they should liquidate and stand aside until they get a more definite feel for the market trend. Most speculative traders avoid carrying a position into the delivery month. This stems partly from fear of getting delivery if they are long in the market and partly from a desire to avoid the increase of margin and increased volatility frequently experienced during delivery months. A plan must include target prices reflecting the points at which you will be satisfied with the profit or will cut the losses and liquidate the position. It is important that you be realistic in setting these prices. Don't get greedy, and don't rely on hopes and dreams.

To add discipline and for protection, it is a good idea to mark your target price objectives with a "stop order" at the same time the original order is entered.

A stop order is simply a standing order to buy or sell that commodity "at the market" when a certain price is reached. As a market order, it is executed at the best possible price after the specified price is reached. For example, if you bought 5,000 bushels of March corn at $2.30 and you wanted to protect yourself against an undue loss—should prices decline instead of rising as you expect—you could give your broker an order to "sell March corn at $2.28 STOP." If the price of March corn futures did decline to $2.28, your order would automatically be executed at the best possible price, which, in a very active and moving market, might be slightly higher or lower than $2.28. Then, your position is closed.

For most commodities, the stop order is given to your broker like any other order. He transmits it to the floor of the exchange where that commodity is traded, and it is held on the books of the floor trader representing your broker's firm. When the market price reaches the price you specified in your stop order, it becomes a market order and is handled as such.

Stop orders can be used to close out your position when you have reached your profit objective, to initiate a new position, or to close out a position that has gone against you. Stop orders add discipline to your trading. They help you stick to your original objectives. The proper use of stop orders and the points at which they should be placed is a subject to which all traders should give careful thought before they enter the market.

In summary, when setting stops, there are two major criteria to consider:

1. The amount you are willing to lose. You cannot avoid a decision on this because the market will force it, if you do not decide.
2. The volatility—both historical and expected. If volatility is high and you set the stops too close to the market price, there is a high probability you will have a lot of small losses. If you set it too far away, you have a low probability of it being executed, but the losses will be large.

The art of setting stops is matching price volatility to your willingness to lose a certain sum of money. This means you must monitor volatility and adjust your stop frequently to reflect changes in volatility. Remember a change in volatility affects your mathematical expectations on a trade. An excellent alternative is to buy options as a stop mechanism. In the long run, you may find it the most probability-efficient manner of protecting against ruinous losses.

PART IV—REVIEW OF RESULTS

After you liquidate the position, review and analyze the results. Find out what you did right and what you did wrong. This may be the most important thing you do. You won't progress to become a skillful trader unless you analyze why the results turned out the way they did. Learn from your mistakes as well as from the things you did right.

It should also be noted that all aspects of a plan are intertwined. Making a small change in one part of the plan may affect the rest of it in a major way. Plans should be internally consistent.

To aid you in developing a plan, included at the end of this chapter are some sample forms for (a) determining your financial suitability for trading, (b) determining the amount of money you have available for trading, and (c) planning your strategy. After you finish the rest of the book, come back to this chapter, develop a plan using the forms provided, and then, in conjunction with the practice trading exercise in Appendix 1 try it out.

A WORD ABOUT DIVERSIFICATION

Diversification of risks is one of the most basic and important means of controlling total risk.

A beginning trader may find it very hard to diversify his futures trading risks, simply because he starts with a very small amount of money —not enough to trade several different markets or not enough to use several different trading systems, models, or rules for entering and exiting positions.

There are several ways to diversify risks. You could trade several different unrelated commodities. You could trade the same commodity but use several unrelated trading rules or models for determining your position. You can commit your capital in two or three tiers—a certain amount for long-term trades, called a "core trend position," and a smaller amount for a variable short-term trend position.

A key word in the above paragraph is "unrelated." It is not diversification to trade two or three different commodities whose price movements are highly correlated, or to rely on trading signals from two or three different trading systems or rules that are highly correlated. If they are highly correlated, they really are not "different." You're really doubling your risk, not reducing it.

So one place to start controlling your risk is in the selection of commodity futures you will trade. Pick two or three of them that have very low correlations in their price movements, or two different trading plans.

SEASONALITY AND TRADING PLANS

As noted earlier, nearly all markets have a seasonal or cyclical aspect to them. You should factor them into your trading plan for entry and exit of positions. Seasonal patterns tend to emerge in any market as it responds to regularly recurring fundamental forces like weather, elections, commercial schedules, governmental funding, etc. The seasonal approach to trading is designed to anticipate, enter, and capture historically recurring trends as they emerge. For example, winter arrives every year and the expected arrival as well as the actual arrival of cold weather creates responses among commercial interests and speculators in a market. Heating oil distributors build inventory to meet the anticipated demand of homeowners and businesses. When winter actually arrives, consumers and the trading public often provide a flurry of buying and, as sales occur, inventories draw down during the cold season. As spring arrives, sellers lower prices to reduce inventories further, and buyers delay new purchases in the anticipation of warm weather. The result is a pattern of price movement reflecting a certain seasonality.

For the trader, the relevant issue is identifying windows of opportunity wherein well-defined seasonal tendencies for tops, bottoms, and trends emerge and play out. These tendencies provide guidance for entry and exit. The exchanges, as well as a number of authors, like Jake Bernstein, have studied the seasonality in futures prices quite extensively over the last few years. The beginner and the experienced trader could both benefit from careful study of seasonal tendencies. For example, studies done by Knight-Ridder analysts on the heating oil market have yielded the following general seasonal tendencies:

First, both fuel oil and heating oil futures tend to make their seasonal bottoms in July during hot weather. Second, the seasonal tops tend to occur in the *cash* market during January, the coldest month. Third, the seasonal top in futures tends to occur by mid-November. Note: Futures tend to peak before the heavy seasonal demand of the cash product begins.

SUMMARY

To summarize, the steps in your trade plan should be as follows:

1. Prepare a personal balance sheet.
2. Determine how much of your net worth and of your cash you can afford to lose.
3. Establish the commodity(ies) futures of interest.

4. Conduct your trade selection research by identifying and testing various rules for entering and exiting long and short positions.
5. Establish the maximum amount of money in dollars and in percentages that you will risk on any single trade or trading methodology (i.e., N in the Risk of Ruin calculation).
6. Establish the trade advantage associated with #5 above.
7. Determine your Risk of Ruin.
8. Determine the Mathematical Expectation associated with #5 above.
9. Establish the stop loss (or gains) point(s) for automatically exiting the trade in whole or in part. This step needs to include:
   - a date or time period for realizing the expected profit;
   - a dollar amount; and
   - a method or plan for adjusting the stop as the market volatility changes.
10. Establish a procedure or rule for adding to positions as profits accumulate.
11. Review your experience. What did you learn?

A FINAL WARNING

There are no sure-fire methods for always making profitable trades. The best you can do is plan and prepare. Get the probabilities in your favor. Probability estimates are fraught with danger. By definition they are soft and unreliable. But for the beginner they are better than nothing.

The process of back-testing trading rules or models is also fraught with danger. There is the tendency to "curve fit," i.e., search for a trading rule until you find one that fits the data. Curve fitting is a self-fulfilling prophecy on a historical data base. But since markets don't read history and conditions seldom repeat exactly as they appeared before, such trading rules often turn out to be unsuccessful or, at least, less successful than planned.

Trade small. Take little risks. Always set exit points to get out no matter what. Be a skeptic on your probabilities of success and allow plenty of cushion that your probabilities are wrong.

Appendix I

The Trading Plan — Part I

Am I Financially Suitable For Futures Trading And How Much Money Can I Afford To Risk On Futures Trading?

The Income Statement
(Average last 3 years)

Annual Income

	My salary	______
	Spouse's salary	______
	Investment income	______
	Other income	______
A.	TOTAL	______

Annual Expense

	Mortgage payments	______
	Insurance	______
	Taxes	______
	Education	______
	Savings	______
	Living Expenses	______
	Vacations	______
	Loan payments	______
	Retirement account	______
B.	TOTAL	______

C. Average annual net income available for investment (A - B):
$ ______

D. Percent of C to be committed to futures trading* ______

E. C × D = $______— amount of income available for futures trading.

---

*The maximum proportion of your available investment income which should be committed to futures trading will vary depending upon individual circumstances. Nevertheless, a prudent man would not exceed 25%.

Personal Balance Sheet

Major Fixed Assets		**Major Liabilities**	
Home	______	Mortgage on home	______
Other real estate	______	Other mortgages	______
Equity in business	______	Loans	______
Other (describe)	______		______
TOTAL	______		______
		TOTAL	______

Liquid assets

Cash in banks	______
Savings accounts	______
Securities owned	______
Other (describe)	______
TOTAL	______

TOTAL Assets ($ ______) — TOTAL Liabilities ($ ______)
= $ ______ Net Worth

Summary

Maximum amount available for futures trading:

Net worth $	______	×	______	%* =	______
Liquid assets	______	×	______	% =	______
Net income	______	×	______	% =	______

Which of these you select as your maximum depends on how you think a reduction in one versus another will affect achievement of your short- and long-run goal. Generally, it would be prudent to select the smallest of the three numbers.

* The maximum proportion of one's net worth liquid assets or net income that one should commit to futures trading will vary with the individual's circumstances. Generally, however, it would be prudent to commit no more than 20% of net worth, 10% of liquid assets, or 25% of net income. Further, if you don't have a net worth of at least $50,000 excluding your home, you probably should not speculate on commodity futures contracts. The exact amount that is right for you depends on your family status, the extent to which the loss of the funds would affect your long-run personal and family goals, your desire to take risks, your annual income levels and your expected future income levels. For example, a man with $100,000 income and a net worth of $200,000, two kids in high school and two in college, two homes and several club memberships is probably less able to take risks than a 30-year-old bachelor earning $35,000 per year and having a net worth of $25,000.

Trading Plan — Part II

Initiating A Position

I. **The commodity** I am interested in trading is: ____________

The contract month I like is: ____________

II. **Market Analysis:**

	COL. I	COL. II	COL. III	SCORE*
Are the supply/ demand factors:	__Bullish	__Neutral	__Bearish	______
Is the seasonal influence:	__Bullish	__Neutral	__Bearish	______
In relation to historial price levels, is the current price:	__Low	__Average	__High	______
Have recent government reports been:	__Bullish	__Neutral	__Bearish	______
Are the chart patterns/technical analysis:	__Bullish	__Neutral	__Bearish	______
			TOTAL**	______

*Assign the following points for each column checked.
COL I = 2 points, COL. II = 1 point, COL. III = 0 points.

**Use the following scale for assessing the expected market direction:

BULLISH	NEUTRAL	BEARISH
10 9 8 7	6 5 4	3 2 1 0
Consider buying	Do nothing	Consider selling

III. Expectations:

Expected Price Change	__10%	__5%-10%	__0%-5%
Probability of Occurring	__75%	__51%-75%	__10%-50%

If you expect less than a 5% change in price or if you think the probability of achieving the expected price change is less than 50%, you are probably better off not taking a position. If you feel you have more than a 75% chance of getting at least a 10% change in price, you probably have a good possibility for a successful trade. In between those extremes it is your best judgment as to whether you think the risk is worth the potential reward.

IV. Action

Based on what I know about market factors, I will take the following position:

I will ______________________ ( ) quantity__________
(buy) (sell) (stand aside) (month)

__________at __________and will enter a STOP at ______
(commodity) (price) (price)

Trading Plan — Part III

Liquidating a Position

The Plan

I (will) (will not) maintain my position into the delivery month. Therefore, my maximum date beyond which I will not hold this position is __________.

A. My target price(s) for liquidation is ____contracts @__________
____contracts @__________
____ contracts @__________

B. If I achieve my target price(s), I will have a net gain on the transaction of __________
____
____

C. The probability of achieving the net gain is __________
____
____

D. If the market moves against me and my stop orders are executed, I will suffer losses of __________
____
____

E. The probability of my suffering such losses is __________
____
____

Given these circumstances, the most I could expect to gain on average over a long run from these transactions is
$(B \times C) - (D \times E) =$ __________*

*If this number is not positive, do not make the trade. The greater this number, assuming the probabilities you assigned are correct, the greater the reward you can expect relative to the risk and the more certain you can be that the trade will be successful.

The Results

I did liquidate my position at: ____ contracts @ ________
____ contracts @ ________
____ contracts @ ________

My gain on the transactions was: ________
I paid commissions of: ________
Interest not earned on my margin money was: ________*

My net gain (loss) on the transaction(s) was: ________
This represented ____% return on my margin money.

*This is an opportunity cost. You could have invested the money in a savings account or some other investment.

Trading Plan — Part IV

Evaluation of Plan

Overall, my plan reflected what I actually did

____ Quite Well ____ Fair ____ Poorly

The mistakes I made were ________________________________
____
____
____

Chapter 6

Choosing a Broker

"My advice to a prospective trader is to get the facts, make sure he or she has emergency funds and an understanding spouse and then get a good broker."

Not long ago, a speaker at an afternoon seminar on futures wound up his speech with the above advice. The first question that came from the audience was, "I've already got the spouse, the savings, and the experience. How do I find a good broker?"

The questioner raised two important points. First, he pointed up the variation that exists among brokers in the commodity futures trading industry. Secondly, he placed his finger on one of the decisions that puzzles most new traders, i.e., what do you look for when selecting a broker?

Several years ago, psychologist William G. Baker III of the University of San Francisco conducted a study of stockbrokers in an attempt to identify the personality traits of successful brokers. He ascertained that brokers who are mature, stable, sociable, self-controlled, enterprising, aggressive, ambitious, competitive, and outgoing are much more likely to have customers who make money; customers whose brokers have the opposite traits or possess only a minority of these traits are more likely to be losers. Although Dr. Baker's research is directly applicable to the stock market, it has strong implications for selecting a commodity futures broker as well.

Look for someone who fits the description above but who also fits your personality, can give you guidance, and is willing to provide you service. Look for a professional.

WHERE TO BEGIN

Many people are reluctant to enter a broker's office, even out of curiosity. Studies show that this attitude stems largely from an unfounded belief that the public is not particularly welcome. The typical descriptions given by many new customers upon visiting a broker's office for the first time are: "active," "confusing," "unfriendly," "noisy" and "no privacy." Nevertheless, most brokers will welcome your visit; after that initial visit you will probably deal mostly with your broker via phone, fax, and mail.

If you already have a stock account with a brokerage firm, your present broker can introduce you to one of the men in his office who specializes in commodities. If his firm doesn't trade in commodities, your broker might be able to recommend a commodity specialist in another firm.

If you don't know any brokers to contact, there are several other ways to approach this decision. You can start by contacting the National Introducing Brokers Association at 30 N. LaSalle, Suite 3500, Chicago, Illinois 60602. NIBA is composed of about 1,400 futures brokers, whose primary role is working with individual traders. They usually are affiliated with one or more of the large national or international brokerage houses who are full clearing members of the exchanges.

You might ask a friend, who already trades commodities, about his broker. You could contact an exchange and ask for a list of firms that handle commodity trades for customers, then give one or several of them a call. You could simply select the names of firms from the Yellow Pages of the telephone book under "Commodity Brokers." Or you might attend a seminar or lecture program sponsored by various brokerage houses. These are usually advertised well in advance in local newspapers and are generally free. Most brokers are selected with someone else's help. Studies done by the exchanges reveal that nearly half of all customers are obtained by referral.

WHAT TO LOOK FOR

The best way to evaluate a broker is to visit him in his office. Think twice before you open an account with a broker you've never seen. There's no substitute for a face-to-face meeting.

One of the most important things about a broker are his credentials. Is he registered with the National Futures Association (NFA) and operating under the rules of the Commodity Futures Trading Commission (CFTC) in Washington, DC? How much experience does he have as a commodity representative? Has he been qualified to handle accounts by a training program? Is he familiar with the literature on commodity futures trading?

You should also find out how much time your prospective broker devotes to commodities. The picture changes rapidly in the futures markets. He should be willing and able to devote the time necessary to follow the fast-moving markets.

If you consider it necessary, a quick check on the broker's background can be made by writing or calling (dial 1-800-621-3570) to determine if he's currently a registered representative in good standing or if he has any outstanding legal actions pending. Registration is required by law.

A broker should know about the materials available from the exchanges, USDA, and other sources. Some excellent work on commodity futures trading and analyses of individual markets has been done by the U.S. government and universities such as Stanford, University of Illinois, University of Wisconsin, Cornell, Texas, et al. He should be able to guide you to those materials, as well as some of the excellent books that have been written in recent years about commodity futures trading.

A good broker will answer your questions directly and honestly, including telling you "I don't know, but I'll find out" when he doesn't know.

It has often been said that brokers who also trade for their own accounts are less desirable, because they suffer a loss of objectivity. Raymond Ross, in his doctoral dissertation completed at the University of Illinois, found otherwise. He found a high positive correlation between the net trading results of broker/solicitors and the results of the customers' trading. Brokers who made money trading for their own accounts tended to have customers who made money, and vice versa. Further, his research showed that the overall net trading results of customers of non-trading broker/solicitors tended to be much worse than those of brokers who also traded for their own accounts.

CONSIDER THE FIRM

In selecting a broker, one must also look beyond the man to the firm. Does his office have good communication facilities for keeping posted up-to-the-minute on prices? What sort of research facilities does the firm have, and how good are they? Surprisingly little has been done to appraise the real value of commodity futures research. Thus, you'll have to make your own judgments. You can probably judge this best by comparison with other firms. It is a good idea to ask to be placed on the mailing lists for research reports and "market letters" from more than one firm, and then make a comparison over time. Obviously it's unfair to evaluate this research and advice solely on the basis of whether the firm was right or wrong in the market during some short time period. No one bats 1.000. But you can compare the firms on the basis of the depth and quality of the research and ask yourself if the conclusions reached are based on sound reasoning. Good research facilities are important. Ross' study also found that speculators who followed "house" research advice made money on two-thirds of their trades.

It could be that you will not want to rely solely on your broker or his firm for research. Perhaps you intend to do your own, or you may want to utilize one of the many independent commodity futures research firms that issue daily or weekly advisory letters to clients. The fees for these advisory services range from a few dollars a month to hundreds of dollars a year. The quality of the research and advice varies almost as much.

If the brokerage firm you choose is some distance away, inquire about being able to call them collect or get their toll-free number. This is a courtesy most firms offer their customers.

One of the most disappointing things that can happen to a new trader is to find that after he's opened an account and made a few small trades, his broker loses interest in him. One man recently complained, "My broker never calls me. As a customer, I don't like that. I like to think he cares about me and my money."

Your broker should keep an up-to-date log on your account and should have that log at his fingertips whenever you call. When you ask him a question about your account, he should be able to discuss with you without hesitation your position in the market, your trading objectives, stops you have placed, and other aspects of your account. He should know what commodities you are interested in, and keep you up to date on the latest news of importance in those commodities.

Another very important service a broker can provide is to help you develop a trading plan. In fact, to test the kind of service you will receive from a broker, ask him to help you develop such a trading plan. He should know how to do it, he should have some simplified forms for planning, and he should be able to discuss with you all of the major points we discussed in Chapters 3 and 5.

It almost goes without saying that you should expect fast and reliable execution of your orders. If you know people who have accounts with a broker, ask them about the order execution they've received from him and his firm. Failure to execute orders quickly and accurately is inexcusable, and a sure sign that you should look elsewhere for your broker. Equally important is fast and timely notification of price and quantity transacted.

WHAT NOT TO LOOK FOR

To this point, it sounds as though the broker should be all things to you. But there are certain things a broker cannot do and which you should not expect from him. He cannot, without legal power of attorney from you, make trading decisions without your prior approval. This means that when giving him an order for execution, you must make sure he understands exactly what you want done.

He cannot promise you profits. In fact, he's guilty of violating certain exchange rules, NFA rules, and a Commodity Futures Trading Commission guideline on advertising if he does not, when discussing profit possibilities, mention the equal opportunity for losses.

He does have other customers to think about and can't spend all of his time pondering your account or discussing it with you on the phone.

He is also human, and no matter how experienced and diligent, can from time to time err in his estimate of the situation.

PROBLEMS

The world is made up of many different kinds of people some good, some bad, and some in between. So it is with commodity brokers.

Some "bad" brokers take a very short run-view of things and are more interested in getting the immediate order without giving proper thought to whether that particular transaction is appropriate for their customers. Some brokers care less about long-run service and more about immediate commissions.

The encouraging aspect of this situation, however, is that those people are being gradually eliminated by natural market forces (their customers leave them) and by the stringent requirements imposed by the NFA and CFTC.

If misunderstandings should arise or mistakes be made by one party or another, the first place to go with a complaint about a broker is to his immediate superior. Most complaints are settled there. If you're right, a settlement of the dispute will be made to compensate you. If further action is necessary, both the exchange on which the transaction was made and the NFA have departments to receive and investigate complaints about broker activities. Both are impartial in these investigations and are deeply committed to fairness and action, when and if guilt is established. However, they need evidence, and the burden of proof is on the customer to show that the broker acted improperly.

The Commodity Futures Trading Commission Act of 1974 required the Commission to establish a reparations procedure for customers who felt they had been defrauded of their funds or in some other way injured financially by persons registered under the Act. Such a procedure was established in early 1976 and notification of your rights to use reparations should be included in the papers you sign when you open your account.

Finding a good broker is not difficult, if you know what you're looking for. A true professional—one who is interested in providing quality service—can strongly enhance the profitability of your futures trading.

OPENING THE ACCOUNT

Once a broker has been selected, it's relatively simple to open an account. Generally, it's a case of filling out some forms and depositing some money.

The first form a customer will usually be asked to complete is a new account information form. This asks for the usual personal information, including references (personal and credit), type of account (whether regular commodity account or managed account), instructions on sending notices and statements, and your signature.

Brokers also must furnish customers with disclosure documents explaining the risks of futures trading and must also give customers the opportunity to select arbitration or mediation rather than a civil law suit as a method of settling disputes.

The second is a customer agreement form. This gives the broker authority to liquidate any positions outstanding if the proper margin requirements are not met.

The amount of money that needs to be deposited depends on the individual brokerage house. Very few will open an account for as little as $5,000. Most insist on an initial deposit above $10,000.

TYPES OF ACCOUNTS

The type of accounts opened may vary, e.g., there are joint accounts, sole proprietorships, partnerships, corporate accounts, and managed accounts. A managed or discretionary account is an account in which the customer signs a power of attorney to the broker or someone else, giving them the right to make trades for the account without first obtaining from the customer the approval on each trade. Don't open such an account unless you know the person and his organization and have confidence in his integrity and ability. Most exchanges have set up special rules covering such accounts.

Many firms also offer guided account programs. A guided account program is one that is essentially managed by a brokerage firm employee, but the customer is required to approve each transaction in advance of execution. Normally, the customer is called and consulted before each trade.

Guided accounts and managed accounts have special appeal and are particularly suited to those people who feel they don't have the time or expertise to manage the accounts themselves and would prefer to have someone else do it for them or at least help them do it. A person seeking such services may also want to consider some of the commodity funds or pools, limited partnership arrangements, or even computerized advisory services.

Most large brokerage houses have established and are marketing commodity funds. Just as the name suggests, an individual can buy an interest in the fund and participate in the profits or losses of the fund activity in proportion to his or her ownership in it. These usually operate as limited partnerships composed of an established number of limited partners and a general partner. Each of the limited partners assumes limited liability for any losses incurred by the partnership. That liability is limited to the investment made. The general partner, however, has unlimited liability.

The attractive thing about limited partnerships and commodity pools is that the individuals investing in them, except for the general partner, have limited liability; they can lose only the amount they have invested. And when a group of people pool their funds, it provides some efficiencies in the management of the money and assures a sufficiently large sum of money so that the account has greater "staying power" than any one of the individuals might have if they were trading separately.

You should be wary of participating in any of these ventures without thoroughly examining the background of the individuals managing the account and the rules and procedures under which the fund's assets will be invested (see Chapter 3).

It's hard to pick up a financial newspaper today without encountering an ad for someone selling a computerized commodity futures trading advisory service. Some people are attracted to the mystique that is associated with computer technology. The advent of the computer as a trading tool was inevitable. The computer is a very efficient means of analyzing large amounts of data and of testing a large number of trading strategies to identify those which seem profitable. Nevertheless, the computer is not better than the person programming it. "Garbage in, garbage out" is an old saying in the computer industry.

Before you lay out very much money for computerized advisory services, check carefully into their past record of achievement. Many such programs are very simplistic and rely heavily on technical analysis largely because the rules of thumb generated by technical analysis are easily programmable on the computer. The more sophisticated and better programs rely on a combination of technical analysis and fundamental analysis. In addition, the good models are sophisticated enough that they contain internal feedback procedures whereby the computer learns from its experience. Thus, as the economic environment changes, the model in the computer conducts trial and error procedures to identify those parts of the model which must be updated to reflect things learned from past experience. These types of models, which have been used successfully to teach a computer to play chess with such skill that even expert players lose to it, are now finding their way into the futures trading field.

If you're looking for outside advice and management help, check carefully into what you're getting before you sign a contract. And, most important, watch the size of the management fee.

Chapter 7

The Order

One of the most important and perhaps least understood aspects of commodity futures trading is the order that a customer gives to his broker to assume or close out a position in the market.

An order is, by definition, an instruction given by a customer to his broker directing the broker to buy or sell a particular futures contract or contracts during a certain time interval. Within these two broad categories of buy and sell orders, however, is a wide variety of order types, each with a specific purpose. So let's examine the above definition, one phrase at a time, to see how each works.

TIME ELEMENT

Time is an aspect of all orders, and there are several ways in which timing may be specified when placing an order.

"Day" orders are good only for the day they are placed. If not executed, they expire at the close of trading on the day on which they are entered.

"Open" orders remain in effect until either executed or canceled or until the contract expires.

"Good 'til canceled" orders are the same as open orders.

"Good through (date)" orders remain in effect until the close of business on the date specified. Variations include orders that are "Good for this week" or "Good for this month."

"Time-of-day" orders call for execution at a specific time or specific intervals during the trading session. For example, "Sell two July pork bellies at the market at 11:30 A.M."

"Off-at-specific-time" orders are similar to "day" orders but have an added time contingency in that they remain in effect only until a specified time during the trading session. If the order is not executed by that time, it is automatically canceled. For example, "Sell two May pork bellies at 55.00. Good 'til 12:00 P.M. Chicago time."

"Fill-or-kill" orders are those to be executed at a specific price or better immediately upon receipt in the pit on the exchange floor. If the order cannot be executed immediately, it is canceled, and the customer is notified of the latest quote. These are also sometimes referred to as "immediate or canceled" orders or "quick" orders. Such orders must be filled in total or in part immediately upon receipt. Any part of the order not filled immediately is canceled automatically.

"On-the-opening" orders must be executed during the opening of trading, which is a short period of time usually counted in minutes at the beginning of the day's trading during which an opening price range is determined in the trading pit. If not filled then, the orders are canceled.

"On-the-close" orders must be executed during the closing of trading, which is a short period of time again measured in minutes or fractions of minutes at the end of the day's trading activity. If not executed before the closing bell, the orders are canceled.

Note: Some brokers and some exchanges will accept only certain types of time-contingent orders. Check with your broker on what he allows. Also, most brokers automatically cancel all open orders at the end of each month.

PRICE

In addition to the time element, all orders must include instructions as to the price at which the transaction is to be made. The order may designate a specific price at which it must be executed, or it may leave the price to be determined by the market. A number of alternative types of price instructions may be used.

The one with which most traders are familiar is an order to buy or sell "at the market." "Market" orders are to be executed at the best possible price obtainable at the time the order reaches the pit. Example: "Buy two Feb. pork bellies at the market."

"Limit" orders are those to purchase or sell futures at a designated price or better. If it is a limit order to buy, the price designated must be below the current market price. If it is a limit order to sell, the price designated must be above the current market price. A limit order enables the customer to execute a transaction at a better price than that prevailing at the time the order is entered, if the market price reaches (actually trades or is bid or offered at) the level specified. Of course, the customer takes the chance that his order will not be executed because the price level he has designated for execution is not reached.

A limit order never becomes a market order. For example, consider the limit order, "Buy two May pork bellies at 54.50 limit." This transaction will be made only at a price of 54.50 or less. If it had been, "Sell two May pork bellies at 54.50 limit," the transaction would be made only at 54.50 or higher.

A "market-if-touched" order is one to buy or sell futures "at the market," when the price reaches the specified level. This order is similar to a limit order in that the designated price to buy must be below the current market price and the price to sell must be above the current market price. Unlike limit orders, however, market-if-touched orders are always executed if the price moves to the designated level because they become market orders at that time. An example of such an order is, "Buy two May pork bellies at 54.50, market-if-touched."

STOP ORDERS

A "stop" order is one to buy or sell at the market when the market reaches a designated price. They are referred to as "stop-loss" orders when placed to close out a position in the event prices move against the trader. A stop order to buy must be entered above the prevailing market price. A stop order to sell must be entered below the prevailing market price. It is these two characteristics that distinguish a stop order from a market-if-touched order.

A stop order to buy or sell at a specified price does not guarantee, however, that the order will be filled at the price specified, even though the market sells or is bid at the stop price. If the market is moving quickly and passes through the stop before the broker has a chance to execute the order, the execution price may be higher or lower than the stop price.

Stop orders are used for three purposes: To protect the profit on an existing long or short position; to initiate a new long or short position; or to stop losses by closing out an unprofitable long or short position. An example of a stop order is, "Buy two May pork bellies at 54.50, stop."

A "stop-limit" order is one that has a designated limit above which the customer will not buy and below which he will not sell. A stop-limit order enables a trader to take advantage of the stop order, yet also to be sure of getting a price within a definite range. Stop-limit orders may be executed when the price is bid at or above the stop price, but they cannot be executed outside the limit specified. In effect, once a stop order is elected, it becomes a limit order. For example, "Buy two May pork bellies at 54.50 stop, limit 54.80" means that if the market sells or is bid or offered at 54.50, buy two May pork belly contracts. If you can't get them done at 54.50 or better, keep trying to buy them up to a price of 54.80, but in no event buy them at a price above 54.80.

"Scale" orders are orders to buy or sell two or more lots of the same commodity at designated intervals. For example, "Buy two May pork bellies at 52.50 and one each 1/2-cent down for five" is an order to buy two May pork bellies at 52.50 and then one more each as the price declines by 1/2-cent intervals until the total of five additional contracts have been purchased.

COMBINATION ORDERS

Combination orders are two orders that are entered at the same time, with the cancellation of one contingent upon the execution of the other. A combination order may also be an order to buy or sell one commodity at a specified price in one month when prices reach a specified level in another month or in another commodity. However, commodity brokers who accept combination orders assume no responsibility for simultaneous or exact price execution, because it is physically impossible for a broker to be in two places executing two orders at the same time.

Combination orders may be classified as "alternate" orders and "contingent" orders. Alternate orders are a group of orders entered at the same time with instructions that, upon execution of any one of the orders, all remaining orders are canceled. Example, "Buy two May pork bellies at 54.50 or two July pork bellies at 55.00."

Contingent orders are entered with the understanding that the execution of one order is dependent upon the execution of the other. They are also referred to as "when-done" orders. These orders may instruct the simultaneous purchase and sale at a stipulated price, or they may instruct the execution of one part of the order before the other part of the order is considered entered. Example: "Buy two May pork bellies at the market when August pork bellies sell above 55.00."

"Spread" orders are used to establish or close out spread or straddle positions and can be used in a variety of ways.

An "inter-market spread" is the purchase of a particular commodity future on one market and the sale of a contract for the same commodity on another market. Example: "Buy two May wheat, Chicago, at the market and sell two May wheat, Minneapolis, at the market."

An "intra-commodity" spread is the purchase of a futures contract for a given month and the simultaneous sale of a futures contract for the same commodity in a different month on the same exchange. Example: "Buy two May pork bellies and sell two July pork bellies when July is three cents over May."

An "inter-commodity spread" is the purchase of a futures contract for a given commodity and the simultaneous sale of a futures contract for a different but related commodity. Example: "Buy three July wheat at the market, sell 20 July corn at the market."

When entering a spread order, the buy part of the order is always given first.

Note: Many brokers and exchanges do not accept complex combination orders. Check with your broker about his practices.

PLACING THE ORDER

It is important when placing orders to give your broker complete and clear instructions whether you want to BUY or SELL; the QUANTITY (quantity in some commodities is given in number of contracts, while in others it is given in number of units of the commodity; for example, "two pork bellies" refers to two contracts; "five wheat" refers to 5,000 bushels or one contract of wheat); the EXCHANGE on which you wish to trade (some commodities are traded on more than one exchange); the MONTH you wish to trade; the length of TIME you want the order to stand; the PRICE: and, of course, the COMMODITY. This may sound like extremely rudimentary advice, but it is surprising how many misunderstandings result from failure to ensure that the broker knows exactly what his customer wants done.

ELECTRONIC TRADING ORDERS

The advent of electronic trading has made the order entry process at once more complex and simpler. It is more complex because each system (and there are several in use) is independent and follows different rules. Most brokers place more responsibility on the customer to track his orders. Orders entered but not executed during the electronic trading session may not be automatically canceled so as to not carry over into the next day's pit trading. Therefore, there is great need for the customer to take serious responsibility for tracking his orders.

It is simpler because the computerized systems cannot handle and will not accept some of the complex contingent and combination orders that a good broker can accept and get executed.

Chapter 8

Forecasting Prices—Supply and Demand

One of the most popular myths in commodity price forecasting is that there is a magic formula for accurately predicting prices and that someone, somewhere, holds the secret to that formula.

A few years ago a member of a major commodity exchange told me excitedly that, after eight years of trading and searching, he had discovered the method for forecasting pork belly prices. A few months later he had to sell his membership on the exchange to pay his debts. Currently, he is working as a brokerage house clerk. Apparently he had staked all he had on his newly discovered secret, only to learn, as did countless others before him, that his magic formula was really a witch's potion.

The price of a commodity at any given instant does not pop from a bubbling cauldron but is the result of decisions on the part of both buyer and seller. Presumably, both traders, after careful analysis of all the factors, have concluded that the price was the best for them under the circumstances.

How did they arrive at their decisions? Most likely through a combination of fundamental analysis and technical analysis. Fundamental analysis refers to the study of those elements that affect the physical supply of and demand for a particular commodity. Technical analysis refers to the study of market activity itself: prices, trading volume, open interest, and other numerical data.

This chapter contains a cursory look at fundamental analysis. Those who would like to delve deeper into the subject can find it in any good basic economics text. This does not mean to imply that fundamental analysis is more important or better than technical analysis in price forecasting. As a matter of fact, most successful traders utilize both approaches the fundamental approach for identifying long-term trends, and technical analysis for timing of trades and identifying short-term trends.

FUNDAMENTAL ANALYSIS

A contractor starting out to build a house has a definite objective in mind, namely, the completed house. Likewise, the price analyst must have a definite objective. It can be narrow and specific, such as an explanation of the movement in beef prices during the last six months, or more general, such as the probable effects on prices of a new government policy or program.

The building contractor needs certain things to accomplish his objective, i.e., a detailed blueprint or plan, tools, materials to work with, and a technique. The price analyst also needs a plan. He needs a knowledge of basic economic concepts in order to avoid costly errors and to assure that he remains on target. He must have material to work with in the form of data and information, and he needs techniques for utilizing the data to build, step-by-step, toward his objective of accurately forecasting commodity prices.

A good place to start understanding this process is with the meaning of a couple of pretty important words: "supply" and "demand."

Demand

The term "demand" is used by different people to mean different things. It is often and not quite correctly considered synonymous with "consumption" or with the "quantity" of a commodity moving into market channels. To an economist, demand refers to the quantity of a product or service that buyers are willing and able to buy at a given place, time, and price. Normally, the quantity people will buy varies inversely with the price; that is, as the price goes up, the amount bought goes down, and vice versa.

In general, consumer demand for a product or a service depends on four main factors and may change when any of the factors change:

1. Real income or purchasing power of consumers—as people have more money to spend, they will usually spend it.

2. The number of consumers—as the number of people grows, so does the total demand for products.
3. The price and availability of substitutes—chicken as a substitute for pork; hence, if the price of chicken goes up relative to the price of pork, people will tend to eat more pork and less chicken.
4. Consumers' personal tastes and preferences—if people suddenly decide they like pork better than beef, their preferences will be reflected in increased demand for pork.

As noted, the price of the product and the quantity bought are closely related. However, this relationship varies, depending upon the commodity. If sirloin steak goes up 50 percent in price, housewives might start pushing their shopping carts right past the steak cooler. However, if the price of table salt were to rise by 50 percent, sales of salt are not likely to fall very much. In one instance, there are several alternatives; in the other instance (salt), there are few and it's a necessity. By the same token, a 10 percent change in the price of pork may cause a 12 percent change in the amount of pork purchased.

The degree to which the quantity bought changes in response to a change in price is described by the frightening term, "price elasticity of demand." This is nothing more than an index number devised by economists to describe how far purchases will go in one direction when price goes in the other. For example, the price elasticity for all beef has been estimated at 95. This means that a 10 percent *increase* in the price of beef is associated with a 9.5 percent *decrease* in the amount of beef bought. Expressed another way, it means that people tend to tolerate moderate beef price increases and go on broiling hamburgers.

A full understanding of elasticity and what it means will enable you to estimate the amount of price change necessary to clear a market of a given amount of product. For a complete discussion of this subject, consult any good introductory text on economics, marketing, or price analysis.

Supply

Just as you can't cut a piece of cloth with one blade of a scissor, you can't determine price by considering demand only. The other blade of the price-determining scissor is supply. Recent experience has shown that the demand for commodities remains relatively constant over short periods of time. This is particularly true in developed economies such as the United States, where consumer habits change slowly and incomes do not fluctuate sharply. Therefore, supply must be given careful consideration in price analysis and forecasting.

Generally speaking, the short-term supply of a agricultural commodity is made up of the carryover from previous growing seasons, the current year's production, and imports. There is no carryover, of course, for unstorable commodities like live cattle or hogs, but in commodities such as grains, carryover is an important part of supply.

Most data published on agricultural, food, and fiber commodities by the USDA and other sources deal with supply, because it is more readily measured than demand. Periodic reports based on producers' stated intentions as well as measurements of actual yields at the end of a season provide a relatively accurate indication of the forthcoming supply of a commodity. Ask your broker for such reports or get on the mailing lists at the U.S. Departments of Agriculture, Commerce, and Treasury to receive their reports directly.

As used by economists, the term "supply" means the quantity of a product or service that would be made available by sellers at a specified place, time, and price. Just as buyers will take different amounts of a commodity depending on the price, so sellers are usually willing to sell different amounts at different prices. Normally, the quantity of a commodity offered for sale varies directly with the price; that is, when the price goes up, the amount offered for sale goes up, and when the price goes down, the amount offered for sale goes down. As in the case of demand, the concept of elasticity also applies.

The quantity of a commodity offered by sellers at a given price is also influenced the commodity's storability. The willingness to sell from stocks on hand depends on the owner's comparison of current prices with what he thinks he might get if he held on to his commodity a while longer. On the other hand, the supply obtained directly from current production is affected more by such things as weather, yields, acres planted, or number of animals bred, quantities and prices of feed, and other costs of production (see Figure 8.1).

The longer-term supply of a product is determined by the total number of potential producers; the capacity of the facilities they operate; their proficiency as producers; the physical characteristics of production of the commodity such as the length of life of fruit trees; their own personal expectations; the relative costs of production for alternative products; and certain social and institutional influences, such as the historical tendency of corn farmers to continue to plant corn.

Armed with an understanding of what it is that makes up supply and demand for a commodity, the analyst is then ready to organize these elements in such a way that he can judge their collective effect on price. In other words, the analyst can develop a "model"—a diagram of what affects prices and how it affects prices. It should be noted that models are simplifications of reality. No model can include all of the relationships that affect price, and, indeed, it would be a waste of time to attempt to do so. The important thing is that the model include the major factors and show the real interrelationships between them. The diagram on the next page is a model of how supply and demand interact to affect the prices of pork. The lines connecting the elements show the interrelationships.

Figure 8.1 The Demand and Supply Structure for Pork

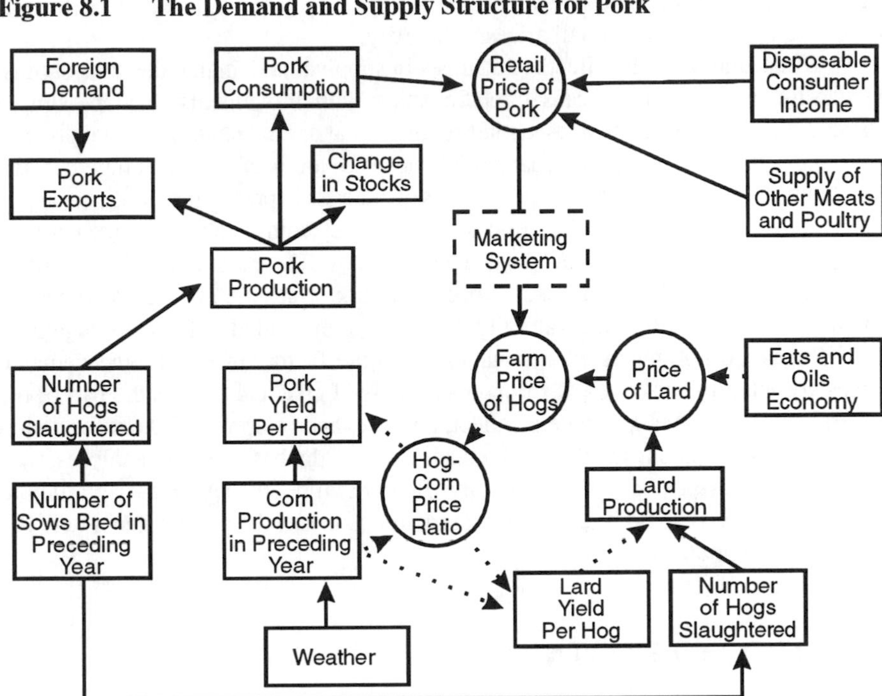

Arrows show direction of influence. Heavy arrows indicate major paths of influence which account for the bulk of the variation in current prices. Light solid arrows indicate definite but less important paths. Dashed arrows indicate paths of negligible, doubtful, or occasional importance.

CONSUMER IS KING

All demand begins, of course, with the consumer. In the absence of a demand by consumers for a product, there would be no demand by retailers, wholesalers, or processors. This demonstrates the importance of beginning a price forecast with an analysis of consumers' demand for the end product or at least working from the point closest to the consumer.

An experienced analyst learns to study those factors that affect demand and supply at each level of the system. He learns, for example, that when the packers are operating plants at less than optimum capacity because of a lack of hogs for slaughtering, they bid up the price of hogs. And that during periods of inflation, the price of beef usually rises more than the price of pork. He also learns that these factors do not operate instantaneously, that there are time lags built in. It takes weeks for a rise in the demand of pork at retail to be fully transmitted back to the farmers in the form of higher prices for hogs. Likewise, an increase in the supply of hogs at the farm level is not transmitted into lower retail prices right away.

When analyzing the effects of changes in supply and demand, the analyst must be careful not to confuse causal relationships with movements that are simply associated. Some years ago a researcher reported that annual changes in the price of pork seemed to be related to changes in the price of beef. Some jumped to the conclusion that changes in prices of beef caused changes in pork prices. Later, analysts discovered that changes in pork prices were almost completely accounted for by changes in market supplies and consumer incomes. The reason for this apparent cause-and-effect relationship was that beef and pork prices are affected by the same domestic demand conditions. Naturally, therefore, they tended to fluctuate together.

Prices are not generated automatically by the factors of supply and demand. Prices are actually "discovered" through a process of give and take on the part of the buyers and sellers. Market traders collect, analyze, and interpret all the information and facts they can about supply and demand. Then on the basis of their analyses, they make bids and offers, back and forth, until finally two people agree that a particular price is satisfactory to both. When the transaction is made, the price is generated. It's like a giant computer.

WHERE TO GET DATA

For the beginning trader or non-professional, doing your own data gathering and analysis is generally out of the question. You really have to rely on your broker, his sources, and his research team. Don't work with a broker that does not keep you informed of fundamental economic reports and news that affect the commodities you trade and, especially, those in which you have positions.Knowing the release date of a report is crucial for the trader. Markets anticipate reports, and prices will adjust prior to release of the report in anticipation of what the report will contain. Sometimes, of course, the market is wrong in its anticipation, and prices that went up expecting a bullish report will immediately go down when the report is found to be bearish. Most smart traders try to be out of the market or at least in a protected position at the time major reports are released. This is just good common sense. Do not try to outguess the market. Take time to study and analyze new information before committing yourself to a position.

If, however, you are interested in doing your own analysis, a lot of the data you will want are available directly from reports of the U.S. Departments of Agriculture and Commerce and several private market reporting agencies. These reports tell in great detail the daily, weekly, and monthly price movements, market receipts, and other associated factors and are useful in following current situations as well as in long-term forecasting. Most of the government reports are available free. Anyone working regularly in the field of price forecasting and analysis should ask to have his name placed on the mailing lists of the government agencies issuing reports. For a list of the available reports, write to: Superintendent of Documents, Government Printing Office, Washington, DC 20250. At the end of this chapter a great many government reports, as well as a number of private sources, available on specific commodity groups, are listed.

Private market reporting services are available for many commodities. In addition, many trade organizations collect and publish information about their industry on a regular basis. Magazines, newspapers, and wire services report information about USDA statistics and the markets on a daily basis. Many of the articles contained in *Futures* Magazine deal in depth with analysis of individual reports and commodities. Your broker should be able to keep you posted on the timing of the reports, and he should also be able to give you a quick summary of the contents of reports after they are released.

In addition, most exchanges provide relatively complete statistical summaries and pamphlets explaining, in a simplified way, the fundamental supply and demand factors affecting prices for individual commodities. For example, the Chicago Mercantile Exchange publishes a daily bulletin containing summaries of the previous day's futures trading and the important cash market statistics. They also publish a yearbook containing the same information for a whole year, special periodic summaries of important USDA reports and an excellent series of pamphlets explaining how to analyze the fundamental factors affecting each of the major commodities traded.

GOVERNMENT POLICIES

As in most aspects of life, the government plays a major role in the pricing of products, and all fundamental analysts learn to watch closely the activities of the federal and state governments in encouraging or discouraging production, controlling imports and exports throughembargoes and quotas, storage programs, and in establishing price ceilings and floors. There are myriad such government programs in existence, and virtually all affect prices in some way.

WHAT TO LOOK FOR AND WHERE TO FIND IT

Other chapters of this book set forth, in basic form, some of the *modus operandi* for analyzing futures price movements. What follows in this chapter provides a guide for selecting the type of information you should plug into a model for a particular commodity.

No attempt is made to be exhaustive in presenting the factors that may affect the price of a commodity. Nor are these data complete in covering all commodities traded on the various exchanges. Rather, the purpose is to be introductory only—to provide the new trader with an awareness of some of the kinds of information to seek out and where to find it.

You will still have to ask yourself these questions:

1. Which of these factors is most important?
2. Why is this particular piece of information important?
3. How does change in a certain factor affect prices?

You will note that sometimes the same factors appear on both the supply and demand sides of the price-making equation. This is because some factors interact to affect both sides. A worthwhile and fascinating but frustrating experiment is to take the supply/demand factors outlined for the commodities indicated on the tables that follow and arrange them in a schematic diagram to show their interaction and relationships to each other. Such an exercise would show you that there is no one interpretation of data, no single model that is "correct." In fact, the differences in interpretation of such information are what make a market. In the final analysis, the greatest satisfaction (aside from monetary gain) derived from commodity futures trading lies in interpreting the available facts better than anybody else and being "right."

GOVERNMENT INFORMATION

The U.S. government is probably the most important source of information for the commodity trader. And best of all, the information is usually available free. Virtually every major governmental agency or department collects information of some kind from the public at large or from the industry of its concern. Careful analysis of this information can be extremely helpful in developing a trading plan.

In addition to the general supply/demand data listed on the following pages, you should also try to understand the people who are trading the markets. To this end, it is suggested that you study the *Commitment of Traders Report* issued bi-monthly by the CFTC. Each day the names of individual traders who have large positions are reported to the CFTC. This information, along with a good deal of other information concerning the cash market activities of the individual, is then used in the CFTC's market surveillance activity.

Once a month the accumulated data about these trader positions, their classification as hedger or speculator, and the percent of the contracts owned by the largest four and largest eight traders are released to the public. Although the data is slightly out-of-date by the time it is released, it does provide some guidance as to whether hedgers or speculators are dominating any one side of the market and how they are changing their positions from month to month. When you couple that information with the price activity and trend, you can get a hint of what large speculators or large hedgers believe will happen to prices and how they are getting into a position to take advantage of it.

It would be misleading to place too much emphasis on the current value of this information. However, the CFTC regularly makes some changes in the reporting system to provide even more detailed analyses of the makeup of the market and to provide it in a more timely fashion.

In addition to government reports on many topics, there are also a number of publications available from private sources or from commodity organizations. Daily newspapers and financial publications provide important information on a regular basis, and most exchanges also have a number of helpful publications available to the public. Although it would be impossible to list all of these sources, here are some of the key sources covering most commodities regularly:

Futures Magazine, 219 Parkade, Cedar Falls, IA 50613

The Wall Street Journal, 22 Cortlandt St., New York, NY 10007

Journal of Commerce,110 Wall St., New York, NY 10005

Barron's, 22 Cortlandt St., New York, NY 10007

The New York Times, 229 W. 43rd St., New York, NY 10036

Commodity Yearbook, Knight-Ridder, Trade Center
25 Hudson, New York, NY 10006

On the following pages you will find a breakdown, by commodity, of the most important factors to watch, as well as some other sources of information in each case.

Chapter 9

Basic Price Patterns—Forecasting Tools

Remember the old comedy record of a Frenchman describing the first American football game he had ever seen? Looking at commodity price movements on a day-to-day basis without an understanding of the underlying patterns can make about the same amount of sense.

These underlying patterns take several forms. Some movements reflect seasonal influences, some are cyclical. There are also trends to be considered. All of these price movements may be further divided into those of short-term and those of long-term duration.

Short-term price fluctuations are due mainly to sudden shifts in the demand for, or supply of, a commodity as a result of reactions to weather conditions, political moves, international developments, rumors, technical "signals," or chance occurrences. Long-term price fluctuations are the result of fundamental or gradual shifts in demand and supply resulting from more enduring factors such as changes in production technology, consumer preferences, or population growth.

SEASONAL MOVEMENTS

All agricultural commodities and many financial instruments have some seasonality in production and marketing. Perishable and semi-perishable commodities not stored by dealers have to be moved into consumption as soon as possible after production. As the available supply of these products increases, consumers will buy the added quantities only at lower prices. When the supply falls off, consumers are willing to pay higher prices. That's why prices are usually more volatile for perishable commodities than for the non-perishables. Figures 9.1 and 9.2 show the consistency over 10 years, five years, and three years of seasonal factors in cattle and pork bellies.

Non-perishable commodities (those that can be stored) are usually lowest in price at harvest time but tend to rise during the rest of the year only by an amount sufficient to cover the accumulated cost of storing. Consequently, the season's supply is fed into consumption in relatively uniform amounts from month to month. As a result, prices are more uniform throughout the year than for perishable commodities.

Financials also have seasonal trends reflecting debt-issuing cycles by governments, elections and political cycles, and business cycles. For example, the U.S. Treasury holds major bond auctions every three months to issue three-year, 10-year, and 30-year debt for financing the government. These auctions have a significant influence on interest rate futures and currency futures.

Seasonal variation in commodity prices is frequently misinterpreted. The true seasonal movement in prices can be observed only by taking average prices over a long period. And keep in mind that this represents history—it does not necessarily predict the future. The average or so-called "typical" seasonal price movement does

Figure 9.1 Cash Seasonal Omaha Pork Seasonals

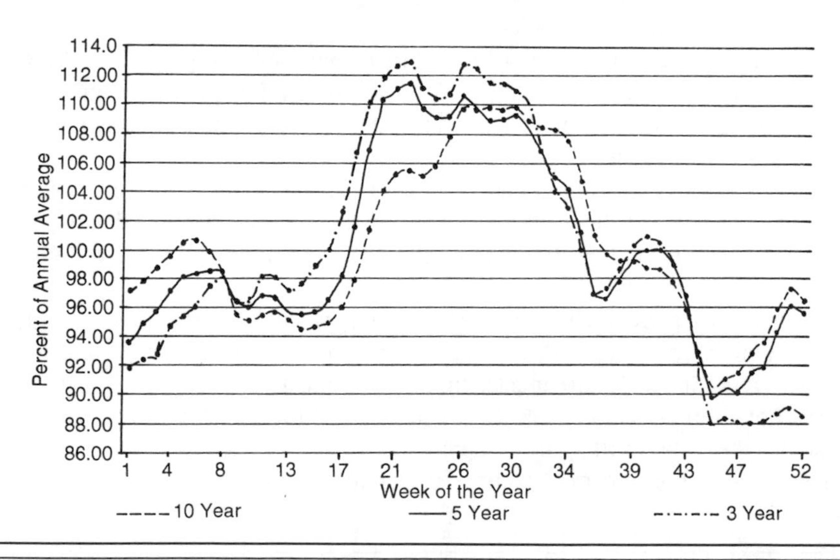

Figure 9.2 Pork Belly Seasonals

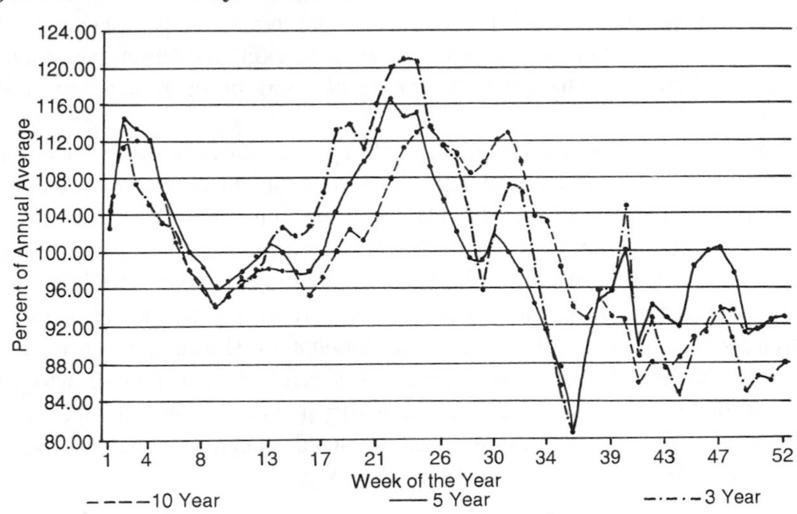

These charts have been prepared by August R. King and Associates for informational purposes only, and should not be considered investment advice. All futures and options are for people who can afford risk. Although every reasonable attempt has been made to ensure the accuracy of these charts, August R. King and Associates and the Chicago Mercantile Exchange assume no resposibility for any error or ommissions

not occur regularly each year. In fact, month-to-month changes in price are quite different in different years. The seasonal price variation merely represents a general tendency.

Wheat provides an excellent example, as it is one of the commodities that tends to follow a distinct seasonal price pattern. Generally, low prices in wheat occur during the summer harvest season, with higher prices in winter and spring.

CYCLICAL MOVEMENTS

Almost any regularly recurring movement can be called a cycle. But in commodities, this term is usually applied to the more-or-less regular rise and fall of production and price over an extended period of time. Cycles are self-energizing, which means that one part of the movement follows or is caused by another part. This makes cycles, to a certain extent, predictable.

There are several well-known cycles in the production and price of a commodity. High prices not only encourage new producers to enter into production but influence existing producers to produce more. As market receipts increase, prices decline until they reach a point where some producers become discouraged and drop out while others simply reduce their operations. As the contraction continues, prices rise until they again reach a level that encourages expansion, marking the beginning of a new cycle. Figure 9.3 showing changes in hog prices and pork production, demonstrates this action.

Often there are time lags associated with cyclical movements. For example, livestock marketings tend to lag behind production on the upswing of the production cycle because, as production increases, a larger proportion of available animals must be retained for breeding purposes. On the downswing, a smaller than average number of animals are retained for breeding and farmer marketings are therefore larger than the total number of animals on farms would indicate. In anticipating the effects of the production cycle on price, you have to take into account this shifting lag of production and receipts. Further, the length of time it takes production to change will vary according to the time it takes to bring the commodity to market. For example, in hogs, it takes three to four years for a cycle to be completed; in cattle, it takes six to eight years. Clearly, business and financial cycles also exist.

TRENDS

Long-term changes in supply or demand, whatever the causes, may result in gradual increases or decreases in prices. Such long-term changes are referred to as "secular trends."

Figure 9.3 Changes in Hog Prices and Pork Production

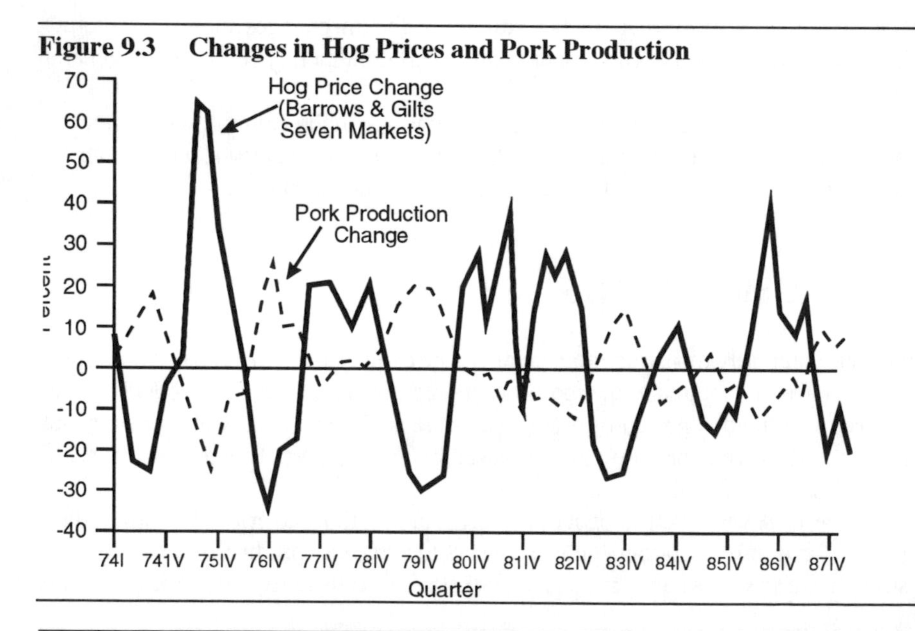

The steady growth in population, the gradual development of new uses for a commodity without a proportionate increase in supply, changing customs, changes in purchasing power, and gradual changes in the technology of production all may have some effect on supply and demand over the years, forcing prices into higher or lower ranges. Meanwhile, of course, the price is fluctuating from day-to-day, season-to-season and, possibly, from cycle-to-cycle.

STATISTICAL TECHNIQUES

Armed with some understanding of the supply and demand factors that can affect commodity prices, you are now ready to apply statistical techniques to analysis of the data. There are many. Selection of a particular technique or combination of techniques depends on the nature of the problem, the nature of the data and, to some extent, on your personal preference.

We'll treat only a few of the more popular methods here. We can only familiarize you with the basics. It would take a separate book—and many have been written—to explain any one of them.

Ratios

For long-run forecasting, a great many experienced traders consider certain ratios, such as the hog/corn ratio, as reliable indicators.

The hog/corn ratio is used in forecasting hog prices. It is calculated by dividing the price of hogs per hundred-weight by the price of a bushel of corn. (If the price of hogs is $20 per hundredweight and the price of corn is $1.50 per bushel, the hog/corn ratio would be 20 ÷ 1.50 = 13.33.)

Changes in this ratio give you an indication of the profitability of hog feeding and help forecast an increase or decrease in the number of hogs fed. Low ratios (below 12) suggest narrow profit margins and low future production, while high ratios indicate higher profits and greater future production.

Moving Averages

A moving average is a flexible trend line that has been "smoothed out." If annual or monthly data are used, the moving average will reduce the effects of cycles, seasonal variations, and irregular movements, giving you a better idea of underlying supply and demand strength. But the longer the period chosen, the greater the likely time lag between a change in the trend of prices and the indication of this change by the moving average.

Active traders prefer to plot moving averages over short time periods. Five-day, 10-day or 20-day moving averages are commonly used although some methods use

Figure 9.4 **US Hog/Corn Price Ratio**
BU of Corn = Value to 100 lbs Hog LVWT

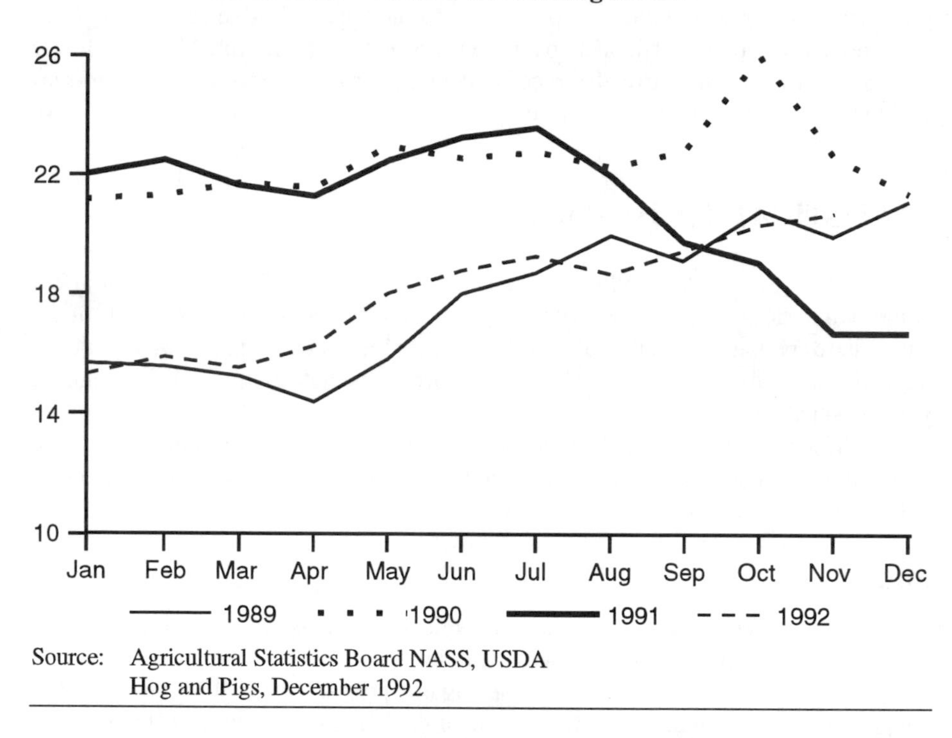

Source: Agricultural Statistics Board NASS, USDA
Hog and Pigs, December 1992

four-, nine- and 18-day moving averages. The example in this chapter is based on a 12-month period. The method, however, applies to any time period.

To build a moving average:

1. Select a time period or number of weeks that seems to best represent the cycle or seasonal element that you are most interested in smoothing out. As an example, if you want to eliminate the seasonality in pork prices to identify the long-term trend, you should use a 12-month period.

2. Average the prices for that 12-month period in order to obtain the first number of the moving average.

3. To figure out the second number in the moving average, drop the price for the first month and average the next 12 prices in the series. And so on.

Table 9.1 ahows how to calculate a 12-month moving average for retail pork prices.

Table 9.1 Building A Moving Average

	Average Price/Pound	Moving Average
January	76.68	
February	76.40	
March	76.03	
April	74.63	
May	74.72	
June	74.72	
July	75.37	
August	74.44	
September	71.64	
October	69.49	
November	66.13	
December	63.98	874.23 ÷ 12 = 72.85
January	63.89	861.44 ÷ 12 = 71.88
February	64.82	849.86 ÷ 12 = 70.82
March	65.29	829.12 ÷ 12 = 69.09

Index Numbers

High on the list of most useful statistical measures are those telling you how much change has occurred from one period to another or how change in one element compares with change in another element. For example, you may want to use an index to compare the production of corn in one year with the production of corn in another.

The usefulness of index numbers is by no means limited to changes in the price or production of single commodities. They are widely used to express changes in such complex economic areas as the cost of living and business cycles. These, of course, involve combining many prices or quantities in such a way that a single number can be used to indicate overall changes. The "cost-of-living index" is perhaps the most well-known of these; the Dow Jones index of leading stocks is almost a household word. We are more concerned here, however, with a simple index that pertains to one commodity.

Suppose, for example, that we wanted to develop an unweighted index to measure the change in the average price of a barrel of oil over eight periods. We would divide each period's price by the initial price and multiply by 100.

Year	Price	Index
1	22.66 ÷ 22.66 × 100 =	100.0
2	25.39 ÷ 22.66 × 100 =	112.0
3	25.86 ÷ 22.66 × 100 =	114.1
4	25.58 ÷ 22.66 × 100 =	112.8
5	27.13 ÷ 22.66 × 100 =	119.7
6	29.95 ÷ 22.66 × 100 =	132.1
7	29.64 ÷ 22.66 × 100 =	130.8
8	32.35 ÷ 22.66 × 100 =	142.7

This would give us a rough but handy single number to indicate these relative price changes.

Indexes are particularly useful in analyzing seasonal patterns. For example, in grain prices seasonal indexes can aid in estimating the profitability of storing a crop versus selling it immediately.

Seasonal indexes can also be used to estimate specific price levels during the year but only when reliable annual price forecasts are available. For example, if the average price of fed steers at Omaha for a particular year is reliably estimated to be $50 per hundredweight and the seasonal price index for June is 97.80, the estimated June price would be $50 × .9780, or $48.90 per hundredweight. Through additional simple statistical techniques, you could also estimate the probability of achieving the price.

The main point of all this is simply that indexes properly constructed and used can be very powerful projection tools.

Correlation

Earlier we said that an analyst must fit together supply and demand to determine how they relate to market prices. Correlation analysis is often used to identify these important factors for inclusion in a supply and demand model.

Correlation is nothing more than a measure of the degree of association (not necessarily cause and effect) between two or more factors. Most fathers, for example, would find a high correlation between a teenage son's request to use the car and Saturday nights.

Correlation may be determined and expressed either mathematically or graphically. Correlation studies are classified as "simple," meaning the study of relationships between only two factors, and "multiple" or the study of the relationship of one factor to a group of other factors. We'll deal here only with "simple" correlation as shown on a graph.

Suppose we want to measure the relationship between the price of lumber and the number of housing starts in the U.S., assuming the preceding data.

The first step is to put the data on a "scatter" diagram, as shown in Figure 9.5. The vertical scale represents lumber prices and the horizontal scale represents housing starts. Dots are inserted in the diagram representing price and housing starts for each month. That is, the dot for any one month is opposite the point on the horizontal scale corresponding to the houses started and opposite the lumber price on the vertical scale. After all the data have been plotted, a line is drawn through the field of dots representing the average relationship between the two factors.

If the level of lumber prices depended only on the number of housing starts, all of the dots would lie on the line, and you would have a very powerful forecasting tool. If you know the number of housing starts, you would then be able to determine fairly accurately the level of lumber prices. But many other factors affect the price, which is why the dots are "scattered" around the line. Therefore, you have to look at other factors, like other uses for lumber, to help improve your price forecasting accuracy. The closer the dots are to the line, the stronger the relationship between the two factors and the more reliable the forecasts on the graph.

If the relationship is positive, the line will run upward to the right and the two variables tend to increase together. If it is negative, the line will run downward to the right, and the two variables tend to move in opposite directions.

This is a good technique to use at the beginning of analysis, because it suggests which relationships and variables are worthwhile exploring in depth and which ones are really mirror images of each other.

ANALYZING THE DATA

One last word of warning. Don't confuse fundamental analysis with statistical analysis. And don't use one without the other. The mechanics of statistical analysis alone would be quite insufficient for effective price analysis. In fact, many successful commodity traders do not use formal statistical techniques. Qualitative or deductive reasoning plays an important role in price analysis, since many relationships or causes and effects cannot be statistically measured. Fundamentals are essential in filling the gaps. Using both, you won't fall into the common trap of arriving at erroneous conclusions drawn from purely statistical manipulations.

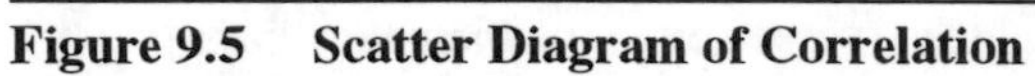

Figure 9.5 Scatter Diagram of Correlation

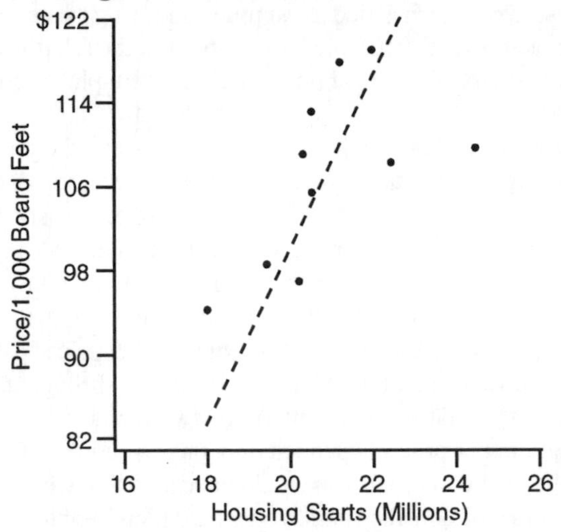

	Average Monthly Price/1000 Bd. Ft. 2 × 4's	U.S. Housing Starts (thousands)
January	$ 82	1,810
February	95	1,794
March	98	1,938
April	97	1,951
May	96	2,046
June	109	2,008
July	118	2,091
August	119	2,219
September	119	2,029
October	106	2,038
November	108	2,228
December	110	2,433

Chapter 10

Technical Analysis

Technical analysts approach commodity price analysis in much the same manner as cryptographers attempting to decipher a code. They have no less expectation that "written" in those squiggly lines is a message containing the ultimate secret to forecasting commodity prices if only the code could be broken.

Their reasoning? That even if you knew where to find all the fundamental information about the supply and production of a commodity . . . even if you had the time to add it all up and also allow for such fleeting factors as weather, strikes, and crop disease . . . you still wouldn't have the clue to market response. Because it is not these things that affect futures prices, but how traders react to them that determines price movement. And, according to the theory of technical analysis, the only place where all the factual supply and demand data plus the mass moods, hopes, fears, estimates, and "guesstimates" of everyone in the market are crystalized is in a commodity's price, volume, and open interest.

Technical analysts thus believe that by studying *how* prices have acted, you can obtain more insight about prospective futures price movements than you can by studying *why* prices have acted a certain way. They believe one can learn more by studying the price movements than by studying the factors that affect prices.

There are two basic types of price charts used in technical analysis: bar charts and point-and-figure charts. (Candlestick charts used in Japan are a third popular choice.) Both kinds of charts are easily constructed. All you need are the price information, some graph paper and a pencil, or a computer and some software.

If you don't want to be bothered or don't have the time to build and maintain your own charts, there are numerous chart services available that provide ready-made charts for a fee. Some of these provide only one type of chart, while others such as Commodity Price Charts, provide a combination of all types of charts and also offer interpretation of the data. Ask your broker or check *Futures* Magazine's annual reference guide.

The first step in constructing any chart is to decide on the frequency of the prices to be plotted—that is, hourly, daily, weekly, or monthly. Normally, if you are interested in short-term trading you would keep your charts on an hourly and daily basis. If you're interested in intermediate or longer-term analysis, weekly price charts may be more suited to your purpose.

This chapter will help you understand the basics of chart building and pattern identification and interpretation. Knowing how the charts are built can be very helpful in interpreting them. Knowledge of construction reveals the flaws and helps avoid misinterpretations. The last section of this chapter covers chart services and software vendors who supply ready-made charts or allow you to use your home computer to build your own systems.

THE BAR CHART

If you've ever seen a commodity price chart, chances are it was a bar chart. They are by far the most popular, because they're easier to keep than point-and-figure charts and because all the information needed to update them can be found in most local newspapers.

Figure 10.1 is a typical bar chart. The numbers running up the right side of the chart are the prices in cents per pound. Similar charts for other commodities would use price scales in keeping with those commodities. For example, a wheat chart would show prices in cents per bushel with minimum variations of 1/4-cent per bushel, a hog chart in cents per pound with minimum variations of 1/40 of a cent (or 2-1/2 "points") per pound.

Across the bottom of the chart is a daily calendar with the weekends left out. That is, each square contains only the five weekly trading days. This prevents a two-day "gap" in the chart between each two sets of weekly data, making the chart easier to read.

At the end of each trading day, a vertical line is drawn on the chart directly above that date on the calendar. The top of this line marks the point of the day's highest price.

Figure 10.1 Chicago December Wheat

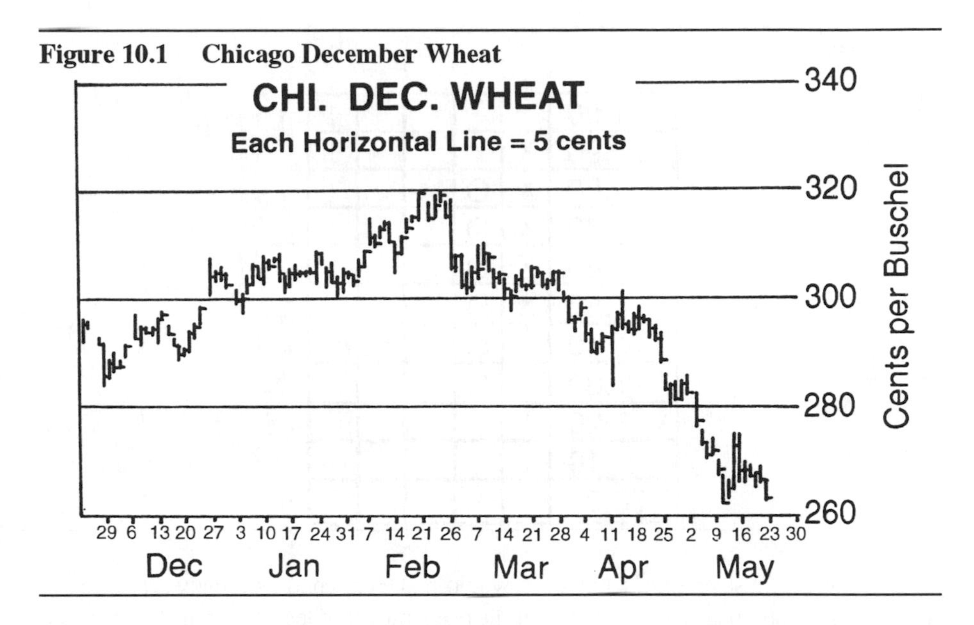

The bottom of the line marks the lowest price at which that commodity traded that day. The closing price is shown by a short horizontal "tick" extending to the right.

THE POINT-AND-FIGURE CHART

"All well and good," say the point-and-figure chartists, "but look at what you've missed. That one little line stands for thousands of trades and price fluctuations. It doesn't tell you nearly enough."

And they have a case. In a sense, a point-and-figure chart is to a bar chart what a moving picture is to a still photograph. Depending on the scale to which it is built, a point-and-figure chart can show you every single price fluctuation in a commodity throughout the entire trading period.

As with bar charts, the vertical axis of the point-and-figure chart shows prices (see Figure 10.2). This time, however, the spaces—not the lines—represent the prices. The reason for this is that prices are marked on the chart by filling in the boxes with an "X" or an "O." Because point-and-figure charts display price changes without regard to time, the bottom scale has no calendar.

Entries are made on a point-and-figure chart whenever a predetermined price change occurs. The best way to understand this is with an example, so let's build a point- and-figure chart for December New York silver.

The minimum price fluctuation for silver is 1/10 of a cent per ounce, or 10 points, so we'll mark off the point scale in 10 point increments. To record every one of the

Figure 10.2

471.00					
.90	X				
.80	X	O			
.70	X	O			
.60	X	O			
.50	X	O			
.40		O			
.30		O			
.20					
.10					
470.00					

10-point jiggles in silver prices, however, would make our chart extremely sensitive . . . so, let's agree not to take any action until the price moves at least 20 points in the same direction.

To begin charting, let's say that right now—right at this very moment—December silver is quoted at 470.50. To show this, we'll put an "X" in the 470.50 box in the first column as our starting point. Then, after jumping around between 470.60 and 470.40 for a few minutes, the price of December silver touches 470.70. This is a 20-point move, so we add another "X" to the first column at 470.70 and then—only then—fill in the 470.60 box to show the travel of the price. If the price continues up and reaches 470.90, another "X" is added at that price and at 470.80. And so forth.

Now, for reversal. Even though we decided that a 20-point change in the price of silver in one direction was worth recording, we now have to decide how far it must go against the trend to be significant. Let's say that it has to reverse at least 40 points to be meaningful. In charting jargon that's called a "four-box reversal." This means that if December silver drops from 470.90 (our last "X") to 470.50, we must make a new mark on the chart. We used "X" to show up-moves, so let's use "O" for down-moves. We place an "O" opposite 470.80, 470.70, and 470.60 for continuity. We have to move to the next adjacent column to do this, because those boxes in the first column are already filled.

Then, if December silver continues down to 470.30 (remember, we're charting 20-point moves in one direction) we mark an "O" in the boxes or 470.30 and 470.40. And so on.

You can readily see that a point-and-figure chart this sensitive would almost require your presence on the trading floor or a ticker in your office for you to keep it accurate and up-to-date. Of course, most people cannot be on the floor of the exchange and, besides, one does not need such a sensitive chart to trade successfully. These types of charts can be made less sensitive to the little wiggles in price and more useful in identifying major turning points in price trends by the size of the price change recorded and the size of reversal needed before the change is recorded. Realistically, for example, a point-and-figure silver chart in recent markets probably would have boxes measured in 10 cents or perhaps even 30 cents per box, not tenths of a cent, and it might take a price change of $.60 per ounce to mark a reversal, not .4 of a cent, as in our example.

But there are some guidelines which apply to all point-and-figure charts, regardless of values assigned to boxes or reversals. For example, suppose you want to build a three-box reversal chart which notes only large significant moves and can be developed from the daily high-low price data carried in your local newspaper. The general rules for developing such a chart are:

A. X's represent price increases; O's represent price decreases.

B. The spread (difference) between the high and the low for the day is the important figure to get from the newspaper.

C. To start the chart, begin with a day in which the spread between the high and the low represents at least three boxes on the chart.[1]

D. If the most recent entry is an X (O), review the daily high (low) first. If the high (low) is at least one box higher (lower) than the last entry, add the appropriate number of X's (O's).

E. If the daily high does not require drawing more X's, then consider the low. If today's low is lower than the highest X by three boxes or more, begin a column of O's beginning one box below and one box to the right of the highest X.

F. If the daily low does not require drawing more O's, then consider the high. If today's high is higher than the lowest O by three boxes or more, begin a column of X's beginning one box above and one box to the right of the lowest O.

G. A simple buy signal occurs when the current column of X's rises one box higher than the top X in the prior column of X's.

H. A simple sell signal occurs when the current column of Os fall one box lower than the lowest O in the prior column of O's.

---

1. You will need to decide how sensitive you want the chart to be and select the size of box and number of boxes for reversal accordingly. The procedures for charting are the same, irrespective of what box you select.

To demonstrate this charting method, consider several actual contracts over a period of time (Figures 10.3 and 10.4). There are a number of buy and sell signals, several of them false. Can you find them?

Although the point-and-figure technique can be applied in any market, among the most useful are those in which good fundamental analysis is difficult to accomplish and where the price moves are subject to a broad spectrum of political and economic factors, e.g., currency, Treasury bills, bonds, etc. Point-and-figure charts become especially powerful tools when combined with good fundamental analysis.

Figure 10.3 September Eurodollars Point and Figure 10 × 3

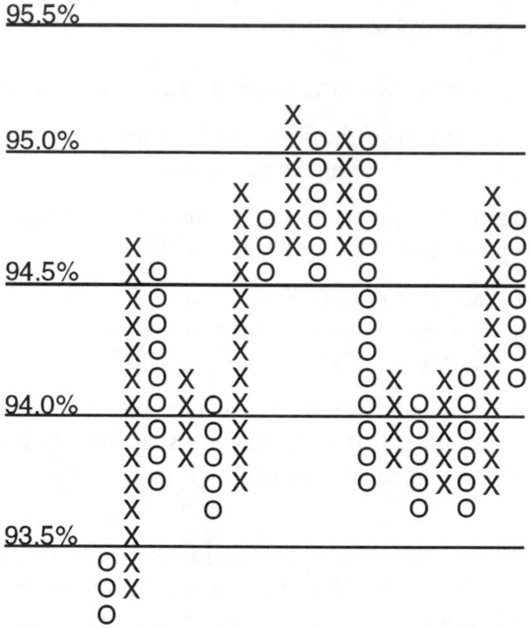

```
95.5%

               X
95.0%          XOXO
               XOXO
             X XOXO     X
             XOXOXO     XO
   X         XOXOXO     XO
94.5%XO      XO O O     XO
   XO        X    O     XO
   XO        X    O     XO
   XO        X    O     XO
   XOX       X    OX  XOXO
94.0%XOXOX        OXOXOX
   XOXOX          OXOXOX
   XOXOX          OXOXOX
   XO OX          O OXOX
   X  O             O O
93.5%X
  OX
  OX
  O
```

INTERPRETING BAR CHARTS— BASIC CHART PATTERNS

By recording price movements as they develop, charts provide a continuous picture of how prices are reacting to market forces. The objective of chart analysis is to discern the trend of prices, and to ascertain when that trend changes. Although it is not the intent here to provide a comprehensive discussion of chart formations and their

Figure 10.4 July Cotton Point and Figure 40 × 2

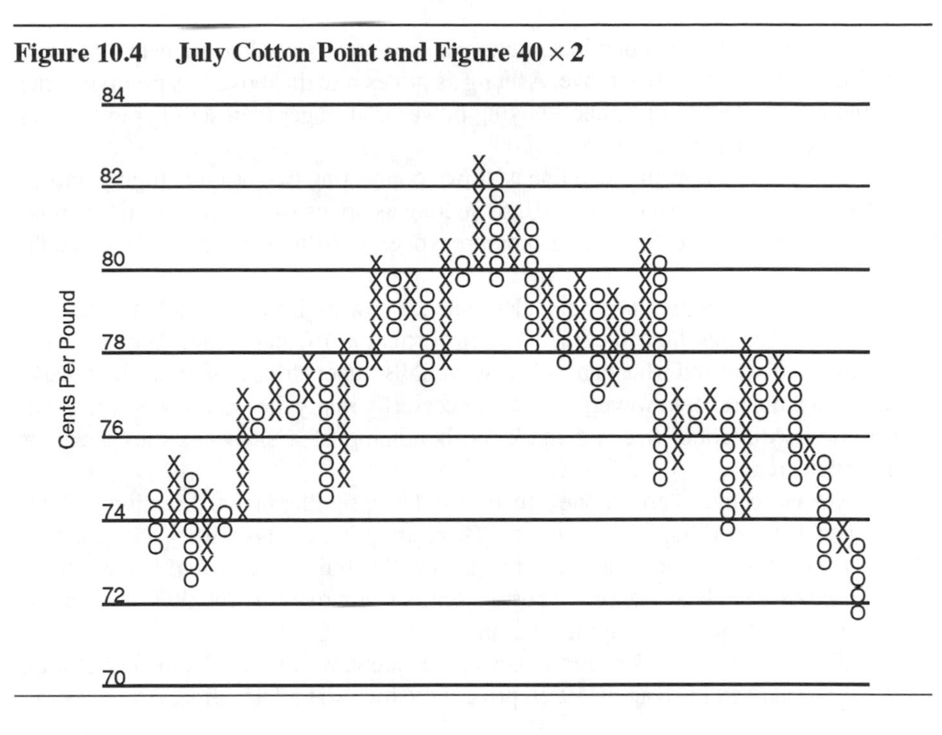

interpretation, a few of the basic formations will be reviewed in order to give you an idea of how many chart analysts think and how they interpret pictures of price moves.

A bit of reflection makes it obvious that there are only three things prices can do: They can go up, they can go down, or they can stay where they are. Whichever happens, it is meaningful to a technical analyst.

If prices are in an uptrend, it is because buyers are more aggressive than sellers at that general price level, and the market is said to be characterized by buying power. When prices trend downward, it is because sellers have the upper hand, and selling pressure predominates. When prices move in a seemingly random, sideways fashion, it is construed that buying and selling pressures are about equal and the market is considered to be in a congestion area.

DEFINING A TREND

An uptrend in the price of a commodity is characterized by a series of higher and higher lows, i.e., attaining levels above previous highs and lows. A market is in a downtrend when the highs and lows get progressively lower when each price decline reaches lower than the immediately previous low price and each increase falls short of the previous high price.

To mark an uptrend in prices, a chartist draws a straight line connecting two or more low points in the price move. As long as prices remain above this trend line, the uptrend is considered to be intact (buying power is stronger than selling power) and one should be long (Figure 10.5).

To identify a downtrend, a line is drawn connecting two or more high points in the price move, as shown in Figure 10.6. So long as prices stay below this downtrend line, the trend remains down; selling pressure is deemed to hold the day, and one should be short.

The end of an uptrend is signaled when a new high "wave" fails to reach or exceed the previous high recorded in the formation of that trend. The end of a downtrend is indicated when a new low wave fails to penetrate a previous low mark. The ending of a trend, however, does not necessarily imply the start of a new trend in the opposite direction. It could mark the beginning of a sideways movement or congestion area.

No market ever starts in one direction and keeps going in that direction without some backing and filling along the way. There are price swings within price swings. There are reactions (short-term price declines) within bull markets, and rallies (short-term price rises) in bear markets. These intermediate moves do not alter the trend of the market but merely interrupt it for a time.

When a trend is broken and prices move sideways for a while, the congestion area so formed can have an effect on price movements at a later time. A congestion

Figure 10.5 September Soybean Oil

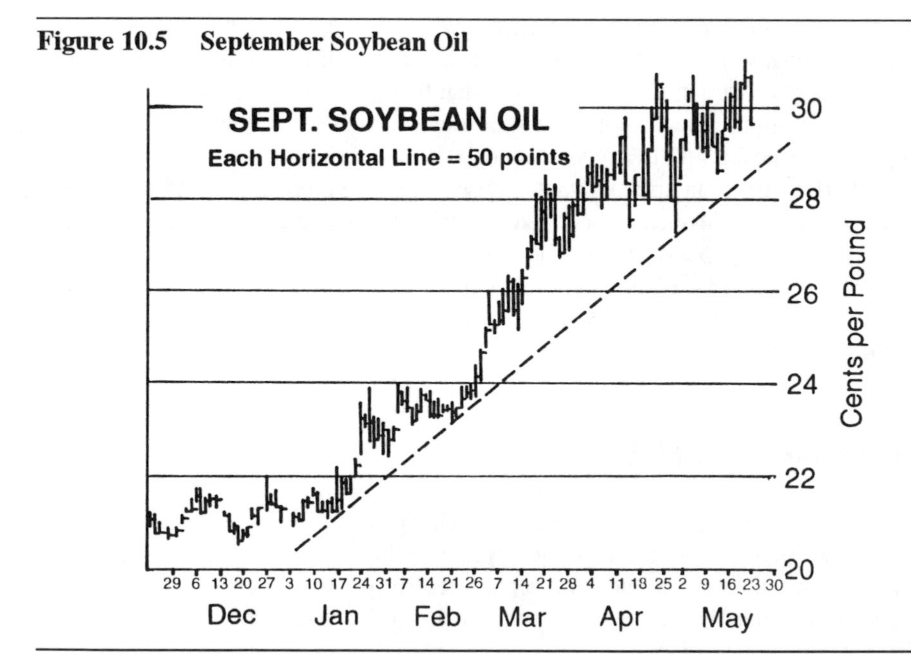

Figure 10.6 September Corn

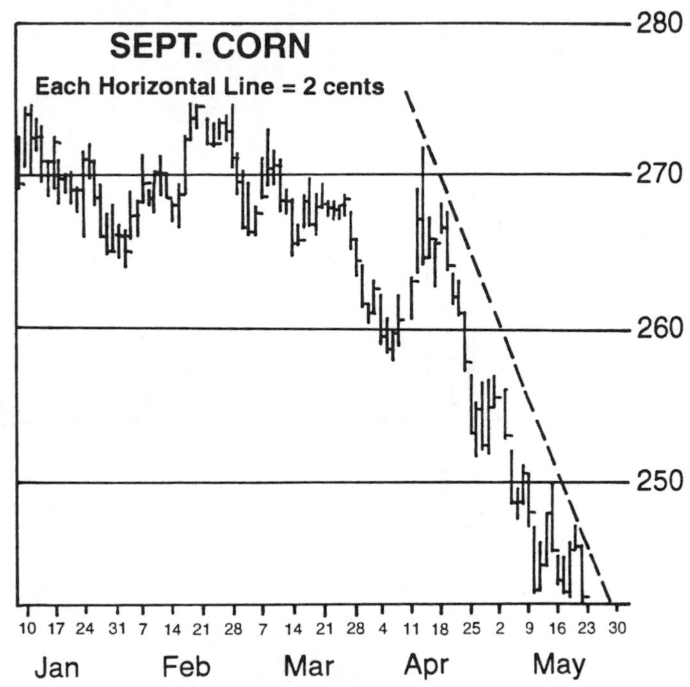

area made during an uptrend can tend to act as a "support" for prices during a later downtrend. A congestion area formed during a downtrend may offer "resistance" to the upward movement of prices when they turn up again. Generally speaking, a support area is a price range where buying pressure increases rather abruptly, and a resistance area is one where selling pressure suddenly appears in force.

CYCLES

Cycles are common in agricultural markets and can be very useful trading tools for projecting potential trend changes. Whole books have been written on this subject. Probably the best is Jake Bernstein's *The Handbook of Commodity Cycles,* published by John Wiley & Sons, 1982.

Figure 10.7 shows the overlay of an approximate half-month cycle with an approximate two-month cycle on corn prices in 1992. Note how well the two cycles worked together in picking short-term trend tops and bottoms with longer-term trend tops and bottoms. Cycle analysis can be a powerful trading tool.

Figure 10.7 Corn Price Cycles

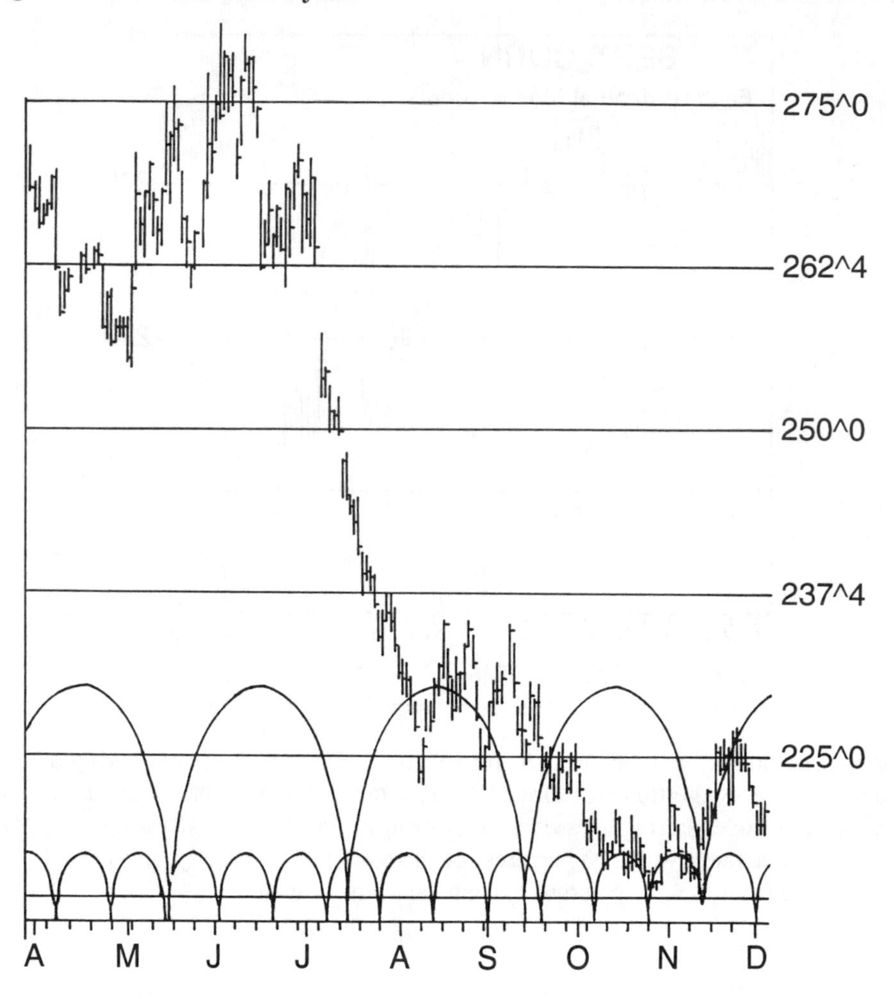

CHART FORMATIONS

As we have stated, one of the major objectives of all technical market analysis is to identify the end of an old trend or the start of a new one. A number of chart formations have come to be accepted by chartists as important indicators of trend changes, as they have in the past marked the top of an uptrend or the bottom in a downtrend.

A price "bottom" is a level where buying power begins to absorb all offerings, the demand for futures contracts begins to exceed the supply, and prices rise. Conversely, a price "top" is an area where selling pressure intensifies, buying power is not sufficient to absorb all offerings, and prices turn downward.

Various chart formations have over time become associated with these important turning points in the market. Perhaps one of the most reliable and easily identifiable is the so-called "head-and-shoulders" formation. When you find this formation it usually means a major market move is beginning.

The head-and-shoulders top formation looks like a "W" with an extended middle leg. As shown on the accompanying chart, it begins with a sharp rally and a following sharp reaction to form the left shoulder. The head is formed by another, more extended rally and decline. Then a third, smaller rally and decline form the right shoulder. The formation is considered to be completed and considerably lower prices in store when prices decline out of the right shoulder and penetrate the "neckline" (see Figure 10.8).

The head-and-shoulders bottom formation is simply the inverse.

Other important chart formations include the ascending triangle, the descending triangle, and "gaps."

A *descending triangle* formation results when the market is unable to make consecutive highs at higher levels. As prices approach previous highs, increased selling pressure appears . . . while at the same time prices encounter strong support at a particular price level each time they descend to that level. Thus, buying power is

Figure 10.8 "Head and Shoulders" Formation

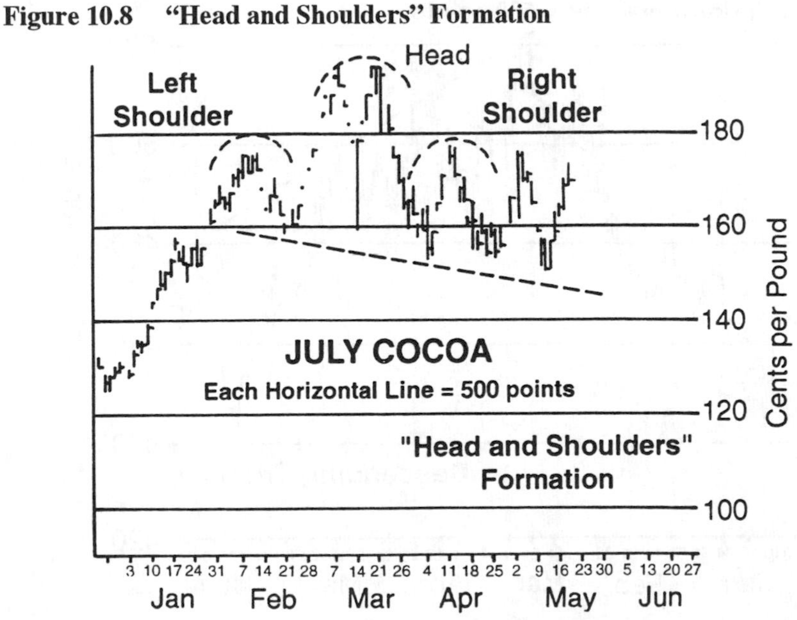

limiting the decline; but because offerings get progressively weaker on each rally, each rally falls short of the one before it.

Descending triangles often develop at the end of extended advances. When prices finally break through the bottom of the triangle, it is frequently an indication that a further decline is imminent (see Figure 10.9).

An *ascending triangle* is indicative of a market bottoming out, and suggests an advance in prices. This formation results when consecutive market lows strike progressively higher, while highs run into repeated resistance at about the same price level. Although selling pressure limits the advance at a certain price level each time, buying power gets stronger and stronger with each reaction . . . and each price dip is therefore shallower than the one before. If prices finally break out on the upside, it is often an indication of higher prices to come (see Figure 10.10).

A *gap* is simply a price area where no trading takes place. In an uptrend, a gap occurs when the day's lowest price is higher than the previous day's highest price. In a downtrend, the case is reversed.

Gaps can be "read" in a variety of ways. A gap out of a top or bottom formation is sometimes called a "breakaway" gap, indicative of a surge in buying or selling power

Figure 10.9 Comex December Silver

Figure 10.10 October Soybean Meal

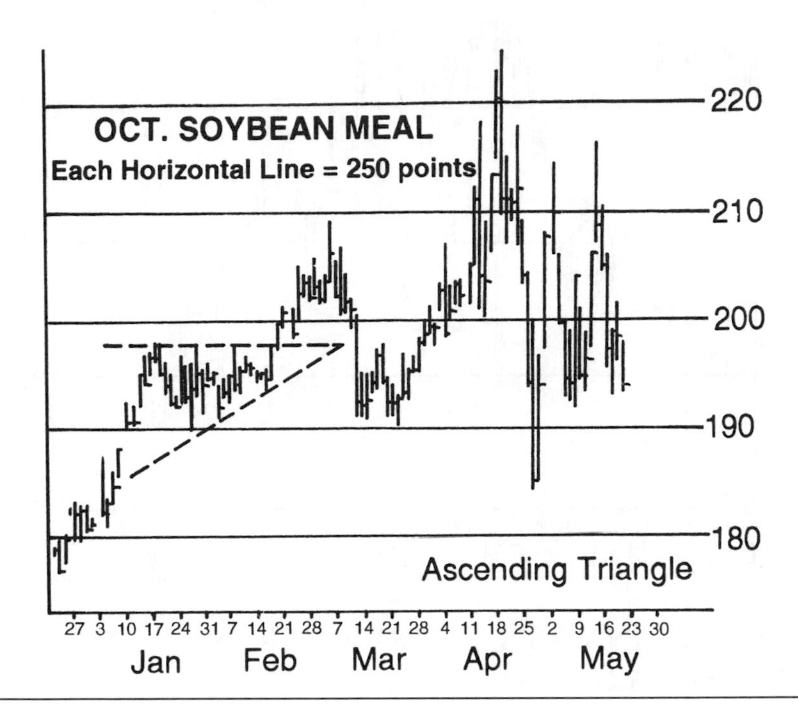

that causes price(s) abruptly to break away from the formation. Gaps formed in steep price moves are often referred to as "runaway" gaps, implying that prices have run off and left all opposing factors far behind. A gap at the end of a long move may be an "exhaustion" gap, the last lunge of an expiring price move (see Figure 10.11).

To a beginning analyst, the subject of charts may seem almost incomprehensible, and you may wonder if the whole thing is nothing more than a figment of a hyperactive imagination. As a matter of fact, a good imagination is an asset in identifying price formations. The patterns are seldom as symmetrical as those chosen for our examples, and it does take some imagination to see them. But with experience, you will find it easier to identify not only the basic formations noted here but also many their variations.

Of course, interpretation of chart formations is only part of the technical analyst's job. You must use your knowledge of past price action, along with considerations of such other important factors as trading volume and open interest, to fully evaluate the relative strength of buying and selling pressure in the market.

Figure 10.11 July Lumber

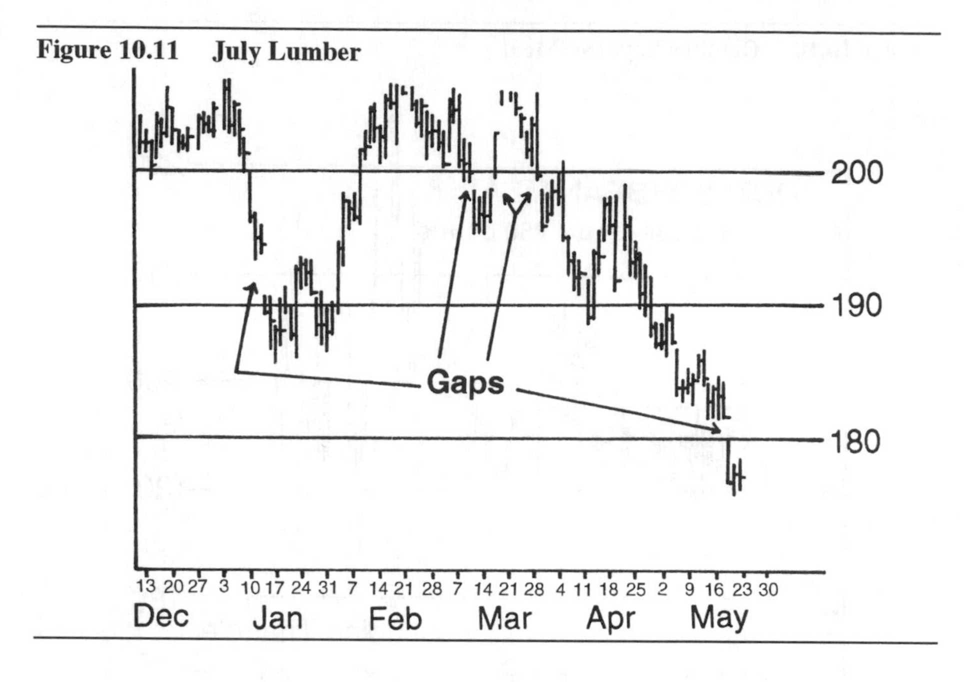

TECHNICAL ANALYSIS, CHART SERVICES, AND SOFTWARE

Until a few years ago when the use of computers became widespread, technical analysis primarily meant hand-drawing charts of prices and analyzing patterns and formations on those charts. In recent years, analysts with backgrounds in physics, statistics, engineering, etc., began applying higher mathematical techniques, statistical analysis, and probability analysis to the price data. Today, a wide variety of indicators have evolved as trading tools to help traders make better buy/sell decisions. These tools can really only be used in conjunction with a reliable data base and a computer to analyze the data and display results. They are far too complex to create through hand calculations.

One's choice of software and data is important, and there is a dizzying array of products from which to choose. Be wary. You can spend thousands of dollars on systems that don't meet your expectations or simply don't work. While this chapter won't review specific software packages (that is done on a regular basis by *Futures* Magazine as well as other publications), we intend here to give only a short checklist of suggested criteria you should keep in mind when looking for a system.

Perhaps the first thing a novice trader should consider is subscribing to a chart service which delivers weekly a book of charts covering the major markets. They usually cost a couple of hundred dollars per year. These chart books usually contain daily price charts, weekly charts, and monthly charts, along with special charts dealing with spread relationships. Usually, they also contain a number of graphs depicting several popular technical analysis tools. During the week, the trader can update the price bar charts, do continual analyses of the unfolding price patterns and make buy/sell decisions. When the new packet arrives the next week, a new set of price formation lines will need to be drawn and the price patterns analyzed anew. Most traders start this way, and a lot of seasoned and very successful traders still do their analyses this way.

Those traders who are more experienced, have the money, are active traders, and are "computer literate" may want to buy a computer and either link it to an outside data base that is updated daily, or even go on-line. Reliable data are necessary for successful trading. Bonneville, Knight-Ridder, CIS, and several other services provide automatic electronic delivery of quotes to your home computer at the end of each day for as little as $50 a month. These data services may be delivered via satellite, FM radio channels, or sometimes even cable TV lines. This sort of service is a huge time-saver and usually well worth it for anyone actively involved in the market. Periodically, of course, one will get some bad data transmissions, so you have to be alert, do some editing, and clean up such dirty data points.

It is a good idea when purchasing software to talk to someone who is a current user of the system and to obtain the software on a trial basis before paying for it.

Once you have reliable data, the next task is selecting trading software. There is lots to choose from, some of it very good, some just very expensive.

- Good trading software should include a library of popular technical trading indicators such as moving averages, relative strength indexes, stochastics, Fibonnaci numbers, etc. See the next chapter for definitions. These technical indicators should be automatically calculated by the trading software.

- Good software allows the user to adjust the design of the indicators in the library. For example, switching from a five-day stochastic to a nine-day stochastic, or a nine-day RSI to a 14-day RSI.

- Trading software can be purchased very inexpensively, but usually such software covers only a few trading indicators and has very limited ability for user interaction to make changes in parameters on indicators. More elaborate and expensive trading software will allow you to develop your own technical indicators and to test them under a variety of scenarios and assumptions. Such software will usually run a thousand dollars or more and require annual payments in addition.

- Good trading software should allow the user to compare simultaneously two or more items in the data base; i.e., allow spread analyses, ratio analyses, options volatilities calculations, etc.

- Good trading software should allow you to divide your screen into several windows in order to review several markets or indicators at the same time.

- Good trading software should allow you to design your own bar charts and point-and-figure charts.

- Lastly, good trading software should allow you to keep track of your trades and monitor the profit and loss in your positions by automatically updating the closing prices on those positions.

It is fair to say that the personal computer has changed our lives and our life-styles. It has also changed the markets. Technology has made the markets more efficient. Information of all types from all over the world gets reflected in the market price faster than ever. At the same time a well-educated, computer-literate generation of traders has emerged and married technology with scientific (and lots of pseudo-scientific) methods of analysis.

Chapter 11

Technical Analysis—The Tools and How They Work*

The last chapter covered the basic chart patterns associated with traditional technical analysis. We now turn our attention to some of the contemporary tools of technical analysts, namely, statistical measures of price activity that have become popular and within reach of virtually everybody due to the popularity and affordability of the personal computer and modem communications technology.

The basic arithmetic tools covered previously are fundamental for doing good price analysis. This chapter covers extensions or refinements of those tools. Most of these refinements involve substantial data calculation effort and, hence, make using a computer imperative. Almost all of these refinements are designed to do one of three things:

---

* For an excellent exposition on this topic see a *Futures* Magazine article by Jon Stein entitled "The Trader's Guide to Technical Indicators," August 1990. This chapter was inspired by Jon's work and reflects some of his thoughts.

1. Identify and confirm trends.
2. Evaluate the gathering strength or impending weakness of a trend.
3. Identify potential timing and levels of turning points in trends.

MORE ON MOVING AVERAGES

Most moving average techniques work best in trending markets. The lagging nature of moving averages makes them useful for at least confirming a change in trend. However, they can yield as many false signals as correct signals, especially if you are using shorter-term moving averages.

Some traders try to filter out the minor aberrations (false buy/sell signals) in a moving average model by establishing a *moving average channel.* They average and graph the closes, the highs, and the lows. This creates a band or channel. Problems can arise when the band becomes so wide that some of the aberrations filtered out are actually substantial moves. At some point, "break-outs" become "turning points" within a band, and a trader who misses it not only can miss the trend, but might enter the trade on the wrong side. Buy/sell signals are usually generated when the price crosses through the entire band. One usually uses this technique when looking for a market about to establish a trend.

Exponentially weighted moving averages give more weight to the most recent prices during a specified period.

Differentials between moving averages can also be used to identify cycles.

MOVING AVERAGE OSCILLATORS

The term *oscillator* usually means simply the difference between two moving averages. For example, when the oscillator crosses the zero line, it simply means two moving averages have crossed. Traders use oscillators as indicators of overbought/oversold conditions and initiate trades when the oscillator reaches a certain extreme positive or extreme negative. Sometimes people combine the oscillator with a moving average of the oscillator! Thus, overbought/oversold signals come when the moving average of the oscillator crosses the oscillator; i.e., long positions are taken on upward crossovers, short positions on downward crossovers.

An increasingly popular oscillator is an exponential moving average of the oscillator. This is often referred to as the MACD or Moving Average Convergence Divergence. The oscillator is based on the exponential moving averages and the moving average of the oscillator is also exponential. Crossover rules are the same as for any of the moving average techniques. Most traders use the MACD for finding divergence and combine this technique with other overbought/oversold indicators.

A SURVEY OF TECHNICAL INDICATORS

As noted previously, many technical indicators are derived from other technical indicators—singles or groups. Almost all of the technical indicators make use of, or incorporate, the basic forecasting tools discussed in Chapter 10, i.e., ratios, index numbers, correlations, moving averages, etc. The purpose of this section is to survey in summary fashion the list of technical indicators most commonly used by traders. This list is not exhaustive, but should motivate the reader to select a few of these indicators for further study.

TECHNICAL INDICATORS	BRIEF DESCRIPTION
1. Accumulation/ Distribution	This is an index designed to identify changes in major trends. Accumulation/distribution studies are designed to search for divergences within the market characteristics that might be indicative of potential trend changes, e.g., a confluence of indicators that suggest smart buyers are gradually running out of steam and are "distributing" their activity to protect their gains and establish short positions, or indications suggesting that smart traders are gradually accumulating a position on the long side of the market in the anticipation that a bull market is about to emerge. The running index is composed by adding or subtracting portions of daily price moves (adding for higher closes, subtracting for lower closes) over some specified period of time.
2. Directional Movement Index (DMI)	DMI is an index designed to measure the strength of a trend by measuring the increase in volatility as reflected in the increases (not the decreases) in the daily trading true range over a 14-day period. The directional movement index is the creation of Welles Wilder, an engineer turned technical analyst. It is actually a combination of three sepa-

rate indicators—an average directional index (ADX), upward movement (+DI), and downward movement (–DI). The +DI measures the strength of upward pressure, the –DI the strength of downward pressure, and the ADX, a ratio of the DMI averaged over 14 days, or the propensity for trending. ADXR is a further refinement of the ADX, resulting from another averaging process. The arithmetic for computing this index is quite cumbersome, though not complex. For those interested, you should check the book by Welles Wilder called *New Concepts in Technical Trading.*

3. Trading Bands

Bands are lines drawn at fixed intervals above and below a moving average. The interval is usually based on a measure of volatility (such as a percentage), or one, or two, or three standard deviations above and below the average. The use of standard deviations rather than a fixed percentage for the interval allows the bands to adjust for volatility as it changes. During volatile periods, the bands move further away from the average. During quiet periods they converge toward the average. The closer the prices move to the upper band, the more overbought the market is. The closer prices move to the lower band, the more oversold the market is.

4. Candlestick Chart

Candlestick charts are a very old tool developed in Japan and very similar to a standard bar chart, with the exception that the distance between the open price on the bar and the closing price on the bar is drawn hollow if the closing price is higher than the previous bar, and drawn solid if the closing price is lower than the previous bar. Interpretations of patterns are similar to traditional U.S. interpretations of charts, though different names are attached to the patterns.

5. Commodity Channel Index

The commodity channel index was originally designed to detect the beginning and ending of cycles and important trends. The index, as it is normally constructed, incorporates a moving average together with a factor reflecting trading ranges. The index is designed to capture about 80 percent of all price fluctuation between an index value of +100 and –100. The general trading rule is that when the index exceeds 100, you establish a long position. When it falls below –100, you go short. Often, this indicator is used by traders as a measure of overbought/oversold. Its reliability is spotty.

6. Moving Average Convergence/ Divergence (MACD)

MACD is the difference between a fast exponential moving average and a slow exponential moving average. During rising markets, the fast moving average will rise more quickly than the slow, resulting in a rising value. During falling markets, the reverse will be true. When the fast line crosses the slow line from below, it is a buy signal. When it crosses it from above, it is a sell signal.

7. Momentum Oscillator

Momentum (also called rate of change indicator) is another overbought/oversold indicator and is often referred to when people are talking about an oscillator. Basically, a momentum indicator tells one whether prices are rising or falling at an increasing or decreasing rate. It is usually calculated by simply adding or subtracting the price changes from one period to the next. So if the closing prices are advancing by increasing amounts, momentum is up; if advancing by decreasing amounts from time period to time period, momentum is down. When there is no change in price, momentum is zero. Crossing the zero line indicates an overbought/oversold condition; hence, one buys when the indicator passes up through the line, and sells when it passes down through it. As with other indicators, the time period chosen for analysis is important. Some experienced traders claim also that one should match momentum cycles to the underlying price cycle of the market.

8. Moving Average Envelope

This refers to price bands placed a certain percentage above and below a simple moving average. As the market approaches the upper band, it is considered overbought. As it approaches the lower band, it is considered oversold.

9. Exponential Moving Average

The exponential moving average is a form of a weighted average in which each older price is given less and less importance and the more recent prices greater importance. Crossovers of the fast or slow exponential moving averages are used to provide buy and sell signals.

10. On Balance Volume (OBV)

On balance volume (OBV) is the creation of Joe Granville, well publicized flamboyant stock market operator. OBV is very similar to the accumulation/distribution technique discussed above, except that it is based on volume (not price), and was designed to try to uncover accumulation and distribution patterns of large stock traders. The OBV attempts to gauge the buying and selling pressure on the market by measuring the volume of trading accompanying any particular price bar. The volume associated with an up price move is considered indicative of buying pressure. Volume associated with a down price movement is representative of selling pressure. Over any given time period, the up volume and the down volume is netted and the resultant differential compared to the price move. If the OBV moves down while price goes up, it signifies buying pressure is weakening. If OBV moves up while the price moves down, it signifies selling pressure is weakening. Some traders find this a very useful tool, but for it to be useful, one must have reliable data on volume. Many futures markets display considerable inconsistency in the reporting of daily volume figures. There are even greater problems if one tries to apply this technique on intra-day trading where volume estimates are very rough approximations.

11. Parabolic System

The parabolic system was designed by Welles Wilder to help traders identify points to exit the market and reverse their positions. It always keeps you in the market. A stop and reverse (SAR) price point is based upon an initial extreme price achieved in some immediate past price movement. That SAR point is gradually increased at an increasing rate as time passes. In a stop and reverse methodology, you liquidate a long position and establish a short position or you liquidate the short position and establish a long position. The system considers time an important factor. So if a position does not remain profitable as time passes, it is reversed. Its success is dependent on the speed with which it adjusts the stop and reverse price.

12. Price Channel

The price channel, like price bands, is often used to detect break-outs of significant support and resistance areas. A penetration of the upper channel line is considered a sign of significant market strength. The penetration of the lower channel line is a sign of significant market weakness. As prices approach the lower line, many traders look for buying opportunities, but immediately stop and reverse their positions if the prices break the line. They do the opposite when prices approach the upper band.

13. Rate of Change

The rate of change indicator reflects the market's price change as a percentage over some short period of time. Many traders buy when the rate of change line crosses the zero line from below and sell when it crosses from above.

14. Relative Strength Index (RSI)

Another overbought/oversold indicator is called the relative strength index (RSI). The RSI attempts to estimate the current strength or weakness in the price movement during a given period. The underlying assumption is that higher closes indicate strong upward price movement, while lower closes indicate weaker prices. The RSI is simply an index of the difference between the sum of all up closes and the sum of all down closes during some short time period, usually nine or 14 trading periods, e.g., minutes, hours, days, weeks, etc. When the index on a 14-day RSI drops below 30 or moves above 70, traders usually consider those to be indications of overbought or oversold extremes. If one were using a nine-day RSI, the extreme levels would be 20 and 80. Although this is a very popular indicator, one needs to be careful in the application of this technique. It is not unusual for RSIs to remain in overbought or oversold territory for days or even weeks before a trend ends.

15. Range Leader

The range leader compares 50 percent of the trading range to the high and the low price of a given time period and weights the result by a volume differential. Range leader bars on a bar chart are used to indicate impending upward moves or downward moves.

16. Key Reversals

A key reversal buy signal is generated when the current period's price low is below the previous period's low and the close is above the previous period's close. The reverse is true of a sell signal. These indicators give large numbers of false signals and are most reliable only when they are accompanied by very large volume.

17. Stochastics

A stochastic is an oscillator which indicates overbought/oversold conditions. It essentially measures the frequency with which price closes tend to accumulate near either end of the price bar on a bar chart; i.e., during periods of price decreases, if the closes tend to accumulate near the low end of the bar, it is considered a bearish signal. The reverse is true for price closes accumulating near the high end of the bar. Traders usually smooth these calculations by means of a moving average technique and then create both fast and slow stochastic moving averages that generate two lines often called the percent K and the percent D lines. Traders use divergences between the lines as indications of overbought and oversold. They also consider the absolute level to be important trading signals. Divergence between the two is considered important when the percent D line makes a series of lower highs while the commodity price makes a series of higher highs. This signals an overbought market. An oversold market occurs when the commodity posts a series of lower lows while the percent D makes a series of higher lows. Generally the buy/sell signals are generated when the percent K crosses the percent D. Most people use this indicator with great caution and then only in conjunction with major trend indicators.

A warning is in order on all of these technical indicators. None of them work well all of the time. All of them work some of the time. All of them are very sensitive to the length of time selected for creating the indicator, i.e., a nine-day indicator will sometimes be more reliable than a 14-day indicator. Generally, all of them have a high incidence of false signals. A significant amount of research on the MACD shows that the indicator isn't very reliable particularly in short swing markets.

The best trading opportunities arise when several of these indicators flash similar trading signals. Generally, the reliability of those signals increases if the systems are based on different parameters, different sets of rules, assumptions, or information. For example, if the MACD, Stochastic, RSI, Momentum, and DMI are all near their extremes flashing buy signals, one should have more faith in the reliability of their signals and, therefore, more confidence in entering into trades.

Application of these analytic tools based on different time windows can be extremely helpful in confirming or strengthening the reliability of signals. For example, if the monthly, weekly, daily, and hourly signals are all flashing the same with a set of these tools, one can have much greater confidence in establishing positions.

In any event, these tools are all designed to provide guidance to traders searching for turning points in a trend. It is virtually impossible for a trader to pick exact turning points. The objective should be to take the middle out of the trend. Prudent use of these technical tools and patience in waiting until a number of them flash the same signals will increase enormously the probability that the trader will make money and capture significant portions of important price trends in most markets.

WARNING

Many technical indicators develop popularity because of the allure associated with their claims to success. However, as noted above, many of them are not successful when used independently of others. One has to remember these are indicators not necessarily reliable signals. Many technical indicators provide a certain scientific panache that some people use to generate sales of systems, excitement about trading, and commissions. To those people whether the tools actually make money for the investors is often secondary. More often, these technical indicators are very reliable as indicators of what has happened, but not very reliable as predictors of what will happen. In many cases, they can be more distractions than aids in dealing with the problems of making money, especially if the tools encourage overtrading. These tools require the user to have considerable emotional aptitude in dealing with the ups and downs of the market.

Volatility

There are really two faces to volatility. Historical volatility allows one to develop probability distributions and provides a statistical estimate of how prices have tended to vary from the norm. Implied volatility, on the other hand, is an up-to-date reading of how current market participants view what is likely to happen. Implied volatilities are calculated from options prices (see Chapters 26 and 27).

If the market has anticipated a piece of news such as a trade surplus figure or a political development, implied volatilities will tend to stay flat or decline, but if the market has not anticipated the event, traders sense of surprise will be reflected in the size of movement; implied volatility will rise accordingly. Implied volatility is most easily calculated from the options markets but needs to be interpreted with some caution. Illiquid markets will send false signals about implied volatility.

Changes in volatility often presage real market trends. For example, when a market is trading into new high territory and well above some of the popular moving averages, price alone might not supply the most useful evidence about where the trend is headed. Knowledge of historical volatility measured in conjunction with price level and implied volatility can, however, be helpful. To illustrate, one would expect that as markets move into higher ground, volatility would also increase if the trend is expected to continue. But if the volatility remains stable while prices climb, that's significant evidence that the "market" believes the increased activity can be absorbed and the trend likely will be short-lived. A market with rapidly rising implied volatility, especially if it is reaching the outer edges of a probability distribution curve, suggests that the market expects an advance to occur that may cause a sustainable market change.

Implied volatility also provides other information. For example, if a market that is trading slightly below the moving averages begins to fall, and if volatility drops sharply during that fall, it suggests that the market believed that whatever triggered that fall already had been discounted. In general, increasing volatility indicates prices will continue to move away from moving averages. Decreasing volatility indicates a move toward their moving averages.

Elliott Wave

Elliott Wave analysis is one of the more popular contemporary methodologies for analyzing market price movements. It was popularized in the 1980s by Robert Prechter, who made consistently correct and very profitable calls on the stock market right up to and including the crash of 1987.

The Elliott Wave Theory (EWT) emanates from research conducted in stocks by Ralph Elliott early in the 1930s. It was popularized in the 1960s in the writings of A.J. Frost and by Frost and Robert Prechter in a book published in 1978.

Essentially, EWT has three important components—chart patterns (called waves), ratios, and time cycles. The theory states that wave patterns come in sequences of 5's and 3's—five waves in the direction of the major trend and three waves in the direction of the correction of the major trend.

Each wave subdivides into similar five-and-three patterns in a continuing series of waves of smaller and smaller degree and, as these subdivisions occur, their count forms a series of numbers called Fibonacci numbers.

These wave formations take on traditional chart patterns familiar to technical analysts and similar to those discussed in the preceding chapters. Thus, by connecting the extreme points of the waves, one can see triangles, pennants, channels, rising and falling wedges, etc. These familiar patterns along with Fibonacci ratios identify areas of support and resistance and price objectives.

Figure 11.1 Elliott Wave Count Illustrated

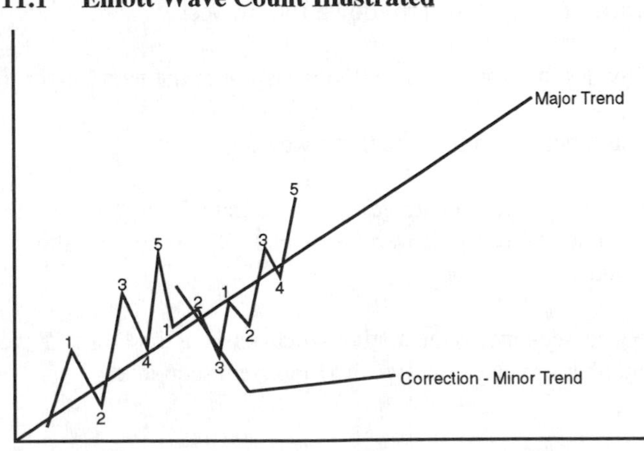

Fibonacci Ratios

A Fibonacci sequence of numbers is 1, 1, 2, 3, 5, 8, 13 . . . N. It is named after a 13th century mathematician named Leonardo Fibonacci, whose statue stands near the Leaning Tower of Pisa in Italy. Fibonacci's sequence represents the reproduction rate of rabbits (a problem he was trying to solve).

All of that has very little to do with commodity trading except that the sequence has some unique properties which seem to reflect price behavior in markets.

First, the sum of any two consecutive numbers equals the next higher number; e.g., 1 + 1 = 2; 2 + 3 = 5, etc.

Second, the ratio of any number to its next higher number, after the first 4 numbers, is approximately .618.

Third, the ratio of any number to its next lower number is 1.618 or the inverse of .618.

Fourth, the ratio of alternate numbers approaches 2.618 or its inverse of .382.

These ratios, when combined with the wave counts, chart patterns, and time cycles yield an elaborate set of "rules" and high probability tendencies that give quite explicit guidance on when to enter a market, whether to be long or short, what price objectives to expect, both in the direction of the trend and the extent of a correction, and in what time frame to expect such movements.

The EWT model is complex and comprehensive. It attempts to pull together into an understandable package the many diverse elements and techniques of traditional technical analysis, mathematical tendencies, and contemporary knowledge. Some analysts think it has a lot of elements in common with other market movement theories like the Dow Theory.

In summary, according to the Elliott Wave Theory:

- A complete bull (bear) market cycle is made up of eight waves, five up (down) waves followed by three down (up) waves.
- A trend divides into five waves in the direction of the next longer trend.
- Corrections always take place in three waves.
- Waves can be expanded into longer waves and subdivided into shorter waves. Sometimes one of the impulse waves extends. The other two should then be equal in time and magnitude.
- The Fibonacci sequence is the mathematical basis of the Elliott Wave Theory and the number of waves follows the Fibonacci sequence.

- Fibonacci ratios and retracements are used to determine price objectives. The most common retracements are 62 percent, 50 percent, and 38 percent.

- Its "rule of alternation" warns not to expect the same thing twice in succession.

The Elliott Wave Theory is comprised of wave forms, ratios, and time, in that order of importance. The theory was originally applied to stock market averages; does not work as well on individual stocks and many individual futures; and works best in those commodity markets with the largest public following, such as gold, bonds, and Eurodollars.

No one theory, however, holds all the answers. Elliott Wave Theory is an excellent model to help get a perspective on a market, but long-term success in trading will be enhanced if you use it in conjunction with other tools. Using it in conjunction with all of the other technical theories in this book will increase its value and improve your chances for success.

MIMICKING THE MIND—NEURAL NETWORKS

One of the most helpful computer tools ever invented was the spreadsheet. In fact, it was the development of Lotus 1-2-3 that really made personal computers popular. Spreadsheets also revolutionized investment analysis because they made number crunching easy.

Neural networks (or computers that "learn") are the next stage in the move toward making computers mimic the human mind ever more perfectly and to making them more agile in deductive reasoning. Wall Street firms have spent tens of millions of dollars to design and adapt neural networks to replace human traders.

Neural networks are systems of computer commands that are designed for processing huge amounts of information and data; seeking answers to basic questions concerning the data; interpreting those answers and remembering them; formulating new questions; interpreting those answers, etc., and then, after thousands of iterations, distilling some meaning out of the data, facts, and information generated in the Q&A process.

Because a computer, unlike a human, does not get bored, tired, forgetful, hungry, sleepy, etc., it can "mine" deeper into the information and data regarding past events and their results and find patterns of price behavior that the human mind will not find or recognize as important.

Real neural networks, as opposed to those that are simply dressed up as such, have an "intuitive" approach to their answers to questions. This intuition is called fuzzy logic. Essentially, the computer makes good guesses of what the correct answer is when the correct answer is not clear-cut. This often leads it to explore relationships that otherwise might not be explored. This fuzzy logic element makes neural networks especially useful for processing imprecise information or information in which relationships are unknown. Figure 11.2 depicts a typical neural network process. The computer would start by searching for answers in the information sets I-V. Those answers would be then further refined by searching through the factors in group A, then group B, then group C, and, finally, a response would be selected. So, for example, you may ask the computer to help you determine whether, during the first quarter of the Clinton presidency, the U.S. dollar will be strong or weak, i.e., should you buy it or sell it? It would then search through the first set of factors, say, current economic status of the U.S., and arrive at a set of responses that need to be further refined by the next set of factors, say, foreign trading partners' economic situations. This, in turn, will generate a set of responses to be further refined or narrowed by the next set of factors, say, the technical market indicators, then to chart pattern recognition, then to Elliott Wave Analysis, and so on, until it finally works its way through each set of questions and information, checking and back-checking its logic, and arrives at an answer, which could be, "I don't know!"

For many years, neural networks have been applied in the military, especially in the Navy in their efforts to explore the oceans and detect submarines. Neural networks are part of the systems for guiding missiles and other high-tech weaponry.

Figure 11.2 Neural Network Illustrated

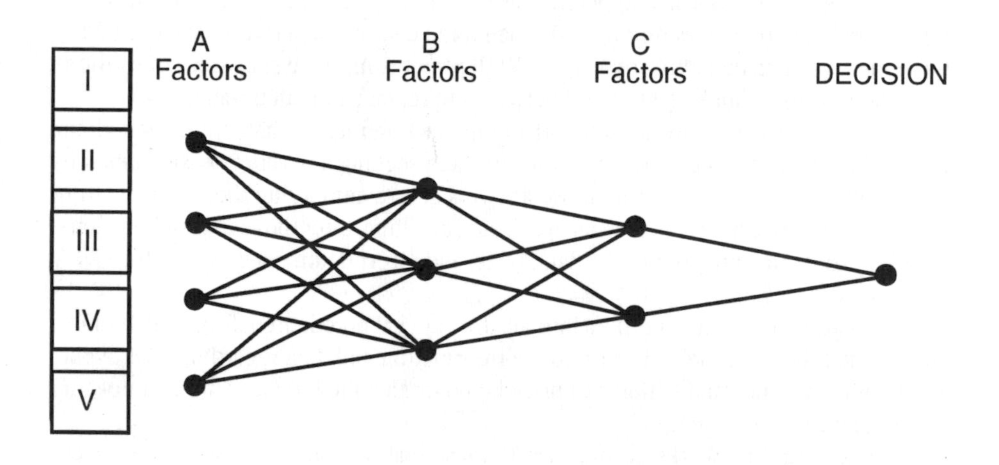

Recently neural networks have been packaged for sale to traders. Prices range from several hundred to several thousand dollars. Many of them work with spreadsheets like Excel. Among those making neural network programs available are:

- Braincel by Promised Land Technologies of New Haven, Connecticut.
- Neuralyst published by Epic Systems Group of Sierra Madre, California.
- Neural Ware produced by Neural Ware, Inc. of Pittsburgh, Pennsylvania.

All of these firms offer beginner's packages and advanced packages. They provide detailed instructions on how to create customized systems to enhance your trading—some of them provide a ready-to-use, fully functioning system, and some also provide textbooks and seminars for further training and education.

Before you buy a neural net system, there are several things you should keep in mind:

1. Many of the computer systems sold as neural network systems are not. They are simply the same old "rule testing technical tools," torturing and curve-fitting data without the "intuition" or fuzzy logic element.
2. The data needs for operating a neural network will be immense.
3. You have to train the neural network to recognize the correct answers to the questions you have asked it to research. You have to train it to fit your problem, feed it lots of facts about the past events and their results, give it time to learn to distinguish correct answers from incorrect answers again and again, and give it time to learn from the mistakes it makes.
4. The old adage about computers—garbage in, garbage out—applies here as well. If you don't train it on good reliable data and with sound logic, it will give you back "bad answers."
5. A good neural network, after it has completed its training, will probably regularly tell you it does not know the answer and cannot give you specific guidance about a particular problem. In other words, it can be just as confused as you in trying to distill meaning out of the gobs of information available in the marketplace. In such cases, it should tell you to stay out of the market.
6. Neural networks can be trained to fit your biases. The frequency, and thus the accuracy, of neural network forecasts can be adjusted to suit your comfort level. If you like trading action, you can set the neural network's parameters and train it to give you short-run recommendations, many of which may be

wrong. If you want only long-term, high-probability trades, you can train it accordingly.

7. Neural networks can make a substantial contribution to your trading analysis by helping you identify the factors that are most important in influencing the neural network's "thoughts" at any point in time. In that sense, even if you don't follow its advice exactly, it may greatly enhance and supplement your "human analytic ability."

Lastly, the major difference between neural networks and regression analysis, a commonly used statistical method for examining data, is that regression analysis averages all past influences and data and assumes they are about the same today. A neural network on the other hand understands that under different market conditions, different factors will have different weights. It keeps learning from its experience and from its mistakes, thus, as the market changes, its thoughts change and it searches through its memory to find similar situations that emerged in previous periods to discern what the most likely result will be. It then makes its "best guess."

ADDITIONAL REFERENCES

Following is a list of some references on technical analysis for additional study:

Bernstein, Jacob. 1982. *The Handbook of Commodity Cycles: a Window on Time*, NewYork: Wiley.

Edwards, Robert D. and John Magee. 1966. *Technical Analysis of Stock Trends*, 5th edition, Boston, MA: John Magee.

Frost, Alfred J. and Robert R. Prechter. 1978. *Elliott Wave Principle, Key to Stock Market Profits*. Chappaqua, NY: New Classics Library.

Kaufman, Perry J. 1978. *Commodity Trading Systems and Methods*. New York: Wiley.

Kaufman, Perry J. 1980. *Technical Analysis in Commodities*. New York: Wiley.

Pring, Martin. 1985. *Technical Analysis Explained*, 2nd edition, New York: McGraw-Hill.

Schwager, Jack D. 1984. *A Complete Guide to the Futures Markets: Fundamental Analysis, Technical Analysis, Trading, Spreads, and Options*. New York: Wiley.

Teweles, Richard J., Charles V. Harlow, and Herbert L. Stone. 1974. *The Commodity Futures Game—Who Wins?—Who Loses?—Why?*, 2nd edition. New York: McGraw-Hill.

Wilder, J. Welles. 1978. *New Concepts in Technical Trading Systems*. Greensboro, NC: Trend Research.

FUTURES PERIODICALS

Futures, the Magazine of Commodities and Options, 219 Parkade, Cedar Falls, IA 50613.

The Journal of Futures Markets, John Wiley & Sons, 605 Third Ave., New York, NY 10158.

Chapter 12

Volume and Open Interest

Two important elements of technical analysis are the daily trading volume and open interest.

A technical analyst would no more think about ignoring the statistics on volume and open interest than he would consider eating his breakfast eggs without salt and pepper. Volume and open interest statistics are, in a sense, seasonings. When mixed with the other information available, they heighten the sense of what's happening in the market.

When we speak of volume of trading, we are referring to the total of purchases or of sales, not of purchases and sales combined. That is, each time a transaction is completed—whether it involves the establishment of a new position or an offset of an old position—the volume is increased by one.

"Open interest" refers to futures contracts that have been entered into and not yet liquidated by an offsetting transaction or fulfilled by delivery. As with volume, the open interest figure is for one side of the market only, not for the long and short sides combined. However, unlike volume, the effect of a transaction upon open interest does depend on whether new positions are being established or old ones closed out.

When trading in a new delivery month begins, there are no contracts in existence, so the open interest is zero. This is in contrast to the stock market, where a new issue may begin trading with many shares available for trading prior to its opening. In the futures market, a new contract comes into existence only when a new buyer and a new seller complete a transaction. If the buyer is offsetting by buying back a previously sold contract or the seller is offsetting by selling a previously purchased contract, there is no change in the open interest.

Thus, the rules for determining changes in open interest are as follows:

1. Open interest increases only when a new contract is made, i.e., a new purchase is matched with a new sale.
2. Open interest decreases when an old purchase is liquidated by a sale and the opposite side of the transaction is an old seller buying back his previous short position.
3. Open interest decreases when a short makes a delivery on a contract and a long accepts delivery.
4. There is no change in open interest when a new purchase is matched with an offsetting transaction (sale of a previous purchase) or if a new sale is matched with an offsetting transaction (purchase of a previous sale).

All open contracts must ultimately be closed out in one of three ways; by an offsetting transaction; by making or taking delivery of the physical commodity; or by cash settlement at maturity.

And, if all this has started the fog horns blowing, maybe an example will help. Let's assume that you now have no position in the market but decide today to buy one futures contract of soybeans. If the seller on the other end of your transaction was closing out a previous long position in soybeans, the open interest would not change. You would have, in effect, "replaced" him in the market. He was long. Now he isn't, and you are.

On the other hand, if your seller was initiating a new short position, there would be a new long (you) and a new short (him) in the market, and open interest in soybeans would go up by one.

Now let's assume it's some time later and you have a nice $800 profit in your soybean position and decide to sell and take those profits. When you do, you close out your long position. If the buyer on the other end was closing out a short position to stop his losses, your transaction would reduce the open interest by one, as the soybean positions outstanding would be reduced by one long (you) and one short (him).

On the other hand, if his was a new long position he would "replace" you and the open interest in soybeans would remain unchanged.

FINDING THE INFORMATION

Statistics on open interest and volume of trading are easily available from the exchanges, from your local broker, and in many major metropolitan newspapers. In addition, the Commodity Futures Trading Commission (CFTC) publishes monthly statistics on open interest and volume of trading for all of the regulated commodities. The CFTC also provides information about the nature and size of traders who hold the open contracts. Any trader who holds a position in any one future of a regulated commodity in excess of a particular amount—an amount set by the CFTC—must report daily his trades and the number of contracts he holds in his position. In making this report, the trader also classifies his positions as either speculative or hedging. These data are then compiled by the CFTC and reported each month. There are some traders who believe this information provides good indications of the relative buying or selling strength of the people in the market.

INTERPRETING CHANGES

In analyzing open interest and volume, you should consider the total figures for all the months of a particular commodity and not the open interest or volume of the individual options (months) separately. A word of caution, however. For best results, the months to be aggregated should all be within the same "crop year." Supply and demand factors in two separate crop years are not always related. You could have an increase in total open interest for the aggregate of the two years, with price trends in each of the years moving in opposite directions. This could cause a misreading of market signals. By separating the figures for the two years, a more reliable technical interpretation can be reached.

Changes in open interest and volume of trading have forecasting value only when considered in connection with price changes. Almost any book on technical analysis provides a summary of rules of thumb for relating change in open interest and volume to price action. Most such rules of thumb and their rationale go something like this:

1. If the open interest is up and prices also are up, this indicates new buying and a technically strong market. The increase in open interest means new contracts are being created, and since prices are advancing, buyers must be more aggressive than sellers.
2. Open interest going up while prices are going down indicates short selling or hedging and a technically weak market. Again, the increase in open interest means new contracts are being established. However, since prices are decreasing, sellers must be more aggressive than buyers.

3. If the open interest is going down and prices are also descending, this implies long liquidation and a technically strong market. Since open interest is declining, offsets and liquidations by old buyers and old sellers are more numerous than new commitments by new buyers and new sellers. Inasmuch as prices are declining, these old buyers (who are now selling) must be more aggressive in their market activities than the old sellers (who are now buyers) in their covering operations.
4. If the open interest is down and prices are up, this indicates short covering and a technically weak market. Again, since open interest is decreasing, old buyers and old sellers must be closing out commitments; but increasing prices suggest that the old sellers who are covering their positions by buying back their contracts are more aggressive than new sellers. Hence, the market is considered to be technically weak.
5. If the volume of trading "follows" the price that is, if volume expands on price strength and declines on price weakness; this indicates the market is in a technically strong position and should go higher. By the same token, if the volume of trading expands on price weakness ,and declines on price strength, the market is considered to be in a technically weak position, ripe to go lower.

Like all rules of thumb, however, there are many pitfalls in their rote application. One of these is the effect of seasonality.

SEASONAL PATTERNS IN VOLUME AND OPEN INTEREST

As in many aspects of commodity futures trading, there are seasonal influences and patterns in open interest and, to a much lesser extent, volume of trading. This is particularly true in commodities that have a seasonal aspect to their production or consumption. For example, the seasonal change in the open interest in grains follows the same general pattern as the seasonal change in the visible supply of grains. Thus, there is a tendency for the open interest in such commodities as wheat, soybeans, corn, and oats to be at its low point for the year just before the harvest of the new crop and for open interest to gradually increase and peak at about the time of the peak in storage stocks. These seasonal changes in the open interest result from changes in hedging requirements. As a commodity is put into storage, the number of hedged transactions made in the market increases. Because hedge positions are frequently longer-term positions, the open interest naturally grows as hedging increases. Then as stocks move out of storage and hedges are lifted, the open interest tends to decline.

The gross seasonal changes in open interest are relatively unimportant in measuring technical market strength or weakness. A more important statistic is the *net* change, after allowing for the seasonal trend. It is difficult to measure precisely these net changes, but if you follow the procedures we outlined in the earlier chapter for developing a seasonal index, you can remove much of the seasonality in the data. After that it's a matter of measuring the deviations from year to year and determining whether the deviation is comparatively large or small.

Generally speaking, volume of trading has little seasonal tendency, and what little there is, is relatively unimportant. There may be a slight tendency for trading volume to increase during heavy crop movements, but such increases are not consistently repeated.

FUNDAMENTALISTS VERSUS TECHNICIANS

As we have pointed out, there are many different systems for forecasting prices. Practically all of these systems, however, are based upon the same general considerations. They assume that two types of forces influence prices: The fundamental conditions of supply and demand and certain technical factors arising out of the characteristics of trading and the psychological reactions of the traders themselves. Many believe, by studying either one or both of these methods, one can predict price changes. The two approaches do not always make good bedfellows, however, and the battle lines have been drawn for years as to which of these analytical methods is more useful. The fundamentalists can point to numerous instances in which they were "right" and the technicians were "wrong." Technicians can show an equal number of cases that went their way.

Most "orthodox" analysts look upon chartists with skepticism, mainly because they think that, in order to predict prices, it is necessary to understand the causes of price change. They argue that anyone such as a chartist who bases his predictions on evaluation of market action (prices, volume, and open interest) rather than upon the causes (supply and demand forces) is suspect. Yet many of these same analysts would grant the validity of the story of the old Indian woman who could predict the appearances of Old Faithful without having the foggiest notion as to what caused the geyser. And most of them would also readily admit that if the ability to predict prices were no better than the ability to evaluate causation, many a successful stock market and commodity trader would be making a living in some other way.

Those who are accustomed to applying rigorous scientific tests to methods of analysis can find plenty of inconsistencies in the various systems of chart reading. Yet these systems seek to provide a means of evaluating short-term market moves which even the most skilled users of fundamental methods do not pretend to be able to predict.

In view of this fact, the least the fundamentalist can do, in all fairness, is to give chart reading a sympathetically critical hearing.

Purist chart readers, on the other hand, might do well to pay more attention to the criticism offered by fundamental analysts. Chartists' explanations of market action often are, well, over-imaginative. Some so studiously ignore fundamental forces that even in the face of violent price-shattering events they may be found calmly making their price predictions for weeks ahead, to within a fraction of a cent!

In point of fact, most successful traders combine fundamental and technical analyses. Many of the arguments propounding the superiority of fundamental analysis to technical analysis, or vice versa, are therefore really moot. The two methods of analysis are complementary.

RANDOM WALKS VERSUS TRENDS

Recently, new fuel has been added to the controversy, namely, the random walk theory. Adam Smith, in his best-selling book, *The Money Game*, included a chapter entitled, "What the hell is a random walk?" He answered the question when he wrote that "prices have no memory, and yesterday has nothing to do with tomorrow."

Put another way, the random walk theory states that today's price change is totally unrelated to tomorrow's price change and that one cannot predict future prices solely on the basis of past prices.

If Adam Smith's economic model is a correct description of reality, there are several obvious implications. It can be shown, for instance, that such price series cannot contain any cyclical or seasonal variation. This implies that so-called technical methods of investment analysis may be far less useful in predicting futures price changes than is commonly believed.

Economists have probably spent more time seeking to determine the validity of the random walk theory than they have on any other single pricing model. Research on the random walk model goes back to the early 1900s. Holbrook Working, Professor Emeritus of Stanford and considered by many to be one of the best of all economists working in the area of futures trading, was the first to do a definitive study of the random walk model as it is related to grain futures prices. He concluded that the random walk model did appropriately describe commodity price behavior for the wheat market. His work led to subsequent attempts to apply the model to the stock market, and the vast majority of the work on the stock market has reached the conclusion that the random walk model is a very good approximation of stock market price action.

Most studies using commodity prices, however, have rejected the model, although not always for the same reasons. Dr. Working himself, for example, reported a tendency for corn prices to deviate from random walk. Dr. Hendrik Houthakker, formerly of the Council of Economic Advisors and currently at Harvard University, and Dr. Seymour Smidt of Cornell University have conducted studies and concluded that on the basis of their information, the random walk model is an incorrect approximation of commodity futures prices. Labys and Granger, in their book, *Speculation, Hedging and Commodity Price Forecasts,* conclude that most price series of commodity futures contracts approximate a random walk, although on some occasions seasonal patterns are found, particularly in daily price-changing series.

Economists and commodity futures traders have argued that purely speculative markets would have to approximate the random walk model, because if they produced price series with predictable patterns, these patterns would soon be "traded" out of existence. The obvious question, then, is: Why has research shown that some commodity futures series do contain predictable components?

There seem to be several possible reasons:

1. Commodity futures markets are not purely speculative markets, since in them goods are actually sold by producers and bought by consumers.
2. The production of many commodities is highly seasonal in nature. Demand is also seasonal, and since the cost of trading is so small, you would not expect all of the seasonal pattern to be "traded out" but only enough for it to be barely profitable to use this pattern in determining a buying or selling policy.
3. It might also be argued that some commodity markets are not sufficiently developed to eliminate completely every predictable component. Dr. Houthakker comments that commodity price developments are watched by relatively few traders, most of whom are quite set in their ways. Even in the most active futures markets, the volume of serious research by participants seems to be quite small. It is therefore possible that systematic patterns will remain largely unknown for a very long time.

In summary, the random walk model is probably not descriptive of most commodity markets, although it is probably descriptive of some markets for selected periods of time. In any event, the random walk theory does not say that price changes are unpredictable if one uses all available information. It only postulates that they are unpredictable if based solely on considerations of previous price changes.

Do all futures prices trend? Yes, to some degree, but some of them are much closer to random walks than others. Research results suggest that most futures and securities price series are a mixture of trends and random walks. The trader's challenge lies in determining which is which.

One unique filtering technique, developed by Mike Poulos of Traders Insight, Inc., for selecting markets that have tendencies to trend is called the Random Walk Index, which allows one to measure and rank the various futures price series by their tendency to trend (see Table 12.1). This tool only ranks the futures with respect to tendency to trend—thus helping a trader identify those futures to which trend-following trading techniques may be applicable—and gives them some idea about the expected length of trends. It will not tell one when to buy or when to sell. Mr. Poulos provides a very simple step-by-step procedure for its application.[1]

Ranking futures contracts in this way and keeping this ranking up-to-date can help a trader determine when he should be applying trend-following methods, when he should be using some other technique, or when he should be standing aside.

Table 12.1 30 Futures Markets Ranked by Tendency to Trend

Channel Length (DAYS)	Square root of Length	Channel Height Ratio to 1 Day									
		Euro$	Yen	Pound	OJ	TBill	$Indx	CrOil	UGas	Corn	Can$
1	1	1.00	1.00	1.00	1.00	1.00	1.00	1.00	1.00	1.00	1.00
4	2	2.27	2.28	2.27	2.24	2.26	2.23	2.24	2.23	2.28	2.22
9	3	3.61	3.61	3.58	3.53	3.57	3.47	3.46	3.46	3.55	3.46
16	4	5.00	4.97	4.95	4.88	4.90	4.73	4.71	4.71	4.81	4.74
25	5	6.46	6.41	6.42	6.30	6.22	6.06	6.05	6.03	6.08	6.02
36	6	8.03	7.96	7.92	7.78	7.59	7.41	7.41	7.37	7.32	7.30
		H.Oil	DM	S.Meal	SFr	Bean	S.Oil	Coffee	Coppr	Belly	Cocoa
1	1	1.00	1.00	1.00	1.00	1.00	1.00	1.00	1.00	1.00	1.00
4	2	2.22	2.23	2.24	2.21	2.20	2.18	2.17	2.18	2.16	2.18
9	3	3.45	3.45	3.48	3.41	3.40	3.39	3.38	3.38	3.34	3.35
16	4	4.66	4.67	4.71	4.61	4.64	4.64	4.58	4.59	4.56	4.52
25	5	5.96	5.95	5.96	5.86	5.87	5.88	5.80	5.80	5.75	5.65
36	6	7.27	7.25	7.21	7.16	7.11	7.09	7.07	7.04	6.92	6.84
		TBond	LHog	Gold	Cottn	Silvr	Wheat	LCat	SP500	Sugar	NYSE
1	1	1.00	1.00	1.00	1.00	1.00	1.00	1.00	1.00	1.00	1.00
4	2	2.14	2.13	2.18	2.17	2.15	2.16	2.14	2.13	2.12	2.14
9	3	3.27	3.28	3.33	3.29	3.29	3.29	3.29	3.23	3.20	3.24
16	4	4.42	4.46	4.46	4.41	4.41	4.42	4.41	4.31	4.30	4.32
25	5	5.59	5.65	5.60	5.55	5.53	5.54	5.49	5.41	5.40	5.42

January 87 - June 92 Spliced Nearby Futures

Source: "Futures Ranked According to Trend Tendency" by Mike Poulos, *Knight-Ridder Financial Products & News,* Fall 1992.

1. See "Futures Ranked According to Trend Tendency" by Mike Poulos, *Knight-Ridder Financial Products & News,* Fall 1992.

Chapter 13

Commodity Hedging—A Primer

Malcolm C. Forbes, founder of *Forbes* magazine, once drew up 10 commandments "for those who earnestly seek to fight successfully the battle of life." His fifth commandment was "Take out life insurance."

If we were to write 10 commandments for those who "earnestly seek to fight successfully the battle of business," our fifth commandment might be "Take out price insurance—hedge."

This chapter will introduce and define the concept of hedging and focus on commodity hedging. The beginning of Chapter 23 provides further specific guidance on the practical decision-making steps of implementing a hedge, whether the hedge be for commodities, financial instruments, or currency.

Most business professionals would not think of operating without insurance against fire, theft, explosion, and other natural disasters. But physical loss or damage to goods are not the only risks they face. The risk of loss due to price change looms equally large.

It is a simple matter, of course, to get policies for fire or other physical risks. Yet, no matter how many insurance companies you go to, you won't find one that will write a policy to protect against losses due to price changes. The reason, obviously, is that fires are usually independent events. When fire burns down an individual's building, it does not destroy the buildings of all that individual's competitors. This means that an insurance company can calculate the probabilities of a claim on an individual basis.

Price changes, however, are not independent in their impact. They affect all competitors at the same time and generally in the same way. That is why you cannot buy price insurance. Still, a form of "insurance" is available through a technique called hedging in the commodity futures markets.

There are many different definitions of hedging, many different circumstances under which hedging can be accomplished, and many different types of hedges. The simple "short form" definition of hedging I prefer is: Transactions or positions in any futures contract that (a) represent a temporary substitute for a transaction or position to be made or taken at a later time in a physical marketing channel; (b) are economically appropriate to the reduction of risk in the conduct and management of a commercial enterprise, and (c) arise from potential changes in the price of assets, liabilities, and services (existing or anticipated) associated with the operation of a business enterprise.

This definition fits all commodities traded on futures contracts, including currencies and interest rate futures. It makes it clear that hedging is associated with risk reduction in the management of a business and that, in order for such risk reduction to occur, the prices in the futures market must be substantially related to the value of the assets, liabilities and services being hedged.

For example, a firm that knows it will need raw materials six months from now hedges (to reduce the risk that price will go up over the next six months) by entering the futures market and buying a contract of those raw materials now, thus establishing its price. Later, when the time approaches that it actually needs the commodity, the firm purchases the actual commodity from its normal suppliers and cancels its obligation in the futures market by selling the futures contract. The futures contract thus acts as the temporary substitute for the later transaction.

Then, a firm carrying inventory that it knows it will need to sell in the coming months hedges by entering the futures market and "selling" that inventory now, establishing its price. Later, when the time approaches that it actually needs the commodity, the firm purchases the actual commodity from its normal suppliers and cancels its obligation in the futures market by selling the futures contract. Again, futures contract thus acts as the temporary substitute for the later transaction.

On the other hand, a firm carrying inventory that it knows it will be selling in the coming months hedges by entering the futures market and "selling" that inventory now, establishing its price. Later, the firm will really sell its inventory through its normal channels and cancel its obligation in the futures market by buying back the futures contract. Once again, the futures acted as a temporary substitute.

So long as the actual material and the commodity futures contract are identical or closely related, hedging can be a very effective tool for reducing price risks. If they are not closely related, the "hedge" will not reduce risk and may increase it. When one hedges, he trades the risk of change in price level for the lesser risk of change in price relationship between two related prices: the cash market price and the futures market price.

The purchase or sale of the futures contract offsets the opposite position in the cash market. Ideally, the loss in one market will be offset by a gain in the other, and the threat of loss through price change will be considerably reduced.

The purpose of hedging, then, is to seek protection against major price changes by neutralizing the impact of price fluctuations.

Let's take a specific example and follow it through. Let's assume you are a small meat packer, and you know you are going to need about 400 head of fat cattle next December to slaughter and pack. Let's further assume, for the sake of discussion, that December cattle on the Chicago Mercantile Exchange are quoted today at $43 per hundred pounds (or 43 cents per pound). At this price, you know you can conduct a profitable beef packing business but you can't be sure what actual, live, on-the-hoof cattle will be selling for come next December.

So you decide to hedge. You do so by buying 10 futures contracts of December cattle (400,000 lbs. or about 400 head). And let's say you did pay 43 cents per pound for them.

Disregarding a few other factors, which we will delve into later, let's assume that by the time December rolls around and you are ready to buy the actual cattle, the cash price for fat steers has risen to 47 cents per pound. Ordinarily, your profit margin on your beef business would be so slim with cattle at this price that you might even consider cutting back on your beef packing. But your hedge has done its job and you can, in effect, buy cattle now for 43 cents pound not 47 cents.

How? Because the increase in the cash price will have been reflected in the December future price, particularly as the delivery month approaches. The extra four cents per pound you have to pay for live cattle your "loss," so to speak, while you waited until December to actually buy will be approximately offset by your four-cent profit in the futures market. So, you can buy your cattle through your normal supply channels for 47 cents per pound, and offset your futures position by selling 10 December cattle contracts for about a four-cent-per-pound profit.

As we said before, this is somewhat oversimplified, but it demonstrates the basic concept of the "buying" hedge.

A "selling" hedge is conceptually the same but would be used, for example, by a silver processor who holds a large inventory of the metal and wishes to reduce the risk of its value declining over time as a result of a drop in cash silver prices. In this case, any loss in his inventory worth would be approximately offset by the profits on his short sale of silver futures.

Whatever the reason, hedging provides protection against major price swings when the price of the product traded in the cash market (the market of immediate payment and delivery, e.g., wholesale market) is closely related to the price of the product described and priced in the futures market.

Business professionals hedge because they want to establish a price that they can be certain to realize within a small range of error. When they hedge, they give up the opportunity for obtaining a better price of course; but at the same time they protect themselves against obtaining a dramatically worse price.

WHO HEDGES AND WHY?

A review of the companies that do, can, or should use the futures market as a tool in corporate strategy reads like a veritable "Who's Who" of U.S. industry. Among readily recognizable names are Swift & Co., Armour, Oscar Mayer, Kroger, A&P, General Foods, General Mills, Kellogg, Kraft, Coca Cola, Nestlè, Hershey Foods, National Biscuit, Weyerhauser, Georgia Pacific, and Boise Cascade. The list goes on and on. Reviews of various published reports (government and private) reveal that thousands of corporations carry "large trader" hedge positions in various futures contracts. Although these figures probably involve some double counting, the significant point is that a large number of corporations do use the futures market for hedging.

Firms use the futures market as a business management tool in a diverse number of ways, depending on the special circumstances of their line of business. Dr. Holbrook Working, the noted agricultural economist, after careful and extensive observation of the business use of the futures market by handlers of commodities, defined and identified a number of types of hedges. Briefly, as identified by Dr. Working, the uses of hedging are as follows.

The Carrying Charge Hedge. This is undertaken for purposes of obtaining at least partial payment for the cost of storing products, as in the case of a grain elevator operator who buys corn in November with the intent of storing it until the following summer. He hedges by attempting to sell the July futures at a price difference sufficient to cover the cost of the product plus all storage costs from November to July.

The Operational Hedge. This involves the placing and lifting of hedges over short time periods as temporary substitutes for merchandising transactions. It is widely used in the milling industry. There is no intent of earning storage charges in the use of this hedge.

Anticipatory Hedge or Forward Pricing Hedge. This involves the purchase or sale of futures in anticipation of a formal commitment to be made later, as in the foregoing example of the meat packer. The operator carries an open position in the futures market for a time without an offsetting cash commitment.

The Selective Hedge. This comprises hedging on the basis of price expectations. The motivation is not so much to avoid risk, as such, but to preclude major losses. Thus, a firm would hedge incompletely; they would not carry short hedges at all when a price increase is expected.

The Risk-Avoidance or "Insurance" Hedge. This is the kind of hedge the silver processor used in the example above to protect his inventory. It involves the carrying of equal and opposite positions in the same commodity in a futures market and the cash market. It is the typical textbook example.

SEVERAL BENEFITS

Dr. Working's description of the use of futures markets as a management tool makes clear that, properly employed, hedging can be one of the most important elements employed by a manager in his overall mix of strategies for achieving company goals.

There are at least six important benefits to properly used hedges:

- First, hedging provides protection from adverse price fluctuations, thus permitting a business manager to escape in large part—rather than having to overcome—the uncertain impact of price changes on his operations. By reducing exposure to price change uncertainty, hedging can help protect profit margins and stabilize income.

- Second, and perhaps equally as important, is the flexibility hedging provides a firm in its corporate strategy of buying, selling, and pricing. Most particularly, it provides flexibility and control in the timing of purchases and sales. Being able to buy earlier or sell later than your competitors or even vice versa may be the key ingredient in obtaining better prices.

- Third, where the product is stored or inventoried, hedging can free working capital that would otherwise be tied up in inventory. Buying a contract for the future delivery of a product requires only a fraction of the value of the product paid out in margins. This allows a businessman to control the same amount of resources with much less capital. This, in turn, has some added benefits in the form of reduced fixed capital investment and interest charges, since the businessman may be able to reduce the size of his storage facilities.

- Fourth, for products that are inventoried or stored, hedging can substantially reduce the costs of storage, since futures prices for different months will tend to reflect such costs. "Carrying charge" hedges are designed for just such purposes. See Chapter 16, "Hedging in Action," for an example.

- Fifth, fixing of costs and prices in advance facilitates business planning.
- Sixth, the benefits that can be reaped from an effective hedging program should increase the borrowing capacity and creditworthiness of a business. A banker will be more willing to offer his best terms against an inventory intelligently and effectively hedged than he will with one not hedged.

All of this means that to the extent hedging reduces the cost of marketing, society and the national economy benefit.

COMMODITY CHARACTERISTICS AND HEDGING

In considering the applicability of the different types of hedges to a particular commodity and in trying to understand the price relationships between cash and futures markets (the essence of hedging), you should study the production and marketing characteristics of the commodity involved. Some commodities are perishable, some storable, some semi-storable, some continuously produced, and some seasonally produced.

A little reflection on the types of hedges and the commodity characteristics mentioned above should make it obvious that only certain types of hedges are applicable to particular commodities. For example, a carrying charge hedge, the traditional hedge used by grain elevators for hedging the seasonally produced and storable grains, is not applicable to non-storable commodities like cattle or hogs. The forward pricing hedge is most applicable here.

It follows that the key to hedging in any of the categories mentioned above is the playing off of price relationships in two different markets so that losses from your position in one market (cash or futures) are offset by gains from your position in the other market (cash or futures). The essence of these two price relationships is called the basis.

THE CFTC AND HEDGING

The Commodity Exchange Act authorizes the Commodity Futures Trading Commission to establish limits on the number of transactions and the size of positions that any speculator can maintain or control in any futures. The Act requires that hedgers be exempt from such regulations. Because of this exemption, the CFTC must define who is a hedger and institute a procedure for granting the appropriate exemption from trading and position limits.

The CFTC has established such speculative limits for many commodities (e.g., cotton, potatoes, eggs, soybeans, corn, wheat, oats, barley, and flaxseed) and for purposes of granting exemptions has defined hedging for those commodities. Generally, the level at which limits are set is sufficiently high so that only very large traders are constrained by them.

The definition established by the CFTC for hedging is conceptually similar (but more complete) to the definition given earlier in this chapter. Specific transactions for which exemptions from the limits are automatically granted by the CFTC generally fall in the following categories:

a. Sales of any futures which offset the ownership or fixed price purchase of the same commodity.

b. Purchases of any futures which offset the fixed price sale of the same commodity or its equivalent byproducts.

c. Certain types of cross-hedges and anticipatory hedges. A cross-hedge is one where the commodity being hedged is not the same as the commodity represented in the futures contract, e.g., sweet corn being hedged in the Chicago corn contract. An anticipatory hedge is a purchase or sale of a futures contract to protect the price of a cash commodity you do not yet own or have not yet sold but anticipate that you will own or have available for sale, e.g., a farmer who has wheat planted but not yet harvested or a processor who will need corn for his milling plant. The CFTC has special filing requirements and may impose special restrictions on such positions.

The CFTC also recognizes a wide variety of other transactions as hedges. For those transactions to qualify for exemption from the speculative limits, however, the trader must obtain permission in advance from the CFTC.

Generally speaking, the procedure for obtaining the exemption is quite simple. Contact the CFTC office nearest you, and the staff will provide you with all the information for filing.

HEDGING IS NOT AN AUTOMATIC REFLEX

More and more businessmen are coming to recognize that decisions on hedging are not and should not be made in isolation from their tax strategies, their accounting methods, and their financing strategies.

A hedge transaction that, viewed alone, seems like a good idea may indeed be unnecessary or even unwise when its full implications are considered in light of its effect on taxes or in light of the hedger's ability to bear the risk without hedging.

The steps in making the decision of whether to hedge are quite straightforward and apply equally well to farming, merchandising, banking, etc. A manager must address the following questions:

a. How much risk exposure do I have, i.e., how much money could I lose if prices go against me?

b. What is the probability that I will suffer a loss, i.e., is there a 30 percent? 40 percent? 50 percent? chance that the price will move adversely by 10 percent? by 20 percent? by 40 percent?

c. What will it cost me to hedge, i.e., interest on margin, commissions, basis variation, spread between the bid and the ask price?

d. Can I afford not to hedge? Should I carry this risk myself?

In answering these questions, the manager has to have a good understanding of his operating costs, his market prospects, his tax strategy, and the overall nature or his risks. It is very possible that in the total operation of a firm one risk will be offset by another, thus obviating the need to hedge either of them individually. (For example, under LIFO accounting methods for valuing inventories, one may find different net exposure than under FIFO.) Sometimes a careful review of market prospects and calculation of the potential adverse price move indicates that the risk of loss is quite small compared to the cost of hedging. If the firm is well-capitalized and can stand that risk quite easily, it may decide not to hedge. On the other hand, even if the risk is small and the firm poorly capitalized, then it would be wise to hedge.

Further, timing of the hedge position can be important. As pointed out earlier, technical market analysis can be a useful means of identifying the proper time to hedge. Consequently, it behooves hedgers to have good charts of prices. It is very possible that, given the outlook for prices and the chart signals, a hedger could afford to carry a certain risk for a short period of time until the market has moved to a more appropriate level for hedging.

Tax rules with respect to hedgers are somewhat different than they are for speculators. The Supreme Court, in the Corn Products Refining Co. case, ruled that hedging transactions which are an integral part of manufacturing or are done for the purpose of price protection, must be treated as ordinary income or loss. Therefore, business firms that keep their records on an accrual basis and value their inventories at market at year-end must take into account gains or losses on the open futures contracts hedged against the cash commodity or against forward sales or purchases. This interpretation has been called into question, however, by more recent court decisions, especially the Arkansas Best case. Check with your tax advisors.

If the hedger values inventories at cost or the lower of costs or market unrealized gains, losses usually are not taken into account until the futures market transactions and their corresponding cash trades are closed. Therefore, taxpayers who value their inventories at the lower of costs or market have an opportunity to defer income tax liability from one period to the next by closing out all loss futures positions and simultaneously placing their hedges into another delivery month.

All of this is quite complicated and very dependent on the overall position and business strategy of the business firm. Accounting rules have a particular importance here. That's why it's so important that the manager of a firm involved in hedging integrate the hedging decisions into the overall strategy of the firm.

The important point here is that hedging should not always be an automatic reflex. The decision to hedge should be considered carefully in light of its costs and its benefits. For a further explanation of this concept and an example of this decision-making process at work, see the beginning of Chapter 23.

Chapter 14

Hedging—The Basis

Here's a practical example from a few years ago that shows you the significance of basis in hedging.

The telephone rang and Bart Jones answered. It was Bob Thompson, his commodity broker, calling to talk to him about hedging the cattle he had on feed.

"Your cattle should be ready for market in June," Bob said, "and right now June futures are at $61.50. I think you ought to sell them now and lock in that price."

Jones thought for a minute. The 80 head he had on feed would be about the equivalent of two futures contracts. June cattle futures prices had been rising steadily, but recently had leveled off in the $61 to $62 range. He doubted they would be much higher by June, and they could be lower. At $61.50 he figures he'd have about a $4 per hundredweight profit margin.

"Okay" he said, "sell two June contracts at $61.50." Ten minutes later Bob called back to tell him the two contracts were sold at $61.50 and instructed Jones to send him $1,500 in margin money. Jones did so and then relaxed, figuring he had sold his cattle at $61.50 and secured his $4 per hundredweight profit.

When June rolled around, Bob called again to suggest that Jones lift his hedge by buying back the futures and delivering his cattle at his normal market—a meat packing plant located about 15 miles away. Since Jones knew that delivery on the futures contract was not the normal route followed in hedging, he did as Bob suggested. He lifted the hedge at $62.50, futures prices having gone up slightly, and he sold his steers, graded USDA Choice, to the nearest packer for a price of $61.

But when Jones calculated his net, he found that he had lost $1 per hundredweight on the futures transaction, not counting his commissions and interest he could have earned on the margin deposit and, he had sold his cattle for $1.05 per hundredweight less than the futures had been on that day. His net profit was only $2.50 per hundredweight. He was puzzled by it all; he wasn't sure whether he had been sold a bill of goods by his broker about "locking" $61.50 or whether the local packer had cheated him by giving him so much less than the futures price.

Jones had make his mistake by assuming that the futures price quoted to him equated with prices at his local market. He forgot about the most important element in hedging: Calculating the basis or adjusting the futures price to represent his local area.

THE IMPORTANT DIFFERENCE

A futures contract represents a specific time, quality, quantity, and location of a commodity. When Jones sold the futures, he was entering into a contract for the delivery of 40,000 pounds of Choice grade fat animals delivered in Omaha, Nebraska, or Sioux City, Iowa (or at certain other delivery points at a premium or discount). Hence, in judging whether the futures price at $61.50 was the "right" price for him at that time, Jones should have first determined how the futures price related to the price where he usually markets his cattle.

Had Jones known that the prices for his local area were usually $1.50 under the futures, he would have known he was not locking in a net price at $61.50 on his hedge and that the $61 price paid by his local packer when deliverable futures were selling at $62.50 was "about right."

The essence of profit or loss in hedging is the basis. This is true for any hedge in any commodity. The basis is the difference between two prices representing different locations, different qualities, different markets, or different times. Hence, if one is hedging a product of different quality in the cash market than is reflected in the futures contract, he must account for that difference in the basis calculations. We will use the term "basis" in this discussion to mean the aggregate of all these, or simply the difference between a trader's local cash price and the futures price at any given time.

Before beginning a hedging operation, close attention should be paid to historic price relationships for the time period covering the proposed hedge.

With futures contracts such as those for live cattle, feeder cattle, and live hogs—which are continuously produced, non-storable commodities—the relationship of the cash price to the futures price has relatively little meaning except during the contract month. Hence, it is sometimes difficult to get a good hedge for commodities such as cattle that are ready for market in a non-delivery month. Accurate estimation of what the basis will be for a particular delivery month is, therefore, most important in effective hedging of these commodities. If the producer accurately forecasts the difference between his price and the futures price at the time of the sale of his product, he will have a virtually perfect price-protecting hedge.

For a semi-storable or storable commodity, such as corn, the basis primarily reflects two main factors: the cost of storage between two time periods and location differences.

Because there are costs for storing actual corn and there are virtually no similar costs for holding futures contracts, cash prices usually gain in relation to futures prices during the storage period. The price of cash corn, therefore, should usually be below the price of futures by the amount of storage cost from any given point in time to the date of maturity of the futures. March futures, for example, will usually be below the May futures by the cost of storage between March and May.

Futures markets are not always "normal." When immediate supplies are scarce, futures markets often become "inverted" that is, nearby contracts are at higher prices than the more distant contracts.

The pork belly market of a few years ago illustrates this point. The February pork belly contract was selling at as much as a 600-point premium to August bellies. March and May were at similarly extreme, but slightly lower, levels. This premium reflected short near-term supplies and high cash prices, as well as traders' expectations that the "hog cycle" was beginning to turn upward and that supplies could be considerably more plentiful by late summer.

Then, as succeeding pig crop reports released during the winter months indicated that, because of a variety of factors, farmers' farrowing intentions would apparently not be met as soon as had been expected, the premium gradually shrunk. By May, the premium over August was only 200 points, still an inverted market but much less so than before.

Fully storable commodities such as wheat, for example are also subject to these influences. In fact, futures for all commodities are affected to some degree by such factors as temporary weather conditions, import/export agreements, near-term shortage or oversupply, and other factors. These should be made a part of any evaluation of your basis in a particular commodity futures contract.

In actual practice, the basis for the par delivery area represented in the futures contract tends to narrow toward zero as the delivery time for the futures contract approaches. The reason for this is simple. If on April 1 the cash price of the commodity is $1 below the April futures price, merchants will buy the actual commodity, sell the

April commodity future, and make a certain profit. As they do this, the two prices rapidly converge until the basis narrows and the profit opportunity disappears.

This convergence of the cash and futures prices during the delivery month means simply that the futures price tends to reflect actual values in the cash market. This convergence does not usually occur during non-delivery months. Hence, in non-delivery months, the basis for non-storable commodities is likely to be unstable and difficult to predict accurately.

CALCULATING THE BASIS

There are two primary methods of determining the basis for any local market: (1) historic price relationships, and (2) actual cost calculation.

To calculate the basis with the first method, you simply obtain past futures prices and compare them with prices at your local market for the same quality product. Usually, you will find that basic patterns repeat themselves year after year. Hence, you can learn to predict basis levels for particular months. If you were figuring the basis for live cattle at Kansas City, Missouri, you might find that Kansas City prices normally have been 50 cents per hundredweight below the prices paid at the specified futures delivery point of Omaha. The basis would, therefore, be 50 cents, and any producer who normally markets at Kansas City would adjust the futures price by 50 cents per hundredweight when figuring his basis. See Figure 14.1 for a historical basis for Texas Panhandle steers versus Chicago Mercantile Exchange live cattle futures for September and December futures. Note that the patterns follow closely each year, and the levels vary only slightly.

To calculate the basis with the second method, you must obtain the actual cost of transporting the cattle from the local market to the location represented by the futures contract. Hence, in this instance, to determine the basis between Kansas City and Omaha via this method, you estimate the costs for transportation (including shrink), interest charges, insurance charges, and the like and use this total to adjust for your actual basis at Kansas City.

If Jones had calculated his basis correctly using costs, he would have had the figures shown in Table 14.1, and he would have known that a $61.50 futures price really meant $60 at his local market.

As mentioned above, there are many factors that cause the basis for any local market to vary over a period of time. These include such things as changes in local supply and demand, changes in local production costs, the predicted size of a future crop, changes in government programs, and local market receipts.

The basis may not work out perfectly because the price relationships described above don't always follow their theoretical models—that is, cash and futures don't always move up and down in unison.

Figure 14.1 Basis Relationship

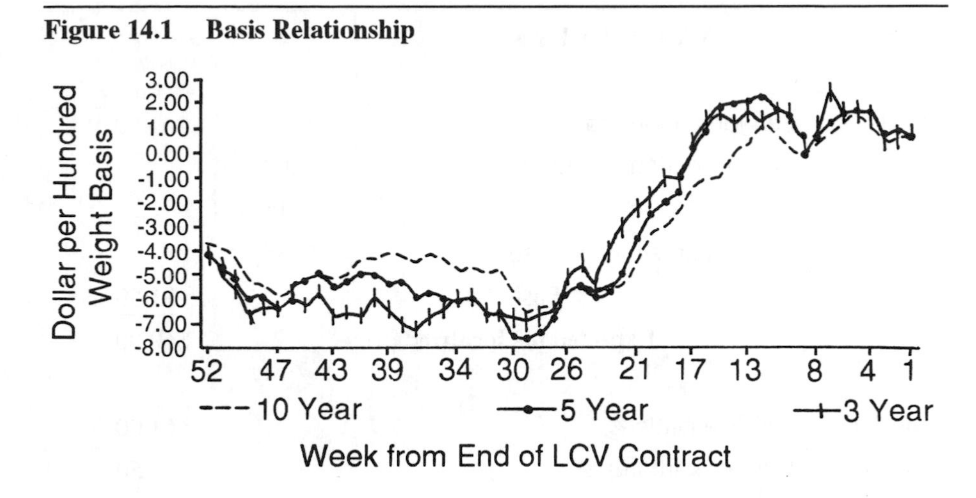

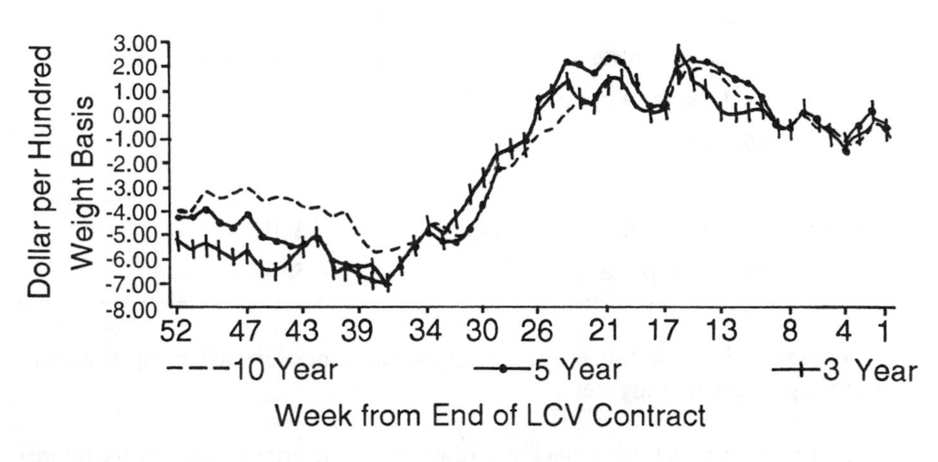

Nor do they always converge exactly at delivery time. And there is the difference in the strength of the relationship between the cash and futures prices for semi-storable commodities like pork bellies as opposed to non-storable commodities like live hogs.

Another bug in the theoretically perfect hedge is the fixed size of the futures contract, which must be used to hedge. A cattle futures contract on the Chicago Mercantile Exchange is 40,000 pounds, which equates roughly with 40 head of fat cattle. If you are feeding 60 head, the sale of one contract leaves one-third of your cattle unhedged. The sale of two contracts would "overhedge" your herd.

Despite all these imperfections, however, hedges do work and even an imperfect hedge may be better than no hedge at all.

Table 14.1 Allowing for Basis

Jan. 15	Sell June futures @		$61.50
	Transportation differential	$1.00	
	Interest & commission	.15	
	Other marketing expenses	.35	
	Basis		$1.50
	Expected net localized price		$60.00
June 10	Sell live cattle @		61.00
June 10	Buy back futures @		62.50
	Loss on Futures	($62.50 – 61.50)	$1.00
	Net realized price for cattle ($61.00 – 1.00)		
Summary:	Expected price from hedge	= $60.00	
	Realized price	= $60.00	

In summary, the Bart Jones example above illustrates several key ingredients in any hedging program. They are:

a. Know your costs of production so that you can determine whether the futures price is allowing you to hedge at a profit.

b. Know what the futures price represents in time, quality, quantity, and location and how that corresponds to the commodity you are hedging.

c. Know your basis—the relationship between your local price and the futures price.

When you know these things, you can apply the basic principles to hedging any commodity.

It should be emphasized that a perfect hedge is not necessarily one in which you get a better price by hedging, but rather it is one in which you achieve your target price through correct calculation of the basis.

It should be emphasized also that hedging is not an operation that should be taken lightly. It takes hard work to hedge effectively. Hedging decisions should be given as much attention as any other aspect of the business. Hedging will not guarantee a profit. If a business manager can't control costs in the cash market, hedging will not help. Hedging will not make a good manager out of a poor manager, but it can make a good manager an even better one.

Chapter 15

Your Banker and Hedging

One of the most important relationships a hedger has is with his banker. A good banker can assist a hedger in a number of ways, not only in lending money but also in providing advice. Bankers are in a unique position to teach their customers how to use futures markets, and it is in their best interest to do so since futures markets and hedging provide a lender with an opportunity to improve the quality of his loans.

A good loan can be made even better by hedging. Producers who have learned this are finding that, with increasing frequency, hedging helps them secure loans.

Futures trading can aid the overall profitability of a business by providing a good deal of flexibility in the timing of purchases and sales, thus allowing a businessman to select the most favorable time of the year for making his price decisions.

As pointed out earlier, when a producer hedges, he "locks in" or assures himself of achieving a price within a fairly small price range. Thus, when he comes to his banker for a loan, he will be able to assure the banker of the exact price, within a small margin of error, that he will receive for the product he has hedged. The banker, therefore, has a greater assurance that the loan will be repaid.

THE LOAN PACKAGE

When a banker makes a loan secured by hedged collateral, it is usually a good idea to coordinate the management of the hedge account at the brokerage house with the management of the loan account at the bank. This coordination has to start at the very beginning, when the terms of the loan are being considered. At that point, the banker will be interested in what the loan is to be used for and from what source the funds for repayment will come.

In considering the first question, it is usual on most hedged collateral loans that the funds loaned be used not only for the business purpose stated by the borrower but also that the banker agree to allow the funds to be used for meeting margin calls on the futures exchange. Just as a speculator should not speculate with too little capital, a hedger should not try to hedge without sufficient capital to meet expected margin calls. A banker who would refuse to take this second step and lend for purposes of making margin calls on hedged collateral could soon find his customer without a hedge (brokers are required to close out accounts when margin calls are not met), thus reducing the quality of his loan and removing any guarantee of the price to be obtained for the hedged collateral.

The second question, pertaining to the source of funds for repayment, goes to the heart of cash flow management. When the futures market price moves in favor of the hedger's futures position, the cash market has moved against him. For example, assume a farmer sells hog futures to hedge against hogs he is fattening. If the price declines, the farmer will have a gain on his futures transaction, but his hogs will be worth less. But the gain on the futures side will be paid into the farmer's brokerage account each day, and that money is available for payment to the bank to reduce the loan amount.

On the other hand, if the price of the futures increases, the farmer will have lost money on his short futures position, and he will be required to pay his broker, in cash, the amount of the loss. This loss will be offset by the increase in the value of the collateral.

For example, suppose a hog farmer plans to buy 700 feeder pigs weighing 40 pounds each and to use his own feed, fattening them to 230 pounds each. Suppose further that, at the time he buys the feeder pigs, he hedges by selling four futures contracts (each contract represents 40,000 pounds or 175 hogs) for fat hogs at $41.65 per hundredweight. If the banker requires the hogs and the farmer's feed as collateral for the loan and lends 85 percent of the value of the fat hogs, the farmer will have a loan of about $57,000.

Now, if the cash and futures prices for the fat hogs decline to $35 per hundredweight, the banker will find that the value of the collateral (56,350 = 1610 cwt. × $35 per cwt.) has fallen below the original amount of the loan—a dangerous situation for the banker. It is likely he will ask for a prepayment on the loan to restore the 85 percent ratio of loan to collateral value.

Since the farmer has hedged, he will have no problem making the prepayment because, as the futures price fell from $41.66 to $35.00, the farmer's brokerage account was credited in cash with the gain on his futures position. The money, except for the original margin in the brokerage account, can be withdrawn and transferred directly to the bank to reduce the loan without actually closing out the futures position.

If per chance the futures market had risen to $45.00 per hundredweight, the farmer would have been called on to meet a margin call because the market would be above the level at which he previously sold. This increase in price would result in the loan ($57,000) being worth only about 78 percent of the value of the collateral (72,450 = 1610 cwt. × $45 per cwt.). The bank should be willing to increase the loan back to the 85 percent level of the collateral value. This amount can then be used to meet the margin calls.

From this example, it becomes clear that management of the hedge and loan accounts needs to be coordinated. The hedge becomes important in upgrading the quality of the loan and assuring repayment. Management of the loan account becomes important in maintaining the hedge. And the key to good management in both is good management of cash flow.

There are several important points for both hedgers and lenders to keep in mind. These include:

1. A hedge will not make a bad loan a good loan. Loans should be made on the basis of whether the underlying purpose for the loan is justified, not on the basis of whether it is hedged or not.

2. Hedging is not for everybody and should not be undertaken solely for the purpose of securing a loan.

3. Whether the collateral is hedged or not will have no impact on the interest rates charged for the loan. Research has shown that the most likely impact will be an increase in the debt-to-equity ratio or the lending of a larger amount of money on a given equity base.

4. The hedger and the lender need to have a thorough understanding of the hedger's cost of operation and his margin of profit represented in any hedge transaction.

The biggest danger confronting both the lender and the hedger is that the "hedger" will succumb to the temptation of "speculation" and thereby take positions in the futures market which jeopardize his loan as well as his whole financial structure. It is not unusual for a producer to sell a futures contract, thus hedging, and after a short time to find that the market has moved against him, causing a loss. He reasons that if he simply "hedged" a little more at this higher level by selling even more contracts, he will recover his loss and even "make a little money" when prices ultimately fall. Alas, prices don't fall but continue rising. He finds himself strapped for cash to meet the margin calls. His banker finds out what he has done when he comes in for a bigger mortgage on the farm.

Another temptation is for the hedger to trade in and out of his position, removing the hedge when prices move slightly against him and trying to put it back on at a better price. The usual result of this activity is huge commission costs and a great danger of being whipsawed, i.e., the hedge won't be "on" when a major market move occurs.

A third temptation is that the hedger, particularly after initial successes, begins to think that since he is so intimately familiar with the market he can "out-speculate those speculators." He therefore begins to speculate heavily out of all proportion to his financial ability, thus jeopardizing his loan and his business.

The banker can protect against these happenings by keeping tight control of the hedge and the hedger. Any banker who makes a loan on hedged collateral should include as part of his control procedures the following:

1. Frequent consultation with the hedger for purposes of reviewing his strategy
2. Insistence that the borrower and the broker sign an agreement requiring that the banker receive a copy of all orders entered into the account
3. That any profits accruing to the account be kept in escrow for the bank until the account is closed and the loan repaid
4. That the broker provide a monthly statement of account activity to the banker

The hedger should also assure the banker that other accounts will not be opened for purposes of speculation. It is also not unusual for a banker to require hedgers to sign agreements that, under special circumstances, allow the banker to "take over" management of the hedge account and even make delivery of the collateral on the futures contract.

Chapter 16

Commodity Hedging in Action

Even if the only real hedging you'll ever do is in an argument with someone else, if you are going to trade futures, it is important to know basically when and how farmers, processors, and others hedge their products and services in the futures markets. Their hedging can have an impact on futures prices that means profit or loss to you. In previous chapters you learned about the importance of basis and the importance of your banker in hedging. Now let's make the process of hedging come alive with some real down-to-earth examples. We'll see how important it is to know your costs of production and to calculate accurately your break-even point as well as your basis. We'll cover commodity hedging in this chapter and financial futures hedging in Chapters 21 and 23.

For the first part of this chapter, you are going to be short-hedging cattle. Then you will be in the meat packing business and will buy futures to protect the price you will pay for hogs you will actually buy at a later date. We could as easily make the example a grain elevator in North Dakota buying wheat from a farmer. The concepts are essentially the same, although the arithmetic would be different. Lastly, we'll demonstrate the use of the grain market to earn storage charges for grain you have harvested. Again, we could easily make the commodity gold or silver or any other storable commodity. The concepts would be the same.

To do an effective job of hedging, the first thing you need is good information. You must know your costs in the cash market . . . the relationships between your price at the local level and the futures price (the basis) . . . and you should have knowledge of what the futures price is and what it represents. The last is especially important, because the futures contract very specifically defines the quality and location of the commodity being traded. If the quality or location of the commodity a hedger is concerned with in the cash market differs from the commodity deliverable in the futures market, he should take that into account in calculating the net localized price he is trying to establish in the futures. And, lastly, you should have a knowledge of the fundamental economic and seasonal factors that affect the prices of your product and how these act over time.

THE SHORT HEDGE—CATTLE

Let's assume you are operating a feedlot, and in January you bought 189 feeder cattle averaging 703 pounds in weight. The accompanying Table 16.1 summarizes your hedge program. You intend to feed them to an average of 1,100 pounds each. Total cost for the purchase of the animals averages $58.09 per hundred pounds, and you estimate that it will cost you $67 per hundredweight to feed them to their finishing weight of 1,100 pounds. Your estimated break-even point is $61.54 per hundredweight (total weight divided by total cost).

Using procedures learned in the previous chapter, you estimate your basis for cattle in your local area at $1.50 per hundredweight. This should be added to your break-even price along with any profit you hope to make. Let's assume that you expect a $30 per head profit (equivalent to $2.73 per hundredweight). Adding the basis and expected profit to your break-even point provides you with a target price of $65.77 per cwt. This is the price at which you must sell the future for your hedge.

The 189 head of cattle is the equivalent of about five contracts of fat cattle (contracts are for 40,000 pounds each). Since you expect that they will reach the 1,100 pound level by June, you select June futures for your hedge. Let's assume that on five successive days, starting in late January, you sell one futures contract each day for an average futures sale price of $65.40 per hundredweight. You are now hedged, i.e., you have sold the cattle you are raising on a futures contract.

Now assume that time passes, the cattle gain weight, and on June 11, 188 head (one died) are sold to a meat packer for $60.60 per hundredweight. On that same day, you buy back your five June futures contracts at $62.05 per hundredweight. Note that the basis ($62.05 - $60.60) is equal to $1.45 per hundredweight—not quite equal to the $1.50 you had estimated. Note also that the sale price of $60.60 per hundredweight

Table 16.1 Summary of Short Cattle Hedge

I. Estimated Costs, Breakeven and Target Prices

Jan 26.—bought 189 feeder cattle weighing 703 lbs at 58.09		$ 77,182.44
Estimated gain 397 lbs. at $67 cwt.		50,272.11
	Total costs estimated	$127,454.55

1,100 LBS. × 189 head (207,099 lbs.) divided into $127,454.55 = $61.54 estimated breakeven cost.

Estimated sale date: June 16 (Use June Futures).

Breakeven	$61.54 cwt.	
Estimated basis	1.50 cwt.	
	$63.04 cwt.	
Profit desired	2.73 cwt.	($30 per head divided by 1,100 lbs.)
Target prices	**$65.77**	

II. The Hedge

You need to sell 207,900 lbs. of June live cattle futures (5 contracts of 40,000 lbs. each) to assure a $65.77 price and a possible profit of $30 per head.

Jan. 31—sold 1 June futures at $64.00
Feb. 2—sold 1 June futures at 64.50
Feb. 5—sold 1 June futures at 65.00
Feb. 5—sold 1 June futures at 65.50
Feb. 8—sold 1 June futures at 68.00

200,000 lbs. sold at average futures price of	$65.40 cwt.		
June 11—bought 5 June futures @	62.05 cwt.		
Difference	3.35	(× 200,000 lbs. =	$6,700.00
		Less commission ($50 per contract)	250.00
			$6,450.00

III. The Results

June 11—sold 188 heads at $60.60 cwt. (delivered to packer June 11) averaging 1,093 lbs.			$124,523.30
Acutal purchase costs	$77,182.44		
Actual feedlot costs	50,340.86		
Actual marketing costs	23.83		
Actual interest	2,551.50		$127,326.60
		Feeding loss	**$ -2,803.30**
		Futures gain	**+6,450.00**
		Net	**$ 3,646.70**

Actual breakeven	**61.63 cwt.**	**Projected breakeven**	**$61.54**
Actual cost of gain	**63.14 cwt.**	**Project cost of gain**	**67.00**
Actual basis	**1.45 cwt**	**Project basis**	**1.50**
Actual profit	**$3,648.70 or $19.39/head**	**Projected profit**	**$5,670 or $30/head**

is $.71 per hundredweight below your break-even point. This loss on the sale of the animals is more than compensated for, however, by the $3.35 profit made on the futures side.

Overall, you would end up with a net profit per head of $19.39—a little more than $10 less than you expected when you bought the feeder cattle. Why? First of all, the cost per pound of gain was underestimated. It actually turned out to be $2.05 per hundredweight higher than had been estimated. The animals were sold at a slightly lower weight than had been anticipated (one animal died), and feedlot, marketing, and interest costs were slightly higher than expected. The result was that the break-even price was underestimated. This demonstrates the importance of accurate estimation of the costs.

Despite the loss in the actual feeding of the cattle, there was a $6,450 net gain in the futures transactions for an overall profit of $3,646.70 or $19.39 per head. Had you not hedged, you would have had a loss of a little over $2,800 or about $14 per head. In this instance, hedging definitely paid off (check through Table 16.1).

HEDGING HOGS

One of the hedges we talked about before is a forward-pricing hedge for a continuously produced, non-storable commodity. So let's work through an example of a live hog long hedge and see how you, a meat packer, can protect the price you will have to pay for hogs. Although this example refers to live hogs, the concepts explained (know your basis, establish a target price, etc.) are applicable to long hedging for any commodity including industrial commodities like copper, rubber, etc., and foods like cocoa, coffee, sugar, etc.

For purposes of illustration, we'll assume that you get interested in hedging hogs on March 7 and decide to find out about protecting the price of hogs you will be buying in June. On March 7, June hog futures are selling for $40.50 per hundredweight (see Table 16.2).

Since you're attempting a long hedge to protect the cost of buying hogs for slaughter, you will be *buying futures*. We will assume there are two costs involved—a commission cost, which you must pay your broker (in our example, that's approximately 12¢ per hundredweight), and interest on margin. (This cost is somewhat hidden and may be non-existent, if your broker pays interest on the margin deposit. It's the amount of money your margin could have earned if it were in a bank savings account, for example, rather than on deposit with your broker.) For our example here, it's about 3¢ per hundredweight. So, the total cost of buying the futures is $40.65 per hundredweight.

As explained earlier, if you were buying hogs somewhere other than in the Peoria area or hogs of a quality substantially different than those priced on the hog

Table 16.2 Futures versus Cash Hog Prices (Prices in dollars per hundredweight)

		Closing June Futures Price	Top St. Louis Cash Price			Closing June Futures Price	Top St. Louis Cash Price
March	7	40.50	40.75	June	2	49.27	48.00
	14	42.95	41.00		3	49.65	48.00
	21	43.85	40.75		4	49.20	48.75
	27	45.50	40.25		5	49.15	49.25
April	4	45.55	41.00		6	49.25	49.25
	11	46.80	42.25		9	50.10	49.50
	18	46.70	42.25		10	50.50	50.25
	25	47.75	42.50		11	50.77	50.00
May	2	47.70	44.75		12	50.80	49.75
	9	47.00	47.25		13	52.20	51.00
	16	48.60	49.00		16	53.55	52.50
	23	48.95	48.75		17	53.70	53.00
	30	49.20	48.75		18	54.65	53.50
					19	56.05	56.00
					20	56.85	57.50

futures contract, you should take into account the location difference (location basis) and quality difference (quality basis) in estimating the net price you would have in the hogs if you received them in actual delivery on the futures contract. We'll assume here that you normally buy hogs in Peoria, and by the time you get them to your plant the price is equivalent to the Peoria top price. We'll also assume that you're buying the same quality as is represented on the futures contract—200–220 pound USDA 1-, 2-, 3-, or 4-graded quality hogs.

As shown in Table 16.3, the target price you expect to pay for hogs by hedging them on the futures market is, therefore, $40.65 cwt.

Now comes the $64 question—or maybe we should call it the $40.65 question: Do you expect to be able to buy hogs in the cash market in June for less than $40.65? Or do you look for cash prices above that? If you expect them to be less and are reasonably certain your expectations will be realized, you probably won't want to hedge. If you expect them to be considerably higher than $40.65, you will. We'll say that you are looking at a price of over $45 per hundredweight in June, so you decide to hedge.

Now let's determine exactly how your hedge would have worked out. Time passes and June 20 arrives. On that date June futures are selling at $56.85. Since you bought for $40.65 and sold at $56.85, you have a net gain on the futures of $16.20 per hundredweight.

Table 16.3 Worksheet for Live Hog Hedge

Futures price for June	$40.50
Commission	.12
Interest on margin	.03
Total cost	40.65
Location difference (transportation and shrinkage from Peoria — or, normal price (differential)	0
Quality difference	0
Target price	**40.65**
Expected cash price	**45.00**
Buy futures (including commission and margin) on March 7	40.65
Sell futures on June 20	56.85
Net gain or loss on futures	+ 16.20
Purchase live cash hogs on June 20	57.50
Minus gain on futures	- 16.20
Actual cost of live hogs	**41.30**

On June 20 you also buy the actual, walking-around live hogs and get them to your plant at the equivalent Peoria top price on that date of $57.50 per hundredweight. That $57.50 per hundredweight is a dollar more than you expected to pay, and $16.85 over what your target price was when you hedged. However, since you have a $16.20 gain on futures, you can apply that to the actual cost of the hogs. This makes the total net cost of the hogs equal to $41.30. Not quite the target price but close. The hedge did its job. It protected against major price risk.

The target price was not met exactly. Why? Because the futures price and the price you paid in the cash market for actual hogs were not exactly equal at the time you offset your futures contract. If they had been equal, you would have paid exactly a net of $40.65 for the hogs. For example, had you removed your hedge on June 6, you would have paid $49.25 per hundredweight for your live hogs (see Table 16.2), but since futures were at the same price, the gains would have exactly offset the losses and the net price would have been $40.65. If you had removed the hedge on June 2, you would have paid only $39.58.

A couple of caveats. Our packer here was long; that is, he had purchased the futures. When the buyer goes into the delivery period—in this instance, any time during the month of June—he may receive delivery of hogs on the futures contract; and he could receive them in Peoria, East St. Louis or any of the other Exchange-approved delivery points. You need to keep this fact in mind whenever you carry a long position into the delivery period for any commodity.

THE STORAGE HEDGE

Now let's turn our attention to another type of hedge—the storage hedge, i.e., using the futures market to help pay the costs of storing a product. This type of hedge is possible because the normal relationship between cash and futures prices for storable commodities is a futures price higher than the cash price and the more distant futures higher than nearer-term futures, reflecting the cost of storage.

Anyone who owns the product will be induced to store it for a period of time only if he expects to be able to sell it at a sufficiently high price to pay his storage costs. Conversely, people who buy the product will have to pay storage charges if they buy it in advance of their time of need. To avoid having capital tied up in storage and other facilities, they are willing to pay a slightly higher price at a later time if someone else will store it for them. Hence, distant futures prices are normally above near-term or cash market prices. As the futures month approaches the delivery period, cash prices will converge toward futures as carrying charges are earned or become less (see Figure 16.1). This phenomenon allows businessmen to put a product in storage, sell it forward on a futures contract and, as the basis narrows, earn a profit to help cover storage costs. It should be obvious that such a hedge is not practical in non-storable commodities.

A word of caution: Not all markets for storable commodities are always normal, i.e., futures prices above cash. Sometimes they become inverted, i.e., cash above futures. In that instance, the storage hedge does not work.

Let's assume that a farmer has harvested 20,000 bushels of corn. On Oct. 10 his local grain elevator offers him $3 a bushel, the going cash rate. At that same time the

Figure 16.1 Cost-of-Carry Illustrated

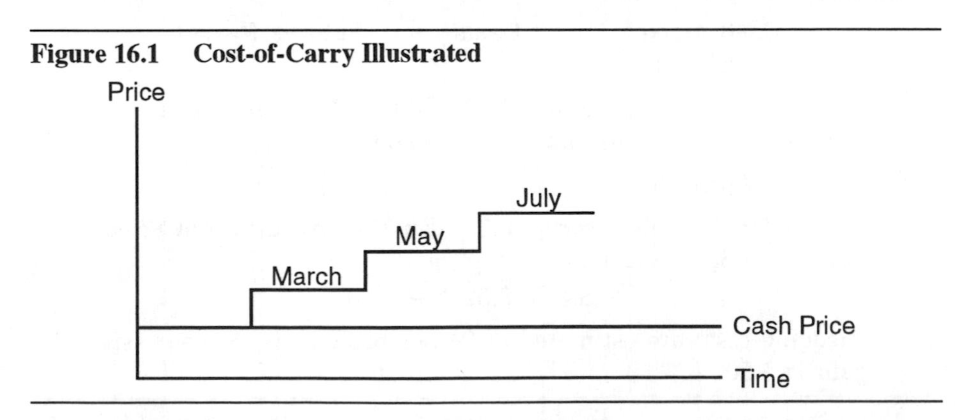

Chicago May futures price is $3.60. Since the farmer owns the corn, he has these alternatives:

a. Selling the cash product for immediate delivery,

b. Selling it on a cash forward contract, or

c. Selling it on a futures contract through a short hedge.

If he does none of these, he will be speculating in the cash market.

In considering his alternatives, let's assume that the farmer decides to store his corn on the farm and hedge it by selling it in the May futures, thus earning at least some of his storing costs. In evaluating May futures, he needs to consider whether a May futures price of $3.60 provides him, after the storage period, with a net local price high enough to cover storage costs, interest, insurance, etc., plus a profit to make the storage worthwhile.

Let's assume that he plans to sell the cash product sometime in April. He calculates that he will need $3.40 as a target price to cover the cost of storage, 35¢, plus 5¢ profit. His present basis (cash to May futures) is 60¢ under May. Historical basis patterns for his area show that the local basis narrows to about 10¢ under May in April. This will give him a target price of $3.50 per bushel ($3.60 - $.10 for location basis). His hedging costs are 2¢ per bushel, thus his net target price is $3.48 per bushel.

Assume he sells four contracts of May futures at $3.60 per bushel. Time passes, April 15 arrives, and the cash price of corn at his local market is $3.45. May futures have fallen to $3.53, indicating a basis of 8¢. He sells his corn on the cash market and lifts his hedge. He nets $3.50 per bushel on the hedge. The transaction is summarized in Table 16.4.

Table 16.4 Hedging Corn

Cash Market	Basis	Futures Market
October 10		
Harvests 20,000 bushels of corn, local price $3 per bu.	$.60	Sells 4 May futures at $3.60
April 15		
Sells 20,000 bushels of corn, local price $3.45 per bu.	$.08	Buys 4 May futures at $3.53
+ $.45	$.52	+ $.07

(Hedging costs are estimated at 2¢ per bushel. Hence net basis gain is $.50.)

Another quicker way of doing the above calculations is simply to look at the change from the buying basis to the selling basis. Add the basis gain to the original purchase price, subtract the costs of hedging, and you will know the net price received. When using a carrying charge hedge, remember these two rules:

a. If the basis is narrowing (selling basis is less than the buying basis), you are earning at least part of your storage charges.

b. If the basis is widening (the selling basis is above the buying basis), your hedge is costing you more money than not hedging.

This points up the importance of knowing your basis patterns and selecting the most opportune time to lift your hedge. These storage hedge rules are equally applicable to grains, gold, silver, etc.

TRYING OTHER EXAMPLES YOURSELF

Now you know what a short hedge, a long hedge, and a storage hedge look like. We could not cover examples in every commodity, hence we covered two livestock and one grain hedge. However, the principles we used throughout are applicable to a wide number of other commodities. Work out some examples for yourself to determine how well the hedge works. You could also plug in some hypothetical situations in which the futures price goes up and you lose money on futures.

You will find that as long as prices eventually converge to your expected basis, your hedge will work out as you expected it would. That's what hedging is all about—knowing your basis patterns. When you hedge, you essentially trade the greater uncertainty associated with absolute price change for the lesser uncertainty associated with basis change or relative price change.

SELECTING A HEDGE BROKER

In selecting a broker for hedging, you should look for someone who is interested and willing to service hedge accounts. Some registered representatives prefer to handle hedge accounts. Others are not willing to spend the time and effort necessary to do a good job. A suitable broker should be able to explain the various aspects of hedging to you, aid you in calculating price relationships, and be willing to help you give and receive delivery, if necessary. A good broker should also be able to provide fast and reliable execution of orders.

WHAT ABOUT DELIVERY?

Although about 98 percent of all futures contracts are offset and not delivered, there are times when it would be advantageous for a hedger to accept delivery . . . when, for a particular location, accepting or giving delivery is the most profitable alternative. At that same time, at another location, it may not be the most advantageous. In deciding whether you want to give or take delivery, you should calculate all of your costs involved in accomplishing the delivery and then compare that to the best price you can get in another market.

Some futures contracts do not allow delivery of the physical commodity. Instead, the remaining longs and shorts at the end of trading simply settle their price differences through a cash payment. These contracts are the norm in financial futures, but relatively new in agricultural futures.

DECISION MAKING ON HEDGING

The internal organization of the decision-making machinery on hedging for a firm is quite important, because hedging should be a part of a firm's total management strategy. It's important that the top people in a firm, including the president and the board of directors, be aware of how and why the futures market is being used for hedging. If they understand that hedges do not always work out perfectly and that there will be times when the gains and losses in the futures market will not exactly offset the gains or losses in the cash market, the chances of futures trading becoming an integral and useful part of the management decisions of the firm are much greater.

For decision making, some firms establish committees to review the basic economic data, estimate risk exposures, coordinate the decisions that need to be made between buying and selling, and make the actual decisions in the futures market. Other firms have one man responsible for trading, with a committee to provide basic outlook data, advice, and guidelines on his use of the futures market.

In all cases, there should be a close liaison between the comptroller of the firm and the man having responsibility for the hedging, because hedging is basically a financial operation and can have an important effect on the finances of the firm. It can also have implications for tax purposes.

HOW MUCH TO HEDGE

A major concern facing all hedgers is deciding just how much to hedge. Should you cover 100 percent of your exposure, or is 50 percent sufficient? How about 10 percent of it, or none?

There are no hard and fast rules. The proportion of risk you hedge is a personal decision. Generally, the answer to the question should be based on some, or all, of the following factors:

a. Your Net Capital The greater your capital base, the more risk you can withstand. If you are well-capitalized and unhedged and prices move against you, the loss may not be catastrophic. On the other hand, if you are poorly capitalized, you probably can't afford to take very much risk. A small adverse price change could mean bankruptcy. In those instances, hedging to protect small positive price margins, or to protect against further losses, may be well-advised.

b. Your Expectation About Prices When you put on a hedge, you have essentially accepted a price. When you decide if you want to accept a price, whether it's one available in the futures or in the cash market, you need to have a standard against which you can compare the available prices. The standard should be either a forecasted price (your forecast or someone else's), a break-even price, a budgeted price, or some acceptable price you have identified. You also need to consider the strength of your expectation, i.e., the probability that the forecasted price, or expected price, will be realized if you do not hedge.

c. Your Cash Flow Expectations Hedges require cash deposits at your broker. If your futures position loses money, that money must be deposited in cash with your broker on a daily basis. If you do not meet variation margin calls, the broker will liquidate your position. You may then find yourself unhedged at exactly the time you need it.

Hence, in deciding how much you want to hedge, keep in mind how the variation margin calls may affect the cash flow needs of the rest of your business.

Chapter 17

Energy Hedging— Some Examples

One of the most successful new futures contracts introduced in recent years was the crude oil futures offered in the early 1980s by the New York Mercantile Exchange (NYMEX). This contract, which benefited from the earlier success of the NYMEX's No. 2 Heating Oil contract, further introduced futures hedging and derivative product risk-management techniques to the petroleum industry. Applying these ideas to crude oil was an almost instant success. The success of this contract led to the development of other energy-related contracts, most notably, contracts for unleaded gasoline and natural gas.

Since then, energy futures trading has grown to be one of the most active groups of futures in the world. Further, energy futures have become a widely used hedging tool.

Oil is one of the world's most important commodities. It is produced in many countries, consumed everywhere, and accounts for a large percentage of international trade. Its prices are very sensitive to political and economic changes.

Crude oil is usually refined, a process that results in two major products: fuel oil and gasoline. The prices of all three products are related and usually follow similar patterns, though not with precise timing. See Figures 17.1 and 17.2. The prices of the products are clearly interrelated because their supply is derived from the same source—crude oil. However, they react to different demand forces, and for that reason

Figures 17.1 Crude, Heating Oil, and Gasoline Futures Prices (weekly data)

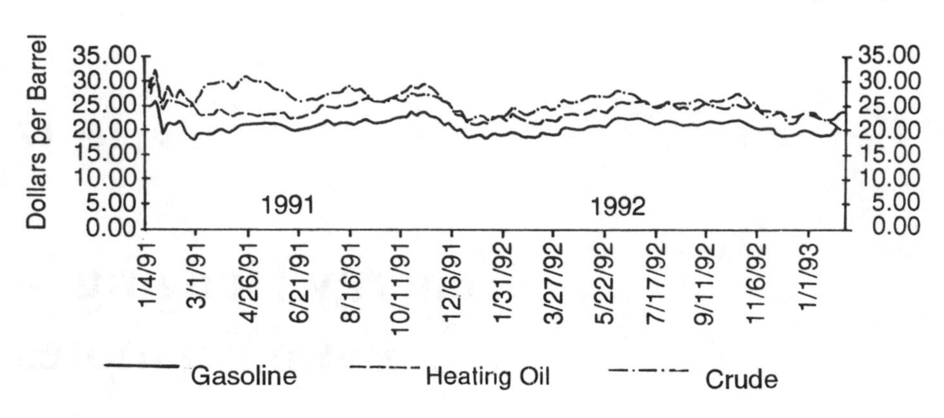

Figures 17.2 Heating Oil Less Gasoline (weekly data)

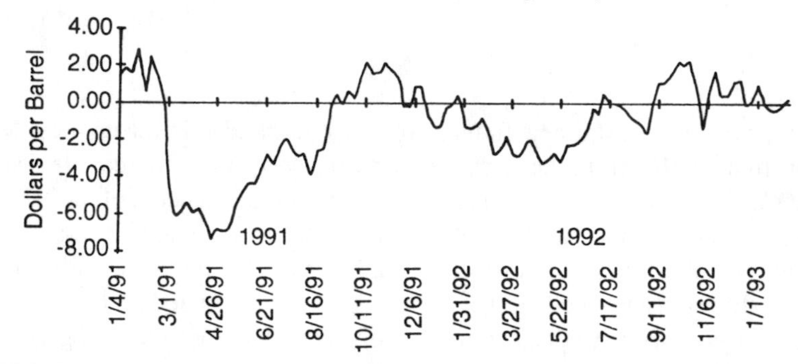

the spread between fuel oil and gasoline prices can be volatile, though usually staying within a limited range. All of this creates price risk (and hedging or trading opportunities) to producers, refiners, distributors, manufacturers, homeowners, etc.

Chapter 18, which deals with spreads, contains an example of the use of these three contracts to implement a trading strategy called "the crack." It is roughly equivalent to operating a refinery. Buying crude futures and selling heating oil and gasoline futures.

The following are some examples of typical energy hedges.

HEDGE #1: REFINER—HEDGING THE SALE OF EXCESS INVENTORY

Assume that Hopeful Energy, a medium-sized refiner located on the Gulf Coast, ordinarily contracts to sell its #2 fuel oil production f.o.b. pipeline. The contracts require that the buyer take a minimum amount of #2 fuel oil each month. The company produces more than the minimum amount because, on average, the contractors take considerably more than their minimums. Assume also that in January some of the buyers decide to take only the minimum quantities specified in their contract. As a result, Hopeful Energy's inventories begin building. They are faced with several alternatives. They can immediately cut back on the refining activity, but this can have the disadvantage of increasing their average production costs per gallon. They can also sell off their excess inventory for immediate delivery, or they can hedge it. Let's assume that their cash/futures basis (Gulf spot price minus the futures price) has been averaging .5¢ per gallon, and that it will cost another .5¢ per gallon to carry the product in inventory over the expected life of the hedge.

If the futures price for #2 fuel delivery in March is at 56¢, then Hopeful Energy knows that its net hedged sale price is 55¢ per gallon (56¢, less basis of .5¢, and cost-of-carry .5¢).

Assume Hopeful Energy sells the futures at 56¢. Time passes and in the middle of February, Hopeful gets an opportunity to sell the fuel oil in the cash market at a net price of 52¢. It then buys back the futures it previously sold at a price of, say, 51.25¢ per gallon. In this instance, the cash/futures basis has widened and the net result is a windfall profit. Table 17.1 below contains a summary of this transaction.

Table 17.1 Refiner's Hedge of Fuel Oil Inventory

Cash			Expected Basis	Futures		
Jan.	Net Expected Price	55¢	–1.00	Sell March Futures	@	56¢
Feb.	Actual Sale	52¢	+ .75	Buy March Futures	@	51.25
		3¢	1.75			+4.75

HEDGE #2: FORWARD SALE TO HEDGE THE PURCHASE OF INVENTORY NEEDS

Assume that Smith is a large independent distributor of fuel oil to retail outlets in the Midwest. The manager tries to beat the competition by keeping his price quotes low during rising markets. He does this by buying inventory and stockpiling fuel oil whenever he thinks prices are likely to be rising in the months immediately ahead. Sometimes he is right. Sometimes he is wrong. Smith's immediate problem is that refiners are reluctant to sell to him for delivery more than a few weeks in advance. Assume Smith's manager wants to take advantage of private forecasts showing tighter supplies and higher fuel oil prices six months ahead. He can't do it through forward contracting in the cash market, because the refiners won't forward contract that far ahead. The futures markets are an alternative for him.

Assume the manager enters the futures market and buys #2 fuel oil futures for delivery six months out at a price of 60¢ a gallon, 4¢ over the current spot price. The 4¢ differential reflects the cost-of-carry and the market's general expectation that prices are likely to be higher six months from today than they are currently. Assume that time passes and the prices do indeed rise in a steady fashion. Each month, as Smith's manager purchases his needs in the cash market, he reduces his futures hedge by an equivalent amount, taking the profits from the long futures position and adjusting the cost of his purchases in the cash market.

HEDGE #3: SELLING INVENTORY IN TRANSIT

Golden Touch Trading Co. buys and sells gasoline in a pipeline originating on the Gulf Coast and ships it to the Midwest. Sometimes it buys gasoline without having already sold it, thus it is exposed to possible decreases in price. Assume that on October 15, Golden Touch Trading buys 100,000 barrels of gasoline from a major refinery on the Gulf Coast at a spot market price of 89.5¢ per gallon. It would schedule to lift it from the pipeline about a week later, say, October 22. It takes approximately one month for that shipment to wind its way through the system and reach the Midwest. Thus Golden Touch would expect to deliver the product to some buyer about the middle of November. Assume also that Golden Touch has not found a buyer for the product yet, but knows that between October 15 and the third week of November, as the product is moving through its distribution system, it will find a buyer. The company can protect itself by selling unleaded gasoline futures on the NYMEX.

If Golden Touch's basis averages about 7¢ and the cost for shipping adds another 3¢ a gallon, this means that for Golden Touch to make a profit on this product, it must obtain a price of 99.5¢ per gallon (89.5¢ + 10.¢).

Assume the NYMEX unleaded gasoline futures for December are selling at $1.00 per gallon. At that price, Golden Touch knows it can make a slight profit on the transaction.

To protect against a price fall, they would sell the gasoline futures at NYMEX, go about their business listing the gasoline and shipping it northward, finding buyers in the cash market, and, as they made the sales in the cash market, lifting their hedge. If their basis calculation is correct, they will achieve their expected market price.

Note in all of these examples, as in any hedge activity, the stability of the expected basis is the key element for success. This expected stability is measured by correlation. If the correlation is 1.00, and the rate of change in the two prices (cash and futures) remains relatively constant as they march through time, you will get very effective hedges. Normally, the stability of the basis, and the expected rate of change in the two prices, is measured by regression analysis. The regression coefficient reflects the rate of change in the two prices, and its inverse establishes the number of futures contracts you need to hedge for a given quantity or exposure amount.

Chapter 18

Fact and Fiction About Spreads

Joe Boswell first appeared on the commodity trading scene about six months ago . . . the morning after a dinner party where he had listened for almost an hour while a well-dressed stranger described commodity conquests in numbers that boggled his mind.

In the succeeding months, Joe became a trader. He won some and he lost some, the latter category unfortunately predominating because—in spite of the reasonable guidance he was getting from his broker—Joe's own preparation for trading commodities did not extend much beyond that party conversation.

It was also during this time that Joe first heard of a "spread." He knew it to be a trading strategy calling for buying a contract for delivery in one month and selling a contract for delivery of the same or a different commodity in another month, and that it is considered a conservative method of trading. A little further investigation revealed to him that by spreading he would be trading two contracts for only a little more commission than he'd pay to trade one, and in the case of the cattle spread he was considering he would need only $300 margin instead of the $700 necessary to trade one contract outright.

Joe figured that was a good deal. He would be getting two for almost the price of one . . . and he would be being "conservative," which suited his Midwestern upbringing perfectly. So he bought June live cattle at $41.00 and simultaneously sold December live cattle at $44.00. Two days later, June cattle were at $39.50 and December cattle were at $45.00. By spreading, Joe had, without delay, lost $1,500. In retrospect, had he taken an outright position of one contract in either of those two months, the most he would have lost over that time period would have been $600.

Joe has since disappeared from the commodity trading scene and is still wondering, among other things, how a "conservative" method of trading could result in his losing more money than if he had not been so "conservative" and been simply long or short.

What Joe didn't know (and what his broker had apparently failed to impress upon him) is that spreading transactions in and of themselves are not necessarily conservative methods of trading. Sometimes the prices for different futures months of the same commodity fluctuate independently, making such spreads more risky than outright positions. This is particularly true for "perishable" commodities like cattle and hogs.[1]

SEMANTICS

The term "spread" and "straddle" are sometimes used interchangeably but frequently confused. The term "spread" is often used to refer to the simultaneous purchase of a futures contract for delivery in one month and sale of a futures contract for the same commodity for delivery in another month (e.g., the purchase of May corn and the sale of July corn). The term "straddle" is frequently used to refer to simultaneous trades which arch across two different markets (e.g., the purchase of July pork bellies and the sale of July hogs).

In order to avoid confusion, we'll use only the term "spread," calling these "intra-commodity spreads" and "inter-commodity spreads," respectively.

The objective of a spread is to make a profit by correctly anticipating variations in the relative market strength of the two positions involved. A spread trader is *not* concerned with the absolute price change in either one of the contracts but only with the relative price changes *between* the two futures contracts.

For example, assume that February pork bellies are trading at 40 cents and May pork bellies at 45 cents. A trader who believes that a five-cent premium for the May

1. Even though brokers offer special margins for spreads, be careful; not all of the things they call spreads are economic spreads.

contract is not justified or will not be justified prior to the expiration of the February contract might buy the February pork bellies and sell the May pork bellies at the prevailing five-cent-per-hundredweight differential. Later, if the absolute price levels change so that February is at 46 cents and May is at 49 cents, the differential will have narrowed to three cents—leaving a two-cent profit (minus commissions) on the transaction.

Obviously, if one is to favor being long one contract and short another, as he must in a spread, he must have reason to believe that forces affecting the two are related. They must be related, or else the two prices will act independently and one will be in the position of having two distinct outright trades and not a spread at all. Buying cocoa and simultaneously selling corn, for example, is not considered a spread. It is merely the establishment of two unrelated trading positions. On the other hand, the purchase of grain sorghum versus the sale of corn (or vice versa) is a true spread because, while there are forces tending to make these two markets act somewhat differently, the two commodities are substitutes for each other in the livestock feed economy and, indeed, their price movements are related.

"TIME" SPREADS

"Time" spreads involve the purchase of a futures contract for delivery in one month and the sale of a futures contract in the same commodity for delivery in another month. For example, the purchase of a futures contract of corn for delivery in May and the sale of a futures contract of corn for delivery in July. The purpose here is to take advantage of discrepancies that arise between the two prices as a result of the difference in the time of maturity of the two contracts. In order for such a spread to have an any economic logic, of course, the supply/demand elements affecting the price for one of the time periods must also have an effect on the prices in the other time period.

Time spreads can be very risky in some commodities and nearly riskless in others. Those time spreads which would be near the low end of the risk spectrum would involve the completely storable, seasonally produced commodities like the grains. Those at the other end of the spectrum would be in the highly perishable commodities, like fat cattle or eggs. In the middle would be spreads in continuously produced, fully or semi-storable commodities that may have variable carrying charges like pork bellies or silver.

For the seasonably produced, completely storable commodities, prices between futures months are related to the cost of carrying the commodity in storage from one time period to the next. Such costs include storage, handling, insurance, shrinkage, interest on investment, and commissions. In a normal market, where the price system provides an incentive to producers who store products, the nearby months usually sell at a discount to the more distant months, the difference between the two representing the carrying costs. In a normal market, therefore, the price of May corn will usually be higher than the price of March corn.

If the price differential between these two months exceeds the total cost of carry, smart commercial traders will buy a March contract and sell a May contract; and then in March, if the differential has not returned to reflect carrying costs, take delivery of the corn, store it for a month, and re-deliver it in May to cover the short sale. The profit on the transaction would be the difference between the sale price plus the sum of the carrying costs and the transaction costs, and the price of the March contract. Because traders will take advantage of such profit opportunities, the carrying costs usually limit the amount by which the price of the May corn contract will exceed that of the March corn contract.

It is important to note, however, that there are no such carrying cost constraints on the amount that March can sell over May. In fact, this sometimes happens. When it does, it is referred to as an "inverted" market. An inverted market results from a shortage of immediately available supplies. It reflects an economic disincentive to storage and encourages storers to sell their grain. Since the far-out months are selling at discounts, the market indicates it expects this near-term supply/demand imbalance to correct itself in the short run.

As indicated earlier, spreads in storable commodities are generally at the low end of the risk spectrum because the prices of different months are related to carrying costs, and usually these carrying costs establish a limit, albeit an imperfect one, on the forward premiums. However, in some storable commodities—such as silver—short-term interest rates constitute a major part of the carrying cost. If short-term interest rates are quite volatile, carrying costs will fluctuate accordingly.

Such time spreads also work well for continuously produced, storable, or semi-storable commodities, such as pork bellies. In such commodities the normal spread relationship will change, however, between months as the in-to-storage movement changes to out-of-storage. Remember that these discounts and premiums being paid in the market reflect essentially the strength of the incentive for holders to store or not store a product. It is for this reason that "normal" carrying charges for the months when the product moves into storage will be different than those for such commodities when the product moves out of storage. This seasonality can be reflected in spread relationships and may offer special profit opportunities. Figure 18.1 shows that since 1988 the May-August spread tends to widen from the middle of March until the beginning of May.

Figure 18.1 CME May—Aug Pork Belly Spreads

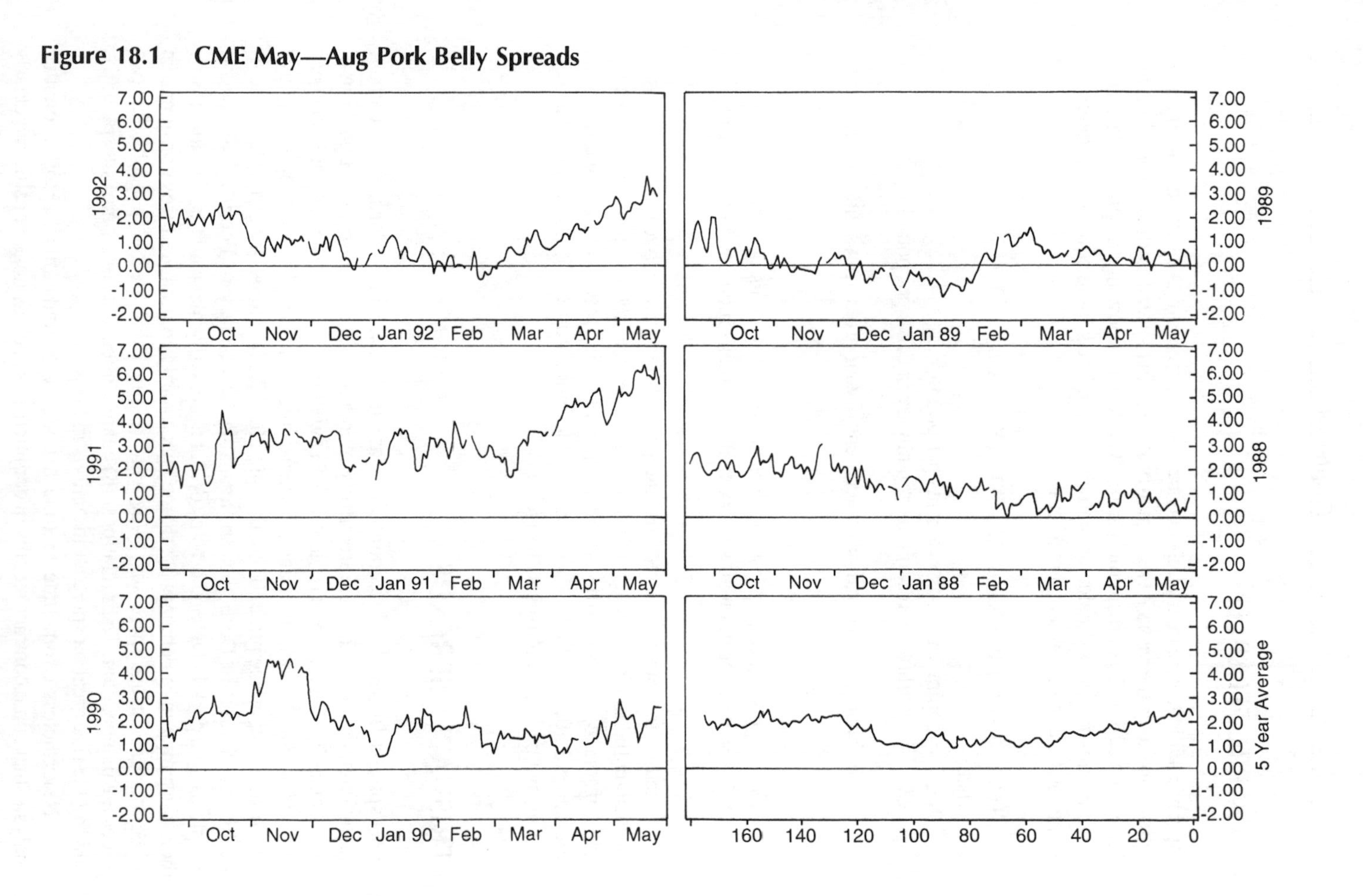

HOW PROFITABLE?

Properly handled, spread trading can be very successful. Academic and industry studies done over the years have regularly shown that spread trading, properly done, often returns 15 to 20 percent on margin. The key to knowing the proper value of a spread is knowing how to calculate carrying costs. The simple equation for determining the total carrying costs in a market is:

Total Carry Costs = X1 + (X2 x A) + (X3 x A)
where:
X1 = commission costs in cents per pound
X2 = monthly interest on margin money in cents per pound

(Note: This may be small or nonexistent if your broker pays interest on margin deposits.)

X3 = insurance and storage costs per month in cents per pound
A = number of months between the contracts included in the spread.

Subtract the carrying costs from the price differential between two months. If that differential is large enough to provide a 20 percent return on margin, make the trade. Of course, you have to be careful about interpreting results of trading tests which were derived after the fact as being applicable in the future. Times change, markets change, and price relationships change.

PERISHABLE SPREADS

Time spreads in perishable commodities are high-risk transactions. Except under special circumstances, they are frequently more risky than an outright net position in the commodity. This is the problem Joe Boswell had earlier. The reason is because supply/demand elements affecting the price of the commodity in one month may have very little effect on the price for another month. Take live hogs, for example. None of the hogs delivered in December are available for delivery in February. Further, if people eat less pork in December, they do not necessarily make up for it by increasing their consumption in February nor do they necessarily continue reduced consumption in February. Because these supply/demand relationships are independent, the two prices are independent. Their relationships change often and sometimes substantially, making the risk great on spread transactions in hogs.

Nevertheless, from time to time a trader will find, after careful economic analysis, that some contract months in commodities such as hogs or cattle are clearly overvalued and some months are clearly undervalued. In this instance, buying the undervalued contract and selling the overvalued contract can be profitable.

An example is found in a recent preliminary report on price relationships between nearby and distant futures in cattle. A model that included the number of cattle on feed, the average market weight of fat cattle, the steer/corn price ratio, plus a seasonable variable was successful in identifying profitable trading opportunities in cattle.

However, you should be aware that such transactions are, in effect, two outright positions and not legitimate spreads, as there is very little natural economic connection between the two positions, and this is true whether your broker calls them spreads or not.

INTER-SEASON SPREADS

The time spreads referred to above are all intra-season spreads. There are also profit opportunities in spreading between seasons or crop years. For example buying this year's soybean crop and selling next year's. These types of spreads do work and are legitimate when the commodity is storable, so that one season's supply can be carried over to the next season for delivery. This is possible in the grains, but not in pork bellies, where exchange rules prohibit it.

Inter-season or inter-crop spreads are not restricted to crops that are grown in the soil. There is a seasonality to the production cycle in broilers, plywood, and other commodities, as well as periods of in-to-storage movement and out-of-storage movement. It is important to note, however, when effecting transactions covering two distinct seasons, that an important event always occurs during this interim—namely, a new harvest or a turn in the cycle, which means major changes in production.

SPREADING LOCATION BASIS

There are instances where the same commodity is traded on two different exchanges, and the contracts call for par delivery at two different locations. In this case, if all other elements of the contracts are equal, the difference in prices on the two exchanges should be equal to the transportation cost between the two locations represented in the contracts. If, for whatever reason, the difference in prices between the two contracts should exceed transportation costs, it will be profitable for commercial traders to buy the lower-priced contract on one exchange and sell the higher-priced contract on the other exchange, thus locking in a profit equal to the amount by which the price differential exceeds transportation costs. If these profit opportunities do not disappear by the time delivery can occur on the contracts, you need only take delivery on the lower-priced market, transport the product to the par delivery point of the other market, and re-deliver in fulfillment of your short position.

For example, if you were in a position to buy CBOT deliverable wheat in Kansas City, ship it to Chicago, and re-sell it at a profit, you would do so. Hence, any time the contract in Kansas City sells below the contract in Chicago by more than the transportation costs, some traders will be buying the contract in Kansas City and selling it in Chicago.

SPREADING QUALITY BASIS

Just as par locations differ between contracts for the same commodity listed under different exchanges, quality specifications also sometimes differ. A smart trader will be aware of what the normal price differential should be for the various grades and qualities of a commodity. If the two contracts don't sell at these normal differentials, he will buy one contract and sell the other. As the time for delivery approaches, the two prices should come to reflect the actual value in the spot market. To the extent those actual values reflect the normal differentials, the trader will have profited.

INTER-COMMODITY SPREADS

As noted above, there are physical relationships between certain commodities. Sometimes the supply and demand elements for two commodities are tied together because they are substitutes for each other, as corn is a substitute for milo or grain sorghum. Sometimes one commodity is derived from the other, such as soybean meal and soybean oil. Sometimes one commodity is the raw material used in the production of a finished product, as with feeder cattle and fat cattle.

Because of these physical and economic relationships, the price fluctuations in the two commodities are related. As a result, a price change in one commodity directly affects the price of another. This places constraints on the extent to which prices in the two commodities can diverge. For example, as the price of corn rises relative to the price of milo, livestock feeders will start substituting milo for corn. This reduces the demand for corn, thus slowing its price rise, while increasing the demand for milo, encouraging it to rise in price.

Likewise, reduction in the demand for soybean oil and soybean meal will be reflected in the demand for raw soybeans and thus limit that product's price moves. Normally, the price differences between soybean oil, soybean meal, and soybeans will reflect processing margins. If a trader expects the processing margins to widen, he should buy meal and oil and sell soybeans.

SPOTTING SPREAD OPPORTUNITIES

Visualizing the spread between months can be done in a number of different ways. One good way is to keep a daily price table noting the closing price on each side of the spread and the difference between the two (see Table 18.1).

Such a table allows you to tell at a glance how the price moves alter spreads.

Table 18.1

February Pork Bellies	May Pork Bellies	Difference	Profit Buy Feb.–Sell May
48.90	50.00	+ 1.10	
49.00	49.80	+ .80	+30
48.00	49.50	+ 1.50	–.70

It is also a good idea to obtain a history of several previous years' price actions. However, you don't want to become too dependent on past history. Disease effects, droughts, monetary problems, governmental programs, and other factors will change price patterns from year to year.

SUGGESTED RULES

When putting in spread orders, the buy side, or the long side, is always mentioned first. The sell, or the short side, is second, and the premiums state either buy or sell. For example, if you wanted to execute a December/June hog spread at +125, the order should read "buy one December live hog, sell one June live hog, 125 premium."

Many profitable trading strategies can be employed using spreads. Spreads, however, are unique. They require a different approach than simply trading long or short positions. One of the biggest problems in trading spreads is exiting them. Most beginning traders are reluctant to exit a spread, even as it goes against them, because they find it difficult to be sure that the fundamental factors are working against them rather than moving simply in a short-term random blip. Hence, they tend to hold on too long and suffer larger losses than expected. Experienced traders will tell beginning traders to first look for strong seasonal tendencies in price patterns, be selective entering a spread, and be very patient. Use exit benchmarks that are based on money or time. In other words, risk a predetermined amount of money on a spread and exit it once that money is gone or a certain time period has passed. If the spread is still within the time benchmark of your seasonal play, look for a new entry point at a better price. Most successful spread traders I know trade two positions—one is a core spread position with established entry and exit points, and the other a second-level position where one side or the other of the spread is traded on a short-term basis. This is called lifting a leg. It is risky, but if done selectively and in moderation, it can always keep you in the market to benefit (or lose) from seasonal tendencies, and provide reasonably good returns on the margin money posted.

OPTIONS SPREADS AND TREND CHANGERS

Most new traders search diligently for a market timing signal designed to get them in at the top of a market and out at the bottom. If it was easy to do, everybody would be doing it and, of course, then it would not be very profitable. Combining the concept of options and spread trading, however, with a little patience, yields a trading strategy that helps one get properly positioned to take advantage of tops and bottoms. This technique is called the option back-spread (buying more options than you sell). To illustrate, assume you believe that bond futures prices are about to peak, but you do not want to take a naked short position, and you do not want to simply buy a put, which, if prices continued to rise, would result in a complete loss of your premium.

An alternative would be to do a put ratio back-spread. The trader would sell a put of one strike and buy two puts at a lower strike. If the market continues to rise, moderatly, you will end up with a small gain or loss depending upon the exact prices and premiums paid or gained from the legs in the spread. If prices begin to fall, the long put options generate profits, and the more they fall, the more you gain. Clearly, if futures fall just little bit, or remain stable, you will end with a loss equal to the difference in the cost of the two puts and the money obtained from the sale of the put at the higher strike. For example, if December bond futures are at 105, and you sell a 106 put at 1-45, and buy two 104 puts at 0-60, you will have an initial net cash outflow of $171.88. If the final December settlement price is 104, you will have a net maximum loss of $469— $297 from the loss that would occur on the 106 put if the price settles at 104-00, plus the $172 differential in the value of the option sold versus those bought. The 104 puts will be worth zero. This will give you a break-even price of 103-17 (see Table 18.2).

Clearly, you would not want to use this strategy if you expected only a minor correction to the major trend. While this strategy is risk limiting, it can still result in substantial losses. In order for it to pay off, you need a substantial reversal in prices. Nevertheless, it is loss limiting and, when used with moderation and with capital conservation principles in place, keeps you capable of being wrong and still available to continue participating in the market when that major change in trend occurs.

Table 18.2 Put Ratio Back Spread

Bond Futures Price 105-00		
Sell 1 Bond 106 Puts @ 1 45/64	=	$1,703
Buy 2 Bond 104 Puts @ 60/64 = 937.50 × 2	=	1,875
Net Cash Outflow	=	172
Futures Price @ Maturity = 106		
106 Put Value = 0	Net =	+ $1,703
104 Put Value = 0	Net =	– $1,875
	Net	– $ 172
Futures Price @ Maturity = 104		
106 Put Value = 2,000 – 1,703	=	–$297
104 Put Value = 0		0
Initial Net Cash Outlay	=	–$172
	Net Loss =	–$469

This strategy works equally well on the long side and for any commodity. That would be called a call ratio back-spread. You would be shorting one call at a particular strike and buying two calls at a higher strike.

MORE ON SPREADS

One interesting and unique spread trading idea is using futures to synthesize a physical production or processing activity. Three examples come to mind: the soybean crush, the paper feedlot, and the oil "crack" spread.

The Crush

The crush refers to a three-way spread involving the purchase of soybeans and the sale of soybean oil and soybean meal in the same ratio as those two products are represented when one crushes soybeans.

Assume you calculate the economic cost of buying soybeans, crushing them (processing them through a soybean mill), and selling the two resultant outputs, soybean oil and soybean meal, and find that given today's interest rates and profit margins, etc., cost 36¢ per unit. Assume also that the futures show a differential of 42¢. If your calculations are correct, then economic forces will eventually cause the futures differential to fall back toward 36¢, because people will buy soybean futures and sell the meal and oil futures, then take delivery of the beans, crush them, and deliver the oil and meal in satisfaction of the futures. As this happens, the differential between 42¢ and 36¢ will narrow.

The Paper Feedlot

The paper feedlot refers to a complex spread that balances the major factors of a cattle feeding operation. Feedlot operators buy feeder calves and they buy feed which is consumed by the cattle, and, five months later, they sell fat cattle. During that period, a 600-pound calf grows into a 1,000- to 1,100-pound steer, after consuming roughly about 45 bushels of grain. This spread would involve the purchase of four feeder cattle contracts and three corn contracts, and the sale of seven live cattle contracts.

The June live cattle/May feeder cattle spread is an example of a seasonal market tendency. Historically, this spread works well from early March to the end of April, but as one might expect, actual trading situations tend to differ from year to year; hence, what worked in 1987 doesn't necessarily repeat itself in 1992. To identify these seasonal tendencies, one should analyze at least 10 years of data in order to get an idea of the expected probability that those tendencies will repeat, identify the time of the year in which they tend to repeat, and establish the time to enter into the position. Using the moving averages, try to enter slightly before the time you actually expect the ideal entry time to occur. Once that process is complete, you need to fine-tune the timing for entry. One successful spread trader I know uses simple five- or seven-day moving averages lagged by several days to filter out whipsaw.

One could use the same simple moving average systems for exiting the strategy. Money-limit stops should also be used to exit in advance of the time when you expect the seasonal move to end. As with all these things, one needs to watch and study patterns, evaluate the history, and then develop various spread-specific indicators that are useful to the trader and with which the trader is comfortable.

The "Crack"

The "crack" involves the purchase of three crude oil contracts and the sale of two gasoline contracts and one heating oil contract. It is roughly equivalent to running an oil refinery. You buy crude oil, refine it, and get fuel oil and gasoline. Traditionally this is called the 3-2-1 spread (see Figure 18.2). This can be stepped up to a more appropriate ratio called the 5-3-2, capturing the reality of refining relationships more closely.

Traders have to realize that despite the conventional wisdom of spreads, these spreads are neither risk-free nor loss-proof. Lower margins for these spreads do not obscure their speculative nature. A major risk in these trades comes from execution risk. It is not always possible to execute these transactions simultaneously at the appropriate prices or in the desired quantities. That's especially true in cattle. In the case of soybean and energy spreads, traders can specify in advance that they are trading

Figure 18.2 2:1:1 Crack and 3:2:1 Crack Spreads (weekly data)

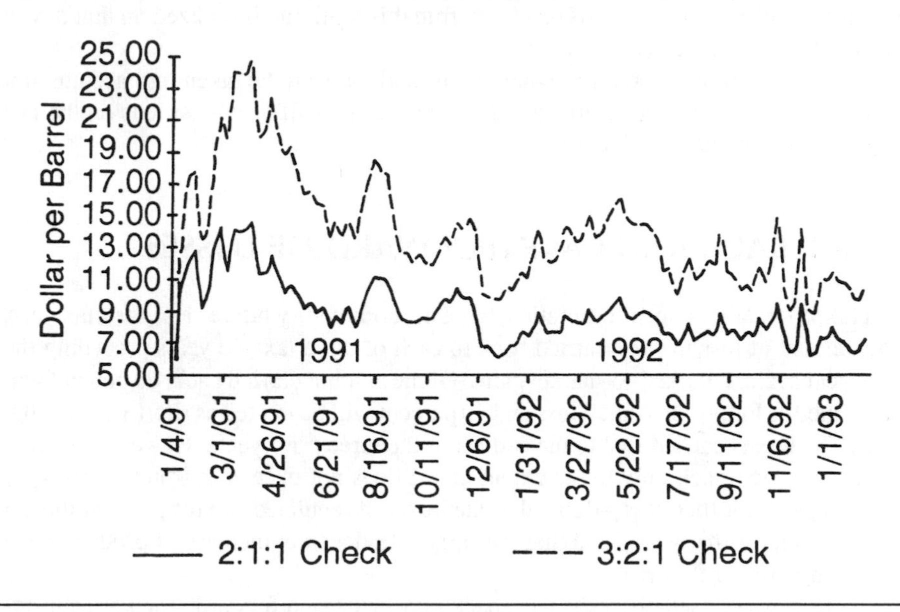

a 5-3-2 or a 3-2-1 and trade the spread directly. In the case of cattle, however, traders must work into three or four positions at two different exchanges. That leaves considerable room for slippage and risk.

SPREADING AND TAXES

The Tax and Revenue Act of 1981 specifies that:

a. Futures transactions have no required holding period.

b. Any gain or loss in futures contracts be treated as 60 percent long-term capital gain or loss and 40 percent short-term capital gain or loss. This ratio applies irrespective of the length of time the futures position is held.

c. Futures losses can be carried back three years against futures gains or carried forward against securities gains.

The tax act marks all commodity futures contracts to market at year-end and treats all of these "unrealized" gains and losses as if 60 percent of the capital gains and losses on them were long-term and 40 percent were short-term "realized" gains or losses; i.e., each futures contract is repriced daily to reflect the market's official closing price. The profit or loss resulting from this repricing is realized on that day in the equity of the investor's account.

The tax rules, therefore, require gains and losses to be taken into account not only when futures positions are closed out, but also on all open positions on the last business day of each taxable year.

CARRYBACK AND CARRYFORWARD OF LOSSES

If a taxpayer, other than a corporation, has a net commodity futures loss for a tax year, the amount of loss may be carried back to each of three taxable years preceding the loss year against marked-to-market gains. Of the amount carried back, 60 percent will be treated as long-term capital loss and 40 percent will be treated as short-term capital loss. The loss is carried first to the earliest of the three prior years. However, the loss may be carried back only to the extent that it does not exceed the "net commodity futures gain" for that year—defined as the lesser of regulated futures gains or the net capital gain for that year—and that the carryback does not increase or produce a net operating loss for that year.

Losses not used up by the carryback may be carried forward. They are considered as 60 percent long-term and 40 percent short-term capital losses and are carried forward under existing rules related to capital losses generally. Carryback of losses may not be available for investors in stocks, bonds, options, and other alternative investments. It is another advantage that exists for investing in commodity and financial futures. Check with your tax advisor on all the rules and regulations. They change.

SUMMARY

In conclusion, then, several points are worth reiterating:

1. Certain normal price relationships exist between futures contracts for the same commodity, based on time, quality, and location differences between the contracts. Because these natural economic factors tie pieces together, the premiums and discounts between futures have approximate natural limits placed on them. Spread transactions to take advantage of these natural relationships can be relatively low-risk yet profitable transactions.
2. Unless the price differences between two contracts are related to natural economic bonds, the risks in spread transactions may be very high. These natural bonds are extremely weak in perishable commodities. Hence, it is

wise to study commodity futures price relationships with respect to time, location, and quality differences before instituting a spreading program. This necessitates reviewing past price transactions and studying marketing patterns for the physical commodity.

3. In nearly all spread transactions, commercial traders have a distinct advantage over public speculators. Commercial traders have easy access to the actual commodity and the facilities necessary for storage, processing, and disposal should they actually decide to give or receive delivery in order to realize their profit from the spread. It is generally a wise practice, therefore, for speculators to liquidate futures positions prior to delivery, unless they have made specific arrangements to accept delivery and hold the product for re-delivery later.

4. Spreading is far from riskless. The low margins required for spread transactions can result in small gains or losses in absolute terms but can have the same proportionate impact on the value of the margin investment as a larger swing in an outright position that requires higher margins.

5. When spreading, try to spread approximately the same dollar amounts on each side of the transaction. Frequently, the contracts will not be of equal value, particularly in inter-commodity spreads. If they aren't of approximately equal value, you may end up in the unfortunate position of having a gain on the small side and a loss on the larger side, which nets out to a pretty good-sized loss. You'll be right, but you'll lose money. You'll win the battle but lose the war.

6. Do not yield to the temptation of establishing a spread in an attempt to recover from a losing outright position. Such tactics virtually always backfire. The spread transaction will not offset the loss, but will only initiate a new position which could work to compound the loss.

7. Consult first and often with your tax advisor. Spreading can be profitable and should be considered as a possible part of every trader's strategy and trading plan. It can hold relatively low risk in certain circumstances. For the beginning trader, spreads in low-risk situations are one of the best ways to learn about the market without being subject to the possibility of sharp market losses.

Chapter 19

Financial Futures— An Introduction

We are all familiar with the dollar bill. We recognize and accept it as payment for debts. These dollar bills are simply pieces of paper manufactured by our federal government and declared by it to be legal tender for the payment of taxes and other debts.

In the commodity futures world, money has always been important as a medium of exchange. In recent years, however, it has taken on even more importance as a tradable "commodity."

The opening of foreign currency and interest rate futures in Chicago has made every commodity trader realize that money is also a commodity and that it, too, has a price just like everything else. Money's price is quoted in two ways: (1) A foreign exchange rate, reflecting the purchasing power of one country's money relative to another country's and (2) an interest rate price, reflecting the value of money as an income-producing asset, and any price quoted at any time will reflect some elements of both.

Just as the value of a bushel of wheat fluctuates relative to the value of a bushel of corn, so too does the value of the U.S. dollar fluctuate relative to the value of the French franc. This price for money is called an exchange rate and represents a sort of external price other countries are willing to pay for our money.

Just as wheat may be used to produce flour, money may be used to earn income by lending it to people who, say, build houses. The price of money here is the interest rate cost of borrowing it. This interest rate price for money reflects the value sellers (lenders) and buyers (borrowers) place on the use of money for a certain period of time. In both cases—the exchange rate price and the interest rate price—supply, demand, and political events determine the level of price.

Money is the ultimate commodity, and no commodity trader's education is complete without an understanding of the futures market for money. Indeed, the money futures markets are the most fascinating and the largest of all. The next few chapters will provide you with a very basic introduction to these markets. This chapter will give an introduction to the role of money in the general economy. An understanding of that role is essential to evaluate the price movements for money. Subsequent chapters will discuss foreign currency trading, Treasury bond and note futures, Eurodollar futures, and stock index futures.

MONEY

If we did not have money, goods would be exchanged through barter, an inefficient and time-consuming process. If a person wanted to trade his output with someone else, he would first have to search among other willing sellers until he found an opposite party with a product he wanted. Second, the two parties would then have to agree on a price representing equivalent values. Even if they agreed that three chickens and two hogs were equivalent to one cow in value, one party might end up with two hogs more than he wanted.

Man, in his wisdom, realized at some point in his development that an intermediate good, which everybody could readily recognize and accept in exchange for all other goods, might make for a lot fewer headaches in bargaining and doing business. Thus, money was born. Producers could sell their output in exchange for the intermediate good (money) to anyone who wanted to buy. They would not need to waste time looking for someone who had a product they actually wanted. Prices of all goods could be expressed in terms of the intermediate good and the amount of payment could be matched to the price. No longer would a fellow get more hogs than he really wanted. He could take the intermediate good and buy precisely the number of hogs and chickens he desired.

Money, as shown above, performs several functions. It serves as a medium of exchange. Everybody accepts it as payment. It serves as a store of value, it can be used to buy things. It serves as a unit of measurement—$1,000 will buy one horse.

Through the years, many different things, ranging from cigarettes to gold, have served as money. At times, more than one intermediate good has been used as money by various countries of the world. But this reduced the efficiency of transactions because producers had to quote the price for each product in terms of each of the monies. Since it was virtually impossible to maintain a stable relationship between the various monies, most countries reverted back to the use of a single intermediate good as money. Today all countries of the world use paper money.

Although all countries use paper money, each country tends to use a different name for its money (e.g., dollar, peso, franc, etc.), and because of differences in political stabilities, natural resources, levels of workers' productivity, opportunities for foreign investment, etc., some countries' money commands a higher price relative to the U.S. dollar than other countries' money.

Some countries, notably European, have recently made great efforts to unite their countries into a unified trading group with a single currency and a single central bank. The currency was called the ECU (European Currency Unit). The process of unification toward a single currency ran into problems in 1992, and resulted in the break-up of their currency agreement. In the fall of 1992, the world's eyes were on France as the French prepared to vote on the Maastricht Referendum. The referendum was to decide whether the French people desired to join a more unified European union. Just a few days before the vote was to take place, Scandinavian countries' currencies came under pressure in the Exchange Rate Mechanism (ERM), an agreement by the countries to maintain certain value relationships among their currencies. Finland and Sweden had already raised their interest rates and still they couldn't maintain the value of their currency relative to the Deutsche Mark. They found their foreign exchange reserves depleted. They had borrowed all they could from other central banks. In a last ditch effort, Sweden raised its short-term interest rate by enormous amounts, to as high as 75 percent. This put pressure on other currencies, especially the sterling, pushing it toward its floor in the ERM, thus forcing Britain and Italy to raise their rates to extremely high levels. But with Germany refusing to lower its rate in order to help maintain the values of these currencies, the pressure on the system become too great, and Finland had to float the marke, which in turn affected the Swedish krona. This ultimately led to Britain having to withdraw from the ERM and devalue its currency. Some of Britain's problems in the ERM arose from the fact that it negotiated terms for entry into the ERM at levels that clearly overvalued sterling relative to the other ERM currencies, thus to a certain extent, Britain created its own problems.

All this turmoil in the currency markets created great economic volatility. Stock markets crashed around the world, and trade and political relationships of all types became unsettled. Some tradeers made and some governments lost large fortunes.The effort toward a single European currency then has clearly sowed: Countries like their independence and having their own currency clearly helps maintain an independent identity.

MONEY IN THE ECONOMY

Money is the grease that makes an economy run smoothly. Imagine the economy of a country as one big machine. This machine represents all the mills, factories, farms, offices, and shops that turn out the goods and services consumed in the society. Everyone with a job works on this big machine. Some are repairmen, some are operators, but all of them are producing goods and services the people use.

Naturally, all of the workers are paid and these workers use their money to buy things produced by the machine. Thus, a nice smooth circle is completed of people working on the machine, being paid by the machine and buying their goods and services from the machine.

If the people buy all that is produced, then everything is in balance and the economy for this country is healthy and stable. Sometimes, however, imbalances appear and interrupt the smooth flow of labor, money, and goods and services. When this happens, prices change and we get increases or decreases in economic activity.

These imbalances may arise because of leakages in flows of spending by the machine or by the people. For example, people may decide not to spend all of their money on goods and services but may decide instead to *save* (hoard) some of their income. Thus, they do not buy as many cars and television sets. Since the flow of money back to the machine is reduced, the machine slows down its production. Fewer people are needed to run the machine, and total income and total buying power are reduced. Economists refer to this set of affairs as a recession.

Usually, however, these savings find their way back to the machine through the hands of businessmen who borrow the funds from the people and re-inject the money back into the spending flow by increasing the size of the machine, i.e., building plants, or buying new equipment and inventory. Depending on how much of the savings businessmen want from people, they raise or lower the price (interest rate) they are willing to pay people for the use of their money. These activities, which are analogous to modernizing and expanding the machine, create new jobs and increase total income, thus bringing the flows of spending back toward a balance.

A second imbalance, or drain on the flows, can be caused by taxes collected by the government. Taxes are paid to local, state, and national governments and have the same slowdown effect that savings have. However, just as with savings, the tax money finds its way back into the system because the government hires people and buys goods and services.

Just as increases in savings and taxes can create imbalances in the system through withdrawals, imbalances can also be created by people refusing to save and simply demanding more goods and services from the government. The government can either refuse the demands or pay for them by raising taxes or by printing money which is then given to the machine in payment for the goods and services. Refusing the demands and raising taxes are not always popular with the people; hence, governments frequently opt to print more money. Frequently, this is more money than is necessary to keep the machine running smoothly. In order to meet this output, the machine foregoes repairs and hires untrained workers. All the income is used to produce goods to meet current demand and none is used for expanding, rebuilding, and updating the machine. This results in reduced efficiency. Ultimately, costs increase and the machine reaches the limits that it can produce. To alleviate this, consumers need to be convinced to postpone their purchases. This is best done by raising prices. This is referred to as inflation. Hence, when too much money gets into the system, the result is inflation.

MONEY, THE MACHINE, AND THE BANKING SYSTEM

It should be obvious from the above that if the flows of money spending match the flows of goods and services produced, prices will remain stable and the machine will run smoothly. If imbalances in flows of money occur, the machine slows down or works at such a furious pace it generates more momentum than it can handle. Thus, the amount of money and the smoothness with which it flows from individuals back to the machine through the land, labor, and capital become most important in determining the health of the economy.

In order to make this all flow smoothly in an economy, every country has a banking system through which they facilitate the flow of funds and adjust the supply of money. Banks serve as depositories for people's savings. They act as intermediaries by making these savings available to businessmen for investment expenditures and the vital function of furnishing business and government with credit. Through their lending function, banks are able to adjust the money supply to make the flow of spending match the flows of goods and services, land, labor, and capital.

Naturally, most governments do not allow banks to operate willy-nilly in this system. Instead, the governments establish a central bank which acts to regulate the actions of commercial banks and to manipulate the expansion and contraction of the money supply. Thus, the ultimate control of the money supply rests with the government.

In the U.S., the Federal Reserve Board (the "Fed"), through its network of regional federal reserve banks, acts as the central bank. Its methods of operation differ only in degree from central banks of other countries. The Fed operates to control the money supply by controlling the amount of excess reserves in the banking system. Long ago banks found it prudent to maintain reserves against their deposits in order to meet the normal cash withdrawals of their customers. Current federal law requires them to maintain certain minimum reserves. The amounts over and above the minimums needed are called "excess" and are funds available for lending. The Fed controls excess reserves by:

a. Adjusting the required ratio of reserves to deposits. By lowering the required reserve ratio, the Federal Reserve decreases the amount of reserves that member banks are required to maintain in their accounts and makes additional reserves available to the member banks. Thus, a reduction in the required reserve ratio from 12 percent to 10 percent would increase the amount of excess reserves and thereby increase the amount of money available for lending. By raising the required ratio, the opposite would occur.

b. The purchase or sale of government securities, T-bills, bonds, etc. When the government buys the securities, they increase member bank reserves and vice versa.

c. Through loans of reserves to member banks.

A commercial bank may be short on reserves relative to its demand for loans and may then borrow from the Federal Reserve. The bank will pay a rate of interest known as the discount rate. The Fed can set the discount rate at whatever level it wants. By raising this rate of interest, borrowing is made more expensive and commercial banks will be less inclined to borrow reserves. They will have to raise the rate of interest to customers, and as the price of credit to customers goes up, usually the demand for such credit will go down. Conversely, by reducing the discount rate, borrowing is made less expensive and banks will be more inclined to borrow reserves and make loans to their customers.

Thus, the central bank of a government acts to regulate the actions of commercial banks and thereby regulates the supply of money to accomplish specific objectives related to levels of employment, personal income, and price stability; i.e., they regulate the machine.

The extent to which the central bank accomplishes these objectives has a great influence on the interest rate price and the international price (foreign exchange rate) of a country's money. The alert trader will watch closely the monetary policy of a country and the action taken with each of the monetary tools. They are among the most important elements in determining long-run strength or weakness in a currency.

INFLATION

Money by itself is really useless. It takes on value only when it is used as a medium of exchange. Thus, the value of money lies in what it can buy.

Ten years ago, one dollar would buy a half gallon of milk, a newspaper, and a package of gum. Today, it won't even buy a half gallon of milk. Ten years from now, it might buy more or less of the same things.

The dollar itself doesn't change. It is still four quarters, 10 dimes, 20 nickels, or 100 pennies. But what the dollar will buy does change. How does that change affect the foreign exchange rate and domestic interest rates? The explanation lies in inflation.

Inflation in a country weakens the domestic purchasing power of the currency for the consumer in that country. People on pensions and others on fixed incomes find that their dollars buy less. People with savings accounts find that inflation reduces the value of their savings.

The Inflationary Process

Monetary economists trace the inflationary process through as follows: First, a change in the rate of the growth in the money supply causes a change in people's incomes in the same direction about six to nine months later. This money "burns a hole in the pocket" and people rush out trying to spend their extra income. It usually takes about another six to nine months before this increased demand catches up with the available supply and prices start to rise. Thus, about a year to a year and a half after the money supply increases, one can expect to see a rise in prices. The Consumer Price Index reflects the general prices of things people buy and thus it becomes the most handy means of measuring inflation. The extent to which the money supply is increased, of course, will affect the extent to which incomes increase, which in turn will affect the amount of money people have to spend and their ability to bid up prices. So a small change in the money supply beyond the amount necessary to maintain economic growth, employment, and stable prices will probably result in small amounts of inflation.

Inflation and Interest Rates

Inflation rates become important in forecasting interest rates because the expectations about levels of inflation get built into the price for borrowing money. Look at it this way. Ten years ago the dollar would buy a newspaper, a half gallon of milk, and a package of gum. Inflation (rising prices) has caused the domestic purchasing power of the dollar to decline so that today it takes two dollars to buy the same amount and quality of goods. So, if you loaned someone a dollar 10 years ago, and if the average annual rate of inflation was 10 percent, when he pays it back today it is worth only about half as much as when you loaned it to him. If you had charged him 5 percent per year interest, you would have collected $.50 in interest and, counting that, would find your dollar worth only about three-fourths as much as 10 years ago.

Had you anticipated the 10 percent average annual inflation rate, you would have asked for at least a 10 percent interest charge in order to maintain your purchasing power over the 10-year period. More likely you would have asked for 15 percent interest, reasoning that you expect that money to provide a 5 percent real rate of return after accounting for the 10 percent expected inflation. It is this latter way that businessmen and bankers react. Thus, expected inflation rates get built into interest rates. That is exactly what happened in the late 1960s and late 1970s.

Inflation and Foreign Exchange Rates

Internationally, the purchasing power of the currency may be reduced if the inflation rate in the home country is greater than in other countries. So the important consideration from a foreign exchange trader's standpoint is the *relative* rate of inflation. If Italy inflates faster than the U.S., Italian products will become more expensive for Americans. Further, Italians will switch from the higher-priced Italian products to the lower-priced U.S. products. Thus, Italian exports to the U.S. will decrease and American exports to Italy will increase. All of this will reduce the demand for the Italian lira and increase the demand for the U.S. dollar.

Therefore, you should watch closely the relative rates of inflation in the U.S. compared to the other countries of the world. If you see that U.S. inflation, compared to Italian inflation, is consistently different and by a large amount, you can see that ultimately the exchange rate between the two currencies is going to have to change to reflect the reduced international purchasing power of the Italian lira. When they do ultimately change, the change may or may not (more likely not) reflect the exact changes in the relative purchasing power of the two currencies.

Of course, the relative rate of inflation is not the only factor to consider in forecasting exchange rates. It waxes and wanes, being a major factor at times, and at other times being a minor factor, overshadowed by other events. Certainly, in the years from 1945 to 1972, when the world was on a "fixed rate" system, the various governments' determination to maintain a fixed exchange rate overshadowed the impact of inflation rate differentials. **Note:** The next chapter will discuss these and other basic elements of foreign exchange trading.

Thus, the money supply and rates of inflation become key elements in understanding and forecasting prices of foreign currency futures and interest rate futures. As early indicators of things to come in money supply trends, watch the action of the Federal Reserve Board, the Wholesale and Consumer Price Indexes, and fundamental economic reports (e.g., Gross National Product, employment, industrial production, etc.) released monthly by the various departments of the U.S. Government.

In summary, through the open, competitive futures market, the general public has an opportunity to make known its hopes, fears, and beliefs about the value of a currency. And with daily reports from a futures exchange of trading volume and price fluctuations, there is a public weathervane providing daily signals of the true value of a currency giving the public a clearer insight into the effect that political actions, monetary policies, balance of trade, and other factors have on the economics of world commerce. All of this, of course, provides for differences of opinion and trading opportunities.

Chapter 20

Money—Trading the Ultimate Commodity

If you buy a pound of cheese from Wisconsin or a gallon of California wine, you naturally pay for it in dollars. The cheese manufacturer and the wine producer expect to be paid in dollars because their expenses and living costs are all settled in dollars. Within the U.S. such single currency transactions are made without a second thought.

On the other hand, if you wanted to buy an English topcoat directly from the British manufacturer, matters get more complicated. You must pay in British pounds (pound sterling) rather than in dollars. Similarly, an Englishman desiring Wisconsin cheese must somehow get U.S. dollars to pay the American producer, if he wants to buy the cheese directly. Most Americans have never seen a British pound note and would understandably be reluctant to accept it as payment if they could not be sure of converting it into U.S. dollars.

Clearly, then, if such transactions are to occur, there must be some means whereby the American who desires to get pounds sterling to pay for a topcoat can convert his dollars into British money and vice versa for the Englishman who wants to buy Wisconsin cheddar.

Simply stated, the conversion of one money into another is the sale of one currency for another. Money is treated like any other commodity. It is bought and sold at a price. This price is called the *foreign exchange rate.*

Thus, when you read that the foreign exchange rate for the deutschemark is $.4500, this means that the price of one deutschemark is 45¢ in U.S. dollars.

Very often, you see headlines which announce the dollar is "weak" or some other currency is "strong." When the dollar is said to be weak, this means that people are selling the dollar and buying other currencies; that is, the dollar price of the other currencies has increased. For example, if the price of one deutschemark goes from 52¢ to 53¢, the dollar has weakened and the deutschemark has strengthened.

This chapter will explain some of the basic elements of the foreign exchange market, including why it exists and how it works. It will cover some of the fundamental aspects of foreign exchange, including a discussion of the recent history of the international monetary system, the development of the futures market in foreign exchange, the economic indicators that help you analyze the relative strength or weakness of a particular country's currency, and some very basic introductory concepts about hedging in foreign exchange.

THE PRICE OF MONEY

Foreign exchange transactions are usually done through a foreign exchange trader located at a bank. Modern-day foreign exchange dealings became common with the development in 11th century Europe of the Champaigne fairs where merchants bought and sold goods in their counterparts' currencies. Bankers attended the fairs to act as money changers, the modern-day equivalent of the foreign exchange trader.

The price of a currency is determined in the same way you determine the price for any other commodity—by the forces of supply and demand. If the people in the U.S. begin to demand more English-made products, the demand for the pound sterling goes up; as the demand for the pound sterling increases, Americans will have to pay higher prices in order to induce holders of sterling to sell. Conversely, if the British developed an overwhelming taste for U.S. goods, they would have to sell more and more pounds sterling for the U.S. dollars to pay for the products they bought. This increase in the supply of sterling being offered for sale would cause the price to drop relative to dollars.

RECENT HISTORY OF INTERNATIONAL MONETARY SYSTEM

Of course, all of the above sounds quite simple and straightforward, but the basic forces of supply and demand are not always allowed to operate freely in the foreign exchange market. Persians in the 6th century attempted to thwart the basic forces of supply and demand by fixing an immutable gold/silver ratio. It failed.

A more recent attempt to fix prices was made in 1944 when a group of economic and finance experts from 47 Western nations met in a New Hampshire resort town called Bretton Woods. Their purpose in meeting was to develop a post-war plan for reconstruction of world trade and national economies. Out of that meeting came a plan for an international monetary system. It had four key points:

1. The establishment of a super-national agency called the International Monetary Fund whose purpose was to oversee the international monetary system and to assure its smooth functioning.
2. The establishment of par values or fixed exchange rates for currencies and an agreement among the countries that they would manipulate the supply and demand for their currencies in such a way as to maintain that rate. They did this by entering the market to buy their currency when its price fell 1 percent (in practice, 3/4 of 1 percent) below the declared par and by selling their currency when the price rose 1 percent (in practice, 3/4 of 1 percent) above the par value.
3. The agreement that the U.S. dollar would be the kingpin of the system and other countries would accept and hold it for payment of international debts.
4. The agreement that the U.S. dollar was as good as gold and that any time a foreign government wanted to exchange its dollars for gold it could do so at the U.S. Treasury at the rate of $35 an ounce.

This system was in effect from 1944 to 1971, and world trade did indeed expand during those years. It expanded largely because the U.S. was willing to run its international business affairs at a loss. The U.S. continually imported more than it exported. It paid for its imports by running the printing presses and printing dollars. As long as others were willing to accept paper dollars, the U.S. received fine wines, nice automobiles, radios, televisions, etc., in return.

Ultimately, however, there were a lot more dollars held by foreigners than the U.S. held gold. Foreigners had from time to time turned in their dollars for gold and gradually the U.S. gold supply disappeared until clearly the dollar was overvalued in terms of gold.

On Aug. 15, 1971, President Nixon declared that the U.S. would no longer abide by the Bretton Woods agreement of 1944. Accordingly, he said that the dollar was no longer convertible into gold; that is, that foreigners would no longer be able to turn their dollars in to the U.S. Treasury and obtain gold. Further, he said that the exchange rate for the dollar would no longer be fixed, instead it would be allowed to "float"; that is, it would be determined by free market forces.

The dollar floated just like a rock—straight down. It was devalued. Since that time, except for a brief period in 1972 when fixed rates were again reinstated, the value of the dollar has been determined more or less by free market forces. The value of groups of other currencies, notably European countries, have been fixed (within a range) in relation to each other, but allowed to float as a group against the dollar. This effort has periodically come apart and required renegotiation. The ERM effort noted in the previous chapter is an example.

The result of a devaluation of the dollar (or any currency) is that the relative purchasing power of the U.S. dollar changes, sometimes dramatically. Imports into the U.S. suddenly cost more (it takes more dollars to buy the same amount of deutsche marks), and exports from the U.S. are lower priced (fewer deutschemarks equal the dollar price). For example, between June 1991 and June 1992, the value of a bushel of wheat at Chicago increased by 26 percent in U.S. dollars and 40 percent in deutschemarks. Thus, it took about 14 percent fewer deutschemarks to buy the same bushel of U.S. wheat in 1992 than it took in 1991. Put another way, the same number of deutsche marks would buy 14 percent more U.S. wheat in 1992 than in 1991.

THE SPOT MARKET

The buying and selling of spot currencies (for immediate delivery or use) is accomplished through banks. Banks all over the world have accounts with each other in order to serve their customers, many of whom are multinational companies that deal in many different currencies. Every day these banks make deposits and withdrawals for their customers. These deposits or withdrawals result in transfers of funds from one country to another and, therefore, the conversion of one currency into another. Hence, banks worldwide are constantly buying and selling currencies and providing a ready spot market.

This buying and selling is done by telephone and teletype. If a dealer in Frankfurt, Germany, wants to buy dollars and sell deutschemarks, he will probably call several New York banks and ask each for its rate. When he finds a bank with a rate that suits him, they agree to the trade and exchange specially coded telegrams confirming the transaction. The bank in Frankfurt will then credit the account of the New York bank with the proper amount of deutschemarks.

If a businessman desires to convert dollars into deutschemarks to pay a bill, he can simply notify his banker and, after receiving proper information, the banker will see that the proper German bank account is credited. For example, if a businessman imports German bicycles and needs deutschemarks to pay for them, he simply notifies his banker who, in turn, contacts other bankers in Germany or elsewhere in the world to buy the deutschemarks for the importer and have them deposited in the German bank account of the bicycle manufacturer. The U.S. bank will then deduct the dollar cost of the deutschemarks from the U.S. account of the importer. The importer will never see the deutschemarks; the bankers will simply debit and credit the appropriate accounts.

EVALUATING FOREIGN EXCHANGE RATES

What makes foreign exchange rates fluctuate from day to day? Why does the U.S. dollar buy less in Germany in 1992 than it did in 1986? Would an increase in the general level of interest rates in England be bullish or bearish? For whom?

These questions and many more are of great importance to anyone dealing in foreign exchange. And, as you may have guessed, the answers are not easily determined. Fundamental analysis of the money markets is more difficult than fundamental analysis in other commodities. There is a definite lack of good data, and the markets are highly sensitive to political elements. Yet, over the long run, fundamental economic factors will be the dominant considerations in determining the value of currency. In the short run and intermediate term, technical analysis can be very helpful. Indeed, the currency markets may be best suited to chart analysis.

It is not possible to cover all of the factors in detail here; however, we will touch on some of the highlights of each of them. For those who would like to dig deeper, there is a considerable amount of literature available at no cost from the futures exchanges like the IMM, banks, brokerage houses, etc.

International Trade and Capital Balances

The single most important long-run indicator of impending exchange rate changes today is the country's trade balance, also called the balance of goods and services. It reflects the relative value of merchandise imports and exports.

If exports are greater than imports, there is a trade surplus. This is a sign of currency strength. A shift in the trade balance to a deficit (imports greater than exports), on the other hand, is an indication of currency weakness.

A second important indicator is the official monetary reserves of a country, including gold, special drawing rights (SDRs) on account at the International Monetary Fund, and foreign currency holdings. These reserves indicate the ability of the country to meet its international obligations for example, its ability to repay loans, to finance imports, and to intervene in the foreign exchange market to support (manipulate the value of) its currency. Official reserves should be building up when there is a trade surplus. Official reserves may, but not necessarily will, be falling when there is a trade deficit.

A third important international economic indicator is the capital balances of a country, including the direct foreign investment and the short-term speculative funds that flow to or from a country. Capital movements are very sensitive to short-term interest rates.

With the almost instantaneous speed of the world's financial system, funds may be transferred nearly anywhere in the world. These funds move in response to changes in the relative interest rates. Capital flows can have tremendous impact on short-term exchange rates. If three-month interest rates in Canada increase to 1 percent over U.S. rates, people will send their money to Canada. As they do so, they must sell U.S. dollars and buy Canadian dollars. An increase in a country's capital account reflects an increase in demand for assets denominated in that currency, such as time deposits or Treasury bills. This increased demand indicates fundamental strength in the currency. Conversely, a deficit in capital accounts indicates a weakening in the demand and expectation that the price of the currency will fall.

Domestic Economic Factors

The underlying influences of the balance of trade, official reserves, and capital flows are the domestic interrelationships between income, prices, and interest rates.

Among the factors to consider in evaluating the domestic health of a country are:

a. The rate of real (after adjustment for inflation) growth in gross national product. Steady growth is an overall indicator of good economic health for an economy.

b. The rate of growth in money supply and interest rate levels. These are important indicators of future economic conditions. The short-term interest rate differential is important in short-term capital flows. Such flows directly affect the demand for a currency.

c. The rate of inflation relative to the index of industrial capacity utilization. Differing rates of inflation in different countries is another very important factor affecting the price of a particular currency. The end result of inflation is an erosion of purchasing power, which ultimately means a weakening of the currency if other countries are not experiencing the same amount of inflation. High inflation with high utilization suggests that inflation is likely to stay high because "the machine" is already working at capacity, yet the people are demanding more goods. This would suggest a weak currency.

The general price level of a country affects the exports of that country. The U.S. is a good example. In the mid-1980s it had nearly priced itself out of the international market in some goods while Japan, on the other hand, making many similar goods, was able to sell at lower prices. This reduced the exports of the United States and increased the imports to the U.S. from Japan, creating an outflow of dollars and what economists call an "unfavorable" balance of trade. From 1986 to 1992, the dollar fell in value relative to many other currencies, but not proportionately with Japan.

Each country should be studied individually and then one country compared against another. Since the IMM futures contracts reflect other currencies relative to the U.S. dollar, other countries' expected and actual economic conditions should be compared to the U.S. and to each other. If the conditions seem more favorable to other countries relative to the U.S., sell the futures. If the conditions favor the U.S., buy the contract.

Political and Governmental Influences

Political and governmental activities affect exchange rates by helping or hindering the international trade of a country and thus its balance of trade. Study carefully such things as import taxes, negative interest rates (a favorite of the Swiss, this means you pay them interest on savings accounts instead of the other way around), interest equalization taxes, embargoes, etc.

The internal political stability of a country also bears on the issue. Even in the more well-established industrial nations of the world, the unsettling influence of political elections is reflected in the foreign exchange market. Major economic policy changes, as well as revaluations (up) or devaluations (down), are often made with an eye to the next election. A change in the political party in power very often brings a change in economic policy. Even the anticipation of a new party being elected to power can affect exchange rates, which leads us to the significance of expectations or what people think is going to happen.

Expectations

Timing is all important. Expectations about changes in price level and the timing of such changes can have a great impact on the market. Many observers, for example, expected the British pound to be devalued just before Britain entered the Common Market. Early in the year numerous money interests began to act in anticipation of the event, and the British government was forced to float the pound months before they would have liked to. Similarly, many people expected the Mexican peso to be devalued during the latter part of 1982 because a change of political administration would make it a convenient time to do so. The market anticipated the event, although not the exact magnitude, long in advance. The peso was devalued three times by about 90 percent during 1982.

INTEREST RATE ARBITRAGE

How would you like a deal where you borrow money at 10 percent, invest it at 8 percent, and make a profit on the deal? Sounds impossible, doesn't it? It's not. In fact, it's done regularly in the foreign exchange market.

To demonstrate, let's suppose your mother-in-law lends you $100,000 in order to get started on an investment on your own so you can support her daughter in the style to which she is accustomed. Let's say also that your mother-in-law isn't completely benign, and she charges you a rate of interest that is .5 percent over the bank's prime rate of 9.5 percent. That would be 10 percent (9.5 percent plus .5 percent).

First you talk to your brother-in-law who suggests you send the money to Canada to be invested in three-month commercial paper (Prime Finance Company) at 8 percent. You suggest that he must be crazy since you're borrowing at 10 percent. You wanted something conservative but not that conservative! Brother-in-law suggests you watch your tongue and let him finish his plan.

What he plans is to sell your U.S. $100,000 for spot Canadian dollars, assuming a rate of $.9944. The U.S. $100,000 will provide you with $100,563.15 Canadian dollars. He will then immediately buy an equivalent amount of Canadian commercial paper, due in 90 days, paying for it with the Canadian dollars, returning an annualized rate of 8 percent. You will hold the commercial paper for 90 days at which time it will mature and be redeemed for Canadian dollars.

Now comes the important point. If you wait until the Canadian commercial paper matures to sell Canadian dollars and obtain U.S. dollars again, your net rate of return may be greater than, less than, or equal to 8 percent, depending on what's happened to the U.S./Canadian dollar exchange rate. If the Canadian dollar has increased in value to, say, $1.0232, a 2.89 percent increase, the net annualized return on the transactions will be 19.56 percent. If it has decreased in value, the 8 percent will be reduced accordingly because you'll be selling the Canadian dollars for less than you originally paid for them. If the spot rate hasn't changed, you'll reap the 8 percent, minus transaction costs, of course, which are usually quite small.

Of course, you tell your brother-in-law you don't want to take the risks that your Canadian dollars will change in value during the time of your investment. Your brother-in-law explains there is a way to avoid that risk and calculate your exact return before you ever buy the Canadian dollars. "How's that?" you ask. By hedging, he says. By selling a futures contract now, you set the price you will receive for the Canadian dollars in 90 days and establish, therefore, the exact net rate of return on your investment.

He explains that at the present time a three-month futures for Canadian dollars is selling at a 2.49 percent annualized premium over the spot. Thus, you can buy the spot Canadian dollars today, immediately resell them for delivery in 90 days on a futures contract, and make a 2.49 percent annualized return on that transaction. The

Canadian dollars you buy today will not be delivered in fulfillment of the futures contract for 90 days, so you invest them in 90-day commercial paper, which yields an 8 percent annual return. The net on all the transactions then turns out to be 10.49 percent.

Now obviously, in the scenario described above, the young man is not going to get rich very fast, mostly because he's paying such a high rate of interest to his mother-in-law. If his mother-in-law were a little less greedy and would give him the money for a reduced interest rate, he'd obviously be doing better.

The procedure just described is referred to by foreign exchange traders as interest arbitrage. It's the purchase and sale of spot and futures in order to take advantage of differences in interest rates between the two countries.

This illustrates a very important principle in using the foreign exchange markets. That is, there's a very strong relationship between exchange rate movements and interest rate movements in different countries. The basic rule of thumb is, "At equilibrium, the currency of the higher (lower) interest rate country should be selling at a forward rate discount (premium) in terms of the lower (higher) interest rate country's currency."

Thus, if interest rates in Canada tend to be 3 percent below U.S. interest rates, you would expect a forward U.S./Canadian exchange rate to reflect a 3 percent discount for dollars. Market forces will assure this result (assuming certain other factors to be discussed below) because if the exchange rates don't reflect interest rate differentials (plus transactions costs) exactly, arbitrageurs like our friend above can make money by borrowing funds in the high interest rate country, transferring them to the low interest rate country, and hedging them on a transaction in the forward exchange market. If enough money moves from one country to another in this manner, the spot prices of the two currencies will change relative to the forward price until the spread between spot and futures exactly reflects the differences in interest rates between the two countries. At that point, the profit opportunities in transferring funds from one country to another will have disappeared, and the exchange rate between the two countries will be at what is called *interest rate parity.*

As noted above, some important assumptions have been made in order to show how interest rate arbitrage is conducted. It works only under certain conditions, including the following two:

a. Free flows of funds between the two countries concerned must be possible. In recent years, more and more countries have been instituting certain barriers and controls on the movement of capital into or out of their country. Obviously, if the controls are effective, great disparities between interest rate differentials and exchange rates may exist for long periods of time, and interest arbitrage will not be possible nor will exchange rates reflect interest rate differentials.

b. Expectations of a devaluation, revaluation, or of the imposition of capital controls on the currencies must be such that they do not outweigh the interest rate differential factor. Sometimes, people hold such strong expectations of changes in the exchange rate due to factors other than interest differentials that interest rate parity considerations are simply overwhelmed.

Hedged interest arbitrage transactions, like those described above, are virtually risk-free. The only major risk you take in those transactions is that a country will introduce strong capital controls that could prevent the fulfillment of the futures contract or the repatriation of the funds.

Opportunities for interest rate arbitrage appear frequently. People who are managing large sums of money, whether for corporate accounts or for personal investment, should become knowledgeable about interest arbitrage. In the years ahead, investment managers and advisors will need to be skillful at moving funds around the world to various security markets and financial centers. That sort of operation will require an understanding of foreign exchange markets and the concept of interest arbitrage.

CAPITAL CONTROLS

Capital controls (restrictions on the convertibility of domestic currency and foreign currency) come in many shapes and sizes and are designed to thwart arbitrage and free movement of money. They range from relatively simple taxes on holdings of foreign currency assets to burdensome bureaucratic rules covering the uses to which foreign currency can be put. Britain had very tight capital controls for 40 years until they were abolished in the late 1970s. The U.S. for many years after World War II used the interest equalization tax as a means of controlling capital flow. That tax was largely responsible for the enormous growth of the Eurodollar market. During the latter part of September 1992, when the European exchange rate mechanism (ERM) came under pressure, the Spanish government, which was one of the first to feel the pressures, announced new capital controls. The next day, Ireland did the same thing. Neither move was notably successful because investors panicked, and the stock markets in the various countries crashed, which only brought more ferocious selling of the currency and forced the break-up of the ERM.

Financial innovation and cheap rapid communication have made it much easier than ever before to evade capital controls, especially those that are of the clumsy bureaucratic rule type. Even the tightest controls let huge flows of capital leak through.

Nevertheless, given that capital controls were so popular for so many years between the 1940s and the 1980s, and given the current belief among government bureaucrats that it is extremely difficult to maintain semi-fixed exchange rates without capital controls, it is likely that greater pressure will be placed on governments to create new forms of capital controls in their efforts to stabilize exchange rates. They may even attempt a Bretton Woods style agreement again. If so, it too will ultimately fail.

Chapter 21

Understanding the "Yield Curve"

If you want to do an intelligent job trading the financial futures market, spend your time studying the yield curve.

In financial markets, yield refers to the annual rate of return on an investment. It is determined by relating the interest rate, the price paid and time remaining on the life of the investment.

For example, if you lend $100 for one year at 7 percent, the yield on that investment is 7 percent. If you invest $95 in a note that will mature at the end of one year and be worth $100, you have a yield of 5.26 percent (5 ÷ 95 = 5.26 percent).

Yields become important because they reflect interest rates in various money market investments. These interest rates reflect powerful linkages that connect the money market, bond market, stock market, mortgage market, and commodity markets. Money moves rapidly from one market to another, seeking its best return. That return is reflected in the yield.

A "yield curve" refers to the shape of the line you get when you plot yields of various Treasury securities—or any other homogeneous group of securities—against their various maturities. Normally, you plot maturity dates or time on the horizontal scale and yields on the vertical scale of the graph (as in Figure 21.1).

When a number of issues are plotted on the graph, you will see that a sort of pattern emerges from the placement of the dots. Draw a line through the dots so that most of them fall on the line. Those that don't should be distributed nearly evenly on either side of the line. Now you have a "yield curve" picture. Figure 21.1 reflects yields for government bonds and notes of various maturities.

WHY STUDY YIELD CURVES?

You should study yield curves for several major reasons. First it causes you to focus attention on the cash market, something which too few futures traders do. Cash market activity provides clues to price relationships in the futures market. Second, study of yield curves focuses attention on the concept of value, undervalue, and overvalue. The yield curve becomes a general guide for measuring individual value.

As you can readily see in Figure 21.1, not all the dots fall on the "curve." Those which do not fall on it are candidates to be investigated as possible buy/sell opportunities. Those represented by dots above the lines are relatively underpriced while those below the line are relatively overpriced.

Figure 21.1 Yield Curve

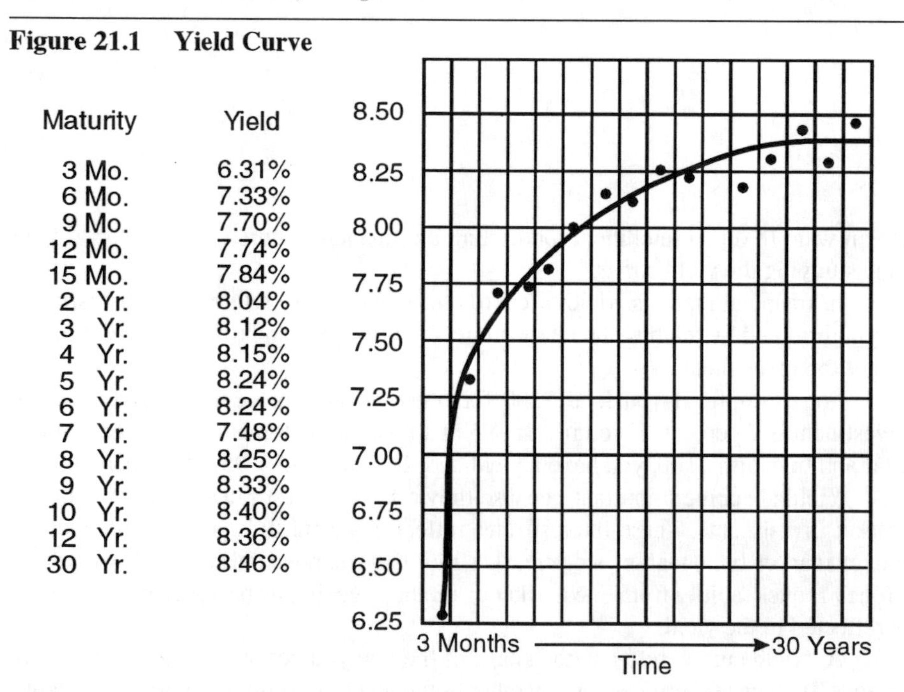

Maturity	Yield
3 Mo.	6.31%
6 Mo.	7.33%
9 Mo.	7.70%
12 Mo.	7.74%
15 Mo.	7.84%
2 Yr.	8.04%
3 Yr.	8.12%
4 Yr.	8.15%
5 Yr.	8.24%
6 Yr.	8.24%
7 Yr.	7.48%
8 Yr.	8.25%
9 Yr.	8.33%
10 Yr.	8.40%
12 Yr.	8.36%
30 Yr.	8.46%

Why the Differences?

Variations of this kind usually can be explained by several things:

1. Differences in coupon rates. Sometimes bonds that were issued many years ago for a special purpose may carry a very low coupon compared to current rates.
2. Difference in the supply of or demand for a particular issue. For example, sometimes particular bonds are in short supply because they are used for the creation of another security. Or because they have special uses, such as the old "flower bonds" which were eligible to be used to settle estate taxes at full value. In such cases, where there are only a few such issues around, the demand for them remains high, their price gets bid up and the yield falls.
3. Differences in the marketability of a particular issue. Trading in some issues is naturally more liquid than in others. Generally, short-term issues have much more liquidity than long-term issues.
4. Risks that the general level of interest rates will change in an adverse direction.

THE CHANGING SHAPE OF THE YIELD CURVE

It is not enough to know what yield curves are and how they are derived. You also need to know why they take on the shapes they do.

As noted previously, the so-called "normal" yield curve is an upward sloping curve to the right (Figure 21.2). Near-term rates are lower than long-term rates. Money market economists refer to this as a "positive carry" market or a positive-shaped yield curve. You can borrow short-term at one rate and lend long-term at higher rates. That's the basis of banking.

Figure 21.2 Normal Yield Curve

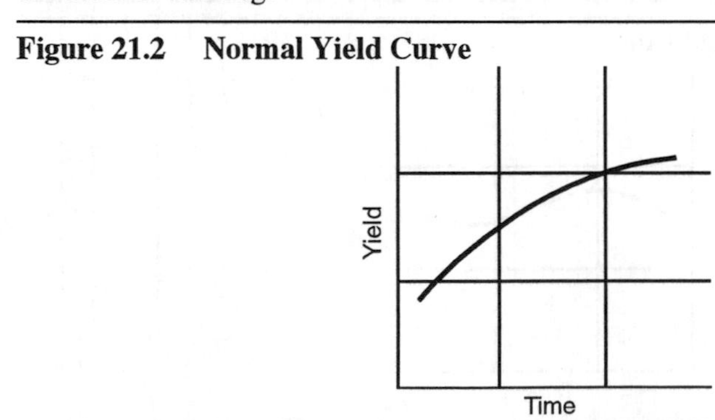

Sometimes, however, the curve takes on a flat look (Figure 21.3). Rates are fairly even across the time spectrum.

Sometimes short-term yields are above long-term yields (Figure 21.4). This is referred to as a "negative carry" market or a negative-shaped yield curve.

And sometimes yield curves become humped (Figure 21.5) when short-term rates rise sharply at first, then fall sharply to a point where the curve for long-term rates becomes flat.

Figure 21.3 Flat Yield Curve

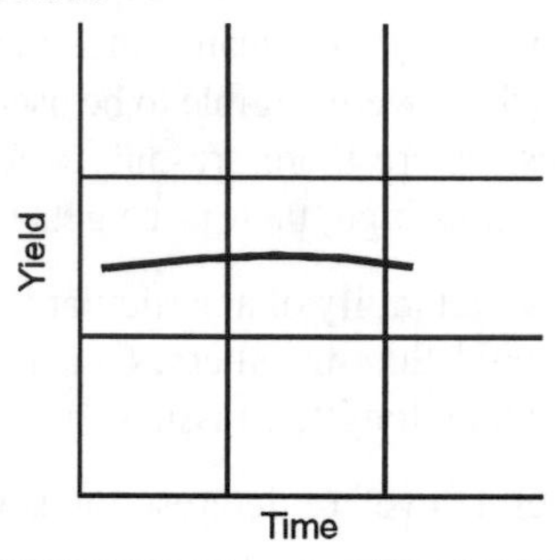

Figure 21.4 Inverted Yield Curve

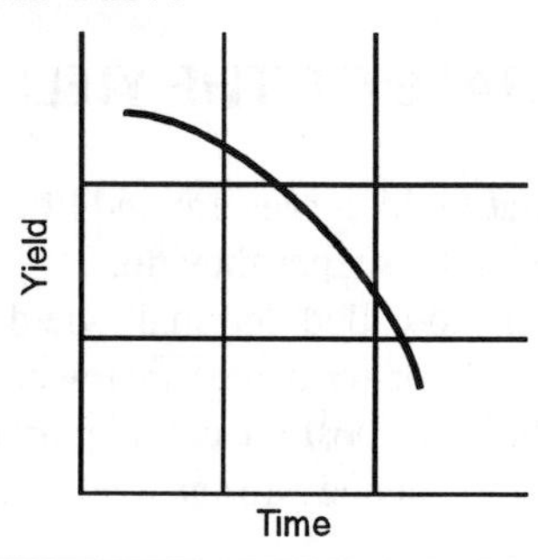

Figure 21.5 Humped Yield Curve

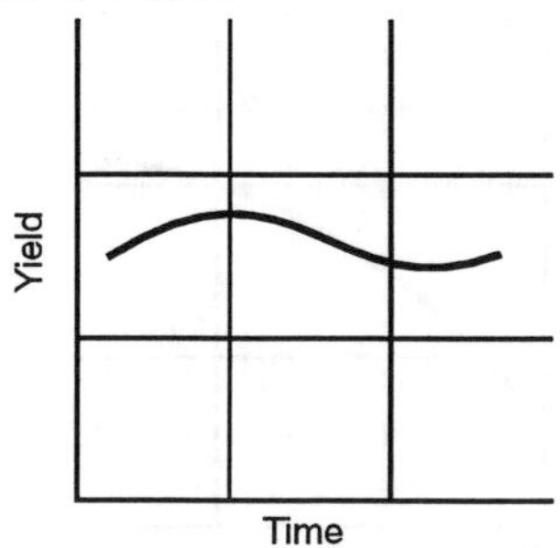

What does all this mean? Simply that knowing and understanding the yield curve, the shapes it takes, and what those shapes mean can provide you with trading ideas. For example, you should expect that a downward sloping yield curve ultimately will return to a normal yield curve.

By studying economic fundamentals, you can begin to identify economic signals that indicate a fall in short-term rates or a change in trends. A logical trading strategy to take advantage of such a change would be a spread between long-term and short-term rates—buy the short-term instruments and sell the long-term instruments.

If the yield curve indeed does return to normal, this strategy is almost sure to be profitable. However, the risk in such a strategy is that the yield curve will become even more inverted. If that happens, losses could be enormous. A more prudent strategy would involve buying the intermediate-term, say the five-year, and selling the long-term, say the 10-year or 30-year.

Not only do yield curves change shape, but they also shift from one level to another (as from A to B in Figure 21.6).

THE FUTURES YIELD CURVE

Just as you can develop a yield curve for issues traded in the cash market, you also can develop a yield curve for the futures market (Figure 21.7). The process of constructing the futures yield curve is similar to constructing the cash market yield curve. The obvious major difference is that you use data from different futures contracts in a futures yield curve—i.e., 30-day Fed funds; 90-day T-bills; two-year, five-year; and 10-year T-notes; and 15- to 30-year Treasury bonds. Just as in construct-

Figure 21.6 Yield Curve Shift

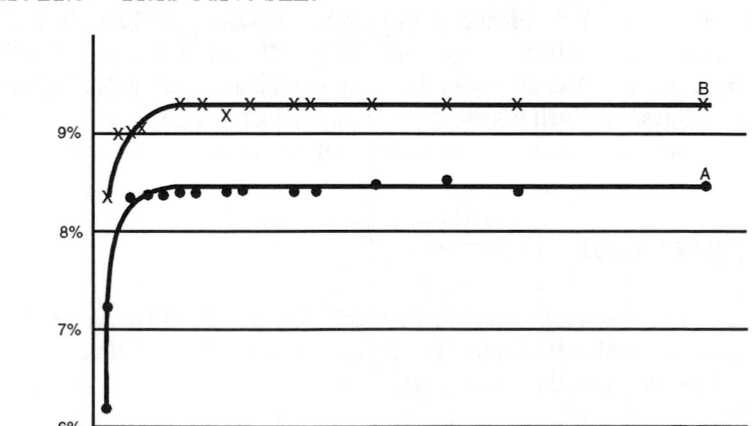

Figure 21.7 Futures Yield Curve

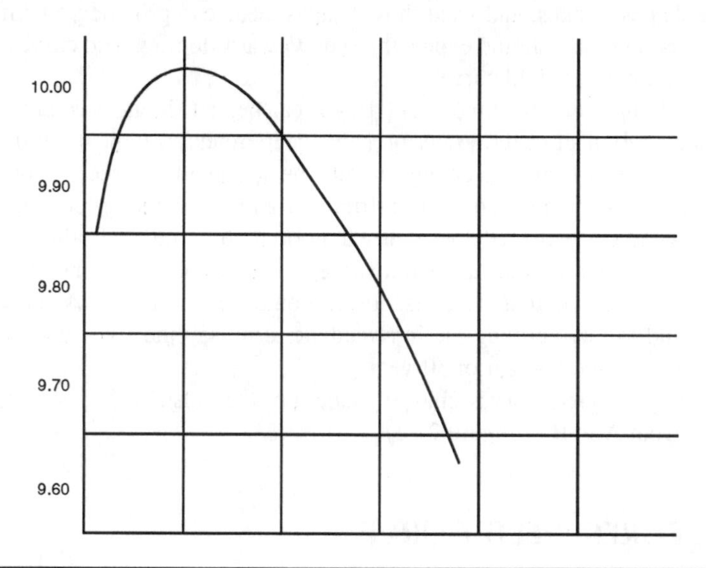

ing the cash yield curve, you need to put them all on a bond equivalent basis, and you need to select issues of comparable quality and creditworthiness; e.g., if you use Eurodollar futures instead of T-bills, recognize that Eurodollars represent private credit.

This futures curve shifts and changes shape just like the cash market curve. Sometimes it anticipates changes before the cash market adjusts. At other times, it follows or moves in loose conjunction with cash market changes.

It's important to use the same contract months for each of the futures instruments for obvious reasons. Each different futures month represents a different future time period and, therefore, a different expectancy curve. If you mix different delivery months—say, June and December—in the same yield curve, you would be mixing apples with oranges, comparing a yield curve that reflects the expected structure of interest rates in June with the expected structure of interest rates in December.

THE STRIP CURVE

The existence of futures markets provides a whole new set of yield curves, reflecting expected rates. But it also allows the development of a third curve called "the strip curve," which provides another benchmark of value.

Table 21.1 The "Strip"

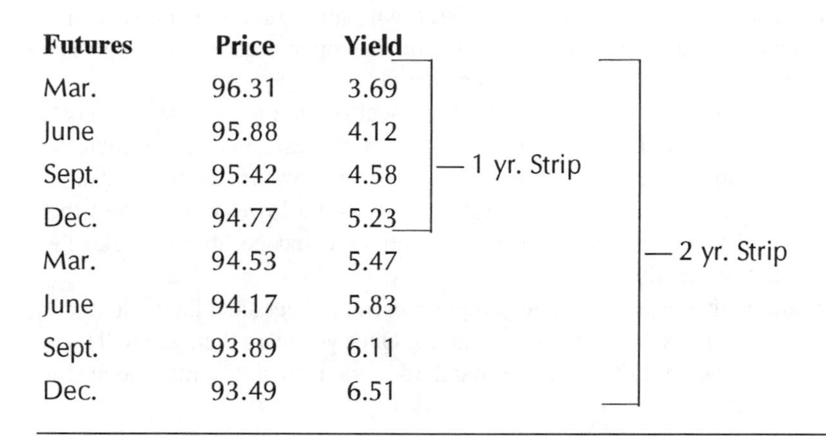

Futures	Price	Yield		
Mar.	96.31	3.69	1 yr. Strip	2 yr. Strip
June	95.88	4.12	1 yr. Strip	2 yr. Strip
Sept.	95.42	4.58	1 yr. Strip	2 yr. Strip
Dec.	94.77	5.23	1 yr. Strip	2 yr. Strip
Mar.	94.53	5.47		2 yr. Strip
June	94.17	5.83		2 yr. Strip
Sept.	93.89	6.11		2 yr. Strip
Dec.	93.49	6.51		2 yr. Strip

By definition, the "strip" is simply a series of successive Eurodollar or T-bill futures contracts. For example, if you were to purchase the December, March, June, and September Eurodollar futures contracts, you would own a one-year strip (see Table 21.1).

Ownership of a one-year T-bill strip actually is the same as owning a 12-month T-bill because the series of futures provides you with rights to purchase a 90-day T-bill every 3 months. The four separate bills cover a total maturity span of 12 months. To obtain that coverage, you simply take delivery of the December futures, thus receiving a bill in December that matures in March. Money from the maturing March bill is then used to take delivery of March futures and receive another 90-day bill maturing in June, and so on.

A major advantage of the strip is that you are completely flexible on the front end of the strip. Because you always are carrying an "actuals" position at the front end of the strip, you can move from T-bills to CDs to bankers' acceptances to Fed funds, or whatever instrument will provide the best short-term yield while keeping the latter part of the strip intact with the "locked-in" yield. That flexibility provides the opportunity to increase the yield over the period.

COMPOUNDING FACTOR

The value of the strip is more than the average of each of the successive futures contracts because of the effect of compounding interest. Each time a T-bill matures, the interest earned during the life of that T-bill is available for reinvestment during the next quarter. Thus, "interest-on-interest" increases the total return of the T-bill strip.

The yield curves for both cash bills and for futures are best compared if converted to bond equivalents first.

There are, of course, some risks associated with this strategy. If rates change significantly, you could receive margin calls on the open futures position. The opportunity cost of such calls needs to be considered.

Further, if you move from one cash instrument to another, transaction costs could get to be expensive. Last, if short-term rates on the cash instrument increase rapidly while the longer-term futures do not change or go down, you could get caught rolling from an instrument with a higher rate to one with a lower rate. To use this strategy, you need to monitor the markets continuously and be able to make the necessary calculations easily.

In summary, the message is quite simple: Learn to understand the yield curve for futures as well as the yield curve for the actuals. Once you learn that, you will have the beginnings of a standard of value. The standard of value then becomes the means of identifying profit opportunities.

Chapter 22

The Interest Rate Contracts

EURODOLLARS AND T-BILLS

Some years ago, a cartoon appeared wherein one fellow standing at a bar looks at his neighbor and says, "What the hell is a Eurodollar?" The addressee responds, "It's a dollar you can't touch or pay your bar bill with, but banks let you borrow it."

A Eurodollar is defined as a U.S. dollar on deposit in a bank outside of the United States. This generally means dollar balances on the books of London branches of major world banks. Since these deposits lie outside the United States, they do not fall directly under U.S. jurisdiction and, therefore, the regulations such as reserve requirements and maximum interest rate restrictions that govern domestic deposits do not apply to Eurodollars. Indeed, it is that regulatory loophole that facilitated and encouraged the explosive growth of the Eurodollar market among banks.

The trading of Eurodollar time deposit futures involves several aspects that are not present in the government securities market. First, Eurodollar deposits reflect private credit, whereas government securities reflect public credit; hence, the credit risk associated with the trading of the underlying cash instrument is greater for Eurodollars than for Treasury bills. That gets reflected in their prices. Usually T-bills trade at higher prices (lower interest rates) than do Eurodollars. Another risk that arises in the cash market for Eurodollars is a sovereign risk. That risk is independent of the bank with which the funds are placed and relates instead to the country under whose regulation that bank operates. There is always the risk that a particular country may establish regulations that would affect the movement of bank deposits into or out of the country. That would cause Eurocurrency rates to rise for that country. This happens particularly when a country's currency is under pressure.

Among the most useful and interesting futures markets ever developed are the contracts for short-term money market investments, Eurodollars and T-bills, which trade at the IMM of the Chicago Mercantile Exchange, and the 30-day Fed funds and LIBOR contracts at the CBOT. No other contracts are so universal in their importance. There is no business enterprise and no borrower, lender, or investor who is not affected by short-term interest rates.

T-bills are direct obligations of the U.S. Treasury. They are sold to investors through the Federal Reserve System, acting as an agent for the Treasury. In this way the Treasury borrows money to help pay the cost of running the government. The Fed sells T-bills, usually having a life of 90, 180, or 360 days, through a weekly auction. Competitive bids are accepted by the Treasury from Thursday until shortly after mid-day Monday when the auction is held. T-bills are sold on a discount basis and are redeemed at par value on maturity—90 or 180 days later. For example, a $10,000 T-bill yielding a 4 percent rate of return with 90 days to run would be purchased for $9,900, and 90 days later would be worth $10,000 as the interest is added on daily to the purchase price. If the interest rate were 6.0 percent, the value of the 90-day T-bill would be $9,850. It would accrue $150 in interest and be worth $10,000 at maturity.

Trading Eurodollar interest rate futures is distinctly different from trading other commodities. One of the most important differences is that, when interest rates go up, the value of the contract goes down and vice versa. To the initiate in finance and to the seasoned futures trader, this seems quite curious. Normally, it would seem that, if the price of something went up and you owned it, you should have a profit on your position. The reason this is not true is because the higher the interest rate, the more earnings will accrue over the life of the security. These future earnings are discounted, and it takes fewer dollars invested today to yield sufficient earnings to bring the price of the security back to par.

THE CONTRACT TERMS

The futures contract for T-bills calls for par delivery of a Treasury bill having a face value of $1,000,000 at maturity, which is 90 days after the delivery date. At the seller's discretion, he may substitute for the 90-day maturity 91- or 92-day Eurodollars of equivalent value.

The Eurodollar futures contract traded at the IMM is based on the London Interbank Offer Rate (LIBOR) for time deposits of $1,000,000 and a duration of 90 days to maturity. Unlike Certificates of Deposit (CDs), these time deposits are non-negotiable. That is why the Eurodollar futures contract became the first futures contract based on the concept of cash settlement—no delivery, but rather just exchange of cash value differences on the last day of trading.

The effectiveness of the cash settlement procedure is confirmed by the great success of the futures contract. As of the end of 1992, it is the futures with the largest volume and open interest on U.S. exchanges.

The "price" of both the Eurodollar and T-bill futures is quoted in terms of an exchange-devised index representing the actual annualized interest yield subtracted from 100. Hence, if you want to know the annual interest yield being represented by a particular futures quote, subtract the quote from 100. For example, an index number of 94.5 represents an annual yield of 5.5 percent. In contrast to interest rates, the index goes down as the contract loses in value and vice versa. Almost all newspapers carrying these futures quotes carry the interest yield price as well as the index price. Bids and offers in the trading pit at the exchange must be made in terms of the index, so be sure that you give your orders to your broker in terms of the index. The minimum price fluctuation of the contract is .01 of the IMM index, or one basis point of annual yield. This is equivalent to $25 on a $1,000 contract.

COMPARING A T-BILL FUTURES QUOTE WITH A EURODOLLAR FUTURES QUOTE

Both the T-bill futures contract and the Eurodollar futures contract are quoted in a similar manner. The cash price equals 100 minus the annualized yield (e.g., 100 - 8 percent yield equals a futures price of 92.00). The annualized yield for 90-day T-bills is a discount yield, whereas that for Eurodollars is an add-on interest yield. The distinction needs to be kept in mind especially when comparing prices (or yields) of the two futures contracts.

For example, suppose the T-bill futures contract is priced at 92.00 and the Eurodollar futures is priced at 91.00. The annualized yields implied by these prices are 8 percent for the T-bill contract and 9 percent for the Eurodollar contract. To compare these yields with each other they need to be put on an equivalent basis. Either convert the discount yield (T-bill futures) to an add-on interest yield (Eurodollar futures) or vice versa.

The conversion from the discount yield of the T-bill futures to the add-on interest yield of the Eurodollar futures is as follows:

$$\text{Add-on Interest Yield} = \frac{\text{Discount Yield} \times 90/360}{[1 - \text{Discount Yield} \times 90/360]} \times \frac{360}{90}$$

$$= \frac{0.08 \times 90/360}{1 - 0.08 \times 90/360} \times \frac{360}{90}$$

$$= 0.08163 \quad (8.163\%)$$

Thus, the 8 percent yield quoted on the T-bill futures contract is equivalent to a Eurodollar yield of 8.163 percent when quoted on an add-on interest yield basis.

SPREADS BETWEEN T-BILL AND EURODOLLAR RATES—THE "TED" SPREAD

As noted earlier, Eurodollar and CD rates reflect private credit, whereas T-bill rates reflect public credit. Generally, because of the credit characteristics of Eurodollars, rates on Eurodollars will exceed rates on T-bills. Further, the spread between Eurodollar rates and T-bill rates, called the TED spread, does not remain constant. It responds to a variety of market forces, most of which are unpredictable, and many of which involve political decisions of the United States and foreign governments. The spread also reacts to changes in currency relationships.

This creates some very interesting and potentially profitable trading opportunities. The margins on the TED spread are very low, mainly because the volatility of the spread differential is much lower than the absolute change in either of the independent futures. If Eurodollars change by 10 points in a day, it would be unusual if the spread to T-bills changed by more than 1 or 2 points.

The TED spread reacts to the business cycle. If business is booming, the spread will tend to be wide. If business is in a recession, the TED tends to be narrowing.

Although the last year is an exception, historically, the TED spread seldom stays below +75 (Eurodollar rates over T-bill rates) for more than a few calendar quarters. Similarly, it seldom remains above 300 for long (Figure 22.1).

HEDGING WITH THE T-BILL AND EURODOLLAR FUTURES CONTRACTS

Both the T-bill and Eurodollar futures contracts can be used in a variety of ways to hedge other money market instruments such as CDs, commercial paper, bankers' acceptances, and so on. For example, a large corporation could use either contract to lock in the rate on anticipated future borrowings. A bank could use the contracts to facilitate the repricing of its CDs. Yet another example would be for a corporate

Figure 22.1 TED Spread (weekly data)

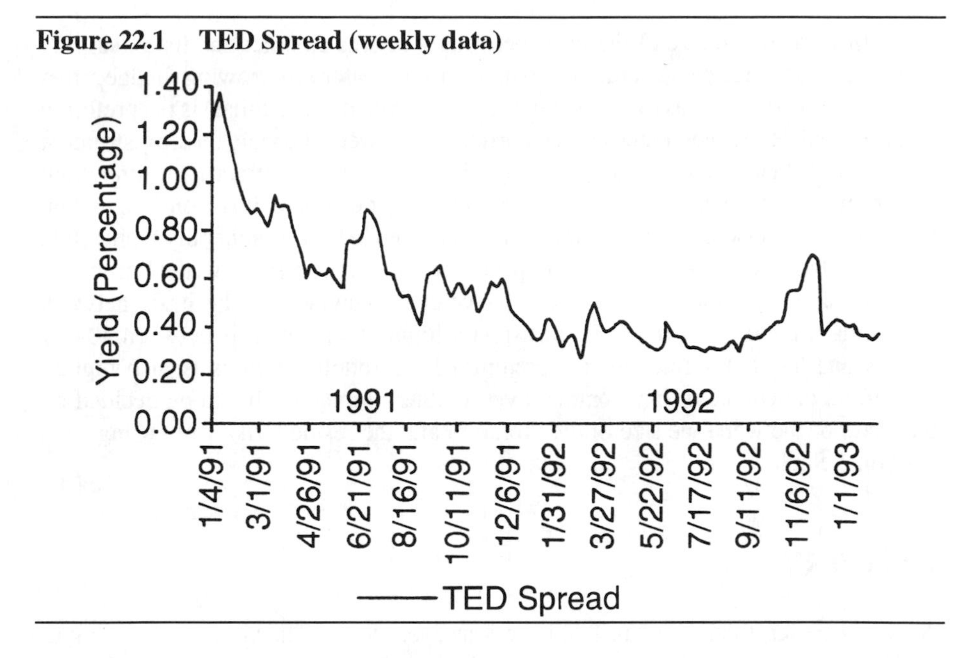

treasurer to lock in the yield on a future inflow of cash slated for investment in money market securities.

Designing effective hedges requires an understanding of the pricing relationships between the instrument hedged and the instrument underlying the futures contract. Correlation provides such a measure. If the correlation between the yields of CDs and LIBOR exceeds that between CDs and T-bills, it is an indication that the Eurodollar contract might be more effective for hedging CDs than the T-bill contract—at least on a pure risk-reduction basis.

Another important factor is basis risk. Since hedging is often viewed as an exchange of price risk (absolute risk) for basis risk (relative risk), one must realize that hedges seldom, if ever, result in the total elimination of risk. Basis risk tends to be higher for hedges where the correlation is lower.

Finally, if futures markets are to be used to effectively reduce risk, there is an implicit price charged for its reduction. The price is built into the basis. It is best seen in the case of an anticipatory hedge. Consider a borrower whose borrowing cost is tied to 90-day LIBOR. Suppose the rate on 90-day LIBOR is currently 10 percent with the Eurodollar futures for delivery two months hence at 89.90 (10.10 percent). The spot rate implies that if borrowing is undertaken immediately the cost would be 10 percent (spot LIBOR). On the other hand, if borrowing is undertaken two months hence, a rate of 10.10 percent could be locked in with certainty through the sale of Eurodollar futures. The 10-basis-point premium may be viewed as a price paid to get rid of the risk that LIBOR could be much higher than the current rate of 10 percent.

In viewing the size of the basis between a futures contract and its underlying instrument as a price paid to eliminate risk in an anticipatory (borrowing) hedge raises the interesting question as to which contract (T-bill versus Eurodollar) is the preferred hedging vehicle. As mentioned earlier, correlation between the yield on the instrument hedged with that of the instrument underlying the futures contract is an important factor, but only from a risk-reduction perspective. For example, it is well-known that the correlation between CDs or commercial paper and LIBOR is generally higher than their correlation with T-bills. So from a pure risk-reduction perspective the Eurodollar contract should be the preferred hedging vehicle. However, if the basis between Eurodollar futures and LIBOR is consistently higher than the basis between 90-day T-bills and T-bill futures, the risk premium in Eurodollar futures is also higher. Therefore, the choice of one contract over another ultimately should be decided on the trade-off between the size of the premium and the residual risk from using each hedging vehicle.

DELIVERY

As noted earlier, the Fed holds T-bill auctions every week. The last day of trading in T-bill and Eurodollar futures for any particular month is the second day following the third T-bill auction of that month. Delivery is the following day.

Delivery for T-bills to settle futures contracts is accomplished through Chicago banks that are registered with the exchange and are members of the Federal Reserve System. Through them you can have the T-bills delivered to your account in any other major city. It is a relatively simple procedure and mirrors the action taken when deliveries are made in the cash market.

The futures contract on T-bills calls for the delivery of bills having 90 days of life remaining. Thus, on delivery you will obtain an instrument that will earn interest over the next 90 days. At the time you buy it, you pay something less than its face value—its discounted value. The difference between what you pay and the face value will be equal to the accrual of the interest during the remaining 90 days. Eurodollars are settled in cash, so delivery does not occur. Speculators should not take delivery, as a general rule.

TREASURY BONDS AND TREASURY NOTES

Treasury bill futures were so successful initially that futures contracts in Treasury bonds and Treasury notes also began. Bond futures were an immediate success, largely because they covered the long-term end of the yield curve and were a natural complement to T-bill and GNMA futures. With short-, intermediate- and long-term points covered on the yield curve, investors now could get decent hedges for an entire portfolio.

The par delivery unit on T-bond futures contracts calls for a $100,000 bond with an 8 percent coupon and minimum maturity of 15 years. (It actually trades equivalent to the 30-year bond price.) There is no maximum maturity. Prices are quoted in 32nds. Thus, each minimum price change is $31.25.

To convert futures prices to actual cash values, the CBOT uses a factor method. The conversion factors that adjust each available government bond to an 8 percent coupon with 15 years to maturity are published regularly by the CBOT. This method of calculation almost always results in the bond with the longest maturity (usually 30 years) being the cheapest for delivery.

Delivery is made through the Federal Reserve's book entry system in the same manner as for Treasury bills.

Treasury bonds are auctioned by the Treasury in the same manner, but less frequently than the weekly auctions for Treasury bills. Bids, however, are denominated in yields instead of dollars.

TREASURY NOTES

U.S. Treasury notes represent the largest and fastest growing segment of the federal government's marketable debt instruments. Like other debt instruments, these are sold to public investors to raise funds for financing government programs and to refinance other maturing debt of the U.S. government. Notes, like bonds, are sold at regular auctions and are issued with a coupon which bears interest semiannually.

There are a number of Treasury note futures listed on the various commodity exchanges. The Chicago Board of Trade lists the two-year, five-year, and 10-year Treasury note futures contracts. The 10-year Treasury futures contract is based on a government security with a face value of $100,000 maturing in 6.5 to 10 years with an 8 percent coupon. The five-year has a face value of $100,000, and the two-year has a face value of $200,000.

Like other coupon issues, Treasury notes are auctioned. With each auction of notes, the coupon associated with those notes change and, hence, the list of deliverable notes changes. Each eligible coupon has a different maturity and a different value. Hence, at delivery, the value of the various deliverable notes must be converted to the equivalent of the contract par coupon. This is accomplished through "conversion factors" provided by the CBOT. A seller delivering any one of these eligible notes calculates the invoice amount for a particular issue by multiplying the futures price by the appropriate conversion factor and adding the accrued interest. These conversion factors also become the means for calculating the correct number of contracts to use when hedging.

All debt instruments with similar maturity and investment quality are affected by the same economic fundamentals. For this reason, one will find that many debt instruments move in unison with one another—their yields rise and fall together. Put another way, they have a high correlation. That high correlation allows one to use Treasury note futures as a hedging tool for the hedging of related instruments.

To some extent, Treasury notes, like other government-backed securities, become a price benchmark for the pricing of other securities. Corporate bonds, federal agency issues, and municipal notes are all priced at a spread to Treasury notes when they trade in the cash market. The size of the spread or the difference between their yields reflects the market's perception of the creditworthiness of the security. A narrow spread indicates that the market judges the security to be closer in credit quality to the Treasury note. A wide spread indicates the market believes the related securities are a more risky investment than a Treasury note.

Money fund managers, cash management funds, and mutual funds all are potential users of the T-bill, bond and note futures. The manager of a money fund whose cash investments are in various types of money market instruments such as CDs, commercial paper, T-bills, etc., can effectively use a futures contract in three-month T-bills, or Eurodollars. By anticipating the size and approximate dates of investment in these and other money marketing vehicles, the fund manager can buy the number of contracts necessary to cover some part of the future interest rate exposure and thereby lock in an acceptable return on at least part of his portfolio.

FACTORS AFFECTING RATES

Yields on Eurodollars and T-bills can fluctuate rapidly as money market conditions change. What makes interest rates fluctuate from day to day? What economic factors can affect the money market? These questions and many more are of great importance to anyone dealing in interest-rate-sensitive instruments.

Among the most important economic factors affecting money market interest rates are (1) Federal Reserve activities; (2) financial needs of the business community; (3) international currency movements, both speculative and trade-related; (4) technical tone of the money market; and (5) the general condition of the economy.

Federal Reserve Activity

By far the most important determinative of money market rates is the Federal Reserve system. In the previous chapter we explained the role the Federal Reserve plays in the overall economy; and we explained, albeit briefly and simplistically, that the Federal Reserve has essentially three tools available to affect interest rates:

First, its Open Market Committee operations, through which it buys and sells government securities, influences interest rates and the availability of credit. When the Fed buys securities from the commercial bank, it results in an increase in loanable funds and a decrease in interest rates. When the Fed sells securities, the buyer's reserve account is debited. This results in a reduction of credit and a firming of interest rates.

Second, the Fed has a far-reaching monetary impact through its control over member bank reserve requirements. It can set them anywhere between 10 percent and 22 percent. These reserves directly affect the availability of loanable funds and, indirectly, the interest rates.

Third, the Federal Reserve sets an interest rate called the discount rate. This is the interest rate that banks must pay the central bank when a commercial bank decides to borrow money in order to maintain its reserves. Changes in the discount rate often are regarded as indicating fundamental shifts in the Fed credit policy. Such shifts are immediately reflected by the financial market, sometimes even anticipated by it. Changes in the discount rate set up a virtual chain reaction throughout the financial market. When the discount rate is increased, banks are generally inclined to sell government securities, especially T-bills, rather than expand their borrowings at the Federal Reserve discount window. The sale of securities reduces security prices while raising their yields, and higher yields in the T-bill market finally spread to other money market instruments and are reflected across the board in higher interest rates. The opposite occurs when the discount rate is lowered.

Business Needs

Industry's demand for cash has a strong influence on short-term interest rate movements. As the demand for loans increases, interest rates generally rise. On the other hand, if loan demand begins to lag because of a slowdown in the general economy, one would expect downward pressure on interest rates. Indicators of short-term business loan demand include new orders in durable goods industries, contracts and orders for new plants and equipment, changes in the book value of inventories, industrial production, and levels of commercial and industrial loans outstanding.

Dealer Activity

Anyone who desires to trade T-bill and Eurodollar futures should become familiar with the activity of dealers in government securities. At the present time there are approximately 35 active government security dealers. The activity and aggressiveness of dealers in bidding on and offering government securities affects the direction and volatility of all interest rates. These dealers are continuously interpreting the Fed's actions, the nation's economic well-being, and social and political events to determine the impact that such things have on prices. One should watch closely what these cash market dealers are doing.

General Economic Conditions

In the previous chapter we discussed some of the significant indicators of the condition of an economy. A stable economic situation would help create stable money market conditions while a period of economic uncertainty usually leads to wide interest rate fluctuations. Such measures of economic conditions as the rate of growth in GNP, balance of trade, levels of unemployment, inflation, housing starts, etc., help determine the strength or weakness of the economy. Some of these factors and an interpretation of them are encompassed in the preceding chapters. A regular weekly, monthly, and quarterly cycle of economic information releases is followed by most government agencies, the Fed, the Treasury, etc. These release dates often show substantial price volatility.

Chapter 23

Hedging Applications for Financial Futures

The preceding chapters on financial futures contain most of the basics you need to start understanding how financial futures markets work. Examples in those chapters also give you a general idea of how those markets can be used for hedging. This chapter provides a slight elaboration of some of the more practical applications of hedging, which will aid the interested reader in exploring these concepts further and in devising new means of application. The chapter starts by setting forth a framework for helping decide whether the cost of hedging is worth it. After that the chapter enumerates typical circumstances that would lead a person to consider a hedge.

TO HEDGE OR NOT TO HEDGE

Hedging is not always worth it or, to paraphrase the English, the game may not be worth the candle. One has to look at expected costs and expected benefits. These expectations change as situations change and new information emerges.

In any hedging decision the manager must answer three very important questions:

1. What is the net exposure?
2. What is the probability of a loss as a result of this risk exposure?
3. Which of the alternative methods available to me for managing this risk will provide the most complete coverage at the least cost and fit our corporate mission?

The following section focuses on currency risk and hedging for convenience of illustration. The concepts and methodology apply equally well to other commodities and financial instruments.

What Is the Net Risk Exposure

Net risk exposure refers here to the amount of money that would be lost if the price changes. Price may be an exchange rate, an interest rate, a price per barrel of oil or per bushel of wheat, etc. It is an objective measure of the impact a devaluation or revaluation will have on the value of a firm's assets and liabilities or inputs and outputs. If a currency is devalued, any liability (such as loans) a foreign firm owes in that currency can be paid back with cheaper money. Conversely, if it has been revalued, the currency needed to pay back that loan will cost more.

Calculating the net risk exposure is one of the most useful exercises a manager can do and, perhaps more than anything else, is the key to successful risk management. The exercise often forces managers to look at their business and corporate mission in a whole new light and yields benefits even if they never enter into a futures hedge.

There are a variety of ways by which the net risk exposure can be calculated. Current assets in a currency minus current liabilities in that currency is one very simple but probably incomplete way. Most firms today use a more sophisticated procedure that takes account of such things as receivables booked, liabilities incurred, and the method by which the balance sheet values are converted from one currency to another and, most important, the timing of the repricing. This is a very complex topic on which whole books can be and have been written. Suffice it to say, before you venture into this area, get your accountant's advice. A thorough understanding of accounting rules and tax laws is of key importance in estimating true risk exposure.

What Is the Probability of Loss on Net Exposure?

This is a subjective evaluation that should be based on an analysis of the economic and political information available about a country or a product. In making this determination, the manager should first estimate the probability that there will be a change in the exchange rate or price. Is there a 50 percent chance that the currency of concern will be devalued this month? this year? An 80 percent chance? And, second, estimate the probability of the size of change in the exchange rate. Will it be 10 percent? 20 percent? 30 percent? or even 40 percent? These may only be good "guesstimates," but they need to be made. In fact, they are automatically made by the decision maker whether he does it consciously or unconsciously.

Hedge Yes, Hedge No

Armed with these pieces of information—net exposure, probability of loss, and probability of size of loss—you can then calculate the expected value of a loss to the firm by multiplying the probability of a loss times the probability of the size of the loss. See Steps a,b,c, and d in Table 23.1. Once you have that answer, you are then in a position to compare the expected value of the loss (this is calculated by multiplying the probability of a loss by the probable size of the loss) to your cost of hedging.

Ultimately, a manager needs to ask, "Which of the alternative methods available, singly or in concert with another alternative, will provide the most complete coverage of the risk at the least cost?" Generally, a manager has a number of alternative hedge vehicles available to him. He can self-protect through various management techniques (diversification, prepayments or delayed settlements, etc.); he can hedge by going to his bank (or a dealer) and obtaining a forward contract or a swap or option contract; or he can hedge on a futures contract. In making this determination, he must examine the cost of each alternative.

The cost of the hedge includes not just the commission cost, the interest foregone (if any) on the margin for the futures contract, and the bid-ask spread, but also any premium or discount that is reflected between the futures contract and the expected spot price. For example, if your expected spot price is 3 percent under the six-month forward price, the "cost of the buy hedge" includes that 3 percent premium. If the cost of the hedge is less than the expected loss, hedge; if the cost is greater, don't.

$$\begin{array}{c}\text{Cost of Hedge}\\ \text{or}\\ \text{Forward Premium}\\ \text{or Discount}\end{array} = \frac{\text{Futures Price} - \text{Spot Price}}{\text{Spot Price}} \times 100 \times \frac{12}{\begin{array}{c}\text{months}\\ \text{to}\\ \text{maturity}\end{array}}$$

To demonstrate, assume that the manager of a firm calculates his net exposure as $10 million based on an expected devaluation of the U.S. dollar relative to the German deutschemark. Secondly, assume that given his evaluation of the economic situation in Germany, he expects the probability of a loss to be 50 percent. In other words, he believes that there is a 50/50 chance that the devaluation of the U.S. dollar relative to the deutschemark will occur by the next year. Assume also that he calculates the probability of the size of the devaluation to be 10 percent.

Table 23.1 offers a summary of the situation and a way to determine whether to hedge:

Table 23.1 Hedge Decision Model

a. Net exposure	$10,000,000
b. Probability of loss	50%
c. Probable size of loss	10%
d. Mathematical expectation of loss (b x c)	5%
e. Cost of hedge	3%
f. Decision—compare d to e. If d is greater than e, hedge. If d is less than e, do not hedge.	

In the example above, the firm would make the decision to hedge because the mathematical expectation of a loss exceeds the cost of hedging, 5 percent vs. 3 percent. If those expectations are correct, the firm would gain 2 percent by hedging. Note that the key to the decision of whether to hedge is found in correct calculation of the probabilities. If the probabilities were different, the mathematical expectations also would be different.

A caveat: One should not enter into a hedging transaction without considering the tax implications and the effects on cash flows. Any business firm that is engaged in foreign exchange transactions would do well to integrate its hedging transactions and its accounting decisions in order to assure it gets the maximum ***net*** benefit of its risk management efforts.

HEDGE RATIOS—DOLLAR EQUIVALENCY—AND THE MATURITY ADJUSTMENT

The hedge ratio refers to the number of futures contracts one needs in order to get an effective hedge. An effective hedge is one where the dollars gained or lost in the futures position are equal but opposite to the dollars gained or lost in the cash market (portfolio, new investment opportunity, balance sheet, etc.).

As noted earlier, the value of a one-point move (1/100 of 1 percent) in the yield of a T-bill futures contract is $25. This is derived from the fact that T-bill futures represent 90-day maturities. A one-year T-bill will have an equivalent value of $100 for each .01 percent movement in yield. Thus, the following value relationships hold:

.01% for 90 days—$ 25
.01% for 180 days—$ 50
.01% for 240 days—$ 75
.01% for 360 days—$100

The value of .01 percent over time becomes very important in hedging. For example, if you were trying to hedge a six-month loan by using 90-day T-bill futures, you would need to use twice as many "dollars worth" of futures contracts to get the equivalent movement in value between the cash position and the futures position. Each .01 percent movement in yield in the cash position would be worth $50 while each .01 percent movement in a single futures position would be worth only $25. Therefore, you need two futures contracts to give equal dollar value change.

The calculation of the hedge ratio for bonds, notes, and other fixed coupon instruments is more complex. It involves calculating the "duration" of the futures and the "duration" of the instrument being hedged, given small changes in interest rates. Duration is a fancy financial term for volatility.[1] It is not the life span of the bond. The ratio of the duration of the futures to the duration of the instrument being hedged equals the correct hedge ratio. As interest rates change, these ratios change. Thus, hedges must be continually adjusted.

Hedge ratios also are affected by things other than maturity. In most cases, the basic hedge ratios estimated by the above procedures are further adjusted by a regression or correlation coefficient.

For non-financial hedges, such as most agricultural commodities, hedge ratios derived from regression or correlation analysis will suffice. In many cases, those ratios will approximate 1.00.

One can get very involved in doing precise calculations of hedge ratios and find that the effort is not worth it, because the adjustments are too small to be meaningful or else so frequent, in both directions, as to be self-defeating (e.g., whipsawing back and forth). Thus, settling on a simple, easily calculated procedure that reflects true average relative value changes over the life of a hedge is probably the most common and sensible approach.

---

1. The formula for calculation is too complex for presentation here. For a thorough explanation of it, see Powers, Mark J. and Mark Castelino, 1991. *Inside the Financial Futures Markets.* New York: John Wiley & Sons.

HEDGING—CURRENCY

In earlier chapters we discussed the concept of hedging and demonstrated its application to some of the traditional agricultural commodities. These same concepts apply to the foreign currency hedger.

The following examples illustrate some potential hedging situations available to different sectors of the economy.

The Buy Hedge

Assume a Chicago tractor maker has a Swiss plant that is doing very well and has access to funds in the form of Swiss francs. It has no need for those funds until Swiss taxes are due in six months. At the same time, assume that the Chicago tractor maker has an engine plant in Milwaukee that is in need of a short-term loan to meet operating expenses. The best move for the tractor maker may be to transfer those funds from the Swiss plant to the Milwaukee plant for six months. In the transaction, the hedger would sell the spot Swiss francs for dollars and buy Swiss francs for future delivery, thus establishing a buy hedge. Table 23.2 shows the summary of these transactions.

Table 23.2 Swiss Franc Buy Hedge

Cash Market	Basis	Futures Market
March 1		
Sell 500,000 Swiss francs for $.50000/SF = $250,000	100	Buy four September Swiss franc futures, 125,000 SF each at $.49900 = $249,500
September 1		
Buy 500,00 Swiss Francs at $.50300/SF = $251,500	10	Sell four Swiss franc futures contracts, 125,000 SF each at $.50290 = $251,450
Loss = 300 points ($1,500)	90	**Gain = 390 points ($1,950)**

In this example the hedger had a $1,500 loss in the cash market that was more than offset by a $1,950 gain in the futures market. His basis declined from 100 points to 10 points for a net decline of 90 points. Each point is worth $1.25 or $112.50 for each contract, or a total of $450.

The Sell Hedge

Assume a Chicago bank has excess funds to invest in the short term, and the highest short-term interest rate currently is being paid in Canada. Let's say 91-day Canadian Treasury bills are yielding 8.5 percent, and U.S. Treasury bills are yielding 7.5 percent. The Chicago banker will buy Canadian dollars in the spot market, transfer them to his Canadian banking correspondent and direct him to purchase 91-day Canadian Treasury bills. At the same time, he will sell Canadian dollars in the futures market for delivery three months hence. The amount of the Canadian dollars he sells in the futures market will include the original number plus enough to cover the interest that will accrue.

The advantage of this hedge is that the banker will have fixed his selling price for the Canadian dollars 91 days from now. This way he can be assured that the interest in Treasury bills will not be lost in the conversion back to dollars, if the price of Canadian dollars goes down during the period. The transaction is summarized in Table 23.3.

Table 23.3 Canadian Dollar Sell Hedge

Cash Market	Basis	Futures Market
December 1		
Buy 191,000 Canadian dollars at $1.00000 = $191,000	100	Sell two CD contracts, March delivery, $100,000 each at $1.00100 CD = $200,200
March1		
Sell 191,000 CD at $.98000 CD = $187,180	10	Buy two CD March futures delivery at $100,000 each $.98010 CD = $196,020
Loss = 2,000 points ($4,000)	90	**Gain = 2,090 points ($4,180)**
Interest Accrued $8,423.10		

In this example, if the banker had not hedged, he would have lost nearly half of his interest income ($8,423.10) when he changed his Canadian dollars back to U.S. dollars because the spot price of the CD went down. However, by hedging in the futures market he actually recovered all of his interest income in the futures transaction and made an overall profit of $180 on the hedge as well ($4,180 – $4,000 = $180). He could just as easily have lost a small amount. The important point is that the hedge protected his interest income from the exchange risk. His basis declined from 100 points futures over cash to 10 points futures over cash, a net decline of 90 points. Each point for each contract is worth $1. Since he had two contracts, each point is worth $2 for a total of $180.

The world monetary system is in a continual state of transition. As a result, the risk of doing business internationally is increasing right along with the increased demands for international trade. As more and more businesses and banks seek means of protecting themselves from currency losses due to exchange fluctuations, the role of foreign currency hedging will undoubtedly grow in importance.

The currency futures markets can be used by a wide variety of commercial interests. The following are just a few categories in which futures hedging could be helpful:

1. Companies building plants abroad.
2. Companies financing subsidiaries.
3. Manufacturers importing raw materials and exporting finished products.
4. Exporters taking payment in foreign currency.
5. Companies dealing in goods bought and sold into foreign countries.
6. Companies abroad financing operations in Eurocurrencies.
7. Stock purchases or sales in foreign countries.
8. Purchases or sales of foreign securities.

The possibilities are virtually limitless. Everyone who deals in or with foreign countries has a need for a hedging mechanism to avoid major losses due to exchange fluctuations.

APPLICATIONS OF AN INTEREST RATE FUTURES MARKET

Any commitment in the money markets exposes both borrowers and lenders to the risk of interest rate changes for as long as the debt instrument is outstanding. To minimize these risks, money market participants could hedge in the Eurodollar futures market.

As noted earlier, hedging is a method by which a borrower or lender of money market funds buys or sells a futures contract as a temporary substitute for a borrowing or lending transaction to be made at a later date. Hence, the money manager or trust fund manager who knows he will be investing in Eurodollars in September may establish the yield on the September Eurodollars in July by entering the futures market and buying the Eurodollar contract for delivery in September. The corporate treasurer who knows he will be borrowing money soon but needs time to work out his financial plan and actually get the loan arranged can hedge against higher rates by selling the futures.

Builders, developers, and other users of short-term construction loans can use the Eurodollar futures market to establish in advance the cost of borrowed money. Interest rates on short-term construction loans generally fluctuate with the prime rate. An increase in the prime rate during the period of construction could push the cost of financing beyond the capacity of the borrower. This risk can be effectively removed by a short hedge.

Hedging can also be used to protect against changes in the rates of other money market instruments such as commercial paper, certificates of deposit, bankers' acceptances, etc. The effectiveness of the hedge will be determined by the extent to which movements in the rates for Eurodollars parallel movements in rates for the other instruments. For example, if a perfect correlation existed between movements in Eurodollars and commercial paper, then a hedge in the Eurodollar futures would be a very efficient device for protecting against changes in commercial paper rates. The closer the relationships, the more perfect the hedge.

Even in instances where the correlation is not perfect and the basis is unstable but the volatility in both markets is high, an imperfect hedge will be much preferred over no hedge at all. For example, if it is normal for commercial paper to trade at a +25 to +150-point range over Eurodollars, one might think that a Eurodollar futures would be a poor hedge mechanism for commercial paper rates, because a range of 125 points shows a significant amount of instability in the basis. However, if the volatility of Eurodollars and commercial paper is such that a 300-point change in absolute rates is a highly probable occurrence, one could easily see that the 125-point basis exposure that would accompany the hedge is much preferred over the 300-point exposure of the non-hedged position.

Since the Eurodollar market is a rate from which many other movements emanate, you can see that a Eurodollar futures contract can be an efficient vehicle for hedging interest rate movements in other money instruments. You need only compare the volatility of the basis relationships to the relative volatility of the absolute rates for each instrument to determine the efficiency and value of the hedge.

HEDGING AGAINST FALLING INTEREST RATES

A financial manager who anticipates having funds to lend (i.e., invest) in short-term money markets at a known time in the future can hedge against the risk that rates may drop in the interim. He does this by buying a Eurodollar futures contract. If interest rates go down between the purchase date and the delivery date, the contract will increase in value. The futures contract's appreciation in value should offset the investor's "opportunity loss," which resulted from the actual decline in interest rates during the period. A hedge minimizes both the downside risk and upside potential gain.

The Buying Hedge

Judicious and selective use of the Eurodollar futures markets can help the corporate money manager match interest rates on borrowings and investments. It can also provide him a view of market expectations on future interest rate levels. Such information is valuable in establishing the maturity mix in a portfolio.

Let's assume that on May 1 a corporate treasurer anticipating cash inflows for short-term investment during the month of June observes that September Eurodollar futures are selling at 93.00 (IMM index) to yield 7.00 percent. He feels this rate will fall during the next month or so to about 6.50 percent. Since he feels that 7.0 percent is a very favorable yield and he wants to "lock in" that yield for his anticipated investment, he buys September futures. On June15, when he has the cash available for investment, he buys Eurodollars maturing in December to yield 5.60 percent annually (IMM index of 94.40). This is 90 points lower than he expected. At the same time, on June 15, he lifts his hedge by selling his September futures at 94.08 to yield 5.92 percent. The 108-point gain on the futures more than offsets the lower-than-expected yield on the investment. The corporation will realize an additional .18 percent yield return ($450 per million) on their Eurodollar investment as a result of the hedge. The futures provided flexibility in timing the forward pricing of their investment yields. Table 23.4 explains this sequence of transactions.

Table 23.4 Hedging Short Term Investment Rates

Cash Market	Basis	Futures Market
May 15		
Anticipated investment yield of 6.50% (93.50 index)	50	Buy one September future @ 7.00% (93.00 index)
June 15		
Buy $1,000,000 Eurodollar CD maturing 12/24/96 @ 5.6% yield (94.40 index)	32	Sell one September future @ 5.92% yield (94.08 index)
–90	**18**	**+108**

As another example, assume that in September a bank wanted to price in advance the last three-month portion of a six-month asset that would be funded by a six-month Eurodollar liability. The bank would be interested in protecting against a fall in interest rates from the period beginning the middle of December through the middle of March and would make the following transactions:

1. In September, borrow six-month Eurodollars and, simultaneously, make a three-month loan.
2. In September, buy one IMM Eurodollar contract for delivery in December.
3. In December, receive the money from the maturing asset (loan) and re-lend that money for three months at the then-current interbank rate; and, simultaneously, sell (offset) one Eurodollar contract on the IMM. The proceeds from the futures should be applied to the new asset to get the net investment rate.

HEDGING AGAINST RISING INTEREST RATES

Borrowers in the money markets can also use interest rate futures to protect themselves against increases in short-term rates with a "short" hedge, i.e., selling a Eurodollar contract for future delivery. If rates rise, the value of the futures contract will drop, and the hedger can make a gain by buying it back for a lower price.

The Sell Hedge

Assume a borrower plans on May 1 to sell $10 million in 90-day commercial paper in September. He expects to sell the paper at 5.5 percent. The current rate on September futures is 5.2 percent. He can hedge that sale and assure himself in advance of the interest rate he will pay by taking a short position in the futures market (see Table 23.5).

In this instance, had the borrower not hedged, he would have paid 1.13 percent more in interest costs than he originally expected. As it is, he paid .26 percent less. The futures provided the flexibility in timing the date on which he fixed his cost. He did not have to wait until the day he came to market with the paper.

As another example of a selling hedge, assume a money manager on June 15 holds in inventory $5 million in Eurodollar CDs maturing in September yielding 6 percent annually (IMM index of 94.00). He knows that before September 15 he will need the funds and will sell these Eurodollars to someone else. He can protect the selling rate and reduce his risk exposure by selling September futures contracts. Assume the September futures is at 93.35 (6.65 percent yield) for a basis of 65 points (see Table 23.6).

Table 23.5 Hedging Commercial Paper

Cash Market	Basis	Futures Market
May 1		
Anticipates selling $10 million of commercial paper. Expected rate in September 5.5% (IMM index 94.50)	30	Sells 10 September Eurodollar contracts at 5.20% (IMM index 94.80)
September 5		
Sells $10 million commercial paper at 6.63% (IMM index 93.37)	4	Buy (offset) 10 September Eurodollar contracts at 6.59% (IMM index 93.41
Loss = 113 points	**26**	**Gain = 139 points**

Table 23.6 Sell Hedge Eurodollar CD's

Cash Market	Basis	Futures Market
June 15		
Inventory of $5 million Eurodollars maturing 12/14/96, yielding 6.00% (IMM index 94.00)	65	Sell five September Eurodollar futures contracts maturing 12/14/96 @ 6.65% yield (IMM index 93.35)
July 1		
Sell inventory of $5 million Eurodollars maturing 12/14/96 @ 6.2 yield (IMM index 93.80)	55	Buy five September Eurodollars futures maturing 12/14/96 @ 6.75% yield (IMM index 93.25)
Loss= 20 points	**–10 points**	Gain =10 points

On June 15 he protects his inventory by selling September Eurodollar futures at a 6.65 percent yield. Time passes and rates rise, causing his inventory to decline in value. On July 1, he decides to liquidate the inventory at a price to yield 6.2 percent. He buys back the futures at 93.25 to yield 6.75 percent. The basis narrowed from 65 to 55 points. The use of the futures reduced the $500 loss in the cash market to a net loss of only $250.

REDUCING BASIS RISK

The whole idea behind hedging is to minimize the risk of unfavorable basis movement. If you can do that, you will have a very successful hedging program. There are several concepts to keep in mind in minimizing such risks.

One way to hold it down is through proper selection of the contract month for placing the hedge. So many hedgers ask, "Which month should I use?" The answer has several parts:

1. Use the futures month that most closely coincides with the maturity of your cash position.
2. Select the futures price that seems most overpriced or underpriced relative to the cash market.

This involves some understanding of what causes futures prices for different months to take on different values. Basically, the price differences between two futures months are reflecting two things:

1. The cost-of-carry
2. Expectations

Cost-of-carry is the difference between the cost to borrow the money to buy the cash instrument and the return received while owning the cash instrument. Cost of borrowing is best reflected in the repo rate. If the cost-of-carry is positive, you would expect futures to be trading at a higher yield (lower price) than the cash. If the cost-of-carry is negative, you would expect futures to trade at a lower yield or a higher price than the cash.

Why? If you can make money by borrowing to buy a cash instrument, you will bid for the futures as an alternative investment until the net futures price provides exactly the same yield. Because futures are not an earning asset until delivery, you will bid only until the two prices are identical after adjustment for time difference and the cost of money over the time difference. If it is a positive carry of 2 percent, you will give up no more than 2 percent on futures to get the 2 percent income.

Expectations sometimes become a more important price influence than cost-of-carry. Instances arise where people expect the cost-of-carry to change, or they expect significant shifts in the level of interest rates. Those expectations usually get reflected in distant months more dramatically than in nearby months. Thus, you need to watch market fundamentals closely to determine which of myriad factors is influencing the market at any particular time.

HEDGING THE PRIME RATE

Banks regularly issue six-month CDs to obtain funds to lend at the prime rate. They do this when rates are high and when they are low. Sometimes they get caught in situations where they have outstanding CDs with several months to run, but their prime lending rate has fallen. In such cases the profitability of these loans has reduced dramatically and will remain that way until the CDs mature and new money can be obtained (new CDs issued) at the lower rates. A banker caught in such a profit squeeze could protect his profit margin by hedging, by buying 90-day T-bill futures. As the prime rate falls, so should rates on 90-day Eurodollars, if the two rates are correlated fairly closely. In such a hedge, a long position in futures will yield a profit which can be used to offset the loss in loan income. As the cost of funding the loan comes in line with the prime rate, he should lift the hedge.

A construction company anticipates that, in about three months, it will need to obtain a substantial construction loan for six months priced on a floating-rate basis at 1 percent over prime. By selling Eurodollar futures, or Treasury bill futures contracts, it can hedge against an increase in the prime rate between now and the time the loan funds will be needed. If interest rates have risen by that time, and futures prices have declined correspondingly, the profit realized when the futures contracts are liquidated will help to cover the higher rate of interest the company will pay for its construction loan.

This may be a risky hedge if it is a short-term hedge, because the prime rate is an administered rate and changes infrequently compared to the market rates for Eurodollars and T-bills. Hence, short-term basis risk may be great. In the long run, say two years or more, such basis risk will average out and provide a much better potential for an effective hedge.

HEDGING THE FED FUNDS RATE

Sometimes a regional bank has excess Fed funds, so it sells them. When the Fed funds rate is high, such sales can be a nice source of income. When Fed funds rates fall, however, revenues fall. A bank can protect against this loss of income by buying 30-day Fed fund futures traded at the CBOT. As rates fall, income from futures helps offset the loss of income from Fed funds. Again, this hedge has a reasonable chance of success only if the correlation between the futures and the Fed funds rate is quite high.

PREFUNDING A PORTFOLIO

Suppose a bank has a liquid portfolio (very short-term instruments) with maturities in September and December. Assume it expects rates to be lower in those months than the rates currently reflected in futures. To protect against that fall in rates, the bank could buy Eurodollar futures and T-bill futures. As rates fall the futures gains will offset the reduced yields received when the bank reinvests the money from the maturing instruments in September and December.

You might ask why the bank doesn't simply purchase replacement securities now for the securities maturing in September and December. Two reasons: First, it may not have extra cash. Second, it might not want to swap the securities in its current portfolio for others because it would have to reflect the loss on its financial statements. Such a loss would not have to be booked if the securities are kept to maturity, when they will be redeemed at par.

CORPORATION HEDGING SINKING FUND OBLIGATIONS

Assume a corporation must purchase $5 million of its 8 percent bonds (six years to maturity) by September 1 to fulfill a sinking fund obligation. The treasurer of the corporation believes there is at least an 80 percent probability that interest rates will be 1 percent lower than current rates by September but does not have the cash available to buy the bonds at this time. That 1 percent fall on a six-year maturity would increase the costs to the fund manager by approximately $210,000.

He can hedge by purchasing approximately 50 contracts of the four- to six-year Treasury note futures.

If rates indeed do decline by 1 percent *and* if that 1 percent decline is reflected fully in T-note futures, then the manager will have an approximate profit of $210,000 in futures to offset the increased cost of his sinking fund bonds.

BANK ISSUING CDs

Assume that a regional bank economic forecasting group concludes interest rates are headed sharply higher with a real possibility that the Fed will tighten monetary policy imminently. Assume that bank also was preparing to issue $50 million in CDs, but does not have them issued yet. It needs two weeks.

How could the bank protect itself against the possibility that rates might rise before it got the CDs sold?

The answer is to hedge by selling Eurodollar or T-bill futures. Table 23.7 shows how the hedge would have worked out.

Table 23.7 Bank Hedge for CD's

Cash Market	Basis	Futures Market
October 5		
Long $50 million CDs due April		Sell $100 million March T-bill futures
5.80	**1.61**	**4.19**
October 12		
$50 million CDs due April		$100 million March T-bill futures
6.80	**1.93**	**4.87**
–1.00	**–.32**	**+.68**

Each basis point for futures = $25 x 68 x 100 = $170,000
Each basis point for CDs = $50 x 100 x 50 = $250,000
$ 80,000

Loss reduced from $250,000 to $80,000

Note: As the CDs are issued, the futures position should be liquidated proportionately.

This example teaches you several important points:

1. The basis changed. Rates in the cash position increased more than rates in the futures market. Hence, gains and losses did not offset each other exactly. This emphasizes the importance of knowing the basis and correlation.
2. This was a cross-hedge. The product being hedged in the cash market was not identical to the items represented in the futures contract. That is a major reason why the basis changed.
3. Because the maturity of the cash item was different from the maturity of the futures instrument, a .01 change in the rate for the two instruments was not equal. The value of .01 for the 90-day T-bill futures was $25. The value of .01 for the six-month CD was $50. Hence, to get "dollar equivalent" coverage, it was necessary that the futures position be double that of the cash position.

Chapter 24

Stock Index Futures and Options

Kansas City is famous for many things, some of which have been immortalized in song, but it now takes a place in the history of finance as the originator of stock index futures. Trading in stock index futures, specifically the Value Line Average (VLA), began in February 1982. The Kansas City Board of Trade worked actively on the concept of trading futures on stock indexes for five years before regulatory hurdles were overcome and trading actually began.

The last major regulatory hurdle was passed in mid-1981 when the Commodity Futures Trading Commission finally granted approval for the concept of cash settlement of futures contracts. Cash settlement means exactly what it suggests: At delivery time, the buyer and the seller exchange cash equal to the difference between the actual price of the product on that day and the price at which they had originally made their contract adjusted for any daily settlements made in the meantime. Thus, in the case of stock indexes, there is no need for the seller to scurry around at delivery time collecting, in the correct proportion, the various shares of the companies that make up the index.

WHAT'S TRADED AND WHEN

The old Wall Street saying that you can't buy the market averages isn't true anymore. Now if you have an opinion on the market as opposed to an individual stock, you can buy or sell the whole market—if you buy and the market goes up, the index will go up and you will make money. It will not be necessary to make an individual decision on each stock. In other words, index futures now allow you to get in on the price action of broad groups of stocks by buying or selling the futures contracts on those indexes.

Since Kansas City inaugurated the trading, other exchanges have also listed stock index futures. The Chicago Mercantile Exchange (CME) offers futures on the Standard and Poor's 500 (S&P 500), and the New York Futures Exchange lists futures on the New York Stock Exchange (NYSE) Composite Index. The quick success of stock index futures in the U.S. has prompted the listing of stock indexes and options on a variety of other stock groupings, including some highly specialized selections in utility indexes and financial indexes. Further, all of the major stock exchanges of the world now have futures contracts on their stock indexes: e.g., the NIKKEI traded in Chicago and Singapore; the FTSE traded in London; et al.

Not all of the indexes are the same. The VLA index, the first stock index futures traded, reflects all of the several thousand stocks included in the Value Line Average. The VLA is one of the most popular market indicators followed by over-the-counter investors. In the VLA, each company is weighted equally; thus, it represents one share of each of the 1,700 companies.

The S&P 500 stock index, a widely recognized representation of the stock market as a whole, is based on the equity prices of 500 different companies: 400 industrials, 40 utilities, 20 transportation firms, and 40 financial institutions. The market value of the 500 firms is equal to approximately 80 percent of the value of all stocks listed on the NYSE.

The S&P 500 is a weighted index of the prices of the 500 firms. Each stock in the index is weighted so that changes in the stock's price will influence the index in proportion to the stock's respective market value. To determine the weight for the stock of any particular firm, the number of its shares outstanding is multiplied by its market price per share. In other words, a stock's market value determines the relative importance of the particular stock in the index; for example, General Motors accounts for approximately 1.35 percent of the S&P 500, while many other stocks account for only .05 percent or less.

The NYSE Composite Index reflects the value of the shares of all companies listed for trading on the NYSE. Similar to the S&P, the company shares are not weighted equally, but rather are included in the index according to the formula reflecting the stock's respective market value. The formula takes into account both the number of shares outstanding and the market price.

So both the S&P and NYSE attempt to measure the total value of the stocks included in their indexes, while the VLA attempts to measure average value. The NYSE measures every common stock on the NYSE. The S&P and VLA measure a designed market sample.

COMPUTING A STOCK INDEX

The best way to demonstrate the computation of an index is to actually show the computation. To illustrate, consider the S&P 500. That index is calculated using the base years 1941 to 1943 equal to 10. The price of each stock is multiplied by the number of shares outstanding for that company. In the case of the S&P 500, the value for each of the 500 shares is added, giving a total dollar value. To create the index, the total dollar value is then compared to the base value and the index is set according to the base index of 10. As a simple example, suppose the index was composed of only five issues (see Table 24.1).

Table 24.1 S&P 500 Index 1986–1992

	Outstanding Shares	Price	Value
Company A	100	30	3,000
Company B	500	10	5,000
Company C	200	50	10,000
Company D	400	4	1,600
Company E	300	20	6,000
	Current Market Value =		25,600

If the 1941–94 market value was $2,500, then 25,600 is to 2,500 what × is to 10.

Current Market Value $\frac{25,600}{2,500} = \frac{\times}{10}$

1941–1943 Market Value $256,000 = $2,500 ×
× = 102.40

To some extent, the indexes are substitutes for each other, i.e., they measure the same thing. The correlation coefficients between the S&P and the NYSE are normally .90 and above (a perfect correlation equals 1.000); hence, they measure nearly the same thing and will be almost equally useful in hedging a portfolio. However, the VLA and the Dow Jones Industrial Average are not so highly correlated with the other two.

VOLATILITY IN INDEXES

Like other futures contracts, index futures offer a way to play price movements with a lot of leverage. Leverage allows you to get more bang for your buck. Substantial movements in the value of your account will occur with small investments in the index. Historically, though, the maximum leverage allowed on the stock index contracts has been much less than for almost all other futures. Generally, the margin on the S&P 500 has been about 8 to 10 percent of contract value. Figure 24.1 shows the movement in the S&P 500 from 1986 through 1992. A 10 percent margin investment for one long contract in 1986, and continuously rolled over, would have yielded a handsome return indeed, provided you had survived the 1987 crash! (Not likely because margins were raised to very high levels during the crash, and anyone who couldn't meet them would have had their positions liquidated.)

The stock market, as represented by the various indexes, is highly variable when measured over long periods of time. For example, a study by the CME shows that the average daily change in the S&P 500 was 2.58 points between February 2, 1981, and March 12, 1982. In terms of futures contract value, that is equal to $1,290 per day

Figure 24.1 S &P 500 Index Spot Price History January 6, 1986—December 31, 1992

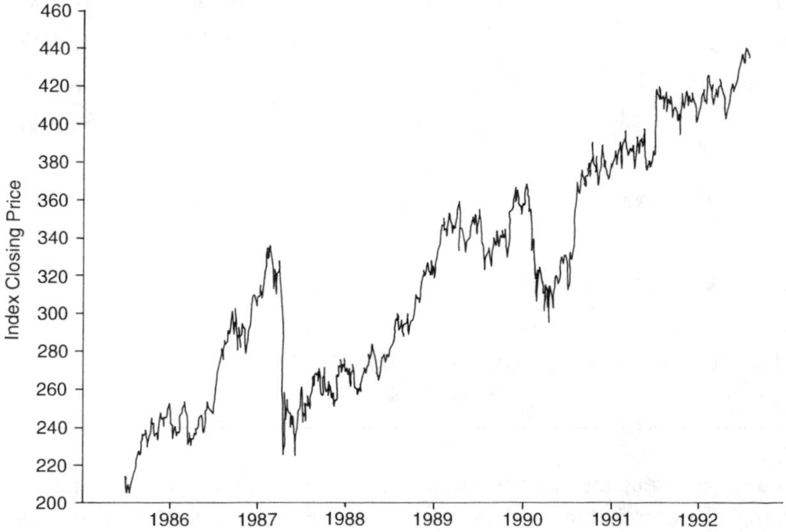

Source: CME Financial Research

(2.58 x $500). In more recent years, the volatility has increased, and it is not unusual for the index to change by $1,500 to $2,000 from day to day.

Although futures prices move in the same direction as the underlying indexes do, the futures tend to be more volatile than the underlying indexes. When investors are bearish, prices frequently drop below, and fall faster than, the relevant index. In contrast, when investors are bullish, they tend to push futures prices above the index, and futures rise faster. This volatility tends to get accentuated in some of the more thinly traded months and more thinly traded futures. As with most elements of volatility, these swings offer opportunities for making money and losing money.

In the long run, stock index futures will trade like all other futures: Prices for the futures will stay in close relationship with the current cash price, plus carrying costs. Generally speaking, when prices of futures stray away from their theoretical values, arbitrageurs push them back into line by buying when the price seems low and selling when the price seems high relative to its cash market value.

CIRCUIT BREAKERS AND CRASH PROTECTORS

In fall of 1987, the stock market crashed, falling over 500 points in one day. Many people immediately pointed at the futures traders as culprits, not for initiating the price decline, but for exacerbating it. Many studies were completed on the causes of the crash and the volatility of the market during the day. The conclusion of the Federal Reserve study, and many others, was that the futures traders were participants, but certainly not the initiators or causers of the problems. They were reacting to outside forces.

The upshot of all the hullabaloo was that the commodity exchanges, stock exchanges, and government regulators each set in place a series of procedures that are designed to protect the stock market from disastrous collapses due to emotion-filled trading. In short, they agreed on a series of steps to shut down the futures markets and the stock markets for short periods of time if the market rises or falls by some predetermined amount. The shutdowns become increasingly more severe, and focus more on market declines than on advances, as the volatility increases. These are referred to as circuit breakers, to reflect the idea that they work like an electrical circuit breaker that automatically shuts off the electricity when a circuit gets overloaded.

This process is simply an advancement on the daily price limit that had been in use for decades on virtually all traditional commodities. Those limits had not been applied to stock index futures because it was thought they could cause price dislocations (and, therefore, great financial risk to arbitrageurs) between the stock market and the futures market, if the futures stopped trading but the stock market continued. Besides, everybody knew that the stock market would generally stay in a reasonable daily volatility range! Didn't they?

Listed below are some of the rules used to engage the circuit breakers:

Table 24.2 Coordinated Trading Halts

A. INTEREXCHANGE COORDINATED TRADING HALTS

DOW JONES INDUSTRIAL AVERAGE—250-POINT DECLINE

If the Dow Jones Industrial Average falls 250 points below its prior day close, the New York Stock Exchange will declare a one-hour trading halt.

If a trading halt is declared and the S&P 500 Primary Futures Contract (PFC) is at its Opening, Initial, Intermediate, Second Intermediate, or Maximum Daily Limit, trading in the S&P 500 Futures and Options will also halt.

- At the end of the one-hour trading halt, trading in the S&P 500 Futures and Options can resume only if at least 50 percent of the S&P 500 Cash Market (by Capitalization) has re-opened for trading.
- Upon resumption of trading the Maximum Daily Price Limit will be in effect.

DOW JONES INDUSTRIAL AVERAGE—400-POINT DECLINE

If the Dow Jones Industrial Average falls 400 points below its prior day close, the New York Stock Exchange will declare a two-hour trading halt.

If a trading halt is declared and the S&P 500 PFS is at its Opening, Initial, Intermediate, Second Intermediate, or Maximum Daily Limit, trading in the S&P 500 Futures and Options will also halt.

- At the end of the two-hour trading halt, trading in the S&P 500 Futures and Options can resume only if at least 50 percent of the S&P 500 Cash Market (by Capitalization) has re-opened for trading.
- Upon resumption of trading the Maximum Daily Price Limit will be in effect.

Table 24.2 Coordinated Trading Halts (continued)

B. TRADING HALTS—ADDITIONAL CONSIDERATIONS

ONE-HOUR TRADING HALT

If the one-hour trading halt occurs within 30 minutes of the normal close of trading, the S&P 500 Futures and Options shall not re-open that day.

If the one-hour trading halt occurs more than 30 minutes but less than one hour before the normal close of trading, the S&P Price Limit Committee after consultation with the Executive Committee shall determine whether an abbreviated re-opening of the S&P 500 Futures contract shall be allowed to settle the futures contracts to market forces. In the event of such a re-opening, there shall be no trading at a price beyond the Maximum Daily Price Limit.

TWO-HOUR TRADING HALT

If the two-hour trading halt occurs within 60 minutes of the normal close of trading, the S&P 500 Futures and Options shall not re-open that day.

If the two-hour trading halt occurs more than 60 minutes but less than two hours before the normal close of trading, the S&P Price Limit Committee after consultation with the Executive Committee shall determine whether an abbreviated re-opening of the S&P 500 Futures contract shall be allowed to settle the futures contracts to market forces. In the event of such a re-opening, there shall be no trading at a price beyond the Maximum Daily Price Limit.

1. OPENING RANGE PRICE LIMIT—500 POINTS (UP or DOWN)
   - The 500-point limit applies for the first 10 minutes of trading.
   - If the Primary Futures Contract (PFC) is Limit Bid or Limit Offer at 8:40 A.M., a two-minute trading halt is required.
   - During the two-minute trading halt, the S&P Price Limit Committee will determine if trading should resume with a Trading Range.

OPTIONS PROCEDURES

Whenever the PFC is officially declared at its Opening, Initial, Intermediate or Maximum Limit, options trading is suspended.

When the PFC trades off the limit or the limit expires, options trading resumes, with a new Opening Rotation (if necessary).

Table 24.2 Coordinated Trading Halts (continued)

2. INITIAL DAILY LIMIT—1200 POINTS (DOWN MOVE ONLY)

   When a 1200-point Limit Offer in the PFC is officially reached:

   - ➥ The Initial Daily Limit remains in effect for 30 minutes or until 2:30 P.M. (whichever comes first);
   - ➥ If the PFC is Limit Offer at the end of the 30-minute period or at 2:30 P.M. a two-minute trading halt is required.
   - ➥ During the two-minute trading halt, the S&P Price Limit Committee will determine if trading should resume with a Trading Range.
   - ➥ When the Initial Daily Limit expires, the Intermediate Daily Limit is in effect, unless the Initial Daily Limit expires at 2:30 P.M.
   - ➥ After 2:30 P.M., only the 3000-point Maximum Daily Limit is in effect

3. INTERMEDIATE DAILY LIMIT—2000 POINTS (DOWN MOVE ONLY)

   When a 2000-point Limit Offer in the PFC is officially reached:

   - ➥ The Intermediate Daily Limit remains in effect for 30 minutes or until 2:30 P.M. (whichever comes first);
   - ➥ If the PFC is Limit Offer at the end of the 30-minute period or at 2:30 P.M. a two-minute trading halt is required.
   - ➥ During the two-minute trading halt, the S&P Price Limit Committee will determine if trading should resume with a Trading Range.
   - ➥ When the Intermediate Daily Limit expires, the Maximum Daily Limit is in effect.
   - ➥ After 2:30 P.M., only the Maximum Daily Limit of 3000 Points is in effect.

4. MAXIMUM DAILY LIMIT—3000 POINTS (UP or DOWN)

   The 3000-point Limit remains in effect until the close of trading.

If the first day of decline ends with the market down the limit, then on the next day the same general rules apply except the daily maximum decline is expanded to 5000 points. Similarly for the third day. The first day the market does not close at its maximum limit, then the next day normal limits apply.

These circuit breakers have been employed many times since the 1987 crash and have worked very nicely. Some of that success is due simply to the fact that people at the exchanges and in government are working together more easily than pre-1987.

TRADING THE STOCK INDEXES

Investors or money managers may be interested in participating in stock index futures for a number of reasons. For example, they might have an overall opinion on the market direction and would buy or sell the market outright—thereby taking a position on market direction. They might want to sell stock index futures to protect an existing investment or in anticipation of a sale of all or part of a portfolio.

Traders may take both a long and short position in the market but in different delivery months. That technique of spreading one month against another works in stock indexes just as it works in other commodities. You can buy near-term futures and sell distant futures, or vice versa, hoping to gain as the price difference between the two months changes. You should be aware that such spreading techniques are not always low risk, particularly in stock indexes where there is substantial uncertainty about future stock prices, interest rates, and dividend levels.

You may also be interested in integrating stock indexes into the overall management of a stock market portfolio. You could take 10 percent of your capital and place it in stock index futures, for example, putting the remainder in money market funds at a high yield. Assume you had $100,000 in high-yielding bonds and felt that the stock market was going up, but you didn't have the time or resources to make the difficult decisions on individual stocks. Instead, you could buy one NYSE contract worth approximately $125,000. Approximately 10 percent of the capital would be necessary to margin those futures positions. The remainder of the money, $90,000, would stay invested at the higher rate of return. This strategy would allow you to participate in the stock market while still maintaining a high yield on your funds. Of course, you have significant risk with this strategy. If stocks fall you will get margin calls.

HEDGING ILLUSTRATED

As noted earlier in this book, a major use of futures markets is for hedging. In this instance, you may want to use the market to hedge your current market holdings or a portfolio of individual stocks. You may hold the stock investments and sell the stock index. If the market goes lower and the value of your individual investments declines with it, you will have a gain on the futures which can offset the loss on the value of the individual shares.

Suppose you owned a 10-stock diversified portfolio with a current market value of $35,000. In addition, suppose it generally reflected the value movements in the NYSE index. If the stock market generally declines by 10 percent as reflected in the NYSE index, your market loss would be about $3,500. You could protect against this loss by selling one NYSE index futures. Suppose at the time of the sale, it had an approximate value of $33,000. If you buy it back after the market has fallen, and if the index has in turn fallen by 10 percent, you will have made $3,300 on your hedge. That hedge will reduce your net market loss from $3,500 to $200.

While this may not work as an exact hedge, ways can be found to efficiently tailor (see the next section) a futures position to a particular portfolio to give you the most efficient hedge possible. Generally, you would not be well-advised to use the futures market to hedge a portfolio unless it could be statistically demonstrated that the stocks that make up the portfolio do move in concert (are highly correlated) with the index used. If that can't be demonstrated in advance, the hedger might find himself in the unfortunate position of losing on both the stocks and the futures. If the portfolio is composed of small, little-known firms that are not included in the underlying index or, if included, are a very small proportion of the index, then it is unlikely that you will find efficient hedges. If, on the other hand, you have a portfolio that is composed of a small but diversified group of stocks that includes such big names as IBM or AT&T, you may indeed find the futures a reasonable hedge. Of course, if in 1992 you had tried to hedge IBM stock alone using any of the indexes, it would not have worked. IBM fell 50 percent or more while the indexes went up. You would have had a double whammy!

THE PORTFOLIO MANAGER AND HEDGING

A portfolio manager is one who takes responsibility for managing money invested in a group of assets usually including a range of securities. His objective is usually capital appreciation and income. In making investments, the manager must consider the risk or safety of the investment while attempting to achieve a reasonable return. Normally, the higher the risk, the higher the potential for return.

When a portfolio manager considers hedging, his objective with the hedge is akin to doing a balancing act with a scale. On one side of the scale, he has a group of investments with a particular risk associated with them. On the other side of the scale, he attempts to construct a futures position which will maintain a dollar balance with changes in the value of the portfolio. The success of his hedge will depend on his success in constructing the proper futures position so that a dollar lost on one side of the scale will be offset by a dollar gain on the other side. He can construct that by selecting those futures contracts which are most closely correlated (as determined by statistical analysis) with the individual or groups of stocks in his portfolio.

Once he has identified the appropriate futures to use, he then must determine the number of futures contracts necessary to balance the scales. That calculation is usually accomplished through a statistical technique called regression analysis. Regression analysis is used to measure past price relationships for individual issues, or groups of related issues, relative to the underlying index chosen for the hedge. That volatility relationship will be expressed as a "beta" and is a statistical measurement reflecting the average relationship. Although this "beta" is based on past history, it is probably the best measure of future price relationships in the long run.

To determine the correct number of futures contracts to sell to balance the scale, the hedger should calculate a weighted beta for his portfolio. If the overall portfolio beta is 1.0 as measured against any of the indexes, it indicates that virtually all of the risk contained in the portfolio is accounted for, or eliminated, if an equal dollar amount of futures contracts are sold. If the portfolio beta is different than 1.0, the number of contracts sold must be adjusted accordingly.

For example, if a portfolio manager found a beta coefficient of 1.20 for his portfolio, he would determine the appropriate number of contracts to sell by dividing the value of the portfolio by the value of the futures contract, and multiplying by 1.20. To illustrate, assume the manager's portfolio value is $20 million and the manager intends to use the NYSE Composite Index, which we will assume is valued at $35,000. Twenty million dollars divided by $35,000, multiplied by 1.2, equals 685.7 contracts. The manager would round that number up and would sell 686 contracts as the appropriate number for his short hedge.

Now, if past relationships hold and the market changes by 10 percent, the value of the portfolio should change by $2 million and the dollar value of the change reflected in the index futures should be $2 million as well.

It would be unusual if the hedge works out as perfectly as just illustrated. Even with all of the statistical techniques mentioned, it is likely there will be some variation in the total amount of gain or loss on the futures side compared to the total amount of gain or loss in the portfolio. This variation will be due in part to the fact that the futures market may move more, or less, than individual stocks in the portfolio. Further, the timing of the two moves may not coincide exactly. One may move today and the other may move tomorrow or next week. This, as noted in earlier chapters, is basis risk. It must be noted that betas and other statistical calculations are based on historical data, and futures seldom reflect past history exactly.

Before leaving this example, it would be reasonable to ask why a manager of a large portfolio would take a short futures position rather than simply sell the stock.

One of the reasons may be liquidity. A highly liquid futures contract can absorb a hedge without significantly affecting the futures market price, while sales in the stock market of the same magnitude could pull down the price of those individual stocks to a much greater extent. Further, many portfolio managers do not find liquidation a feasible alternative because they are restricted to stocks of a particular kind. The cash generated from the sale of those stocks may not be immediately reinvested in other alternative areas. The futures market gives a manager the opportunity and the flexibility to make potential adjustments in his portfolio without going through complete liquidation.

The Long Hedge

Stock index futures also can be used by the portfolio manager as a means of pricing future acquisitions of stock for his portfolio. Most managers receive periodic inflows of capital resulting from contributions to pension funds, dividends received, etc. If in the portfolio manager's estimation the market is cheaper now than it will be at the expected time of the inflow, then he may wish to use the index futures to price the cost of his purchases now. Later, when he actually receives the funds and makes the purchase of the securities, he will offset his futures. In doing so, he protects himself from a rise in the market before he receives his funds for investment. Of course, should the market fall during that time period, he will have losses on his futures which will offset the opportunity gains he had from purchasing stock at a lower level. As with all properly constructed hedges, he gives up the opportunity to make windfall profits while at the same time protecting himself against substantial losses.

STOCK INDEX OPTIONS

Options on the stock index futures have become a very popular trading vehicle. Stock index futures, options on the futures, portfolios of individual stocks, and options on the individual stocks provide a very rich intellectual environment for portfolio managers to develop hedging, arbitrage, and investment strategies for a vast array of time horizons. These derivative instruments when combined with a portfolio of stocks or bonds allow the portfolio manager and private investor (if he is big enough) to custom-design investments with risk/reward profits that match the investors needs and desires.

Chapters 25 and 26 cover the options markets. The strategies discussed there apply equally to stock index options, though they really only scratch the surface in terms of sophistication and potential applications.

Chapter 25

Commodity Options

The history of commodity trading in the U.S. is replete with stories of intrigue and conflict, of great fortunes gained and lost. None of the stories are more engrossing than those involving commodity options trading.

Commodity options trading has been conducted in this country on an intermittent basis since the early 1860s. At that time the Chicago Board of Trade passed a rule prohibiting its members from trading options. A few years later with a new Board of Governors the rules were changed again, this time permitting members to trade options. Throughout the rest of the 19th century, trading options on the CBOT was a sometime thing as battles raged between pro-options traders and anti-options people. They fought through the legislature, in the courts, in the board rooms, and with other exchanges.

In 1936 it was charged that options played a role in a particularly blatant and successful attempt to manipulate the grain markets on the CBOT. Congress held hearings on the matter and subsequently passed the Commodity Exchange Act, which barred all trading in options on commodities under the regulation of the Commodity Exchange Authority.

In 1974, during hearings to revise the Commodity Exchange Act, Congress once again addressed the question and at first seemed to lean toward extending the ban to all commodities. Ultimately, however, after a good deal of testimony extolling the economic virtues of commodity options, Congress decided to review the ban on options for all previously regulated agricultural commodities while leaving a decision on other commodities up to the discretion of the Commodity Futures Trading Commission. In 1982, the CFTC authorized a pilot program and has since allowed options trading on virtually all approved futures contracts.

THE LANGUAGE

Although options may be written on actual commodities or on futures contracts, this section will focus on options on futures contracts. Trading strategies and concepts are basically the same, however.

Options trading has its own terminology, which is considerably different from that of futures trading. For example, a "call option" is an obligation of the grantor (seller) to provide a long futures position to the grantee (buyer) at a predetermined price on or before the exercise date of the option contract, if and when the buyer chooses to exercise his right. Thus, a call option is a right to buy. It establishes a buying price for the buyer of the call.

A "put" option is an obligation of the grantor (seller) to provide a short futures position to the grantee (buyer) at a predetermined price on or before the exercise date of the option contract, if and when the grantee chooses to exercise his right. Thus, a put option is a right to sell. It establishes a selling price for the buyer of the put.

A "double" option allows the purchaser the right to acquire either (not both) a long or short futures position at a specified price on or before a specified date if and when he chooses to exercise his right.

The "strike price" is the predetermined price at which the futures position is transferred from the seller to the buyer if the option is exercised.

The term "exercise" refers to the buyer's decision to require the seller to fulfill the terms of the contract. If a call option is exercised, the option seller must provide to the buyer an underlying futures position at the strike price specified. When a put option on a futures contract is exercised, the seller of the option must provide a short futures position at the strike price specified.

The "premium" is the amount of money paid by the buyer of an option to the seller for the right to exercise the option at the strike price. The seller receives the premium regardless of whether the option is actually exercised. That is a one-time payment to the seller. Irrespective of what happens to price, there are no further payments by the buyer unless he exercises.

The "expiration date" is the last day of the option's life. The buyer of an option must decide whether to exercise or to abandon his right to exercise the option either on this date or before. Options which allow exercise only at expiration are called European options. Options that permit exercise during the life of the option are called American options.

An option is said to be "at-the-money" if its strike price is equal (or approximately equal) to the current market price of the underlying futures contract.

A call is said to be "in-the-money" if its strike price is below the current price of the underlying futures contract (i.e., if the option has intrinsic value). A put is "in-the-money" if its strike price is above the current price of the underlying futures contract (i.e., if the option has intrinsic value).

An "out-of-the-money" option is a put or call option that currently has no intrinsic value. That is, a call whose strike price is above the current futures price or a put whose strike price is below the current futures price.

The "intrinsic value" of an option is the dollar amount that could be realized if the option were to be currently exercised (see "in-the-money").

An option "margin" is the sum of money that must be deposited and maintained in order to provide protection to both parties to a trade. The exchange establishes minimum margin amounts. Brokerage firms often require margin deposits that exceed exchange minimums. In turn, they post and maintain customer margins with the clearing corporation. Buyers of options do not have to post margins since their risk is limited to the option premium.

"Margin calls" are additional funds that a person with a futures position or the writer of an option may be called upon to deposit if there is an adverse price change or if margin requirements are increased. Buyers of options are not subject to margin calls.

"Naked writing" of an option refers to writing a call or a put on a futures contract in which the writer has no opposite cash or futures market position. This is also known as uncovered writing.

An option "series" refers to all options of the same class having the same strike price and expiration date.

An option "spread" refers to a position consisting of both long and short options of the same class, such as having a long position in a call with one strike price and expiration and a short position in another call with a different strike price and/or expiration.

An option "straddle" is a combination in which the put and the call have the same strike price and the same expiration.

The "time value" of an option is the amount by which an option premium exceeds the option's intrinsic value. If an option has no intrinsic value, its premium is entirely time value.

The "writing" of an option refers to the sale of an option in an opening transaction.

THE GREEK LANGUAGE AND OPTIONS

There are a number of Greek words used to describe changes in options value. These include:

1. Delta

Delta is the change in the market price:

$$\text{Delta} = \frac{\text{Option Price Change}}{\text{Market Price Change}}$$

For example, if the market price changes by 1 and the option price changes by .3, the Delta is .3 or 30 percent. This 30 percent actually reflects the expected (market generated) probability that the option will expire in-the-money.

Now this also tells us something useful about hedging. As noted elsewhere in this book, hedging is essentially the establishment of a counter-balancing position. So, if one knows that an option moves .3 for each one point of change in the market price, then the appropriate hedge ratio one should use is the reciprocal, or

$$\frac{1}{.3} = 3.$$

This means that three options are needed to get a complete 100 percent counter-balancing hedge position.

Delta neutral means your option position is hedged. The long Deltas (the sum of the Deltas associated with the calls you own) equal the short Deltas (the sum of the Deltas associated with the puts you own). The Delta tells one how much price change can be expected with a move in market price or how long or short your position is. Positive Deltas mean you have a bullish position and will profit if prices go up. Negative Deltas mean you will profit if prices go down.

2. Gamma

Gamma is the name given to the rate of change in the Delta. So it really reflects the rate of change of the rate of change. If an option has a Delta of .55 and a Gamma of .05, then the option would have a Delta of .6 if the underlying futures goes up one full point.

3. Vega

Vega is a measure of volatility. It is the change in option price associated with a 1 percent change in volatility. Historical volatility is usually measured by the standard deviation (log normal). Implied volatility is the volatility that is imbedded in a given option price. You can calculate the implied volatility in any option premium by holding all elements of the price model constant and solving the equations for volatility, i.e., run the option model backward.

When volatility is very low, and you expect that it will explode upward soon, a logical strategy would be to buy out-of-the-money calls and sell further out-of-the-money calls. This is a very short-term trade with limited risk of loss equal to the difference in the value of the calls bought and the value of the calls sold, and limited gain equal to the difference in the strike prices less the difference in the premiums. With high volatility, the Deltas of out-of-the-money options often move closer to .5, thus causing the premiums between strike prices to narrow.

4. Theta

Theta is the change in the option premium associated with the passage of time. It is referred to as the rate of time decay associated with an options premium and is basically a function of the square root of time remaining on the option's life. It is usually expressed in option premium points to indicate how much the premium would lose in one day if all other factors remained the same and the futures price was constant. Thus a Theta of .02 on an option would suggest that it would lose two ticks in value for each one day of time remaining.

OPTIONS VERSUS FUTURES

There are some important differences between an options contract and a futures contract. A futures contract is a bilateral contract requiring action by both parties and obligating both the buyer and the seller to fulfill the conditions by delivery and payment. An option contract, on the other hand, is a unilateral contract. Unlike a futures contract, the buyer and the seller of the option do not have an equivalent obligation to perform. The purchaser of an option has the right but not the obligation to require the seller to perform under the contract, and the seller is obligated to do so only if the buyer exercises his right. The converse, however, is not true. The seller of an option cannot require the purchaser to exercise. Only the buyer has the right to require fulfillment of the contract terms.

Perhaps the most distinguishing feature of an option contract is the limited liability of the purchaser. The potential loss to an option purchaser is limited to the "premium" he pays the seller at the time of the purchase of the option. His potential for gain, theoretically, is limited only by the extent of the price movement of the underlying contract. In contrast, on the futures contract the holder of a position (either long or short futures position) remains liable to margin calls as long as his position remains open.

In short, therefore, the purchaser of an option contract can lose at a maximum only the amount he pays for the option. This is so because, if the price does not move in his favor, he fails to "exercise" his option. Instead, he simply abandons it. An analogy can be drawn with an insurance contract. The writer of the insurance policy receives the premium for undertaking the risk but has to stand ready in the future to make any payments due the person who bought the insurance if that person submits a valid claim. If he does not submit the claim, the insurance company still keeps the premium.

One major advantage of options over futures markets for the businessman is that, when prices are extremely volatile, options can reduce the demands on cash flow. For example, if you have purchased a futures contract and it declines, you will have to pay in more margin, which, of course, must be paid in cash. If, on the other hand, you have purchased a call option, you will have a one-time payment; no matter how far the price falls, you will not be asked to post more money. The converse of this is, of course, also true. If prices go up, the futures position will yield cash to you while no such thing will happen with the option. Options thus provide more certainty in planning cash flow exposure.

Options permit a range of investment and resource management strategies not available from futures. Options used in conjunction with futures and actual inventories of a product afford a wide range of strategies for a merchandiser, producer, or processor in managing inventories. They can provide greater control with lower capital requirements than do futures alone.

To a large extent options are substitutes for stop orders on futures. You can attempt to limit your risk on a futures position by placing a stop loss order at whatever level you choose. Then, if the market touches that level, your broker would automatically offset the futures contract at the price stipulated or at the next best possible price.

In essence, the purchase of an option serves the same purpose as the stop loss order serves in the futures contract. They are both there to limit losses. The differences between the two, however, are:

1. A stop loss order may not always be exercised at the price stipulated so the loss cannot be absolutely fixed in advance. The size of the option premium, however, is fixed in advance, and the loss cannot exceed the size of the premium.

2. A poorly disciplined trader may decide not to use stop loss orders and to meet margin calls when he should not, thus sticking with a losing position in the hope that the market will reverse. This can lead to very large losses. An option, on the other hand, does not give that discretion to the holder. Once he buys the option, the marketplace decides whether it will be profitable to exercise it. The holder has no more decisions to make if the market moves against him or fails to rise to the exercise price.
3. One can get whipsawed in a market using stop loss orders. The market can set off a stop order, causing the offset of the futures contract, and then the market could turn around and go the opposite direction. Due to the offset, you would be without a position in the market and unable to take advantage of the rise.

In sum, the option is a more certain way of limiting losses. The value of this certainly has to be weighed against the size of the premium paid. It may be a very high price to pay for the luxury of not having to exercise the self-discipline in using stop loss orders or for the potential that you will get whipsawed.

Other differences between options and futures will become apparent as you read some of the strategies for trading options discussed in the next chapter.

PICKING AN OPTIONS BROKER

An earlier section discussed selecting a broker for futures transactions. Chances are you will find that your futures broker also handles commodity options transactions and is well-prepared to provide the trading support you need. In a few instances he may also handle cash options.

Picking an options broker should be done with care. There are many scam operators who sell options on coins, precious metals, etc. They often are not registered and are selling in violation of state and federal laws. Shop around and find out:

1. What kind of services the firm offers and what kind of commission they charge for those services.
2. How much experience the broker has had in trading options.
3. Whether the broker is registered with the NFA/CFTC. Is he a member of any professional options organization or an exchange? If so, you can contact them for further information about the firm; e.g., is the firm in good standing? Are there any public records of past disciplinary action?

After you have picked your broker and before you decide to enter into any particular option transaction, check out the following:

1. What kind of contract is it? Is it a U.S. or a foreign option, and is it an exchange-traded or a dealer option? The difference here can be substantial. A U.S. option is more easily monitored, and all parties to it are under the regulation and scrutiny of the Commodity Futures Trading Commission. An exchange option has a ready secondary market in contrast to most dealer options and, therefore, your option position can be easily offset. In addition, exchange-traded options are standardized contracts with information readily and easily available about the underlying commodity. The opposite is true of many other options.

2. Who guarantees the transaction, and what is the financial solvency of that party? The guarantor of options on futures will be an exchange clearing house. If it is a U.S. exchange, the federal government is monitoring the exchange's, the broker's, and the clearing house's financial condition. That does not mean, of course, they couldn't still go bankrupt. If it is a foreign exchange, find out how the guarantee works and exactly how your account will be settled if there is a bankruptcy. An independent option dealer who is selling non-exchange options is the guarantor.

3. How much does the premium represent as a percentage of the value of the underlying commodity or futures contract? In some independent options dealers, these fees are unconscionably high.

4. What is the break-even point for your option? That is, how much will the price have to change before the option will become profitable?

5. How will the option premium, if you are buying, be passed to the seller and, if you are a seller, under what conditions will you receive the premium?

6. How much is the premium being marked up over what it cost at the time of origination? This is particularly important if you are not buying it directly on an exchange, such as would be the case with foreign options and dealer options.

7. How much commission are you paying and what services are you getting for the commission?

8. What are independent research people indicating the future prices of the underlying commodity will be? Remember, the premium represents the expected value of the expected volatility of prices. If most people expect very little price change, premiums should be quite low.

9. How do you exercise your option, and what do you get when you exercise? Study the terms and conditions of the contract.
10. When and how will your broker notify you of the execution of your contract and the current status of your account?
11. Where can you get regular information about the value of your option and the price of the underlying commodity? If this is not available, beware. In short, know as much about your dealer as you do about your business partner and only deal with someone you know, trust, and are comfortable with. He is using your money. Pick a professional who knows the business.

WHAT'S AN OPTION WORTH? DETERMINING THE OPTION PREMIUM

It should be implicit in the foregoing that one needs to evaluate very carefully the factors that affect the value of the option premium. These include:

1. The current price level of the underlying commodity relative to the strike price of the option.
2. The length of time the option has left before it expires. The longer the life of the option, the more time you are buying and the greater time there is for the market to reach the strike price.
3. The volatility of the price for the underlying commodity. The more volatile the price, the greater chance that the market will reach the strike price within a given time period.
4. The expectations generally held that the commodity price will rise above the strike price. This is related to each of the three preceding elements.
5. Interest rates, higher interest rates generally mean higher premiums.

Fair Market Value Concept

To understand option value, you need to focus on the concept of fair market value.

Fair market value is defined as the expected break-even price for both the buyer and the seller. The word "expected" is important here because, by definition, we are dealing with the occurrence of an event that is some time in the future. This means we have to focus on probabilities. As noted earlier, probability distributions reflect long-run estimates of the results you would expect to achieve over a large number of transactions. In the short run with only a few transactions, you may have distortions and mispricings. These are opportunities for profit.

The first step in calculating the fair market value for an option is to establish the probability that a particular price will be achieved. Recall that, at expiration, an option price must be either zero or positive. Hence, the effort here is to establish the probability that at expiration the difference between the strike price and the market price will be either zero, or some positive number.

The reasons for trying to figure out how to value an option are two-fold. First, it will demonstrate clearly how one determines advantageous option trading opportunities. Second, it will demonstrate the need for a computerized methodology if you are going to be regularly involved in trading options.

To illustrate the importance of getting the pricing right, and how important getting it even a little bit wrong can be, consider the following. Assume that the S&P Futures are at 400, and a 410 call is at $20 fair market value. Assume also the market rises to 450 and you exercise the call, giving you a $20 net profit (450 –410 – 20). You have a profit ratio of 2-to-1. If, however, the call had been mispriced and you bought it at less than fair market value, say $10, your net profit would be $30, a 3-to-1 ratio, or a 150 percent difference.

The formula for determining the value of the call premium is as follows:

Call Premium = the greater of zero or the difference between the market price at exercise minus the strike price multiplied times the probability(ies) of achieving a final market price greater than zero.

For example, assume that the market price for the S&P is at 400 and that the strike price you are interested in is 400. Assume further that at expiration only two final prices are possible, P_1 = 350 or P_2 = 450; and that there is a 50/50 probability either could be achieved. The fair market value of this option is calculated as follows:

Call Premium = (Probability of P_1) $\times$ the greater of (0, 350 - 400)
\+ (Probability of P_2) $\times$ the greater of (0, 450 - 400)
Call Premium = .5(0) + (1 - .5)(50)
Call Premium = $25.

NOTE: The second probability is equal to 1 minus the first probability.

In other words, over the long run, half the time both the buyer and the seller of this option should expect to make $25 and half the time they should expect to lose $25. The expected long-run return on this option is equal to zero and it is priced at a fair market value. But if the option were actually priced to you at $20 and you bought it, in the long run you should expect the probabilities to work in your favor and you will have a net profit (over the long run) of $5.

If in the above example, you had four potential prices—$P_1 = 350$, $P_2 = 375$, $P_3 = 425$ and $P_4 = 450$—all with an equal probability (P) of occurrence, then the proper calculation for the premium would be as follows:

$$\begin{aligned}\text{Call Premium} &= P(P_1)\max(0, 350\text{-}400) + P(P_2)\max(0, 375\text{-}400)\\ &+ P(P_3)\max(0, 425\text{-}400) + P(P_4)\max(0, 450\text{-}400)\\ &= (.25)(0) + (.25)(0) + (.25)(25) + (.25)(50)\\ &= 0 + 0 + 6.25 + 12.50\\ &= 18.75\end{aligned}$$

You can see that the greater the number of possible price scenarios there are, the more complex this calculation becomes. It also means that the more time remaining on the life of an option, the more potential price scenarios there are and all the more reason why these sorts of computations can be accomplished only with a computer (see Figure 25.1).

Figure 25.1 Option Pricing Probability Diagram

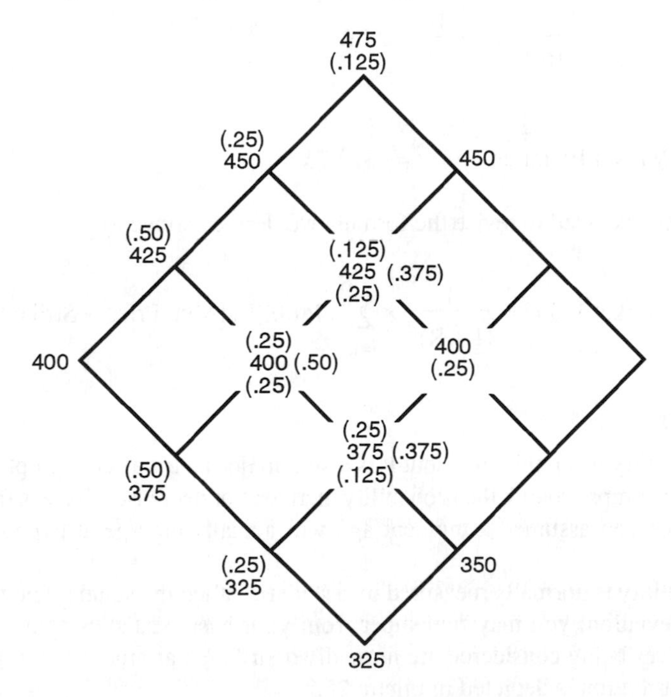

Interest Costs

As noted above, interest costs are an important element in the pricing of options. The $25 option premium derived in the earlier examples says two things. First, in the long run you expect to get zero returns. Second, since you didn't include an interest calculation for the use of your money during that time, the seller gets the use of your money free. Generally, people do not want to work for free and in the process give up the opportunity to earn interest on their money. Therefore, option formulas should always include an interest adjustment. The formula for that interest adjustment is as follows:

$$\text{Interest Adjustment} = \frac{1}{1 + R^{t}} \times \text{The Premium}$$

Where R = the interest rate
t = Number of Years

So, if we assume a 10 percent interest rate per year, then the $25 option value we derived above is really adjusted as follows:

$$\frac{1}{(1 + .10)^{1}} = \frac{1}{1.10} = .909$$

$$\$25 \times .909 = \$22.73$$

Fair Market Premium = $22.73.

Hence, we need to revise the formula we derived above to:

$$\text{Fair Market Value} = \frac{1}{(1 + R)^{t}} \times \sum_{i=k}^{N} \text{Prob.(P) (Mkt. Price} - \text{Strike Price)}$$

Volatility

Future volatility is an unknown, but it is also a major factor affecting options prices. As the price jumps around, the probability increases or decreases that a different price than the one you assumed a moment ago will actually emerge at expiration of the option.

Volatility is normally measured by a statistic called the standard deviation. The standard deviation, you may remember from your basic statistics courses, assumes that the prices being considered are normally distributed around an average price. A normal distribution is depicted in Figure 25.2.

Figure 25.2 Normal Distribution Curve

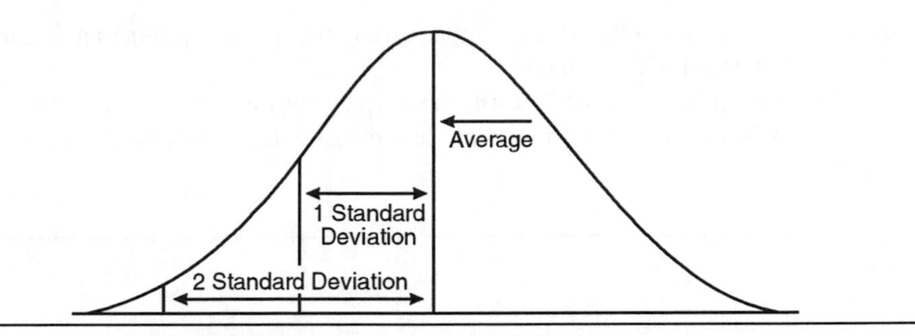

Now, we know that futures prices are not normally distributed so the bell-shaped curve shown above is not really a relevant or correct assumption. The reasons are three-fold. First, the bell-shaped curve shown above suggests that prices can actually go below zero. We know that is not true. Second, it suggests that normally free prices can go below and stay below cost of production in the long run. We know that is not true. Third, we know also that there are natural impediments such as price supports, political actions, subsidies, etc. that cause prices not to follow a normal distribution.

To get around these problems and others, mathematicians use logarithms and create what are called log normal distributions. They calculate the standard deviation using what are called log normal distribution assumptions. This is far too complex to get into here, so suffice it to say that the formula shown earlier actually gets changed and is expressed in logarithmic relationships.

Time

The last factor to consider in pricing options is time. In brief, the more time remaining, the more value there is to an option. The reason for this is that the longer the time period, the more price possibilities that could occur. Hence, sellers of options extract an insurance premium associated with the possibility that their price range assumptions will be wrong. This calculation really gets into complex higher mathematics. So we will skip it.

To summarize, we end with an option formula stated as follows:

$$\text{Option Value} = \frac{1}{(1+R)^{t}} \times \sum_{i=k}^{N} \text{Prob.(P) (Mkt. Price} - \text{Strike Price)}$$

$$+ \text{ adjustment for expected volatility} + \text{adjustment for time}$$

FUTURES VERSUS PHYSICALS VERSUS FINANCIALS

Are the factors that go into pricing options different if you are pricing an option on financials? on physicals? on futures?

The answer is yes. Table 25.1 lists the adjustments one would make to the basic option formula shown above for each of the three categories: futures, physicals, and financials.

Table 25.1

Futures	Physicals	Financials
Price	Price	Price
Strike	Strike	Strike
Volatility	Volatility	Interest Rate
Interest Rate	Interest Rate	Time
Time	Time	Time
	Holding Cost	Yield

Note that options formulae for physicals and financials also require adjustment for the cost of storing or holding a commodity over time and, in the case of financials, for dividends or coupons earned.

Why does an option on actuals differ from an option on futures? There are several reasons. First, the liquidity (ability to get in and out of the market without unduly affecting price) is often much different in cash markets than in futures markets. Second, the deliverable supply in futures markets and the potential for manipulation in either cash or futures markets may be different. Third, the cost of exercise of an option is different. In the case of an option on a futures you are expected to post margin. In the case of an option on a physical commodity, you pay for it in full. Fourth, tax issues and tax treatment of gains and losses in futures may be quite different than the tax treatment associated with gains or losses on physical transactions. Fifth, the dates of expiration may be much different in physical transactions than in futures. Sixth, the attraction of using options on futures as part of a portfolio management strategy is oftentimes much greater than using options on physicals as a part of a portfolio management strategy. Seventh, options done on physicals often are tailored to particular commercial needs and, therefore, have very little resale value.

ARE OPTIONS FOR YOU?

This chapter should have impressed upon you two things. First, options are, or can be, a very useful trading tool especially for limiting potential losses. You can use them instead of stop orders to get in or out of the market at a known cost.

Second, the pricing of options is very complex, not for amateurs, and can't really be done conveniently without a computer or sophisticated calculator, sophisticated software, and data.

There are several of other things you probably ought to think about. These are:

1. The majority of options traders lose.
2. The professional options traders who win are those who are the writers of options and professional market makers.
3. Most professional traders who use options use them as a method of hedging speculative positions as well as portfolios.

CREATING SYNTHETICS

One can combine futures and options to create synthetic options or synthetic futures. For example, if you buy a call and sell a futures, you have created a synthetic put; i.e., you have limited your loss on the upside if prices rise while maintaining opportunity for significant gains if prices fall.

A synthetic call would be just the opposite. If you buy a put and buy futures you have limited your losses if prices fall, but have opportunity for unlimited gain if prices rise.

Those who desire more risk and potential for greater reward in the creation of synthetic securities can institute what is called a dynamic hedging strategy. Prior to the 1987 stock market crash this was referred to as portfolio insurance. The strategy uses futures to create the equivalent of the cash flows associated with an option. By utilizing the Delta and Gamma from an option one can create the effect of an option. For example, suppose you had borrowed $10 million and the interest rate you paid changed every 90 days based on Eurodollar rates. To hedge that liability with futures for 90 days, you would need to sell 10 Eurodollar contracts. That would give you full 100 percent coverage on your hedge. To convert this hedge into the equivalent of an option at the strike price equal to today's Eurodollar rate, you would establish a futures hedge of only five contracts (equal to the Delta) and then adjust a number of contracts up closer to 10 or down closer to zero as the Delta moved up from .5 toward 1, or down from .5 toward zero. In other words, adjust it according to the Gamma.

As noted, this is a risky strategy. If it works perfectly, your results will be very closely equivalent to the purchase of an option. However, as in most things, perfection is elusive. For one thing, the Delta changes by small amounts whereas Eurodollar contracts can be traded only in full units. For another, the futures markets are sometimes discontinuous. If the market moves limit up or limit down, you may be unable to establish a futures position at prices that move in lock-step with the change in Delta. Lastly, there is great danger of being whipsawed. If the market is very volatile, you may be able to establish your position only after a price move occurs, and then promptly find that the market reverses and you again are unable to remove your position until after it moves. That's a disaster. That's also what happened to many people during the 1987 stock market crash when they attempted to employ this technique in using the S&P futures to hedge their stock portfolios.

Chapter 26

Strategies for Trading Options

The trading applications of options are numerous, and motives for buying and selling options are as varied as they are for trading commodity futures contracts. In addition to the limited risk advantages options offer to speculators, they also perform certain economic functions and can be used for hedging purposes.

Commodity options contracts can serve as a risk-shifting medium for individuals and firms dealing in a cash commodity similar to hedging with futures markets. A call option, by providing its buyer the right to acquire a commodity or futures contract at a fixed price, can provide price protection to a person who has a short position in the cash market, e.g., one who has signed a contract to deliver a product. Buying a put option can also provide the same manner of price protection to its purchaser as can a short futures position. Both of them establish a sale price. In contrast to futures, however, options contracts provide price protection only to purchasers because only purchasers have the right to exercise an option. Sellers of options have a firm price for their product only if the buyer exercises the option, but they cannot require a buyer to exercise. Thus, the risk transfer is not as complete or as symmetrical in options as it is in futures.

USING OPTIONS IN BUSINESS

Following are some examples of how the options market might be used for hedging. Concepts apply equally well to options on "actuals" or options on futures.

Purchasing a Put to Protect Profit Margin

Suppose a producer or processor of raw materials—a sugar refiner, a mine operator, or an animal feed manufacturer—wishes to secure a manufacturing margin by selling his product forward but wants the right to cancel the deal should prices rise. He can achieve this by purchasing a put option for a forward delivery date. In the event that prices fall, he would exercise his option and thus have a secured sales contract. (If it is an option on a futures contract, he will have a short futures position that he can deliver on or offset as a normal hedge. If it is an option on the actual product, he will deliver the product to the seller of the option.) But if prices rise, he could abandon the option and sell his product (either physically or through a futures hedge) at the higher level ruling in the market. The cost of this choice would be the option premium.

Buying a Call to Protect a Price

Exactly the reverse of this example would apply to someone who processes raw material and needs to buy those materials forward for delivery at a future date. The use of a call option to secure the purchases allows him the choice of abandoning the option if prices decline or of exercising his option if prices rise.

Buying a Put to Protect a Contingent Risk

Suppose a firm were preparing to make a sealed bid to buy large quantities of a product but wouldn't know for some time (perhaps weeks) whether its bid had been accepted or for how much. In such a situation the firm could buy a put on the product. If, in the interim between the submission of the bid and the acceptance of it, prices fall and the firm is awarded the winning bid, it will be able to exercise the put at the higher price, thus obtaining a sale price at the higher level and buying the needed supply at the new lower price. If, on the other hand, prices should rise and it should receive either no part of the bid or a partial fulfillment of it, the put can be abandoned and the product sold in the open market at the higher prices. In this latter instance the firm will have lost the premium paid for the put but will have gained protection from a price fall during the interim.

This same concept would be applied to any firm which sells largely by catalog or by direct mail. In such a situation, the pricing on the final product must frequently be done long in advance of manufacture and of shipment. If raw material costs change substantially during that time, profit margins can be adversely affected. Buying a call option on the raw material in such a situation provides protection against such dramatic price increases. If prices do increase, the firm can exercise the call at the lower price. If they fall, the call can be abandoned.

Buying a Call to Protect a Short Position

Suppose a merchant sold a quantity of sugar for deferred delivery to a food processor at a fixed price, but the merchant had not yet acquired sufficient sugar to cover the sale. He faces the risk that sugar prices may rise before he can make necessary purchases. Although he could hedge this risk with a long futures position, the merchant may be reluctant to lock in his profit margin in that manner because he suspects that sugar prices are more likely to fall than to rise, in which case he would have to meet margin calls. By purchasing call options rather than futures, the merchant can protect his short cash position at the additional cost of the option premium, while still reserving the opportunity to take advantage of lower sugar prices should his expectations materialize.

Writing a Call Against Inventory

A holder of an inventory, such as a producer or a manufacturer, may use the options market to generate income on inventory by *selling a call option* on that inventory, thus giving the buyer the option to purchase the inventory. If the option is abandoned by the buyer because the price falls, the seller will still carry the inventory but his net cost-of-carry and ownership will be reduced because he has received the option premium and interest on it. This is a form of price speculation, and any businessman undertaking it should so realize. If prices rise and the option is exercised, then the seller must deliver the physical goods against the contract. This, of course, is an attractive procedure only if, at the time the option is sold, the striking price of the option is higher than the spot price, since the option seller obtains this differential together with the option premium and interest.

In short, options provide a businessman:

1. More flexibility in strategy than do futures contracts alone.
2. More certainty in planning cash exposure than do futures.
3. More control over the decision-making environment.

This is particularly true when buying options, because only the buyer may determine when and whether to exercise. Options allow the buyer to buy time during which he can wait for the future to be revealed. If the future turns out to his advantage, he exercises the option. If not, he abandons it, suffers the loss of at least part of his premium, and makes his transaction through another channel.

STRATEGIES FOR SPECULATING IN OPTIONS

In general, the trading of options is a complex topic. Whole books have been written on the subject. All that can be done here is to introduce you to the topic and language to make you aware of some of the rich variety of ways in which options can be a part of your investment strategy.

If you expect prices to go up, you should buy a call or sell a put. If you expect prices to go down, you should buy a put or sell a call. Those two rules of thumb seem simple enough. But beware! If you sell a put expecting prices to go up but they actually go down, you run the risk that the put will be exercised. You do not have that risk buying a call. The same thing is true if you sell a call expecting prices to fall. If they go up, you have the risk of being called to fulfill your contractual obligations.

Buying a Gold Call

A call gives the purchaser the right to obtain a long position in the underlying futures contract. Hence, if you expect prices to rise, you would purchase a call, giving you the right to buy a futures contract at the strike price stated at any time before the call expires.

Suppose on September 1 that December gold futures are trading at $470 per ounce and that, after careful analysis of the market, you come to expect December gold to trade above the $500 per ounce level. There are two ways to take advantage of this expectation: (1) You can buy a futures contract at $470 for delivery in December. That will cost you approximately $2,000 in margin plus a $45 commission. If the price falls to $450 per ounce, you will have lost your entire $2,000 margin plus your $45 commission. If, on the other hand, the price does rise to the $500 level, you will have made $3,000 minus commission; (2) an alternative to buying the December futures contract would have been to buy a call option on the December futures. Suppose you could purchase, for $20 per ounce ($2,000 = 100 ounces per contract x $20) a call option with the strike price of $470. You would then be potentially long December futures contract at $470 with a break-even point of $490 ($470 + $20).[1] Now if the price rises to the $500 level, the option will be worth $3,000. You can sell (offset) the option to obtain the $3,000, deduct the $2,000 cost, and you end with $1,000 profit. Or you can "exercise" (notify the other party [seller] that you wish to buy the December futures at $470 per ounce). You can sell the futures acquired by exercise and accept your profit of $30 per ounce ($3,000) on the transaction for a net

1. Some options (e.g., cash market options) are sold with a strike price equal to the immediate price of the future. Thus, the break-even point is closer to the current price than would be true in the above example. In either event the break-even point is still calculated by adding the premium and commission costs to the strike price.

of $1,000. If the price fails to rise above the $470 level, you will simply be out the amount of your premium, $2,000, plus commissions. If it rises to $475, the value of the option will fall to $500 and you will suffer a $1,500 loss.

The maximum loss to the call buyer can never exceed the premium cost—in this instance, $2,000 plus commissions. That maximum loss will occur only if the option expires worthless, which would happen if the market does not move above the $470 level. If the market does move above the $470 strike price but does not reach the $490 level before the expiration date, the loss decreases as the price rises to the break-even point. As the price rises above the break-even point, the option becomes profitable, and the profit increases as the price continues to advance.

Hedging a Profitable Call Option

As noted above, the major advantage in trading options is the unlimited opportunity it provides for gains with a fixed risk of loss. Another distinct advantage offered by options is the flexibility they provide for trading futures and options against each other at the same time. For example, if a taker has a profitable option position, he can "trade against it" (take an opposite position in the futures—the same as "hedge it"), thus opening many more possible opportunities for profit than simply through the exercise of the option. The following examples show how this can be done.

Hedging a Profitable Call By Selling a Future

Assume that on October 15 the December gold futures contract advances to the $500 level. As a buyer, you can take advantage of this advance and "lock in" your profit on the option without exercise by selling a December futures contract at the $500 level. In effect, you hedge your option position. Now, if futures fall back to $460, the option will be "out-of-the-money" (below the $470 strike price), but you will have a $40 gain on your short futures positions. You will realize the same profit as if you had exercised at $500 and then immediately offset.

The advantage of this technique over an immediate exercise on October 15 when it reaches $500 is that the option is kept "alive" until the declaration date, thus providing you the opportunity to trade against it at a later time.

If indeed the market moves lower (say to the $470 level), the short futures contract can be covered by the purchase of a futures contract. This transaction will generate a profit on the futures side (remember that you went short the futures at the $500 level and bought it back at $470) and leave the original option position unchanged. Now, if the price goes back up (say to the $495 level) so that on the declaration date the market is above the striking price, the call can be exercised at a profit. Thus, you have made a profit on your option and also on your trade against the option. If on the declaration date the market is below the original striking price, the option would be abandoned, causing a loss of the premium. That loss, of course, would be offset by the profit made on trading against the option.

Hedging a Profitable Call By Buying a Put

Earlier, it was shown that you could "hedge" a profitable call by selling a futures against it. Another way to hedge a profitable call option is with the purchase of a put option. The maximum price for this protection is the premium on the put plus commissions. If the market does subsequently drop, the put can be profitably exercised. Even more importantly, if the market continues to rise, the maximum loss on the put is still only the premium plus commissions, and the profit on the call will continue to accrue.

Note that when you hedge a profitable call position through the sale of a futures contract, you give up all potential benefits that might accrue from a continuation of a price rise and, in addition, you have to meet margin calls. Not so when you hedge with the purchase of a put. The other side of this coin, however, is that the cost of a futures hedge may be far cheaper than the cost of the premium for the put option.

What happens to the call option if, on the declaration date, the futures contract is trading at a price higher than the striking price but below the break-even mark? In such a case, it will always benefit the option holder to offset or to exercise the option even if the premium is not fully covered. In the above example, if December gold is trading at $475 on the declaration date, the call should be offset or exercised. Even though a net profit will not result, the cash thus generated will help reduce the total loss on the option. In this instance, had the call been abandoned, the loss would have been $20 per ounce. However, by exercising or offsetting it, the loss is only $15 per ounce.

USING THE FUTURES TO CONVERT A CALL TO A PUT

If you sell a futures position short against the purchase of a call, it has the effect of converting the call to a put. (The opposite is also true. Buying a futures against the sale of a put has the same effect as buying a call.) Remember, a put gives the purchaser the right to sell the product at a later date at a price determined today. Thus, he has unlimited (down to zero price) potential for gain if prices fall and limited risk if prices rise.

Using the futures to convert a call into the equivalent of a put works like this. Assume that you buy a call for $20 with a strike price of $470 per ounce and that later you sell a futures at $490 per ounce. At that point you have a position equivalent to the purchase of a put; i.e., if prices rise, your call option position will become more valuable at the same time your short futures position becomes less valuable. They will offset each other, and you will have given up your premium. In effect, the financial result will be the same as it would have been if you had bought a put. If, on the other hand, prices fall, you will have a loss on the option position and a gain on the futures position—the same as if you owned a put. To the extent the price fall exceeds the cost of the call option, you will have a net profit on the transaction. The break-even point, minus commission, will be $470, the same as if you had bought a put for $20 per ounce and a strike price of $490. The cost of the "put" is the premium for the call option plus interest on margins and commissions on the futures and the options.

OPTIONS ON FINANCIAL FUTURES

Among the most active on the options scene are options on financial futures such as interest rates, stock indexes, and foreign currencies. To further illustrate the rich variety of strategies available, this section focuses on options strategies for long-term U.S. Treasury bond futures. These same strategies can be applied to currencies and stock indexes.

Rising Interest Rates—Declining Bond Prices

a. Buy put options. Assume you are anticipating an increase in long-term interest rates and a corresponding decrease in futures prices. To take advantage of your expectations, you could buy a put option on U.S. Treasury bond futures. Assume you buy a March 100 put at a premium cost of $2,000, reflecting an interest rate on long-term bonds of about 8 percent. Assume, by expiration in March, the interest rate has increased to near 8.6 percent, and the futures price has decreased to 94-00, so you should be able to sell the option at a value of $6,000. Your profit on this transaction will be $4,000 ($6,000 less your $2,000 premium) minus transaction costs.

If, by the time March rolled around, interest rates had decreased to approximately 7.7 percent, the contract would be selling for about 103-00 and your put option with a strike price of 100-00 would expire worthless. You would have lost the entire $2,000 paid for the option.

In many cases, you might decide not to wait until expiration to close out your position. If, in the above example, interest rates started falling with expiration a month or so away, you might have decided to sell the option before it reached a value of zero. By selling the option at $500, for example, you would reduce your loss to only $1,500 ($2,000 premium minus $500) plus the transaction costs.

b. Sell futures and buy call options. By selling a futures contract you can profit from any increase in long-term interest rates because as interest rates go up, U.S. Treasury bond prices decline. The purchase of a call option in conjunction with a short futures position makes it possible to limit the otherwise unlimited risk involved in selling futures contracts. In effect, the call option provides insurance against major loss.

For example, suppose you were expecting higher interest rates, and you sold a September U.S. Treasury bond futures contract at the price of 100-00. At the same time, to protect yourself against major losses that could result if futures prices rise, you might decide to pay a $2,000 premium for the purchase of a September 100-00 call option. The most that you can now lose if futures prices rise instead of fall is the $2,000 cost of the call option. Table 26.1 shows a summary of how this transaction could turn out under various scenarios.

A major advantage of this strategy is the "staying power" it can provide. That is, these two transactions provide the ability to maintain a futures position despite adverse short-term price movements. One survives in order to maintain the potential that the position may still eventually become profitable.

In the absence of the protection provided by the call, you might be faced with a large margin call on your futures position. If such a margin requirement can't be met, you would be forced to liquidate the futures position at a loss. The call protects against that because, as the futures position loses value, the call increases in value. The call acts as a hedge against major losses.

c. A "bear" put spread. If you expect rising interest rates and, therefore, declining bond prices, you could profit by purchasing a put option with a high strike price and selling or writing a put option with a new low strike price. The maximum net profit is the difference in the strike prices less the net cost of the two options. The maximum loss is the net cost of the two options.

For example, suppose in June you expect rising interest rates through the month of September. Assume the September futures price is at 100-00. To profit from your expectations, let's say you buy a September 100 put for a premium of $2,000, and you sell a September 94 put and collect a premium of $400. Your net premium is $1,600.

If the futures price in September turns out to be 94-00 or lower, your profits will be the difference between the strike price of the options ($6,000 less the net premium cost of the two options), or $1,600. The net profit will be $4,400. If, on the other hand, futures prices at expiration are 100-00 or above, both options will expire worthless and you will suffer your maximum loss of $1,600.

SUMMARY OF OPTIONS STRATEGIES UNDER VARIOUS PRICE SCENARIOS

As is obvious from the foregoing, the number and variety of trading techniques that can be employed using options and futures, singly or in combination, is large. In

Table 26.1 Summary of Sell Futures—Buy Call Option

Sell Sept. T-Bond Futures @	100-00
Buy Sept. 100 T-Bond Futures Call @	$2,000
Profit or Loss at Expiration	
Futures rise to 106-00	
Buy Futures @ 106-00	$6,000 Loss
Sell Call @ 6-00	$4,000 Gain
	$2,000 Net Loss
Futures do not change	
Buy Futures @ 100-00	No Gain - No Loss
Sell Call @ 0	$2,000 Loss
	$2,000 Net Loss
Futures fall to 98-00	
Buy Futures @ 98-00	$2,000 Gain
Sell Call @ 0	$2,000 Loss
	0 Net
Futures fall to 92-00	
Buy Futures @ 92-00	$8,000 Gain
Sell Call @ 0	$2,000 Loss
	$6,000 Net Gain

general, you can now tailor a limited-risk trading strategy to almost any price trend (or non-trend) scenario that could occur. Table 26.2 has been compiled to help the reader better understand the variety of strategies available, and the situations in which they should be used. These strategies apply to price situations in all commodities, including stock index options and futures.

Table 26.2 Summary of Option Strategies Under Various Price Scenarios

Interest Rate and Bond Price Expectation	Possible Strategy	Interest Rate and Bond Price Expectation	Possible Strategy
Declining Prices	Buy Put Options	Rising Prices	Buy Call Options
Declining Prices	Sell Futures and Buy Call Options	Rising Prices	Buy Futures and Buy Put Options
Declining Prices	A "Bear" Call Spread	Rising Prices	A "Bull" Call Spread
Declining Prices	A "Bear" Put Spread	Rising Prices	A "Bull" Put Spread
Steady to Slightly Lower Prices	Sell Futures and Write Put Options	Steady to Slightly Higher Prices	Buy Futures and Write Call Options
Steady to Slightly Lower Prices	Write Call Options	Steady to Slightly Higher Prices	Write Put Options
Relatively Flat Prices	A "Neutral" Calendar Spread	Prices will be highly volatile, could change in either direction	Buy a Put-Call Straddle
Relatively Flat Prices	Write a Put-Call Straddle		

NOTE: Interest rates and prices on bonds, T-bills, GNMAs, etc., move in opposite directions. So the above strategies for rising prices (falling prices) should be considered when interest rates are expected to fall (to rise).

Declining Interest Rates—Rising Bond Prices

a. Buy-call options. If you anticipate a decrease in long-term interest rates, your strategy should be to purchase call options on U.S. Treasury bond futures. A call option, as noted above, gives you, the buyer, the right to buy the underlying futures contract at the specified strike price. You will realize a profit if the intrinsic value of the option at expiration is greater than the premium you paid for the option. For example, if it is now June and you expect interest rates to be lower in September, assume you pay a $2,000 premium to buy a September 100 call option reflecting an interest rate of about 8 percent. If, when September rolls around, the interest rate has declined to around 7.4 percent, the futures price should have increased to 106-00. You should then be able to sell the call option at its intrinsic value of $6,000. Your profit would be $4,000 less the transaction costs.

Suppose, however, that when September arrives, the futures price was 100-00 or below. In that case your call would expire worthless and you would lose your entire $2,000. If, on the other hand, the futures price is at 102, your call would be worth the same price you paid for it. If the futures price has increased to 110-00, your call should be valued at 10-00, an $8,000 profit.

b. A "bull" call spread. Perhaps a more conservative approach to a situation where you expect interest rates to decline and bond prices to rise would be one known as a vertical bull spread. With such a strategy, you would know in advance the exact maximum net profit you could possibly make, and the exact maximum net loss possible on the transaction.

Like all bull spreads, bull call spreads (meaning the investor is bullish on bond prices) involves buying one option and writing or selling another option. In this case, you would buy a call option with a low strike price and sell a call option with a high strike price.

Your maximum net loss potential is the net premium cost, that is, the difference between the premium you pay for the call you buy and the premium you receive for the call you sell.

The maximum net profit you can make in this transaction is the difference between the strike prices of the two options less the net premium cost.

For example, suppose in March you expect lower interest rates and higher bond prices, and you find that the June futures price is trading at 96-00. Suppose, further, you buy a June 96 call at a premium of $2,000 and sell a June 102 call at a premium of $500. The maximum net profit would be $4,500, the strike price difference of $6,000 less the net premium cost of $1,500, and your maximum net loss would be $1,500, the net premium cost. In order to realize maximum profit, the futures price at expiration must be equal to or above the strike price of the option written, in this case 102-00. If it isn't, the investor's resulting profit or loss will depend on whether the value of the purchase option at expiration is more or less than the premium cost. See Table 26.3 for a summary of such a strategy under various price scenarios.

WHAT OPTION TO TRADE?

An important decision for an investor selecting among strike prices and maturity dates is the determination of which option to select. Which is preferable: an option with a short period of time until expiration or an option with a long period of time until expiration? An option with a high strike price (an in-the-money option) or an option with a lower strike price) (an out-of-the-money option)?

Table 26.3 Summary of Bull Spread—Call Options

	Paid	Received
Buy June 96-00 call	$2,000	
Sell June 102-00 call		$500
Net Premium	$1,500	

Profit or Loss Summary

Futures @102-00	
Sell June 96 call	+6,000 Gain
Buy June 102 call	0
Net Premium Cost	–1,500
	4,500 Net Gain
Futures @ 96-00	
Sell June 96 call	0
Buy June 102 call	0
Net Premium Cost	1,500
	1,500 Net Loss
Futures @ 90-00	
Sell June 96 call	0
Buy June 102 call	0
Net Premium Cost	1,500
	1,500 Net Gain
Futures fall to 99-00	
Sell June 96 call	3,000
Buy June 102 call	0
Net Premium Cost	1,500
	1,500 Net Gain

Generally, the premium costs will be higher the longer the time remaining until expiration. Such an option provides the buyer more time for his price expectations to be realized and thus, a greater likelihood of his actually earning a profit. Generally, the longer time remaining until expiration, the lower the cost of each additional time unit. That is, a six-month option usually does not cost twice as much as a three-month option.

Decisions about purchasing an at-the-money or an out-of-the-money option are equally important. The option premium is usually higher for an at-the-money option than for an out-of-the-money option. An at-the-money option stands a greater chance of yielding a profit. However, an out-of-the money option usually costs less to buy or to exercise, and involves a smaller potential loss, but also, a smaller potential profit.

When trading options, it is wise to keep in mind some fundamental principles with respect to price behavior:

1. The value of the option is directly related to the expected volatility of the market and the probability that a particular price level will be reached during a given time period.
2. When trading options on futures, examine closely the price structure (relationships) between futures months. If the more distant months are at a higher price than the nearby months, a buyer of a put has, everything else remaining equal, a better probability of a profitable trade. But, of course, everything else is not always equal. Price relationships may remain the same, but price levels, which are the important element, may change. The question is, will they change during the life of the option?

CALCULATING RETURN ON INVESTMENT

In comparing transactions in the futures market with transactions in the options market, you should compare them on the basis of return on investment (ROI), which is calculated by dividing the dollar investment into net profit before taxes. Thus,

$$\text{ROI} = \frac{\text{Net income before taxes}}{\text{Total dollar investment}}$$

It is important to note that the break-even point on the futures is close to the purchase price. The futures market price needs to move only a small amount (commission plus interest on margin) to reach the break-even point. On an option, it has to move at least the amount of the premium and, if the strike price is above the current level, then it must move the amount of the premium plus the difference between the strike price and the current market level before the break-even price is reached.

Figures 26.1 through 26.12 give a pictorial illustration of the profit and loss characteristics associated with the basic futures and option strategies. As the reader will note, the first two graphs show the virtually unlimited risk associated with a position in futures. The remaining graphs show how the options provide variants from very limited risk to unlimited risk. Of course, the opposite of risk is profit!

A little cogitation on these figures and one can quickly see how combining futures and options positions can provide very interesting opportunities for developing exactly the risk/reward profile one wants in an investment.

SUMMARY

To summarize, when considering options relative to futures, remember:

1. Options provide known and limited risk. Futures do not unless you use stop orders, and then they do only if the stops actually are executed at or close to the stated level. This is sometimes hard to do if a market is fluctuating wildly and is locked in to limit moves.
2. To obtain this known and limited risk, you pay a premium. Weigh the size of the premium against the confidence of using stops and your desire to avoid being whipsawed. The size of this premium will be related to a lot of factors, the most important of which are price volatility, the remaining life of the option, and the probability that the price will reach the strike price before expiration date.
3. The value of the option is directly related to the expected volatility of the market and the probability that a particular price level will be reached during a given time period.
4. When trading options on futures, examine closely the price structure (relationships) between futures months. If the more distant months are at a higher price than the nearby months, a buyer of a put has, everything else remaining equal, a better probability of a profitable trade. But, of course, everything else is not always equal. Price relationships may remain the same, but price levels, which are the important element, may change. The question is, will they change during the life of the option?
5. The break-even point on a futures transaction may be reached with a much smaller price move than in the case of an option. The break-even point in futures is close to the purchase or sale price. On an option, the break-even point is the amount of the premium plus the difference between the strike price and the current market level plus commissions and other costs.

Figures 26.1–26.6

26.1 Long Futures

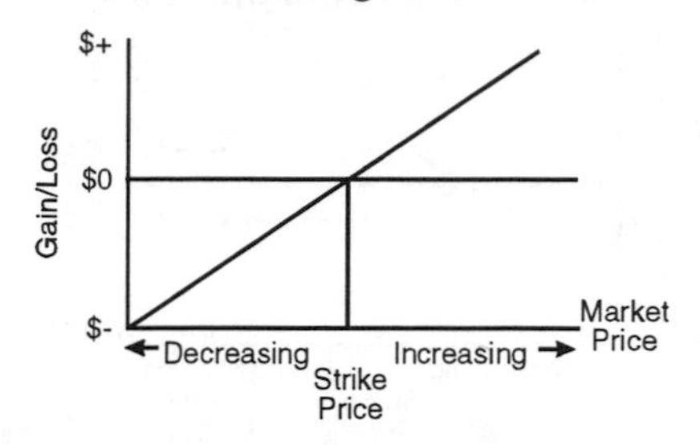

Profits grow as price rises.
Losses grow as price falls.

26.2 Short Futures

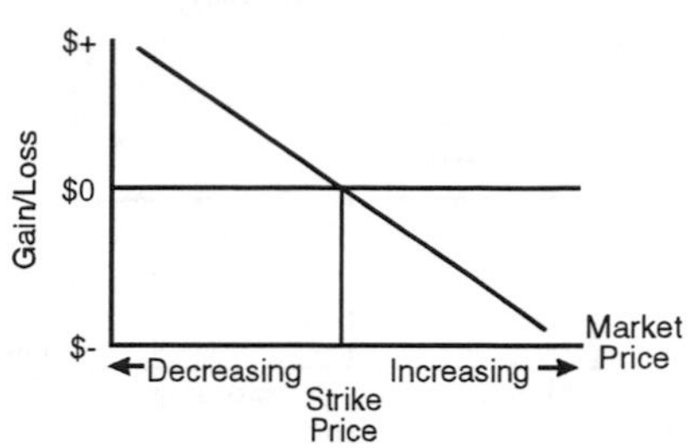

Losses grow as price rises.
Profits grow as price falls.

26.3 Long Call

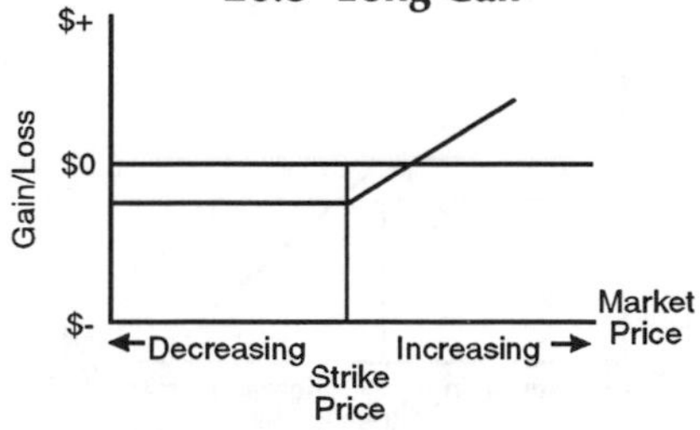

Profits grow as price rises.
Losses limited to option cost as price falls.

26.4 Long Put

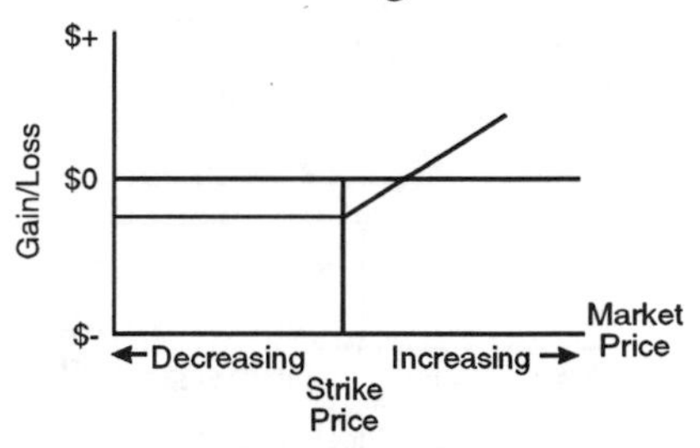

Losses limited to option cost as price rises.
Profits grow as price falls.

26.5 Short Call

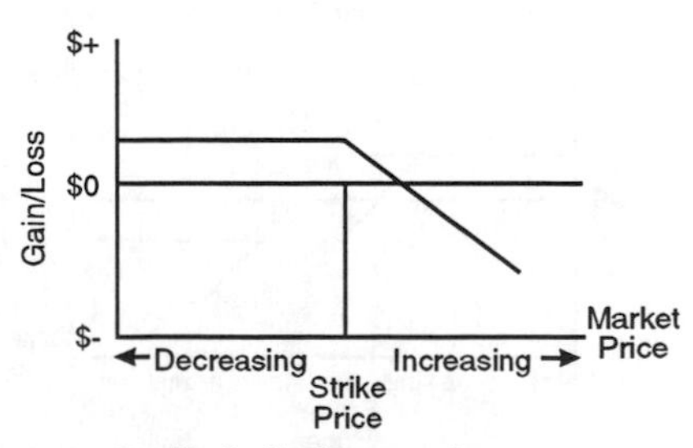

Profits limited to premium earned as price falls.
Losses grow as price rises.

26.6 Short Put

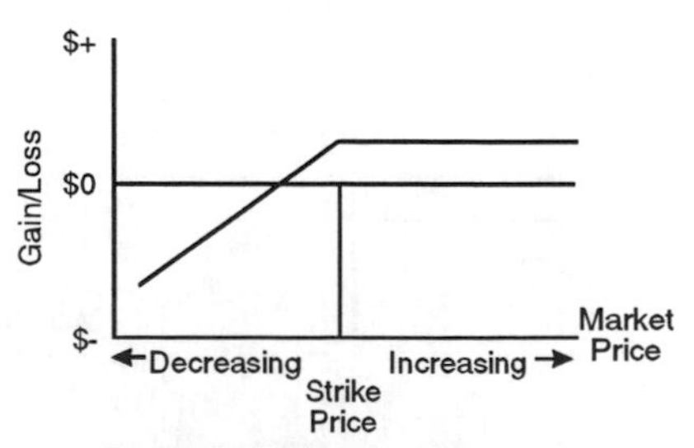

Profits limited to premium earned as price rises.
Losses grow as price falls.

Figures 26.7–26.12

26.7 Short Call/Long Call

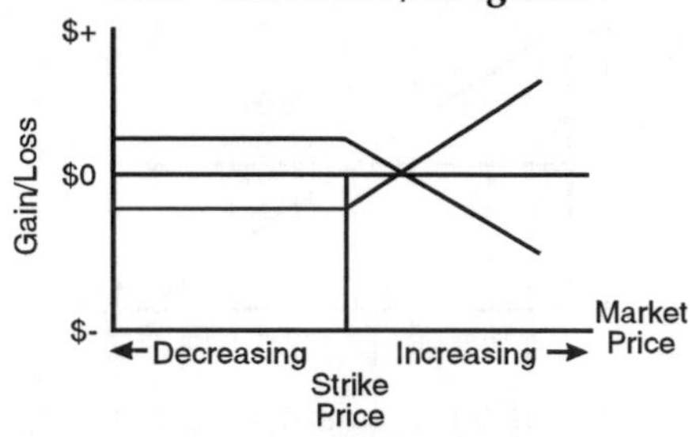

Net gain or loss is limited to difference between premium paid and premium earned.

26.8 Long Put/Short Put

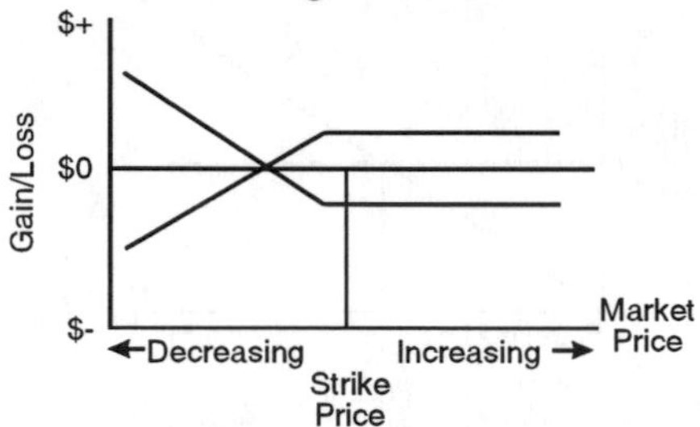

Net gain or loss is limited to difference between premium paid and premium earned.

26.9 Long Call/Long Put

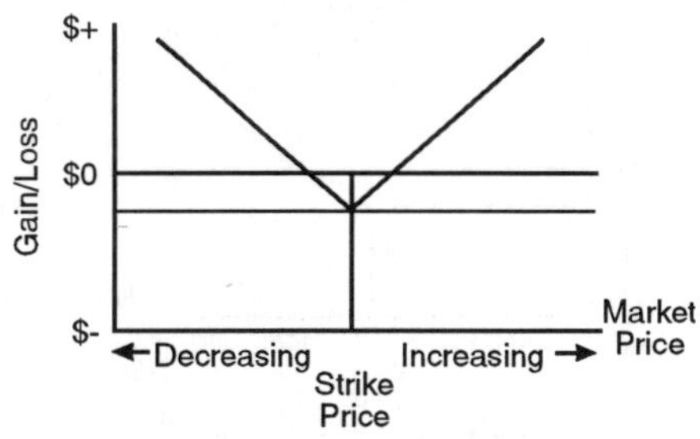

Profits rise as price moves either up or down.

26.10 Short Call/Short Put

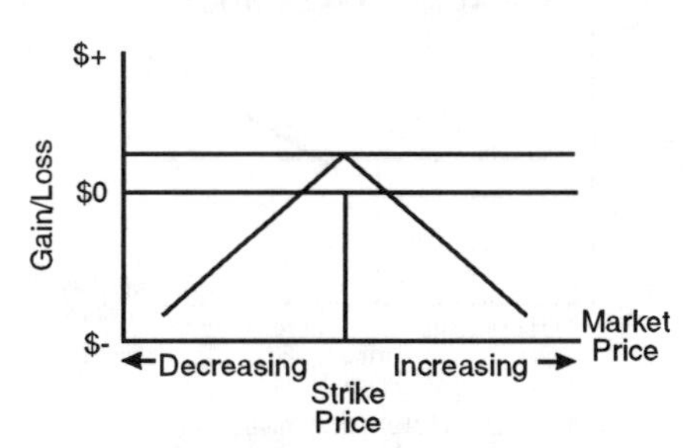

Losses rise as price moves either up or down.

26.11 Long Call/Long Put

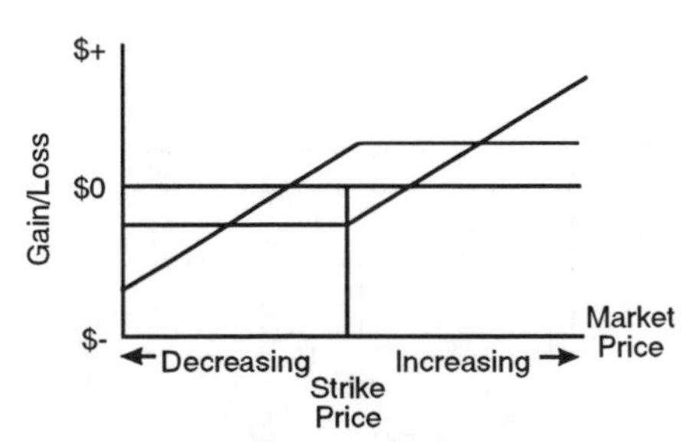

Profits grow as price rises.
Losses grow as price falls.

26.12 Long Put/Short Call

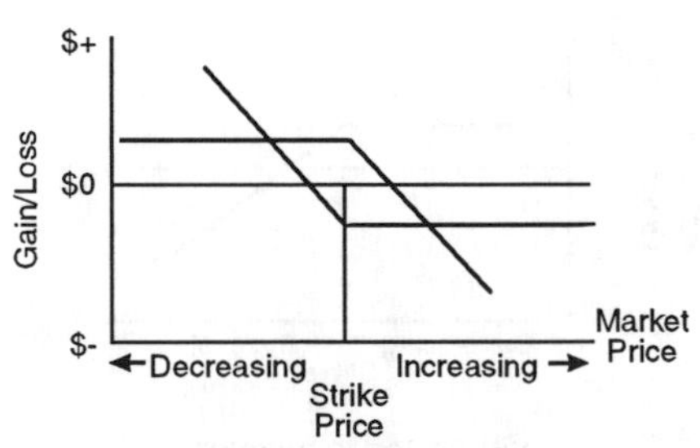

Profits grow as price falls.
Losses grow as price rises.

6. Trading a futures against an option provides flexibility to an investment strategy and allows the holder of the option to make full use of all the "time" paid for when the option was purchased.
7. There are advantages to using a put option instead of futures to hedge a profitable call option and vice versa.
8. There are a number of commercial business uses for options, especially in developing deferred pricing contracts. Some, but not all of the uses, duplicate the advantages offered by futures hedges contracts.
9. Before you open an account and make a trade in options, shop around and ask a lot of questions of the dealer and about the particular option deal being offered. There is no substitute for self-protection.

Chapter 27

Historical Development of Commodity Futures Trading

Mention commodity futures trading to someone not actively engaged in the market and the first and often only reaction you get is that it is a high-risk form of financial speculation. True, speculation is a major aspect of futures trading as we know it today, but underlying current speculative activity is a sound economic purpose that has its roots in ancient times and has evolved slowly over centuries. Trading and marketing practices naturally change with the basic economic needs of people involved in the pricing and handling of goods. Our current trading system did not miraculously appear.

If you were to select any single commodity from among those traded on exchanges today and trace its market development, you would find it has passed through five distinct states: gift-giving, barter, cash (or spot) markets, contract (or forward) markets, and futures (and derivatives) markets.

Thus, the establishment of a futures market in a given commodity is only the current stage of a natural evolutionary process. It's a never-ending process that could very well lead to an as yet unknown sixth stage in decades ahead.

CHARACTERISTICS OF ORGANIZED FUTURES TRADING

Although organized futures trading differs significantly and substantially from other forms of trading, the concept of futurity or deferred performance in transactions is not new or unusual, nor is it the key element in distinguishing futures trading from other forms of trading.

Elements of a transaction (pricing, payment, title transfer, and delivery) can be arranged in any order of time sequence. Hence, one can agree today on the price of a new car, receive the car and title to it two weeks from now, and pay for it six weeks later when the credit card bill arrives. The element of futurity, then, is a necessary though not sufficient condition for a futures contract. Futurity is not what really distinguishes organized futures trading from any of a number of trading arrangements.

Organized futures trading, as it exists on several exchanges in the United States and abroad, may be distinguished from the widespread trading that involves other elements of futurity in the following respects.

1. **Futures trading is conducted on an organized exchange,** with a common set of rules governing all the transactions. Although a car dealer may contract to sell an automobile for delivery in three months, this is *not* futures trading. This is a customized contract or forward contract between one buyer and one seller, usually done in accordance with standard trade practice and subject to contract laws in the various localities but not under uniform exchange rules.
2. **Futures have specific rules governing trading**. Most important of these (which do not apply to most forward dealings) are:
   a. Trading must occur at one place (the trading pit or ring) by open outcry within specified hours. All bids and offers are thus known to all participants, and all transactions are public knowledge.
   b. Various anti-competitive practices are forbidden, e.g., no member may fill or match a customer's order without first offering it openly in a pit.
3. **Futures contracts are standardized with respect to size, date, delivery location, and delivery procedure**. Only price is negotiated at the exchange. In ordinary forward dealings, of course, any peripheral terms and conditions can be negotiated.
4. **Futures trading is impersonal.** The exchange clearing house becomes a party to every contract that is negotiated at the exchange—buyer and seller do the negotiating, but once the deal is struck, each has reciprocal obligations

with the clearing house—not with one another. In other forward dealings the parties continue to rely on their personal relationships for fulfillment.

5. **Futures contracts are legally canceled by offset.** A member who sells one July pork belly futures contract incurs an obligation to deliver 36,000 pounds of pork bellies to the clearing house during July. This he may ultimately do to fulfill his contractual obligation. But if he buys a July contract prior to the completion of trading in late July, he then has equal and offsetting obligations to the clearing house so he is out of the market with no obligation.
6. **The exchange clearing house acts as a common guarantor of all contracts. Members of the clearing house must maintain minimum amounts of working capital and must deposit funds to "margin" their outstanding trades.** Exchange members who are not clearing members must affiliate with clearing members for purposes of verifying and guaranteeing all contracts. No credit is extended in this process; the margin deposit is a performance bond, not a down payment. When delivery occurs in satisfaction of a futures contract, full cash payment is required as the title is transferred. Prior to delivery, no title has been transferred and no credit is extended.

The term "futures contract" then is applied to a special type of forward contract bought and sold under the rules of organized exchanges having a clearing house. It is a legally binding contract to buy or sell a stipulated amount of a carefully specified product or service, during an agreed future period, subject to the rules and regulations of the exchange where the contract is made, and with price determined by public auction on the floor of the exchange.

When did it all begin? Surely, gift-giving and barter, the first two stages, are as old as civilization itself. The third stage cash markets can be considered the true beginning of organized commodity markets.

EMERGENCE OF ORGANIZED MARKETS

Until about the early 1600s, trade throughout most of Europe and Asia was not heavy enough to support resident merchants or local markets. Periodic market fairs served as the trading outlets for large geographic areas. These fairs originated with the movements of itinerant merchants, who bartered their local goods for exotic things in distant lands. Coin was very scarce and the majority of transactions involved simple barter. Fairs were popular in ancient Greece and during the Roman Empire. Marco Polo brought back to Europe accounts of the gigantic Kinsai Fairs in China.

Gradually, a network of highly specialized and well-organized fairs emerged. Fair rules confined traders to the fairgrounds and specified times were designated for trading various commodities. In addition, they required that bids and offers be made publicly with every participant given an equal opportunity to accept bids and offers. Rules also banned traders from contracting outside the fairgrounds in attempts to corner a supply of a given commodity and thereby control its price.

Eventually, guilds (trade associations) were organized to promote the interests of the emerging merchant class. Business disputes were settled in courts especially established by the merchant class for that purpose, and a merchant code of law evolved from decisions handed down in these courts.

As trade grew, pieces of paper called "fair letters" came into being as a medium of exchange. These letters had the effect of postponing settlement in cash to a later date, actually providing an extension of credit. Traders were now free to travel from fair to fair settling their accounts by canceling debits and credits with the fair letters, leaving any remaining balance due to be settled eventually by payment in coin. As this medium of exchange was born, so was the cash (spot) market. Frequently, merchants would display samples of their wares, taking payment in coin or letter upon delivery when the title passed to the purchaser.

EARLY FUTURES TRADING IN JAPAN

Although the roots of futures trading can be traced to the medieval fair systems, it remained for Japan to develop sophisticated forward markets and the organized system of futures trading as we know it today. The Japanese experience carried them through stages four and five of market development, completing the five-stage evolutionary process.

Japan holds claim to the first recorded use of modern futures trading concepts, in the year 1697, approximately a century and a half before the common use of forward contracts in the United States.

During the 17th century, Japanese noblemen were forced into the position of being absentee landlords. This was the result of the ruling shogunate's decree that these noblemen spend at least six months of every year in residence in the capital city so that the shogun could keep a watchful eye on his noblemen in an effort to prevent the possibility of their conducting a revolt or uprising against him.

In keeping with the custom of the times, the noblemen maintained very high standards of living. They depended heavily on their rice crops for income, but rice was harvested during only a brief portion of the year, and they often ran short of cash while living it up away from home. This was understandable. They were maintaining dual households, entertaining lavishly, and indulging in extravagant wardrobes.

As a solution to their cash shortage problems, the nobles began the practice of issuing receipts against their rice crops, stored either in the country or in rented warehouses. Wholesale and retail merchants who eventually needed the rice would buy the tickets against anticipated needs. Eventually, these tickets became a form of currency. It soon followed that merchants began to extend credit to the nobles in advance of ticket sales. Some of the merchants were successful in manipulating the market and, in the process, became quite wealthy. One of the wealthiest of merchants in the city of Osaka set his house up as a center for rice market transactions. This was actually the world's first futures market. Later, this first exchange moved to the Dojima district in Osaka and became known as the Dojima Rice Market.

In many ways, this early exchange was strikingly similar to the modern futures exchange of today. The market functioned under legal sanction of the national government, and trades were executed in an orderly, well-disciplined manner according to rules established by the exchange. Transactions were cleared through a clearing house, with each trader establishing a line of credit with the clearing house of his choice. These clearing houses were non-profit organizations which did, however, charge commissions for their services.

The major difference between this first futures market and those that were to develop later was the fact that no physical deliveries could be made. This, of course, relegated the trading to gambling, and the government closed all exchanges for a brief period in the early 17th century. Later, after government regulations of the market were expanded and physical delivery was made acceptable in lieu of a cash settlement, trading was restored.

DEVELOPMENT OF FUTURES TRADING IN THE U.S.

Although following at a much later date, a pattern of market development evolved in the United States similar to that experienced by Japan. The use of forward contracts, which arose in response to marketing needs as commodity markets became larger and more complex, ripened eventually into organized futures trading.

As the population in the U.S. grew and spread westward—and the economy became more highly industrialized, with increased production capabilities—it became evident that an economic system based on local self-sufficiency was no longer viable. There were new economic needs to be filled—needs for additional capital, additional credit, and for a means to absorb increased price risks caused by longer time periods between production and sale, expanded market areas, and ever-increasing competition.

Stock exchanges took care of the capital needs. The national banking system answered the demand for expanded sources of new credit. Initially, the use of various forms of forward contracts represented an attempt on the part of commodity handlers to satisfy the need to reduce price risks.

The Midwest grain market and the development of commerce in Chicago provided the impetus for the evolution of modern commodity futures trading in the

United States. The use of actual, full-fledged futures contracts was preceded by approximately 25 years of merchants' dealing in what were then referred to as "to-arrive-contracts," or what are now commonly called "forward contracts."

Soon, speculators outside the grain trade began participating in the bidding and holding of these contracts, passing them on to other parties before the delivery date. Bear in mind that this trading was taking place prior to the opening of any exchange. By the mid-1850s, contracts frequently changed hands several times before settling with a person interested in taking delivery of the actual commodity.

MIDWEST GRAIN MARKET

During the 1830s and 1840s, prior to the opening of the railroads, grain farmers in the Midwest faced severe marketing problems. Every year at harvest time, grains arriving in Chicago created a market glut. Farmers had to take whatever they could get for their grain because the quantity available far exceeded the current demand of the market. Lack of adequate storage facilities made it impossible to store the grain to hold it for future sale. As a result, it was not an uncommon sight during the height of the grain-hauling season to see thousands of tons of spoiled grain dumped into Lake Michigan.

As could be expected, the exact opposite of the above situation took place in late spring and early summer. All the harvest stocks were gone. Available grain was in great demand and short supply. Anxious millers competed with one another to buy the available grain at astronomical prices.

As a result, farmers began to arrange sale of their crops prior to production. These forward sales involved a firm commitment on the part of the farmer to deliver a specified amount of grain at a future time period say 10, 20, 30 or 60 days later. This left the farmer free to concentrate his attentions on the harvesting of his crop, assured that it was already sold. In this way, many of the producers' and users' problems resulting from alternate oversupply/undersupply situations were solved through the use of forward contracts.

Now buyers could take advantage of scheduling grain deliveries at designated intervals, which in turn enabled them to program grain arrivals and outbound shipments. Grain elevator operators and owners were able to plan with maximum utilization of their storage facilities in mind, thereby assuring themselves of a more profitable enterprise. In like manner, processors could count on having available a steady supply of the commodity for processing forward sales.

With the opening of the Illinois-Michigan Canal in 1848, and the expansion of railroads, Chicago rapidly became a grain terminal supplying the East Coast and export trade. Processing facilities developed quickly to support local livestock feed demands as well as for shipment east.

But those involved in the handling of these commodities found that the "to-arrive" contracts did not solve all their problems. For example:

1. Qualities were not standardized and deliveries were unreliable.
2. Terms of payment varied.
3. Prices were not common knowledge.
4. Contracts were not easily resalable.

Refinements were made in the contracts to meet specific marketing needs. Eventually, these evolved into our modern futures contracts.

DEVELOPMENT OF CHICAGO COMMODITY MARKETS

The first commodity exchange in the United States was the Chicago Board of Trade, organized in early 1848. Rather than an organized marketplace for trading, however, the early exchange functioned more as a meeting place where grain merchants could discuss their mutual problems. As the volume of grain trade increased in the city, confusion reigned supreme. Trades were made everywhere, even on street corners and in saloons. It finally became apparent that trade was going to have to be conducted in a single location—the Board of Trade.

The Board developed a set of standards for wheat and began a system of weighing and inspecting grain. The substitution of weight for volume measures made possible the issuance of warehouse receipts, useful in change of title and as collateral in trade financing.

Gradually, as the problems inherent in the original forward contracts were overcome, a smaller and smaller number of market participants actually entered into contracts with the intent of taking delivery.

In the late 1850s and early 1860s, there was still considerable contracting taking place outside the Board of Trade, for it wasn't until October of 1865 that the Board adopted its general rules. By that time, all the essential ingredients of futures trading had been incorporated in its rules. October 1865 should more realistically serve as the actual date for the origin of modern futures trading.

Today, the Chicago Board of Trade deals in billions of dollars worth of commodities annually. Their most active contracts are not agricultural commodities, but rather financial futures and services. The process of trading has not changed much, although modern technology is employed, but the influence of market participants and the exchanges has broadened considerably.

CHICAGO MERCANTILE EXCHANGE

Another of the giants among modern commodity exchanges is the Chicago Mercantile Exchange (CME), which got its start toward the end of the 19th century. Like the Board of Trade in accommodating grains, it developed in response to the distribution and pricing problems inherent in the egg industry around the turn of the century. With the development of refrigeration techniques, Chicago became a forwarding market for eggs. As a result of large seasonal accumulations, egg dealers and storers of eggs found themselves faced with increasing problems of financing and price risk.

The exchange, known first as the Chicago Produce Exchange and later as the Chicago Butter and Egg Board, was initially established to determine price quotations, define grades for butter and eggs, and establish regulated trade practices. By 1916, trading in time contracts in these commodities was firmly established within the exchange. Trading was temporarily halted, however, with the imposition of the Food Control Act during World War I. After the resumption of trading in 1919, there was widespread dissatisfaction because of the non-fulfillment of contracts, caused primarily by sharp price advances. The butter and egg men within the Butter and Egg Board felt that insufficient attention had been given to establishing rules for organized trading in their commodities. Their solution was to reorganize the Board and eventually form a separate organization which they named the Chicago Mercantile Exchange, also looking toward an expansion of well-regulated and organized futures trading in commodities other than butter and eggs.

The real impetus to CME growth was the establishment of meat futures contracts in 1961 and financial futures in 1972. Both have been highly successful. It is known worldwide as the birthplace of financial futures and as the most innovative and influential exchange in the world.

Today, actively traded commodities on the CME also include a large number of meat and livestock products, as well as eight foreign currencies, T-bills, Eurodollars, stock index futures, and many other financial instruments on the exchange's International Monetary Market division.

Globex, the electronic exchange joint venture between the CME and CBOT discussed in Chapter 1, is representative of the next generation of exchanges and worldwide markets. Such markets will utilize the technology of communications and the advances in international legal theory to conduct trading, pricing, and title transfer.

OTHER EXCHANGES

In addition to the CBOT and the CME, other exchanges have developed over the years, each specializing in certain areas. Some exchanges have traded for a few years and then closed due to lack of volume, but at present there are 10 major futures exchanges in the U.S.—five in New York, three in Chicago, and one each in Minneapolis and Kansas City. The New Orleans Commodity Exchange still exists but trades on the floor of the MidAmerica Commodity Exchange in Chicago rather than in New Orleans. London is also a major center for futures trading; other exchanges are located in Paris, Winnipeg, Toronto, Hong Kong, and Singapore. Practices on some foreign exchanges may vary considerably from U.S. practices.

WHAT'S TRADED AND WHERE?

Tables 27.1 through 27.3 list a majority of exchanges and the items traded therein. A number of commodity and financial exchanges not listed in these tables have been started or re-opened in Russia, Eastern Europe, Latin America, and The Peoples Republic of China. Most of them have very little activity and do not act as true futures markets, but rather as local spot markets.

Table 27.1 Exchanges

Exchanges and Name		Country
AMEX	AMERICAN STOCK EXCHANGE	U.S.
ATA	ARGICULTURAL FUTURES EXCHANGE, AMSTERDAM	NETHERLANDS
BELFOX	BELGIUM FUTURES & OPTIONS EXCHANGE	BELGIUM
BM&F	BOLSA DE MERCARDORIAS & FUTURES, BRAZIL	BRAZIL
CBOT	CHICAGO BOARD OF TRADE	U.S.
CME	CHICAGO MERCANTILE EXCHANGE	U.S.
COMEX	COMMODITY EXCHANGE, INC.	U.S.
CSCE	COFFEE SUGAR & COCOA EXCHANGE	U.S.
DTB	DEUTSCHE TERMINBORSE	GERMANY
EOE	EUROPEAN OPTIONS EXCHANGE	NETHERLANDS
FFMA	FINANCIAL FUTURES MARKET AMSTERDAM	NETHERLANDS
FINEX	FINANCIAL INSTRUMENT EXCHANGE	U.S.
FOX	LONDON FUTURES AND OPTIONS EXCHANGE	ENGLAND
FUTOP	GUARANTEE FUND DANISH OPTIONS AND FUTURES	DENMARK

Table 27.1 Exchanges (continued)

Exchanges and Name		Country
HKFE	HONG KONG FUTURES EXCHANGE LTD.	HONG KONG
IFOX	IRISH FUTURES AND OPTIONS EXCHANGE	IRELAND
IPE	INTERNATIONAL PETROLEUM EXCHANGE	ENGLAND
KCBT	KANSAS CITY BOARD OF TRADE	U.S.
KRE	KOBE RUBBER EXCHANGE	JAPAN
LIFFE	LONDON INT'L FINANCIAL FUTURES EXCHANGE	ENGLAND
LME	LONDON METAL EXCHANGE	ENGLAND
MACE	MIDAMERICA COMMODITY EXCHANGE	U.S.
MATIF	MARCHE Á TERME INTERNATIONAL DE FRANCE	FRANCE
MEFFRF	MEFF RENTA FIJA, SPAIN	SPAIN
MERFOX	MERCADO DE FUTUORS Y OPCIONES S.A., ARGENTINA	ARGENTINA
MGE	MINNEAPOLIS GRAIN EXCHANGE	U.S.
MONTREAL	MONTREAL EXCHANGE	CANADA
NYCE	NEW YORK COTTON EXCHANGE	U.S.
NYFE	NEW YORK FUTURES EXCHANGE	U.S.
NYMEX	NEW YORK MERCANTILE EXCHANGE	U.S.
NZFE	NEW ZELAND FUTURES & OPTIONS EXCHANGE	NEW ZEALAND
OSAKA	OSAKA SECURITIES EXCHANGE	JAPAN
SFE	SYDNEY FUTURES EXCHANGE	AUSTRALIA
SIMEX	SINGAPORE INT'L MONETARY EXCHANGE	SINGAPORE
SOFFEX	SWISS OPTIONS AND FINANCIAL FUTURES EXCHANGE	SWITZERLAND
SOM	STOCKHOLM OPTIONS MARKET	SWEDEN
TFE	TORONTO FUTURES EXCHANGE	CANADA
TGE	TOKYO GRAIN EXCHANGE	JAPAN
TIFFE	TOKYO INT'L FINANCIAL FUTURES EXCHANGE	JAPAN
TOCOM	TOKYO COMMODITY EXCHANGE	JAPAN
TSE	TOKYO STOCK EXCHANGE	JAPAN
WCE	WINNIPEG COMMODITY EXCHANGE	CANADA

Table 27.2 Commodities and Instruments Traded Financials

Currencies		Stock Indices		Interest Rates	
Country	**Name**	**Country**	**Index**	**Country**	**Instrument**
Australia	A$	Australia	All Ordinaries Share Price Index	Australia	Bank Bills, 90-day
Brazil	Dollar-Cruzeiro	Brazil	Bovespa Stock Index		Treasury Bond, 3-yr
Canada	C$	Denmark	KFX Stock Index		Treasury Bond, 10-yr
Germany	D-Mark	Europe	EOE Stock Index	Belgium	Gov't Bond
	DM/JY Cross (New)		Eurotop 100	Brazil	Interest Rate
Japan	Yen		FTSE Eurotrack	Canada	Gov't Bond
	Dollar/Yen	France	CAC 40 Stock Index		Bankers Acceptances
Netherlands	Guilder, option		CAC 40 Index, short-term	Denmark	Gov't Bond, 9% 1995
	Dollar/Guilder		CAC 40 Index, long-term		Danish Gov't Bond 9%, 2000
Switzerland	SF	Germany	DAX	Europe	ECU, 3-month
Spain	SP/US$		DAX, options on futures		ECU, Bond
	SP/DM	Hong Kong	Hang Seng Index		Eurodollar
United Kingdom	BP	Japan	Nikkei Stock Average		Euromark
United States	Dollar		Nikkei 225		Euroswiss
	US$ Index		TOPIX Stock Index		Euroyen
			TSE 35 Index	France	PIBOR, 3-month
					Gov't Bond
		Netherlands	Dutch Stock Index Options		
			Dutch Top 5 Index	Germany	Gov't Bond
			Dutch Top 5 Index		National Bond, Bobl
		New Zealand	Forty Index	Ireland	DIBOR
		Spain	IBEX 35	Italy	Gov't Bond
		Sweden	OMX Index	Japan	Gov't Bond

Table 27.2 Commodities and Instruments Traded Financials (continued)

Currencies		Stock Indices		Interest Rates	
Country	**Name**	**Country**	**Index**	**Country**	**Instrument**
		United Kingdom	FTSE 100	Netherlands	Gov't Bond
		United States	S&P 500	New Zealand	Bank Bill 90-day
			S&P 400		Gov't Stock 5-year
			Value Line	Spain	MIBOR, 90-day
			Mini Value Line		National Bond, 10-year
			NYSE Composite	Sweden	Interest Rate
			Major Market Index	Switzerland	Interest Rate, 5-year
			XMI Index	United Kingdom	LIBOR, one-month
					Sterling, 3-month
					Long Gilt
				United States	Interest-Rate, 30-day
					Treasury Bill, 90-day
					Treasury Note, 2 -year
					Treasury Note, 5 -year
					Treasury Note, 10 year
					Treasury Bond
					US Muni Bond
					Index

Table 27.3 Commodities

ENERGY	METALS	SOFTS Foods, Grains, Meats & Misc
Crude	Aluminum	Barley, EEC
Crude, Brent	Copper	Barley, Thunder Bay
Crude, Sour	Diammonium Phosphate	Barley, Western
Gasoil	Gold	Broilers
Gasoline, unleaded	Gold, options on actuals	Canola/Rape Seed
Heating Oil	Gold, 5-day options	Cocoa
Heavy Fuel	Lead, standard	Coffee, Arabica
High Sulphur Fuel Oil	Nickel, primary	Coffee C
Natural Gas	Palladium	Coffee, Robusta
Propane	Platinum	Corn
	Silver	Cotton
	Silver, 5-day options	Feeder Cattle
	Tin	Flax Seed
	Zinc	Live Cattle
		Live Hogs
		Livestock
		Lumber
		Oats
		Orange Juice
		Pigs
		Pork Bellies
		Potatoes
		Rough Rice
		Rubber
		Soybeans
		Soybean, Meal
		Soybean, Oil
		Sugar
		Sugar, White
		Wheat
		Sugar
		Sugar, White
		Wheat

COMMODITY FUTURES TRADING AND THE LAW

From its earliest beginnings in the form of forward contracts and even following the opening of organized commodity futures exchanges, futures trading repeatedly faced attack from hostile legislators. Among the earliest of such attacks was a proclamation in 1610 which prohibited short selling in Holland. Almost always, general laws prohibiting organized futures trading on exchanges have been repealed within a short time after their passage. However, one such bill, banning futures trading in onions, did become law in the U.S. in 1958. It is still in effect, although recent studies by the U.S. government have shown that arguments used to persuade Congress of the need for the legislation were invalid and incorrect.

The general public's mistrust of futures trading stemmed in part from a misunderstanding of the concepts, particularly short selling, and in part from abusive practices on the part of exchange members who had little regard for the public welfare during the early stages of commodity futures trading. The uninformed, therefore, quickly equated speculation in futures with gambling, an unfortunate equation which still persists today, though to a lesser extent.

From 1884 to 1953, Congress introduced some 330 bills with the intent to restrain futures trading in one way or another. From 1890 to 1924, at least 30 separate investigations were undertaken in the grain trade. The Hatch Bill, which passed both houses in 1891 and almost became a law, would have imposed a tax upon all futures contracts in specified commodities. Fortunately, exchange officials recognized the need for getting their houses in order and so tightened internal controls and effected reforms in their organizations and the trading.

In 1916, the Cotton Futures Act and, in 1922, the Grain Futures Act were passed, bringing trading in these commodities under government regulation for the first time. Although widely bemoaned by the exchange community at the time, these acts proved beneficial to both the exchanges and the public. The Grain Futures Act was subsequently amended in the 1930s and renamed the Commodity Exchange Act. This legislation outlawed certain manipulative practices and established rules for safeguarding customer funds held by brokers. The act, which covered a broad range of commodities, was administered by the U.S. Department of Agriculture's Commodity Exchange Authority.

Not all commodity futures trading in the United States fell under the aegis of the Commodity Exchange Authority. Only trading in those commodities specifically mentioned in the Act were within its jurisdiction. The Act has been amended from time to time to include additional commodities and to broaden its scope. The most recent major amendment occurred with the passage of the Commodity Futures Trading Commission Act of 1974. What is also notable is that virtually every other country is copying the U.S. regulatory and legal framework for enabling, monitoring, and regulating the exchange activity.

THE COMMODITY FUTURES TRADING COMMISSION

The Commodity Futures Trading Commission Act was passed in October of 1974 largely as a result of high price levels reached in 1972 and 1973 when so many raw materials were in short supply. The furor that grew out of Russian grain deals and the scandals that enveloped commodity options trading in the United States during the early 1970s also caused Congress to feel that the operation of the futures markets had become a matter of great public importance.

The CFTC Act amended the Commodity Exchange Act and established federal regulation over all commodities, rights, and services traded on futures contracts.

Basically, the CFTC Act recognizes that properly functioning futures markets are in the best interest of the United States. The objectives of the CFTC Act are: (1) to foster competition in the marketplace; and (b) to protect people who participate in the markets from fraud, deceit, and abusive practices.

To administer the newly amended Commodity Exchange Act, an independent regulatory commission called the Commodity Futures Trading Commission was created. The Commission consists of a chairman and four other commissioners, each appointed by the President with the advice and consent of the Senate and each serving five-year terms. The Commission is headquartered in Washington, DC, and has branch offices in New York, Chicago, Kansas City, Minneapolis, and Los Angeles.

The new Act strengthened the exchanges' role as quasi-public institutions and brings almost all of their activities under regulation of the federal government. Every contract market (exchange) has to be specifically approved by the Commission. Everybody involved in execution of futures contracts and in dealing with the public has to be registered with the Commission and has to pass examination and fitness requirements established by the Commission. The new Act extends materially the concept of the public interest to be protected by including not only farmer interests but the interests of all people—producers, processors, merchants, other market users, and consumers.

All contract markets must demonstrate that the futures contracts for which they seek designation for trading are not contrary to the national public interest and serve an economic function. All bylaws, rules, regulations, and resolutions that relate to the terms and conditions of the contracts and other trading requirements must be submitted by the contract market to the CFTC for approval. In addition, the Commission has the authority to go directly into court to enjoin any contract market or any person from violating the Act or restraining trade in a commodity for future delivery. The Commission has the authority, in emergency situations, to direct contract markets to take such actions as are necessary to maintain or restore orderly trading. Substantial monetary penalties can be assessed.

The Commission has established a number of operating programs to achieve the objectives of the Act. These are briefly described on the next page.

a. Market Surveillance This refers to the continual monitoring and analysis of the people who trade the various markets, the prices generated by the trading, and the supply/demand elements affecting the prices. The purpose of the surveillance is to maintain orderly markets that are free of manipulation.

b. Rule Reviews The Act requires the CFTC to approve all rules, regulations, procedures and bylaws of the exchanges. Basically, they are reviewed for their equitability, their effect on competition, the extent to which they further the objectives of the Act, and the degree to which they reflect normal commercial practices.

c. Registration and Audit All persons acting as futures commission merchants, floor brokers, associated persons, pool operators, trading advisors, and options dealers must register with the Commission. Each of them is subject to independent financial audits conducted by CFTC or its legal designate.

d. Research The Commission has established a research program designed to assess the status and role of competition in the industry and seek out ways of improving it. In addition, the research effort serves to systematically investigate the functioning of the market and market users.

e. Education The act authorized the Commission to establish an education program to inform people about the important functions performed by futures trading and the role of the CFTC in overseeing trading to assure that it furthers the objectives of the Act.

f. Enforcement The enforcement program is designed to secure compliance with the law by the conduct of investigations to uncover violations of the Act and the prosecution of wrongdoers. In addition, the enforcement program administers the reparations program of the Commission.

g. Reparations The Act authorized the commission to establish a procedure for receiving and reviewing claims for damages that arise from various violations of the Act by any person or firm registered with the CFTC. Reparation requests may be filed for any amount, but the claim must be filed within two years after the alleged violation occurs. Reparations procedures are intended as an alternative to arbitration or court proceedings and not as an additional procedure if others are in the process of being completed. The CFTC encourages arbitration between the disputing parties.

This complaint-handling process, along with many other regulatory functions, has been delegated by the CFTC to the National Futures Association (NFA) (more about that in the next section). CFTC reparations complaints should be filed with the:

Commodity Futures Trading Commission
Reparations Unit
2033 K Street, N.W.
Washington, DC 20581

When the complaint is filed, it should include the name and address of each person alleged to have violated the Act; the specific violations claimed; all relevant facts concerning the alleged violation, including dates, places and circumstances; and any documentation which supports the amount and manner of damage suffered by the claimant. The complaint should be notarized and should include a statement that no arbitration proceeding or civil court proceeding is underway.

The CFTC will review the complaint, if appropriate, or refer it to the NFA. If CFTC action is warranted, each person complained against will receive a copy of it. Such persons have 45 days to answer the complaint. Counterclaims are allowed. Mediation and alternative means to settle disputes outside of court are actively encouraged.

If the parties do not settle their differences, formal proceedings will begin, and the case will be assigned to an Administrative Law Judge for oral hearings. After the Administrative Law Judge rules on the case, either side may appeal the verdict to the Commission for review. The Commission decision may also be appealed to the U.S. Court of Appeals.

Although less government intervention in the marketplace is a desirable goal, the existence of a governmental agency to oversee exchange activities and to assure the enforcement of exchange rules is certainly healthy. In addition, such an agency, particularly if it is a strong agency using its power wisely, aids in establishing the credibility of the exchanges and the valuable economic functions they perform. It also assures the public that an independent entity is mindful of their interests.

SELF-REGULATION AND THE NFA

The existence of government regulation should not reduce or remove the responsibility for self-regulation. It is clear that when Congress passed the Commodity Futures Trading Commission Act of 1974, it intended that the commodity futures industry have a responsibility to itself and to the public to perform certain self-regulatory functions. It is also clear that Congress intended that the Commission require the exchanges to accept that responsibility. This is good. Self-regulation is more desirable than government regulation. To assure that goal, the CFTC Act authorized the creation of the National Futures Association (NFA).

The motives behind and the net effect of most government regulations have generally been commendable and positive. Unfortunately, sometimes government regulations turn out to be incapable of achieving their intended goals. Frequently, they generate greater costs than resulted from the original problem. (And sometimes those costs are considerable.) One commodity exchange that spent $2,500 on legal fees to meet Commodity Exchange Authority requirements the year before the CFTC came into existence spent $75,000 on legal fees to meet CFTC regulatory requirements the year after, and now spends millions. The long-run impact of these effects needs to be analyzed by regulatory agencies.

Frequently, government regulations are too inflexible to accommodate changes in the business environment and the general economy. Thus, they stifle innovation. Sometimes a previously beneficial regulation becomes outdated or even counter-productive and yet remains in effect. This results from the pressure of special interests. Historically, business enterprises have sought to avoid competition and have sometimes been aided in doing so by government or even self-regulation. At other times rules and procedures create vested interests and economic benefits, which reform would endanger. In all of these instances, reform of the regulations would increase the productive use of government resources and would free private resources for better and more productive tasks.

In short, government regulation is expensive, and many of the costs to society are hidden.

Self-regulation may also be expensive, but it is usually more efficient. The costs and benefits of self-regulation in commodity futures usually accrue to the proper people—those most directly affected—instead of the general populace. To this effect, the CFTC has designated the National Futures Association (the "Association") as a registered futures association. Among the Association's activities are qualification screening and registration, financial surveillance, enforcement of customer protection rules and uniform business standards, arbitration of disputes, and educational activities. The Association is financed through the payment of assessments and dues by its members and by registration fees. Figure 27.1 depicts the organizational chart for the NFA. The Board of Directors (27 people) represents all aspects of the industry and has three public directors. The NFA staff has the major responsibility for auditing the members' financial status and operating practices. They conduct about 1,000 audits annually and register about 15,000 new industry participants each year. Perhaps their most important function, though, is in dispute resolution. They are the second line of defense (after the brokerage firms and exchanges themselves) for an individual to get redress of a grievance. The address of the NFA is 200 W. Madison St., Suite 1600, Chicago, Illinois 60606.

Regulatory agencies, both public and industry, need to do more to identify the scope and seriousness of the actual problems they are trying to solve and to consider the total cost and total benefits of their actions. Only those regulations should be instituted for which benefits outweigh costs.

Regulators need also to consider the "why" test more often than the "why not" test when reviewing proposed regulations. They should seriously ask "why" particular regulation is needed and whether there are a number of alternative solutions to the

Figure 27.1 NFA Organization Chart

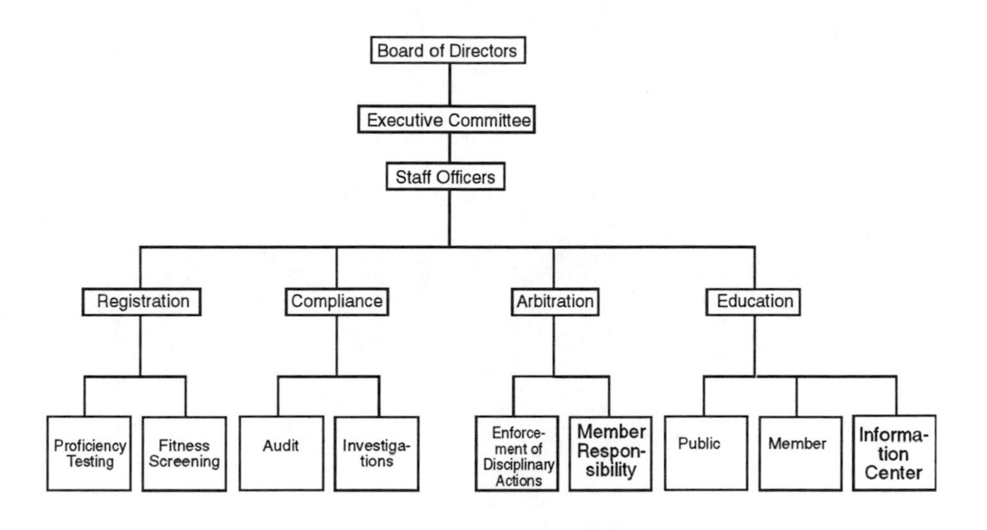

problem other than establishing another regulation. Conversely, in order to create an environment conducive to encouraging innovation and experimentation in the marketplace, regulators should consider a "why not" test when reviewing proposals for new contracts and new types of business arrangements at the exchanges.

Perhaps most important, regulatory agencies, regulatees, and private citizens need to pass the message that there is no substitute for self-protection, and government regulatory agencies cannot protect all people from all things. Citizens ought to be expected to put forth a reasonable amount of effort toward self-protection. Perhaps in trying to determine whether a particular regulation is necessary or not, regulatory agencies should apply an "ability to self-protect" test, which would determine whether a reasonable individual exercising prudence and common sense in a particular situation could be reasonably expected to be able to protect himself without the need for government regulations. Every person has a responsibility to himself and to his fellow citizens to protect himself as much as possible.

To facilitate self-protection efforts, the CFTC should continue to emphasize requiring full disclosure of all relevant aspects of commodity futures and commodity options transactions. In this way, natural forces of competition, which are the most effective means of regulating, will flourish.

Chapter 28

The Commodity Futures Exchange

It is said that in the early 17th century, when futures trading was just emerging in Japan, traders wore the long, flowing, classic Japanese robes with very wide sleeves. As a trade was consummated, each trader allowed the opposite trader to put an arm up his sleeve. This was a sign of good faith, conveying to the opposite party that there were no tricks "up his sleeve" in the transaction.

As business increased and clothing styles changed, no doubt the Japanese found this a cumbersome or needless process. At any rate, in modern commodity futures trading the signs of good faith and contract guarantees are much more tangible. They now take the form of cash, and contract guarantees are provided by a clearing house, the heart of any commodity futures exchange.

The commodity futures exchange of today is a meeting place for buyers and sellers of futures contacts. Its role is to provide the facilities through which futures trading can be conducted; to establish trading rules; to supervise business conduct on the trading floor, and to collect and disseminate information about the market. The exchange itself never enters into the trading. It does not influence or establish prices. Market participants and economic forces influencing the market do that.

NATURE OF THE ORGANIZATION

The internal structure of all exchanges is basically similar. Therefore, the following discussion of exchange organization and operations, although primarily descriptive of the Chicago Mercantile Exchange, adequately describes virtually all commodity futures exchanges.

Most commodity exchanges are not-for-profit organizations. The shares in the corporations are called memberships. The total number of memberships varies from exchange to exchange and is generally fixed by the exchange governing board.

Membership on an exchange, which is an individual privilege, allows the member, among other things, to appear on the exchange trading floor, to act as a floor trader, to pay reduced commissions on his trades, and to participate in the management of the exchange.

Changes in membership occur only as privately—held exchange seats become available for purchase on a bid-and-offer basis. The actual price for a membership may fluctuate considerably from time to time. For example, in 1982 a seat on the Chicago Mercantile Exchange sold for a high of $160,000. These same memberships were being bid and offered in the $60,000-$70,000 range through 1971.

Applications for membership are submitted to the exchange, which then conducts a thorough investigation of the applicant's financial background and character. An applicant who meets financial and other requirements must then receive the approval of the Board of Governors.

Exchange Administration

The exchange is governed by a Board of Governors elected from a slate of nominees selected from its membership and, on most exchanges, from several non-member candidates who represent the public-at-large or the various commodity interests affected by the contracts traded on the exchange, e.g., banking, farming, etc. The Board is responsible for establishing major policies and making and amending exchange rules. In addition, it may act in a judicial capacity in conducting hearings involving member misconduct. The responsibilities and broad powers of an exchange governing board may differ slightly from one exchange to another, but they are generally pretty much alike.

Exchange Staff

Daily administration of the exchange is in the hands of an appointed and salaried president, employed with the approval of the exchange board. The president, as chief executive officer of the exchange, is assisted by such other officers and staff as he deems necessary. Generally, the major departments are: audits and investigations, education, public relations, quotations, research, and statistical.

The most important functions of these departments include:

Audits and Investigations. This department (a) monitors the financial status of member firms and uncovers financial weaknesses early enough to enable corrective action to be taken; (b) undertakes market surveillance, including the review of all discretionary and omnibus accounts, which must be registered with the exchange; (c) aids the Clearing House Committee by providing information gleaned from its review of all applications for clearing house privileges, broker applications, and solicitor applications, and (d) screens applicants for membership and reviews applications from member firms to open branch offices.

Statistical Department. Maintained by all major commodity futures exchanges, it reports and disseminates daily market price data and such information as may become available from governmental and other sources about supply and demand factors.

Quotations Department. The department is responsible for supervising the instantaneous release of market price quotations over national and international wire services, as well as supervision of all price data posted on the exchange floor.

Research Department. The research department conducts or assists in making feasibility studies with respect to new contracts that might be traded and also aids in the analysis and implementation of changes to be made in existing contracts.

Education Department. This department is charged with the responsibility of providing educational materials and services to various segments of the public concerned with or interested in the function and operation of the markets. The groups the department attempts to reach include commercial hedgers, bankers, speculators, the commodity brokerage industry, and the academic community.

Public Relations Department. Charged with supervising all matters concerning the public relations function of the exchange, the department's primary responsibility is to promote public awareness of the vital economic role fulfilled by the modern commodity futures exchange, and its place in our society as a financial institution of integrity and responsibility.

Exchange Committees

The exchange members themselves play an important role in the functioning of the market through a member committee system employed by most commodity futures exchanges. During his term in office, the Board chairman, with the approval of the Board, usually selects the members who will serve on the various committees.

Certain committees are common to most major exchanges; though they may go by different titles, their functions are almost identical. These include an arbitration committee, membership committee, rules committee, business conduct committee, public relations committee, floor practices committee, clearing house committee, pit committee, floor brokers qualification committee, and contract specifications committee.

Arbitration Committee. Reconciles controversies arising between two or more members through arbitration proceedings.

Membership Committee. Reviews all applications of prospective members, investigates their qualifications, and makes reports and recommendations on their findings to the Board.

Rules Committee. Drafts new rules or changes to rules passed by the Board and may also refer or offer suggestions for new rule changes to the Board.

Business Conduct Committee. Supervises the business conduct of members. It also conducts investigations and may take action against member firms to assure that contract integrity and orderliness of trading are maintained.

Clearing House Committee. Has sole discretion in determining qualifications of clearing house member applicants and in adopting those regulations setting forth what qualifications must be met. This committee also reviews applications of clearing members, associate brokers, registered representatives, and applications for assignment of member rates. Some exchanges maintain their clearing house as a separate corporation. In such instances these duties are performed by that corporation.

Floor Practices Committee. Supervises all matters relating to floor practices and trading ethics, conducts investigations and hearings, and resolves any errors or price discrepancies discovered either during or after a trading session.

Public Relations Committee. Supervises the public relations department in the implementation of advertising and publicity activities; investigates, at the request of the Board, activities related to publicity, and advises or makes recommendations to the Board concerning publicity.

Contract Specifications Committee. Reviews existing contracts and makes recommendations to the Board regarding contract changes.

Floor Brokers Qualification Committee. Supervises all matters pertaining to qualifications of brokers and traders.

Pit Committee. Supervises the opening and closing of trading and immediately resolves grievances arising from price infractions during trading.

THE TRADING FLOOR

The central point of a trading floor is the trading pit or ring—a specified area in which the floor brokers do their buying and selling. All bids and offers are made by open outcry and by hand signals in the trading pits. Computerized exchanges substitute for the floor execution process, but the rest of the procedures for clearing, settlement, margining, and delivery are the same as for pit trading.

As bids and offers are made and trades are consummated, prices are recorded by an observing reporter (an employee of the market) and reported on the quotation boards adjoining the pits. This information is also wired instantaneously to other markets and trading centers throughout the country and abroad.

Most floor brokers have telephone, facsimile, and other communication lines adjacent to the trading area from which they receive customer orders for trades and confirm executed trades. Also on the floor, adjacent to the trading pits, are a bank of electronic monitors providing access to important information, news, and prices of other markets. The latter carry the most up-to-date information and commentary from financial centers all over the world.

EXECUTION OF TRADES

When someone decides to trade on the exchange (having first opened an account with a member firm—a simple procedure explained in Chapter 6—he places his order with a registered representative of the member firm. A proper order should specify whether to buy or sell, what commodity, the number of contracts, at which price and the length of time the order is to run. When the account representative accepts the order, he confirms it orally and also in writing through the mail. This enables the customer to double-check the accuracy of the order and also signifies that the representative has accepted responsibility for it.

The order is immediately recorded and time-stamped upon receipt. (The order is electronically time-stamped at each relay point except at execution so that a full record can be kept of its progress.) Then it is sent to the exchange floor, where it is relayed in written form, via a runner, to the floor broker in the pit. Upon execution, the floor broker endorses the price on the order form, returns it via runner to the floor phone-man, who in turn relays it to the office. As soon as the registered representative is informed of the trade execution, he provides the customer with verbal confirmation and later confirms it in writing. If the order is a market order, this entire process—from the time the customer enters the order until it is executed in the pit and confirmation is relayed back to the customer—can take less than one minute. The diagram on the facing page illustrates this order execution process.

During the day and at the end of each trading day, member firms report all transactions to the clearing house, which reconciles (or matches) the trades and assumes the opposite side of the trade for both the original buyer and seller. This facilitates the offsetting of futures positions by the traders and greatly simplifies the settlement and delivery process.

DUAL TRADING

One of the issues that Congress discussed extensively in its deliberations over the CFTC Act of 1974 had to do with dual trading, i.e., the practice of a floor broker, FCM, associated person, etc. trading for his own account at the same time that he solicits and executes orders for customers. Such a practice seemingly has some inherent conflicts of interest. All exchanges have adopted policies governing dual trading; some prohibit it. All require record-keeping procedures to facilitate regulators' detection of abusive trading practices such as trading ahead of customer orders. Lastly, CFTC has issued a rule for public comment banning, by late in 1994, all dual trading for futures trading over 8,000 contracts per day.

THE CLEARINGHOUSE[1]

Most of us are familiar with the clearinghouse operations our nation's banking system use to expedite the flow and transfer of funds from one bank to another within the system. In the case of a futures exchange, the clearing operation exists to perform a similar function in that it facilitates the flow and transfer of funds resulting from its member firms' execution of trades. As is true in the case of the bank depositor, the individual commodity trader has no direct contact with the clearing organization; it serves as a central point for depositing and dispensing funds to be credited or debited to the accounts of member firms.

An additional function served by the exchange clearinghouse is as guarantor of contract performance. In other words, the fulfillment of contract obligations of a clearing member is guaranteed through the collective financial resources of all clearing members, regardless of what happens to the other clearing-member party to the contract. There is no direct comparison here with banks' clearing operations, as the responsibility of guaranteeing transactions rests solely with the individual bank with regard to each of its customers.

1. Exchanges in many other parts of the world do not use clearing houses. This is risky, and most such exchanges have very little public business.

The exchange clearinghouse performs a third important function which is in no way comparable to the banking system's clearing operations, namely, assigning and overseeing contract deliveries.

The formal relationships between the clearing house and the exchange may differ from one exchange to another. For example, the International Commodities Clearing House in London is a privately owned clearinghouse, separate from ownership of any exchange. It provides clearing services for a number of independent exchanges in several countries. On both the International Monetary Market and the Chicago Mercantile Exchange, the clearing house is an integral part of the exchange, operating under the direct jurisdiction of the exchange's Clearing House Committee. At the Chicago Board of Trade, the clearinghouse is a separate corporate entity with its own board of directors. No matter what formal arrangements exist, all commodity exchange clearinghouses in the U.S. operate in a similar fashion and perform nearly identical functions.

Membership in the clearinghouse is normally confined to exchange members, although the majority of exchange members are not clearinghouse members. Those exchange members who are not clearinghouse members must still have their trades cleared (verified and guaranteed) by a clearinghouse member. To put it another way, each member must either be a clearing member or be affiliated with a clearing member.

Clearing members do not pay commissions for trades executed, but do pay clearance fees and floor brokerage fees if an independent floor broker is used for trade executions. They also collect a fee from exchange members who clear trades through them.

The function of the clearinghouse begins as trading closes for the day. Clearinghouse members submit a trade confirmation card for each trade executed. Customers' names do not actually appear on these cards as buyer or seller, but only the name of the clearinghouse member in whose name the trade is executed for the customer and other information matching the trade to original order tickets.

Once these confirmation cards have been matched or verified, the original parties to the transactions—the member brokers—cease to deal with one another directly. Instead they each deal exclusively with the clearinghouse. In effect, they are now long or short to the clearinghouse, because it has assumed the position of second party to each member's transaction. The liquidation of contracts is facilitated through this system, because a trader can now offset his contract without the necessity of obtaining the agreement of the original second party to the contract. The clearinghouse then merely notes that the original trader's obligation is canceled.

The clearing member firm is ultimately responsible for fulfillment of a contract with the clearinghouse, not the individual customer. The customer's responsibility lies solely with his broker. The brokerage firm, after executing the trade, then deals exclusively with the clearinghouse.

FINANCE

Whenever a transaction is made in the market, both parties to the trade are asked to post a "good-faith" bond in the form of cash, Treasury bills, listed securities, or letters of credit. This "good-faith" money is usually referred to as margin, although on some markets it is called "security deposit," a term which more accurately describes it and distinguishes it from margin in the securities market.

The clearinghouse establishes and maintains strict control over these minimum security deposits (margins), both for initiating and for maintaining positions. Member firms are required to collect these minimum amounts from customers. Brokers may, and frequently do, charge customers more than the minimum, but they may not collect less. Clearing member firms must, in turn, deposit and maintain a specified level of funds in the clearinghouse to back up their aggregate net market position.

The purpose for requiring these funds is to insure performance under the terms of the futures contract. It is a safeguard or surety to both buyer and seller (and to the carrying broker) that there will be funds available to make proper settlement when the contract is terminated. When the contracts are offset or delivered upon, this money is returned to the trader along with his profit on the transaction, or is applied toward his debts if he has lost money.

A trader who has a paper profit on his transaction may withdraw his gain over and above the minimum security deposit required at any time before he offsets his position. On the other hand, if his transaction shows a paper loss, his account will be debited accordingly, and he may be asked to deposit additional funds in order to maintain the value of his account at the required minimum amount.

The clearinghouse requires daily settlement in cash for all price variations in every contract traded. This means that each day the clearinghouse credits the account of clearing members showing a net gain due to favorable price movements during that day's trading and requires immediate payment from those members showing a net loss on their positions.

Since there is, of course, a buyer for every seller, the monies paid out must be equal to the monies collected, and the clearinghouse must show neither a gain nor loss. It must balance before a new trading day begins.

Brokers use the cash payments received from the clearinghouse to pay out trading profits to customers. Conversely, they have to pay additional money to the clearinghouse to cover losses sustained by customers.

In summary, today's modern commodity futures exchanges have come a long way in developing managerial techniques for handling the tremendous explosion in volume of trading seen in recent years. The exchanges themselves are modern structures, which make use of the most modern data processing technology available.

Appendix I

Commodity Trader's Scorecard

This scorecard (on p. 342) is a practice trading exercise. It is designed to give you a basic "feel" for commodity futures trading. The more sophisticated kinds of futures trading transactions, such as day trades, straddles, and spreads, have been eliminated in order to keep your practice trading as simple as possible. To best utilize the scorecard, first familiarize yourself as much as possible with all the aspects of commodity futures trading explained in this book. Then:

1. Develop a trading plan. Determine your financial suitability, select a commodity, its delivery month, the number of contracts you wish to "sell or buy," and your strategy for trading. This should be based on your knowledge of the commodity's supply, demand, and technical situation along with your best judgment of which direction prices will be moving in the futures. Remember, it is just as feasible to sell first with the intention of buying later as is the opposite transaction.
2. To make the hypothetical trades, determine the price of your contracts on the initial date of the transactions. Look for the daily prices in the business section

of your newspaper. All major newspapers carry this information. Use closing (sometimes called "settlement") prices. Remember that, while the value of a contract may be many thousands of dollars, the "earnest money" (margin) you have to put up is a much lesser amount. Thus, only a small change in price can provide a large change in your investment, either positive or negative. Your profit or loss in dollars is determined by the difference between the purchase and sales price.

3. Commodity futures prices are quoted in cents per pounds, dollars per hundredweight, cents per dozen, and dollars per thousand board feet, etc. To keep track of how much money you make or lose with each change in price, you need to know how large each contract is and what unit the price quote represents. For example, if the price of pork belly futures moves from 34¢ per pound to 34.5¢ per pound, the price movement would be considered 50 "points." Since each pork belly contract is for 40,000 pounds, each movement of one "point" up or down is worth $4.00, and a 50-point move would, therefore, amount to $200.

4. Enter the information from items 1 and 2 on your scorecard. Obviously, you will not be able to fill in the net profit or loss until termination of the transactions. Assume a minimum commission per contract of $40. (Most brokers have negotiated commission rates for large orders.)

5. To calculate your profit and loss, take the lower price and subtract it from the higher price after you have terminated your position. Multiply the difference by the value per "point" (see step 3 above), and then multiply that number by the quantity of contracts you sold or bought. If you bought for less than you sold, you have a profit and vice versa. Deduct your commission from the profits. Add it to your losses.

6. When you have terminated your position and calculated your net profit or loss, enter the results in the proper column of your scorecard.

7. Evaluate your plan.

8. Be honest. Don't cheat. You're not fooling others; you're fooling yourself.

EXAMPLE: Buy (long)

Step 1:	$31.62	bought 5 July bellies 9-16
	31.02	sold 5 July bellies 11-2
	$ .60	difference in points
Step 2:	4.00	price per point
	× 60	points
	$240.00	loss
Step 3:	40.00	commission
	× 5	contracts
	$ 200.00	total commission
Step 4:	240.00	loss
	× 5	contracts
	$1,200.00	loss
	+200.00	Commission
	$1,400.00	Net Loss

EXAMPLE: Selling (short)

Step 1:	$31.62	sold 5 July bellies 9-16
	31.02	bought 5 July bellies 11-2
	.60	difference in points
Step 2:	$ 4.00	price per point
	× 60	points
	$ 240.00	profit
Step 3:	$ 40.00	commission
	× 5	contracts
	$ 200.00	total commission
Step 4:	$ 240.00	profit
	× 5	contracts
	$1,200.00	profit
	–200.00	Commission
	$1,000.00	Net Profit

Commodity Scorecard

Bought				Sold				Commission	Loss (Including Commissions)	Profit (Including Commissions)
Date	Qty	Commodity	Price	Date	Qty	Commodity	Price			
9-16	5	Pork Bellies July	31.62	11-2	5	Pork Bellies July	31.02	$200	$1,400.00	

Glossary of Commodity Futures Terms

These definitions are not intended to state or suggest the correct legal significance or meaning of any word or phrase, but only to help in understanding the commodity and foreign currency futures markets and the nomenclature used in them.

(To) Accumulate Buy futures contracts heavily in a specific commodity at regular predetermined intervals.

Acreage Allotment Government limitation on planted acreage of some basic crops.

Actuals Physical products bought and sold in the spot market.

ADP Acronym for Alternate Delivery Procedure, a contract delivery method permitting the buyer and the seller, by agreement, to settle their delivery commitment independently of the exchange.

Allowances The discounts (premiums) allowed the buyer for grades or locations of a commodity lower (higher) than the par or basis grade or location specified in the futures contract. Also called differentials.

Annualize To put on an annual basis. Usually pertains to interest rates, which are quoted on a yearly basis, or "per annum." A profit of $4 on a three-month investment of $100 would, on an annualized basis, be 16 percent.

Appreciation An increase in value. If the deutschemark appreciates relative to the U.S. dollar, it will take more dollars to buy the same amount of deutschemarks. See Revaluation.

Approved Delivery Facility Any bank, stockyard, mill, store, warehouse, plant, elevator, or other institution that is authorized by the exchange for delivery of exchange contracts.

Arbitrage The simultaneous purchase or sale of a contract in different markets in order to profit from discrepancies in prices between those markets. See Interest Arbitrage, Covered Interest Arbitrage, Spreads, Straddles.

At-The-Market An order to buy or sell at the best price obtainable at the time the order is received. See Market Order.

Balance of Payments A record, presented in balance sheet form, of the value of all the economic transactions between residents, business firms, governments, and any other institutions in a country and the rest of the world.

Basis The difference between the spot price and the price of futures.

Basis Grade The grade of a commodity used as the standard of the contract.

Bear One who believes prices will move lower. See Bull.

Bear Market A market in which prices are declining.

Bid An offer to purchase at a specified price. See Offer.

Book Transfer The transfer of title to buyer without physical movement of product.

Break A rapid and sharp decline.

Broker A man or firm who handles the actual execution of all trades.

Bull One who expects prices to rise. See Bear.

Bull Market A market in which prices are rising.

Buy In To cover or close out a short position. See Offset.

Buy-On-Close To buy at the end of the trading session at a price within the closing range.

Buy-On-Opening To buy at the beginning of the trading session at a price within the opening range.

CCC Commodity Credit Corporation. A government-owned corporation established in 1933 to assist American agriculture. Major operations include price support programs, supply control, and foreign sales programs for agricultural commodities.

CEA Commodity Exchange Authority. An agency of the U.S. Department of Agriculture, which formerly administered the Commodity Exchange Act before being replaced by the CFTC in 1975.

CFTC Commodity Futures Trading Commission established in 1975 to succeed the CEA and take over regulation of all commodity futures and options trading in the U.S. The Commission consists of a chairman, vice-chairman and three other members, all appointed by the President.

C & F "Cost and freight" paid to move a commodity to a port of destination.

CIF	Cost, insurance, and freight paid to move a commodity to a port of destination and included in the price quoted.
Call	An exchange-designated buying and selling period during which trading is conducted in order to establish a price or price range for a particular time. Also an option to buy a security or commodity at a predetermined price within a given time period.
Car	A loose, quantitative term sometimes used to describe a contract, e.g., "a car of bellies." Derived from the fact that quantities of the product specified on a contract often correspond closely to the quantity carried in a railroad car.
Carrying Broker	A member of the commodity exchange, usually a commission house broker, through whom another broker or customer elects to "clear" all or some of his trades.
Carrying Charges	Cost of storing a physical commodity over a period of time. Includes insurance and interest on the invested funds as well as other incidental costs.
Cash Commodity	The actual physical commodity, as distinguished from a futures commodity.
Cash Market	Market for immediate delivery and payment of commodities.
Central Bank	A financial institution that has official or semiofficial status in a federal government. Central banks are the instruments used by governments to expand, contract, or stabilize the supply of money and credit. They hold reserves of other banks, act as fiscal agents for their governments, and can issue paper money.
Central Rate	Similar to par value, as established by the International Monetary Fund.
Certified Stocks	Quantities of commodities designated and certified for delivery by an exchange under its trading and testing regulations at delivery points specified and approved by the exchange.

(To) Clear To be verified and guaranteed.

Clearinghouse An adjunct to a commodity exchange through which transactions executed on the floor of the exchange are settled. Also charged with assuring the proper conduct of delivery procedures and the adequate financing of the trading.

Clearing Member A member of the Clearinghouse or Association. All trades of a non-clearing member must be registered and eventually settled through a clearing member.

Clerk A member's employee who has been registered to work on the trading floor as a phone man or runner.

(The) Close A short period at the end of the trading session during which the closing price range is established. Sometimes used to refer to the closing price. See Opening.

Closing Range (or Range) The closing price (or price range) recorded during the period designated as the official close. See Settling Price.

Commercial Stocks Commodity in storage in public and private elevators or warehouses at important markets and afloat in vessels or barges in harbors and ports.

Commission The fee charged by a broker to a customer when a transaction is made.

Commission House A concern that buys and sells actual commodities or futures contracts for the accounts of customers. Its income is generated by the commissions charged customers. Often used synonymously with brokerage house.

Commitment A trader is said to have a "commitment" when he assumes the obligation to accept or make delivery by entering into a futures contract. See Open Interest.

Commodity Exchange Act Federal act passed in 1936 establishing the Commodity Exchange Commission and placing futures trading in a wide range of commodities under the regulation of the government.

Commodity Pool An enterprise in which funds contributed by a number of persons are combined for purposes of trading futures or commodity options

Commodity Pool Operator (CPO) An individual or organization which operates or solicits funds for commodity pool.

Commodity Trading Advisor (CTA) A person who advises others as to the value of or advisability of buying or selling futures contracts or commodity options or acts with customer granted authority to trade on the customer's behalf. A CTA places trades for other people's accounts.

Contract A term of reference describing a unit of trading for a commodity future, similar to "round lot" in securities markets. Also, actual bilateral agreement between the buyer and seller in a futures transaction.

Contract Grade That grade of a commodity which has been officially approved by an exchange as deliverable in settlement of a futures contract. See Basis Grade, Par.

Contract Month The month in which futures contracts may be satisfied by making or accepting delivery.

(To) Cover The purchase of futures to offset a previously established short position.

Covered Interest Arbitrage Interest arbitrage transaction that is hedged against exchange rate fluctuation. For example, an American arbitraging to take advantage of higher interest rates in Germany would cover by selling deutschemarks forward at the same time that he purchased them in the spot market. Usually done in short-term instruments. See Arbitrage, Interest Arbitrage.

Crop Year The period of time from one harvest or storage cycle to the next; varies with each commodity.

Cross-Rate In foreign exchange, the price of one currency in terms of another currency, in the market of a third country. For example, a London dollar cross-rate could be the price of one U.S. dollar in terms of deutschemarks on the London market.

Customer's Man — A person employed by and soliciting business for a futures commission merchant. See Registered Representative.

Day Order — Orders that are placed for execution, if possible, during only one trading session. If the order cannot be executed that day, it is automatically canceled.

Day Trading — Refers to establishing and liquidating the same position or positions within one day's trading.

Deferred Futures — Future contracts which expire during the more distant months. See Nearbys.

Deficit — Where "outgo" exceeds income, or expenses exceed receipts. In balance of payments, it implies that more of a country's currency went abroad than foreign currencies came into the country.

Delivery — The tender and receipt of an actual commodity, warehouse receipt, or other negotiable instrument covering such commodity, in settlement of a futures contract.

Delivery Commitment, Buyer's — The written notice given by the buyer of his intention to take delivery against a long futures position on delivery day.

Delivery Commitment, Seller's — The written notice given by the seller of his intention to make delivery against a short futures position on delivery day.

Delivery Month — A specified month within which delivery may be made under the terms of the futures contract.

Delivery Notice — The written notice given by the seller of his intention to make delivery against an open short futures position on a particular date.

Delivery Points — Those points designated by futures exchanges at which the physical commodity covered by a futures contract may be delivered in fulfillment of such contract.

Delivery Price — The price fixed by the Clearinghouse at which deliveries on futures are invoiced, and also the price at which the futures contract is settled when deliveries are made. See Settling Price.

Demurrage The charge incurred for delaying the loading or unloading of a vessel.

Depreciate Decrease in value. A currency depreciates when its "price," or exchange rate, in terms of other currencies, goes down.

Devaluation A formal "official" decrease in the value of a country's currency. For example, when the British pound sterling exchange rate, or price in terms of U.S. dollars, falls from $2.80/pound to $2.40/pound.

Differentials See Allowances.

Discretionary Account An account over which any individual or organization, other than the person in whose name the account is carried, exercises trading authority or control.

Discount Less than par. If a future delivery is selling at a discount to the spot delivery, then it's selling for a lower price than the spot price. See Premium.

Dominant Future That future having the largest number of open contracts.

Dumping Selling goods in a foreign country cheaper than they are sold at home. Under the rules of the General Agreement on Tariffs and Trades (GATT), dumping occurs when the wholesale price to the importer is lower than the wholesale price charged to the buyer in the country of origin.

Equity The residual dollar value of a futures trading account, assuming its liquidation at the going market price.

Eurodollar U.S. dollar deposits held ***abroad***. Holders may include individuals, companies, banks, and central banks.

Evening Up Buying or selling to offset an existing market position. See Liquidation.

Exchange Rate The "price" of one currency stated in terms of another currency.

Ex-Pit Transactions Trades executed, for certain technical purposes, in a location other than the regular exchange trading pit or ring.

First Notice Day The first date, varying by commodities and exchanges, on which notices of intentions to deliver actual commodities against futures are authorized.

Floating The establishment of exchange rates by free market forces. "Clean floats" involve no government intervention to manipulate the exchange rates. "Dirty floats" involve government manipulation of the price.

Floor Broker A member who executes orders for the account of one or more clearing members.

Floor Trader A member who executes trades for his own account, or for an account controlled by him. Also referred to as a "local."

Foreign Exchange Foreign currency. On the foreign exchange market, foreign currency is bought and sold for immediate or future delivery. Also sometimes referred to as non-U.S. futures exchange market.

Forward In the future.

Forward Market Refers to informal (non-exchange) trading of contracts for future delivery. Contracts for forward delivery are "personalized," i.e., delivery time and amount are as determined by the customer.

Free Supply The storage supply of a commodity outside of government-held stocks; the amount available for commercial sale.

Futures A term used to designate the standardized contracts covering the sale of commodities for future delivery on a commodity exchange.

Futures Commission Merchant A firm or person engaged in soliciting or accepting and handling orders for the purchase or sale of commodities for future delivery on, or subject to, the rules of a futures exchange and who, in connection with such solicitation or acceptance of orders, accepts any money or securities to margin any resulting trades or contracts. Must be licensed under the Commodity Exchange Act.

F.O.B. Free-on-Board. A term describing the cost of placing commodities on board whatever shipment conveyance is being used.

Give Up At the request of the customer, a brokerage house that has not performed the service is credited with the execution of any order.

Grading Certificate A paper setting forth the quality of a commodity as determined by authorized inspectors or graders.

G.T.C. Good-'til-Canceled. An order to your broker to buy or sell at a fixed price. The order holds until executed or canceled.

Group of 10 The 10 leading industrial nations of the free world. Specifically, the United States, Canada, England, Belgium, France, Germany, Italy, The Netherlands, Sweden, and Japan.

Hardening Describes a price which is gradually stabilizing.

Heavy A description of a market in which prices are demonstrating either an inability to advance or a slight tendency to decline.

Hedging A means of risk protection against extensive loss due to adverse price fluctuations. In the futures market, a purchase or sale for future delivery as a temporary substitute for a merchandising transaction to be made later.

Interest Arbitrage The operation wherein foreign debt instruments are purchased to profit from the higher interest rate in the foreign country over the home country. The operation is profitable only when the forward rate on the foreign currency is selling at a discount ***less than*** the premium on the interest rate. For example, if the interest rate in West Germany is 2 percent ***higher than*** in the U.S., interest arbitrage profits are possible if the forward rate for deutschemarks is higher than a 2 percent discount over the spot rate. This is one fundamental factor affecting forward rates of exchange. See Interest Rate Parity.

Interest Rate Parity The formal theory of interest rate parity holds that under normal conditions the forward premium or discount on a currency in terms of another is directly related to the interest rate differential between the two countries. For example, the forward rate discount (or premium) on Swiss francs in terms of dollars would equal the premium (or discount) of interest rates in Switzerland over (or under) those in the U.S. This theory holds only when there are unrestricted flows of international short-term capital. In reality, numerous economic and legal obstacles restrict the movement, so that actual parity is rare. See Interest Arbitrage, Covered Interest Arbitrage.

International Monetary Fund An organization of 126 countries created to (1) promote international cooperation; (2) facilitate expansion and balanced growth of international trade; (3) promote exchange stability; (4) avoid competitive exchange depreciation; (5) assist in establishment of a multinational system of payments and elimination of foreign exchange restrictions; and (6) provide members with resources to correct short-term imbalances of payments. Created at Bretton Woods, New Hampshire, in July 1944.

Intervention Limits Outer limit of variation of the par value (as agreed upon by the IMF or a group of trading partners) of the spot price of a currency. At this point IMF members are obligated to keep the price within this limit. The intervention takes the form of open market sales or purchases of the currency. For example, if the deutschemark is at the lower intervention limit, the German central bank will buy deutschemarks, usually with U.S. dollars, to decrease the supply of deutschemarks and thereby raise its "price" above the lower limit. If the upper limit were approached, the government would sell deutschemarks.

Introducing Broker A CTFC/NFA registered broker who solicits and services customer brokerage accounts but "introduces" (passes on) their orders to Futures Commission Merchants for execution, clearing and recordkeeping.

Inverted Market A futures market in which the nearer months are selling at premiums to the more distant months.

Invisible Supply Usually refers to uncounted stocks in the hands of wholesalers, manufacturers, and ultimate consumers, and sometimes to producers' stocks that cannot be counted accurately.

Last Trading Day The final day under an exchange's rules during which trading may take place in a particular futures delivery month. Futures contracts outstanding at the end of the last trading day must be settled by delivery or, in the case of cash settlement, by an exchange of cash value differences.

Limit Order An order given to a broker with restrictions upon its execution, such as price and time.

Liquidation Same as offset. Any transaction which offsets or closes out a long or short position. A market in which open interest is declining.

Liquidity A market is said to be liquid when it has a high level of trading activity, allowing buying and selling with minimum price disturbance.

Local A floor broker who usually executes trades only for his own account.

Long One who has bought a futures contract to establish a market position and who has not yet closed out this position through an offsetting sale. Opposite of Short.

Long Hedge The purchase of a futures contract to offset the forward sale of an equivalent quantity of a commodity not yet owned. Used as protection against an advance in the cash price. See Hedge.

Long the Basis — The purchase of a cash commodity and the sale of a futures against unsold inventory to provide protection against a price decline in the cash market. Synonymous with Short Hedge.

Maintenance Margin (Maintenance Security Deposit) — A sum, usually smaller than, but part of, the original margin (security deposit) which must be maintained on deposit at all times. If a customer's equity in any futures position drops to or under the maintenance margin level, the broker must issue a call for the amount of money required to restore the customer's equity in the account to the original margin level.

Margin — On all commodity exchanges, except the International Monetary Market, a cash amount of funds that a customer must deposit with the broker for each contract as a sign of his good faith in fulfilling the contract terms. It is not considered as part payment of purchase. On the IMM, an amount of funds that must be deposited by a clearing member with the clearing house for each contract as a guarantee of fulfillment of the futures contract. See Security Deposit.

Margin Call — A demand for additional cash funds because of adverse price movement. See Maintenance Margin.

Market Order — An order for immediate execution given to your broker to buy or sell at the best obtainable price.

Maximum Daily Price Fluctuation — The maximum amount the contract price can change up or down during one trading session, as fixed by exchange rules.

Minimum Price Fluctuations — Smallest increment of price movement possible in trading a given contract. For example, the minimum price fluctuation on one gold contract is .10/troy oz. or $10.00 per contract. See Point.

M.I.T. — Market-if-Touched. A price order that automatically becomes a market order if the price is reached.

Monetary Policy — Governmental actions to control a country's domestic economy by adjusting the money supply. Used in conjunction with fiscal policy, which injects funds into an economy via public works, grants, and federal contracts with the government as the buyer of goods and services.

Nearbys The nearest delivery months of a commodity futures market.

Negotiable Warehouse Receipt A legal document issued by a warehouse describing and guaranteeing the existence of a specific quantity (and sometimes a specific grade) of a commodity in the warehouse.

Nominal Price Price quotation on futures for a period in which no actual trading took place.

Notice Day A day on which notices of intent to deliver pertaining to a specified delivery month may be issued.

Offer Indicates a willingness to sell a futures contract at a given price. It is the opposite of Bid.

Offset See Evening Up, Liquidation.

Omnibus Account An account carried by one futures commission merchant with another futures commission merchant in which the transactions of two or more persons are combined and carried in the name of the originating broker rather than designated separately. See Futures Commission Merchant.

Open Contracts Contracts which have been bought or sold and are still outstanding, not having been delivered upon or offset. See Open Interest.

Open Interest Number of open contracts. Refers to unliquidated purchases or sales, never to their combined total.

Open Order An order to your broker that is good until it is canceled or executed.

(The) Opening The varying time period at the beginning of the trading session officially designated by the exchange during which all transactions are considered made "at the opening." The precise time varies with the amount of activity at the opening. See Close.

Opening Price The price (or range) recorded during the period designated by the exchange as the official opening.

Option	Sometimes used as a synonym for "Futures Contract Month," as in the June Option. Technically the term is incorrect in the sense that "Options" are agreements with a seller or buyer permitting the holder to buy or sell, if he chooses to do so, at a given price within a given period.
Original Margin	The margin needed to cover a specific new position.
Overbought	A market that has had sharp advance. Rank-and-file traders (who were bullish and long earlier) have turned bearish.
Oversold	A market that has had a sharp decline. Rank-and-file traders (who were bearish and short earlier) have turned bullish.
P & S	Purchase and Sale Statement. A statement provided by the broker to a customer showing the change in his net ledger balance after the offset of a previously established position.
Par	Refers to the standard delivery point or points, or to quality specifications of the commodity represented in the contract. Serves as a benchmark upon which to base discounts or premiums for varying quality. In foreign exchange, an exchange rate arbitrarily set by the country of issuance and ratified by the IMF.
Parity	Par Rate.
Per Annum	Per year. Usually refers to interest rates, a basis of comparison of rates among various debt instruments of less than one year duration.
Point	The minimum unit in which changes in futures prices may be expressed; e.g., 1/10th of a cent per ounce for silver.
Position	One's interest in the market, either long or short, in the form of open contracts.
Position Limit	The maximum number of contracts, as prescribed by an exchange or the CFTC, either net long or net short, in one commodity future or in all futures of one commodity combined, which may be held or controlled by one person or firm in its own name. Does not apply to bona fide hedgers.

Premium Above par. Used to quote one price in reference to another. In foreign exchange above spot. If the forward rate for Italian lira is at a premium to spot lira, it is selling above the spot price. See Discount.

Primary Market Important distribution centers at which spot commodities are originally accumulated for shipment into commercial channels.

Prime Rate The interest rate charged by banks to their biggest and most creditworthy customers. Other interest rates are scaled up from the prime rate. It is a good indication of general interest rate levels within a country.

Put An option to sell a commodity or security at a predetermined price within a specified period of time.

Pyramiding Using the profits on a previously established position as margin for adding to that position.

Rally An upward movement of prices following a decline.

Range The high and low prices recorded during a specified time.

Reaction A decline in prices following an advance—the opposite of rally.

Reciprocal Any number divided into "1." A number multiplied by its reciprocal equals one. In foreign exchange, it is a handy way of expressing currency prices in terms of each other. For example, if one British pound = $2.6057, then $1 = 1/2.6057 = .3838 pounds.

Recovery Usually describes a price advance following a decline.

Regulated Commodities Those commodities over which the CFTC exercises regulatory supervision for the purpose of seeing that trading is conducted in the public's interest.

Registered Representative See Customer's Man.

Roundturn The purchase and sale of a contract. The long or short position of an individual is offset by an opposite transaction or by accepting or making delivery of the actual commodity.

Reserves (Official) Official foreign exchange reserves are kept to insure a government's ability to meet current or near-term claims. The primary reserve currencies are the U.S. dollar, the German deutschemark, and the Japanese yen. Gold is used in official reserves. As long as reserves grow faster than current claims, their adequacy increases. When claims grow faster, reserve adequacy decreases. Therefore, a particular volume of reserves has little significance because the "adequacy" concept is a relative one. Official reserves are a debit entry on a country's balance of payments; i.e., they are an asset.

Revaluation A formal "official" increase in the exchange rate or price of currency.

Scalp To trade for small gains. Involves establishing and liquidating a position quickly, within the same day or sometimes the same hour.

Security Deposit On the IMM, the amount of funds that must be deposited by a customer with his broker for each futures contract as a guarantee of fulfillment of the contract. It is not considered as part payment of purchase. Used interchangeably with margin.

Security Deposit Call A demand for additional cash funds because of adverse price movement. See Maintenance Security Deposit.

Settling Price The daily price at which the clearing house clears all trades and settles all accounts between clearing members for each contract month. Settlement prices are used to determine both margin calls and invoice prices for deliveries.

Short One who has sold a futures contract to establish a market position and who has not yet closed out his position through an offsetting purchase or delivery. The opposite of being long. See Long.

Short Hedge The sale of futures contracts to reduce the possible decline in value of an approximately equal amount of the actual commodity held.

Short Selling Selling a contract with the idea of buying it back at a later date.

Seller's Option Refers to the seller's right to select from among a range of alternatives regarding quality of the commodity, time, and place of delivery.

Short Squeeze A situation in which a lack of supplies tends to force those who have sold to cover their positions by offset in the futures market rather than by delivery.

Short The Basis The forward sale of a cash commodity hedged by the purchase of a future against the cash position. Synonymous with Long Hedge.

Sold-Out Market Market situation in which liquidation of weakly held positions has been completed and offerings have become scarce.

Speculation Any investment that aims at profit through price fluctuation. It is the assumption of an existing risk in expectation of a profit.

Speculator One who attempts to anticipate price changes and through market activities make profits; he is not using the futures market in connection with the production, processing, marketing, or handling of a product.

Spot Market of immediate delivery of the product and immediate payment. Also refers to the nearest delivery month on a futures contract.

Spread 1. Difference in the prices of a currency between various future deliveries, or between the spot market and a future delivery. 2. To take a simultaneous long and short position, aimed at a profit via fluctuation of differential in two prices. For example, the purchase of May corn and the sale of September corn if it is felt the difference in price between the two would widen (if May were at a premium to September).

If it is felt that price difference will narrow, you would sell May and buy September. Also sometimes called a Straddle.

Stop-Loss Order An order which immediately becomes a market order when the "stop" level is reached. Its purpose is to limit losses. It may be either a buying order or a selling order. For example: "Sell two December British pounds at $2.6000 Stop" indicates that the buyer has bought two contracts at a price higher than $2.6000 and wants to limit the loss to that amount. An order to buy or sell at the market when a definite price is reached either above or below the prevailing price when the order is given.

Straddle In futures trading, the same as the spread. Straddles (spreads) are between delivery months.

Surplus Excess. In reference to balance of payments, income exceeds total payment to foreigners.

Swap An interest rate swap is an agreement between two parties to exchange interest payments on a fixed (notional) amount of debt. In its standard (generic) form, one party to the swap agrees to pay a fixed interest rate in exchange for receiving a variable (floating) rate on the swap's notional amount. The reverse position is taken by the counterparty. Typically, the floating rate side of the swap is tied to three- or six-month LIBOR (London Interbank Offer Rate). In foreign exchange, an exchange of bank balances. For example, when a bank sells Swiss francs for U.S. dollars, the actual funds are not shipped both ways across the Atlantic Ocean. Instead, the U.S. bank and a correspondent bank in Switzerland, via a swap agreement, exchange a franc balance in the Swiss bank for a dollar balance in the U.S. bank.

Switching Liquidating an existing position and simultaneously reinstating that position in another contract month of the same commodity or currency.

Technical Rally A price movement attributed to conditions developing from within the futures market itself. These conditions include changes in open interest, volume, and extent of recent price movement.

Tender Delivery against futures.

Tick See Point. Refers to minimum change in price.

Trade Balance The net amount of ***goods*** exported and imported. Does not include import and export services, capital flows, or official settlements.

Treasury Bills Government debt obligations. They are sold at something less than their value at maturity, the difference thereby being the yield. For example, a one-year U.S. Treasury Bill worth $10,000 at maturity may sell at $9,600. The $400 difference would be the yield, which is 4.17 percent (400/$9,600). They are considered a good barometer of interest rates.

Trend The general direction of the market.

"To-Arrive Contract" A transaction providing for subsequent delivery within a stipulated time limit of a specific grade of a commodity. In reality, the "to-arrive" sales contract was the forerunner of the present-day futures contract.

Visible Supply Usually refers to supplies of a commodity in licensed warehouses. Often includes afloats and all other supplies "in sight" in producing areas.

Volume The number of purchases ***or*** sales of a commodity futures contract made during a specified period of time.

Wire House A firm operating a private wire to its own branch offices, or to other firms' commission houses; a brokerage house.

INDEX

A

Absolute risk, 243
Account, 32
 see Brokerage, Hedge, Managed, Retirement, Size
 equity, 5
 opening, 82
 size, 8
 types, 82-83
Accumulation/distribution, 129
Add-on interest yield, 242
Administrative
 fees, 32
 Law Judge, 327
Advisor, *see* Commodity Trading Advisor, Managed
ADX, *see* Average directional index
ADXR, 130
American Stock Exchange, 8
Analysis, *see* Data, Elliott, Fundamental, Market, Price, Technical
Analytic tools, 135
Annual
 dividends, 41
 rate, 34
 return, 36, 42
  see Average
Anticipatory hedge, 156, 159
Arbitrage, 16, 34
 see Hedged, Interest rate
Arbitrageur, 269
Ascending triangle, 121
Asked price, 8

Asset
see Liquid, Portfolio
classes, risk, 49-50
correlation, 49-51
Asset allocation, 42
see Commodity Trading Advisor
At-the-money option, 279
Audits, 32, 326, 333
Average
annual return, 49
directional index (ADX), 130
return, 42

B

Back-testing, 61
Backwardation, 46
Bands, *see* Trading
Bank(s), 11, 213, 214, 223
Banker(s), 171-174, 237
Banking system, 213-214
Bankruptcy, 284
Bar chart, 112-113
interpretation, 116-117
Barter, 311
Base loss point, 60
Basis
see Cash/futures, Hedging, Spreading
patterns, 11
risk, 243
Basket
investing, 45-52
trading, 16
Bear
market, 118
cycle, 138
put spread, 300
Beta, 275
Bid, 335
price, 8
Blue chip stock, 4
Board of Trade, 317
Bond
see Corporate, Government, U.S. Treasury, Zero coupon
commodities comparison, 16-17
equivalents, 238
futures prices, 202
markets, 16, 231
prices, 16
declining, 299-300
rising, 302-303
stock comparison, 17
yield, 17
Bottoms, 119, 120
Box(es), 115
Breakaway gap, 122
Break-even
point, 284, 305
price, 305
Breakout, 41, 128
Bretton Woods, 221, 222
Broker, 6, 28, 33, 34, 41, 42, 67, 86, 172, 178
see Commodity, Floor, Hedge, Member, Options
judgement, 80-81
margin deposit, 32
problems, 81-82
selection, 77-84
process, 78-79
Brokerage
account, 172
arrangements, 37
fees, 32, 33, 36
firms, 29, 80, 82, 279
see Commodity futures firm, Firm
employee, 82
house, 8, 83, 223
clerk, 91
rate, 28
Bull
call spread, 303

market, 118
cycle, 138
Buy order, 85
Buy-and-hold passive investment, 51
Buy-call options, 302-303
Buying
hedge, 155
power, 117, 118
Buy/sell signal, 128

C

Call
see Margin
buying, 294-297
conversion to a put, using futures, 298-299
hedging, 297-298
option, 278, 297
buying, 299-300
writing, 295
Candlestick chart, 130
Capital, 5, 38, 55-61, 315
see International, Net, Working
amount, 60-61
availability, 54, 55-56
balances, 223-224
commitment, 58
controls, 228-229
losses, 206
need, 54-56
return, 41
Capitalization, *see* Undercapitalization
Carryback of losses, 206
Carryforward of losses, 206
Carrying charge hedge, 156, 158
Cash
commodity, 293
flow, expectation, 185
forward contract, 182
market, 69, 182, 311
activities, 98
options, 283
price, 155, 179, 241
rate, 181
settlement, 8, 265
Cash/futures basis, 189
Cattle, *see* Short hedge
CBOT, *see* Chicago Board of Trade
Certificate of deposit (CD), 237, 241-244
CFTC, *see* Commodity Futures Trading Commission
Channel, 128, 154
see Commodity channel, Moving average, Price
Chart
analyst, 117
formation, 120-124
patterns, 116-117, 140
readers, 150
services, 124-126
Chicago Board of Trade, 12, 245, 277, 317, 337
CBOT, 12, 13, 46, 200, 240, 245, 277, 318
International Commodity Index, 46
Chicago Butter and Egg Board, 318
Chicago commodity markets, development, 317
Chicago Mercantile Exchange, 7, 9, 155, 166, 167, 240, 266, 318, 337
CME, 7, 9, 12, 13, 266, 268, 318
nature, 332-334
Chicago Produce Exchange, 318
Circuit breakers, 16, 269-273
Clearing House Committee, 337
Clearinghouse, 336-337
CME, *see* Chicago Mercantile Exchange
Collateral, 173
see Hedged
Combination order, 88-89
Commercial
business, 11

enterprise, 154
interest, 69
paper, 226
price risk, 10
schedules, 69
Commission, 28, 65, 193, 195, 284
cost, 178
Commitment of Traders Report (C.O.T.), 98
Commodity, 21, 25, 94
see Chicago Board, Goldman, Inter-commodity, Intra-commodity, Non-perishable, Perishable, Semi-storable, Storable
bond comparison, 16-17
Channel Index, 130-131
characteristics, 158
exchange, 2-3, 16, 91, 245, 269
Exchange Act, 158, 277, 278, 324, 325
Exchange Authority, *see* U.S. Department of Agriculture
Futures Trading Commission, 6, 8, 79, 81, 146, 265, 278, 284, 325-327
Act of 1974, 81, 324, 325, 327
CFTC, 6, 16, 33, 36, 45, 79, 98, 99, 146, 158, 159, 278, 283, 325-329
characteristics, 158-159
hedging, 153-162
usage, 175-186
index, 45
index futures, 45-52
limited partnership, 3
market, 16, 17, 22, 231
options, 277-292
terminology, 278-280
trading, 277
pool, 28
Pool Operator, 28
CPO, 28, 37
price, 45
movement, 101
Price Chart, 112
Research Bureau, 16-17
see Real time
CRB Index, 17, 47-48
CRB Index Futures, investment potential, 48-51
CRB Index Futures, performance, 51-52
Futures Price Index, 45, 46, 48
stock compar, 54ison, 1-20
trader, 10
scorecard, 339-342
trading, 4, 8, 55, 193
Trading Advisor, 28
see Managed Accounts Report
administration, 42
asset allocation, 42
CTA, 28, 31-34, 37-39, 41-43
evaluation/negotiation, 41
fees, 32
qualitative factors, 37
selection, 34-39, 41
Commodity futures, 1, 4, 21, 61, 77
contracts, 3, 205
daily price limits, 6-7
exchange, 331-338
investments, 2
markets, 3
relative size, 5-6
research firms, 80
time factor, 6
trader description/psychology, 8-10
trading, 2-4
historical development, 311-330
legal aspects, 324
transactions, 2
value, 40
Compounding factor, 237-238
Confirmation cards, 337
Congestion area, 117-119
Consumer, 93
importance, 95-96

Price Index (CPI), 216
Contingent
order, 88, 89
risk, 294-295
Contract, 14, 165, 193, 199, 204
see Commodity futures, Forward, Futures, Interest rate, Open
liquidations, 337
market, 311
obligations, 336
terms, 281
Convergence, *see* Moving average
Conversion factors, 245
Core trend position, 68
Corporate bonds, 48, 49
Correction, 138
Correlation, 108-109
coefficient, 267
Cost, *see* Commission, Operating, Search, Storage
Cost-of-carry(ing), 190, 195
Cost-of-living index, 107
C.O.T., *see* Commitment of Traders Report
Cotton Futures Act, 324
CPI, *see* Consumer Price Index
CPO, *see* Commodity Pool Operator
Crash of 1987, 15-16, 268, 269
Crash protectors, 269-273
CRB, *see* Commodity Research Bureau
Credit, 315
risk, 239-240
Cross-hedge, 159
Crossover, 128
CTA, *see* Commodity Trading Advisor
Currency, 7, 17-20, 211, 221
market, 16
Customer agreement form, 82
Cycle(s), 103, 104, 119
see Bear, Bull
Cyclical movement, 103-104

D

Data
analysis, 64, 109-110
sources, 96-98
Day order, 85
Dealer activity, 247
Debt, *see* International
Deflator, 51
De-leverage, 37, 58
Delivery, 184
see Eurodollar, U.S. Treasury
Delta, 280, 291, 292
Demand, 92-93, 101, 104, 200, 213
see Supply, Supply/demand
price elasticity, 93
Deposit, 222
see Broker, Margin
funds, 313
Derivatives, 16
market, 311
Descending triangle, 121
Differentials, 128, 202
Directional movement index (DMI), 129-130, 135
Discipline, lack, 25-26
Disclosure Document, 34, 82
Distribution, *see* Accumulation
Distributors, 11, 69, 188
Divergence, 17
see Moving average
Diversification, 38, 39, 49, 68
see Risk
Diversified
investment, 41
portfolio, 274
Dividend
see Annual
payments, 7
DMI, *see* Directional
Domestic economic factors, 224-225
Double option, 278

Dow Jones
Index, 107
Industrial Average, 15, 268
Theory, 138
Downtrend, 118
Drawdown, 38
DTB, 13
Dual trading, 336
Duration, 101, 241

E

Earnings, *see* Interest
Economic factors, *see* Domestic
ECU, *see* European Currency Unit
Education, 326
department, 333
Efficient frontier, 40
Electronic trading, 12-15
orders, 89
Elliott Wave, 137
Analysis, 140
Theory (EWT), 137, 138
Energy
futures, 187
hedging, 187-192
Enforcement, 326
Envelope, *see* Moving average
EOE, 13
Equity, 8
see Account
interest, 4
ERM, *see* Exchange Rate Mechanism
Eurocurrency rates, 240
Eurodollar, 62, 239-240, 318
see TED
contracts, 291
futures, 210
futures, T-bill futures comparison, 241-242
futures contract, 241
delivery, 244
hedging, 242-243
interest rate futures, 240
market, 228, 239
rates, 291
rates, factors, 246-248
time deposit futures, 239
European Currency Unit (ECU), 211
EWT, *see* Elliott
Excess
inventory, 189
reserves, 214
Exchange, 8, 86, 318-319
see American, Commodity, Futures, New York, Stock
administration, 332
clearing house, 312
committees, 333-334
departments, 333
items traded, 319-323
locations, 319-323
market, 2
Rate Mechanism (ERM), 211, 228
rate, expectations, 225
rate, political/governmental influences, 225
rate price, 210
staff, 332-333
Execution price, 87
Exercise, 278, 196
Exhaustion gap, 122
Expansion, 104
Expenses, 36
Expiration date, 279
Exponential moving average, 132
Exponentially weighted moving average, 128

F

Face value, 245

Fair letters, 314
Fair market value, 285-287
  calculation, 286-287
Federal Reserve, 7, 16, 214, 245, 246
  activity, 246-247
  Board, 4, 216
  book entry system, 245
  discount window, 247
  Fed, 16, 214, 244
  Fed credit policy, 247
  funds, 235, 237, 240
  System, 240, 244
Fees, *see* Administrative, Commodity Trader Advisor, Brokerage, General, Managed, Penalty, Sales
  schedule, 34
Fibonacci
  numbers, 125, 137
  ratios, 138-139
FIFO, *see* First in
Fill-or-kill order, 86
Finance, 338
Financial futures, 34, 62, 109-218
  hedging application, 249-264
  introduction, 209-217
  market, 231
  options, 299-300
Financials, 21
  futures comparison, 290
  physicals comparison, 290
Firm, selection, 79-80
  see Brokerage, Commodity futures
First in, first out (FIFO), 160
First-time trader, 27
Floor
  broker, 334, 335
  trading, 13
Flower bonds, 233
Fluctuation, *see* Price
Food Control Act, 318
Forecasting
  see Price
  tools, 101-110
Foreign
  currency holdings, 223
  currency trading, 210
  exchange market, 226, 227
  exchange rate, 209, 220
    see Inflation
    evaluation, 223-225
Formation, 117
  see Chart
Forward
  contract, 316
    see Cash
  market, 311
  pricing hedge, 156
  rate discount, 227
  sale, 190
Four-box reversal, 114
FTSE, 266
Fund(s)
  see Futures, Guaranteed,Public
  free flows, 227
Fundamental
  analysis, 25, 83, 91, 92-95, 223
  factors, 62, 63, 201
  research, 7
  trader, 62
Fundamentals, 62
  technicians comparison, 149-150
Futures
  see Bonds, Cash/futures, Commodity, Financial, Interest rate, Managed, Stock, 179
  contracts, 1, 4, 5, 8, 21, 45, 51, 145, 154, 164, 165, 176, 195, 205, 227, 294, 296, 312, 313
  exchange, 14
  financials comparison, 290
  funds, 28, 30, 31, 40
    see Public
    product design, 41
  losses, 205

market, 7, 11, 12, 23, 27, 156, 175, 311
prices, 275
options comparison, 281-283
physicals comparison, 290
position, 294, 297, 298
price(s), 69, 151, 172, 176, 181
movements, 97-98
selling, 297, 299
trading, 1, 23, 31, 312
see Organized
social/economic benefits, 10-12
transactions, 205
yield curve, 235-236

G

Gamma, 280-281, 291
Gap, 112, 121, 122
General partner, 30, 83
fees, 32
GP, 30, 32, 37
General price level, 225
Geometric average, 47
Gift-giving, 311
Globex, 12-15, 318
Glossary, 343-361
GNMA futures, 244
Gold call, 296-297
Goldman Sachs Commodity Index (GSCI), 45-47, 52
Good(s), 213
through date order, 86
'til canceled order, 86
Good-faith
bond, 338
money, 338
Government
bonds, 49
information, 98-99
policies, 97
GP, *see* General partner
Grain Futures Act, 324
Growth, rate, 224
Guaranteed funds, 29, 32

H

Harmonic average, 47
Hatch Bill, 324
Head-and-shoulders formation, 120, 121
Heating oil market, 69
Hedge, 11, 41
see Buying, Inflation, Long, Selling, Short, Storage
account, 8
broker, selection, 183
position, 148
refiner, 189
transaction, 159
Hedged
collateral, 172
interest arbitrage transactions, 228
Hedger, 99, 173
description, 156-157
Hedging, 10, 171-174
see Commodity, Energy, Hogs, Portfolio manager
application, *see* Financial future
basis, 163-170
calculation, 166-169
benefits, 157-158
decision making, 184
definition, 154
function, 11
illustrated, 273-274
quantity, 184-185
reasons, 156-157
Hogs, hedging, 178-181

I

IMF, *see* International Monetary Fund

IMM, *see* International Monetary Market
Implied volatility, 136
Import taxes, 225
Income, 55, 92, 212, 215
Index
  see Average directional, Chicago Board, Commodity, Commodity channel, Commodity Research, Cost-of-living, Directional, Dow Jones, Goldman, Major, Managed, Real time, Relative strength, Standard, Stock, Weighted
  futures, volatility, 268-269
  numbers, 107-108
  weights, 46
Indicator, 63, 65, 105, 128
  see Spread-specific, Technical
Inflation, 16, 17, 41, 45, 49, 51, 215-217
  foreign exchange rates, 216-217
  hedge, 50-51
  interest rates, 215-216
  rate, 224
Inflationary process, 215
Institutional
  influences, 94
  investor, 45
  portfolio, 48
Insurance, 195
  see Life
  hedge, 157
  premium, 289
Interest
  see Commercial, Equity, Hedged, Investment, Open
  earnings, 31
  equalization taxes, 225
  rate, 3, 7, 16
    see Inflation
    arbitrage, 226-228
    contract, 239-248
    declining, 302-303
    futures, 18-20, 154
    parity, 227
    price, 209, 210
    rising, 299-300
  trend, 17
Interest on margin, 178
Interest-on-interest, 237
Inter-commodity spread, 89, 200
Inter-market spread, 88
International
  capital, 223-224
  debts, 221
  economic indicator, 224
  Monetary Fund (IMF), 221, 223
Monetary Market (IMM), 223, 240, 241
    futures, 225
    index, 241
  monetary system, history, 221-222
Inter-season spreads, 199
In-the-money option, 279, 303
Intra-commodity spread, 88-89
Intraday price limits, 16
Intrinsic value, 279
Inventory, 69, 154, 295
  see Excess
Inventory in transit, selling, 190-191
Investing, *see* Basket
Investment, 5, 30, 38, 274
  see Buy-and-hold, Commodity futures, Commodity Research Bureau, Diversified, Passive, Unit
  decisions, 3
  interest, 195
  managers, 228
  portfolio, 40, 55
  strategy, 282
  yield, 46
Investor, *see* Institutional

K

Kansas City Board of Trade, 265

Key reversal, 134

L

Last in, first out (LIFO), 160
Leverage, 3-5, 6, 37, 58, 61
  see De-leverage, Profit
  factor, 5
LIBOR, *see* London Interbank Offer Rate
Life insurance, 55, 153
LIFFE, *see* London International Financial Futures Exchange
LIFO, *see* Last in
Limit order, 87
Limited
  liability, 28, 83
  partnership, 28, 29, 83
    see Commodity
Liquid assets, 55, 56
Liquidation, 337
  strategy, 66-67
Liquidity, 14, 31, 233
Loan package, 172-174
London Interbank Offer Rate (LIBOR), 240, 241, 243, 244
London International Financial Futures Exchange, 12
  LIFFE, 12
Long hedge, 276
Long-term trader, 62
Loss limiting, 202

M

Maastricht Referendum, 211
MACD, *see* Moving average
Major market index, 62
Managed account, 38
Managed Accounts Report (MAR), 29
  Index of Qualified Universe CTAs
  MAR, 39, 34
  Trading Advisor Qualified Index, 29
Managed futures, 2, 27-44
  fees, 32
  growth, 29-34
  performance, 33-34
  structure, 29-32
Manager, *see* Portfolio, Professional, Trading
MAR, *see* Managed Account Report
Marche a Terme International de France, 12
  MATIF, 12
Margin, 3-5, 193, 273, 279, 282, 313
  see Broker, Interest on margin
  calls, 62, 172, 279
  deposit, 178
Market
  see Bear, Bond, Bull, Cash, Commodity, Commodity futures, Currency, Heating oil, Inter-market, Major, Spot, Stock
  analysis, 7, 25
  letters, 79
  order, 86, 87
  position, 63
  price, 87
  surveillance, 326
  timer, 42
  trader, 96
  value, 4
Market-if-touched order, 87
Mark-to-market settlement, 8
Mathematical expectation, 57-58
MATIF, *see* Marche a Terme International de France
Maturity, 8, 240, 245
Member broker, 337
Membership organization, 3
MidAmerica Commodity Exchange, 319
Midwest grain market, 316-317
Momentum, 213
  oscillator, 131, 135

Money, 210-212
in the economy, 212-213
management, 53
management plan, 54
market, 223, 231, 233
investment, 231
rate, 246
price, 220
trading, 219-230
Mortgage market, 231
Moving average, 105-107, 128
see Exponential, Exponentially
channel, 128
convergence divergence (MACD), 128, 131, 135
envelope, 132
oscillator, 128-129
rule, 64

N

Naked
short position, 202
writing, 279
National Futures Association, 78, 327, 328
NFA, 33, 78, 283, 327, 328
rules, 81
self-regulation, 327-329
National Introducing Brokers Association, 78
NAV, *see* Net Asset Value
Neckline, 121
Negative carry, 234
Net Asset Value (NAV), 30, 32
Net capital, 185
Net worth, 55
Neural networks, 139-142
New Orleans Commodity Exchange, 319
New York
Futures Exchange, 46, 52
Mercantile Exchange (NYMEX), 187, 190
Stock Exchange (NYSE), 6, 7, 266, 267
Composite Index, 266, 275
index, 274
index futures, 274
NFA, *see* National Futures Association
Nikkei, 266
Non-perishable commodity, 102
NYMEX, *see* New York Mercantile Exchange
NYSE, *see* New York Stock Exchange

O

OBV, *see* On-balance volume
Off-at-specific-time order, 86
Offer(s), 335
Offsetting, 10
factors, 39
Oil crack spread, 204-205
On-balance volume (OBV, 132
On-the-close order, 86
On-the-opening order, 86
Open
contracts, 146
interest, 145-152
see Seasonal patterns
changes interpretation, 147-148
information, 147
statistics, 145
Market Committee, 247
order, 86
Operating cost, 10
Operational hedge, 156
Option(s)
see Commodity, Stock
broker, selection, 283-285
business use, 294-295
contract, 278
futures comparison, 281-283

interest costs, 288
premium, 284, 288, 295
determination, 285-289
series, 279
speculation strategy, 296-298
spreads, 202-203, 279
straddle, 279
strategies, 300-303
time, 289
trading choices, 303-305
trading strategies, 293-310
value, 285-289
value, Greek terminology, 280-281
volatility, 288-289
Order, 85-90
see Electronic, Spread
placing, 89
price, 86-87
Organized futures trading
characteristics, 312-313
emergence, 313-314
Japan, 314-315
U.S. development, 315-316
Oscillator, 128
see Momentum, Moving average
Out-of-the-money option, 279, 297, 303
Overbought/oversold, 131
signal, 128
Overtrading, 136
Overvalue, 232
Ownership transfer, 3

P

Paper
feedlot, 204
trade, 26
Par delivery, 240
Par value, 221, 240
Parabolic system, 133
Partner, *see* General
Partnership, *see* Limited
Passive investment, *see* Buy-and-hold
Payment, *see* Dividend
Penalty fees, 31
Penny stock, 3
Performance, *see* Managed futures, Real time
Perishable
commodity, 102
spread, 198-199
Physicals
financials comparison, 290
futures comparison, 290
Point, 113, 114, 245
Point-and-figure chart, 113-116
Pool, *see* Commodity
Portfolio, 21, 45, 49
see Institutional, Investment, Stock market
asset, 50
management strategy, 190
manager, hedging, 274-276
Position, 57, 145
see Hedge, Market, Naked, Trader, Trading,
Trend
addition, 60
initiation, 54, 62-66
trader, 9
Positive carry, 233
Premium, 194, 226, 227, 278, 279, 282, 284, 285, 302, 303
see Option
Price
see Asked, Bid, Bond, Cash, Commercial, Commodity, Commodity Research, Execution, Futures, Market, Order, Target, Technical
analysis, 7, 97
channel, 133
discovery, 10

elasticity, *see* Demand
expectation, 185
fluctuation, 101, 113, 155, 158
forecasting, 91-99
limits, *see* Commodity futures, Intraday, Stocks
movements, 62
see Seasonal
patterns, 101-110, 201
protection, 293
relationships, 11
risk, 154, 243
structure, 46
system, 195
trend, 115
Private risk, 239
Probability, 56-57, 58, 60, 63, 70, 285, 287
Processors, 11
Producers, 11
Professional managers, 28
Profit(s), 2, 12, 27, 30, 32, 58, 65, 105, 125, 146, 164, 303, 305
leverage, 58
margin, 294
objective, 66
opportunities, 196, 227
Property rights, 3
Prospectus, 37
Public
funds, 29, 32
futures funds, 33
relations department, 333
risk, 239
Purchasing power, 92
Put
see Call
buying, 298
option, 278
buying, 299

R

Random walk, 150-152
Range leader, 134
Rate of change, 133
Ratios, 105
Real time CRB Index Futures performance, 51-52
Registration, 326
Reinvestment, 237
Relative
risk, 243
size, *see* Commodity futures, Stock
strength index (RSI), 125, 133-134, 135
Reparations, 326
Research, 326
department, 333
Reserve(s), 214
Retirement account, 55
Return, 31, 39
see Annual, Average, Capital, Stock
on investment (ROI), 36
calculation, 305-306
Return/risk ratio, 40
Reversal, 115
see Key
Reward, *see* Risk/reward profit
Reward/risk ratio, 36, 38
Risk, 2, 5, 8, 37, 55, 56, 153, 204, 228, 273, 293, 306
see Absolute, Asset, Basis, Commercial price, Price, Relative, Reward/risk, Speculation
attitude, 54
control, 38
diversification, 68
exposure, 160
reduction, 154, 244
ruin, 58-60, 70
shifting, 10
spectrum, 3, 4, 195
Risk-avoidance hedge, 157

Risk/reward profits, 276
Roll yield, 46
Rule review, 326
RSI, *see* Relative strength index
Runaway gap, 122

S

Sales fees, 32
Savings, 55
Scale order, 88
Scalpers, 9
Scatter diagram, 109
SDR, *see* Special drawing right
Search cost, 11
Seasonal
  element, 106
  indexes, 108, 149
  movements, 102-103
  patterns, 108
    open interest, 148-149
    volume, 148-149
  price movement, 102
Seasonality, 69, 106, 199
Secular trend, 104
Security, 7, 31
  deposit, 338
  Exchange Act, 4
  Exchange Commission
    SEC, 16
  gains, 205
  industry, 8
Selective hedge, 157
Sell order, 85
Selling
  hedge, 155
  short, 7
Semi-storable commodity, 165, 195
Services, 213
Settlement, *see* Cash, Mark-to-market
Share, 3
Sharpe ratio, 36-38, 48
Short hedge, cattle, 176-178
Short
  position, *see* Naked
  sale, 7
Short-term trend, 92
Shoulders, *see* Head-and-shoulders
Shrinkage, 195
Signal, 101, 115, 128, 135
Size
  see Relative
  account, 34
Small trader, 27
SOFFEX, 13
Software, 63, 64, 124-126
SOM, 13
Soybean crush, 203-204
Special drawing rights (SDRs), 223
Speculation, 21-26, 173, 311
  loss/gain, 25-26
  risk, 23
Speculative, 8
  stock, 3
  trader, 66
Speculator, 9, 11, 27, 69, 99, 244, 293
  loss/gain, 24-25
  motivation, 22-23
Spending flow, 212
Spot market, 222-223, 311
Spread(s), 3, 188
  see Inter-commodity, Inter-market, Intra-commodity, Oil, Option, Perishable, TED, Time
  additional information, 203-205
  fact/fiction, 193-208
  opportunities, spotting, 201
  order, 88, 89
    rules, 201-202
  semantics, 194-195
  traders, 202
  trading, 34, 198
    profitability, 198

transaction, 198
Spread-specific indicators, 204
Spreading
location basis, 199-200
method, 61
quality basis, 200
tax effects, 205-206
technique, 3
transactions, 194
Standard & Poor's
futures, 292
S&P, 62, 267, 286
S&P Index, 7
S&P 500 Index, 17, 33, 34, 42, 266, 268
Standard deviation, 40, 49, 288
Statistical techniques, 105-109
Statistics, *see* Open interest, Volume
Stochastic(s), 125, 134-135
Stock
see Blue chip, Penny, Speculative
bond comparison, 17
commodity comparison, 1-20
daily price limits, 6-7
exchanges, 2, 16, 315
index
computation, 267-268
trading, 273
index contracts, 268
index futures, 210, 265-276, 318
index options, 265, 276
market, 4, 42, 231
portfolio, 273
relative size, 5-6
returns, 40
time factor, 6
trading, 2-3
value, 6
Stop
loss order, 282
order, 67, 87-88
Stop-limit order, 87, 88
Storable commodity, 165, 181, 195, 196, 199
Storage
cost, 181
hedge, 181-183
Straddle, 194
see Option
Strike price, 278, 285, 296, 303
Strip (yield) curve, 236-237
Supply, 92, 93-95, 101, 104, 200
Supply and demand, 10, 91-100, 149
Supply/demand, 63
equation, 10
imbalance, 196
Survivor bias, 25
Synthetics, creation, 291-292

T

Target price, 180
TASS, 34
Tax and Revenue Act of 1981, 205
T-bill, *see* U.S. Treasury
T-bond, *see* U.S. Treasury
Technical
analysis, 83, 91, 111-126
tools, 126-144
analyst, 117, 145
factors, 63
indicator, 64
survey, 129-135
warning, 136-139
price analysis, 25
trader, 62
Technicians, fundamentals comparison, 149-150
TED (T-bill, Eurodollar) spread, 242
Theta, 281
Tiers, 68
Time
element, 85-86

factor, *see* Commodity futures, Stocks
spreads, 195-197
value, 279
Time-of-day order, 86
To-arrive contracts, 316
Tops, 119, 120
Track record, 35
report, 36
Trade, advantage, 59
calculation, 63-66
development, 63
execution, 335-336
exit, 66-67
Trader, *see* Commodity, Commodity futures, First-time, Fundmental, Long-term, Market, Position, Small, Speculative, Spreader, Technical
position, 98
Trading, 2
see Commodity futures, Electronic, Floor, Futures, Money, Options, Overtrading, Paper, Spread, Stock, Stock indexes
bands, 130
day, 112, 338
decision, 25
floor, 335
manager, using, 41-42
method, 8
pattern, 38
personal suitability, 2
plan, 26, 53-76
position, 195
rules violations, 12
signals, 28
strategies, 201
volume, 14
Transactions, 3, 8, 96, 182, 284, 331
see Commodity, Futures, Hedged, Spread, Spreading
costs, 299
Trend, 104-105, 150-152
see Price, Short-term
changers, 202-203
confirmation, 128
definition, 117-119
identification, 128
Trend position, 68
see Core
Triangle, 121
see Ascending, Descending
Turning point, 128

U

Uncovered writing, 279
Undercapitalization, 25
Undervalue, 232
Unit investment, 36
U.S. Court of Appeals, 327
U.S. Department of Agriculture, 7, 94, 96
Commodity Exchange Authority, 324, 328
USDA, 94
U.S. Department of Commerce, 7, 94, 96
U.S. Supreme Court, 160
U.S. Treasury, 7, 16, 94, 221
bill (T-bill), 48, 235, 237, 239-240, 318
see TED
auction, 244
contract, 243
delivery, 244
futures, 18
futures, Eurodollar futures comparison, 241-242
futures, factors, 246-248
futures contract terms, 240-241
hedging, 242-244
rate, 36, 51
bond (T-bond), 25, 31, 32, 210, 235, 244-245
futures, 299, 300

notes, 235, 244-246
note futures, 210

V

Value
see Commodity futures, Intrinsic, Market, Net Asset, Overvalue, Stock, Undervalue
Line Average (VLA), 265, 268
yield curves, 232
Vega, 281
VLA, see Value Line Average
Volatility, 3, 67, 136-137, 285
see Implied, Index futures
range, 269
Volume, 145-152
see On-balance, Seasonal patterns, Trading
statistics, 145

W

W formation, 120
Weighted
see Exponentially
index, 46
When-done order, 88
Wholesale price indexes, 216
Withdrawal, 35-36, 214, 222
Working capital, 313
Worth, see Net
Writing, 280

Y

Yield, 241, 273
see Add-on, Bond, Investment, Roll
Yield curve
see Futures, Strip
changing shape, 233-235
study reasons, 232-233
understanding, 231-238

Z

Zero-coupon bond, 30, 31

About the Author

Mark J. Powers has more than 30 years of experience in the futures industry. He has been honored by *Futures* Magazine as one of the most influential people in the development of the futures industry during the last quarter century and was noted by *The New York Times* as one of the "Founding Fathers of Financial Futures." He served as Senior Vice President of the Chicago Mercantile Exchange, where he was responsible for designing and developing many of the initial rules, regulations and contracts for the IMM, a number of them major innovations that have now spread throughout the world. He has been a member of most of the major U.S. Commodity Exchanges, a Director of four exchanges, Vice Chairman or officer of several exchanges and numerous industry organizations. He also served as the first Chief Economist of the Commodity Futures Trading Commission. He has authored several bestselling books on commodities, including the all-time industry bestseller, *Getting Started in Commodity Futures Trading*. He is Editor of *The Journal of Futures Markets,* which is devoted to the publication of scholarly and practitioner research on futures and options markets. He is the Chief Executive Officer of Powers Research Associates and of Powers & Dubin Asset Allocation and Management Co., one of the oldest and largest commodity fund trading managers in the U.S. He received his Ph.D. in Agricultural Economics from the University of Wisconsin with a minor in law. He is also a former professor of economics, having taught at South Dakota State University.

***Futures* magazine**
Newsletters
Price Charts
Information Services

Futures magazine is the world's largest circulation magazine for derivative traders and money mangers. For subscriptions and other timely information resources, call 1-800-221-4352, EXT. 1025 or 319-277-7892.

or write:

Futures Magazine
219 Parkade, Box 6
Cedar Falls, IA 50613 USA
Fax 319-277-7896

Futures Books/Futures Learning Center
Videotapes, audio cassettes, books, schools, workshops, conferences

For information about other valuable selections by Futures Books, as well as videotapes, audio cassettes, schools, workshops, and conferences, call Futures Learning Center at 1-800-635-3936 or 319-277-6341.

or write:

Futures Learning Center
219 Parkade, Box 6
Cedar Falls, IA 50613 USA
Fax 319-277-7982